Precarity in European Film

Film, Class, Society

Edited by
Elisa Cuter, Daniel Fairfax, Guido Kirsten
and Hanna Prenzel

Editorial Board
Constanza Burucua, Sabine Hake, Gertrud Koch,
Sieglinde Lemke, Philip Rosen, Michael Wayne

Volume 1

Precarity in European Film

—

Depictions and Discourses

Edited by
Elisa Cuter, Guido Kirsten and Hanna Prenzel

DE GRUYTER

This publication was funded by the German Research Foundation (DFG).

ISBN 978-3-11-135571-9
e-ISBN (PDF) 978-3-11-070781-6
e-ISBN (EPUB) 978-3-11-070791-5
DOI https://doi.org/10.1515/9783110707816

This work is licensed under the Creative Commons Attribution-NonCommercial-NoDerivatives 4.0 International License. For details go to https://creativecommons.org/licenses/by-nc-nd/4.0/.

Library of Congress Control Number: 2022933167

Bibliographic information published by the Deutsche Nationalbibliothek
The Deutsche Nationalbibliothek lists this publication in the Deutsche Nationalbibliografie; detailed bibliographic data are available on the internet at http://dnb.dnb.de.

© 2023 with the authors, editing © 2022 Elisa Cuter, Guido Kirsten and Hanna Prenzel, published by Walter de Gruyter GmbH, Berlin/Boston
This volume is text- and page-identical with the hardback published in 2022.
This book is published with open access at www.degruyter.com.

Cover image: production still from Deux jours, une nuit (Two Days, One Night) by Jean-Luc and Pierre Dardenne (2014). We thank the Dardenne brothers and the production company "Les Films du Fleuve" for their kind permission to use it for the cover.
Typesetting: Integra Software Services Pvt. Ltd.
Printing and binding: CPI books GmbH, Leck

www.degruyter.com

Contents

Drawing a Map of Precarity in European Film: Preface and Overview —— IX

Guido Kirsten
Studying the Cinema of Precarity —— 1
An Introduction

Martin O'Shaughnessy
Precarious Narratives in French and Francophone Belgian Cinema —— 31

Manuel Garin
Housing Precarity and Construction in Spanish Cinema —— 49
From Francoism to Contemporary Documentary

Nino Klingler
Aspects of Poverty and Precarity —— 65
Puzzle-Pictures from Portugal

Elisa Cuter
From Poverty to Precarity —— 85
Bridging the Gap Between Arthouse Films and Domestic Blockbusters in Contemporary Italian Cinema

Ursula-Helen Kassaveti
Varieties of the Precariat in Contemporary Greek Cinema —— 105

Özgür Çiçek
Transformation of the Precariat in Istanbul —— 125
Naivete, Idealism, and Corruption with and within the City

Christian Ferencz-Flatz
Film as Social Visibility —— 143
Two Forms of Precarity in Romanian (and Bulgarian) Cinema

Aleksandra Miljković
Precarity in Post-Yugoslav Cinema —— 161
Everyday Life in Post-Socialist, Post-War, and Transition Societies

László Strausz
Move on Down —— 179
Precarity and Downward Mobility in Contemporary Hungarian Feature Films

Katarína Mišíková
Social Martyrs in Slovak Social Film Drama and Documentary —— 199

Melanie Letschnig
Pandemic (Dis)Proportions —— 217
On the Depiction of Precarized Work and Living Conditions in Austrian Film

Marcy Goldberg
Precarity and Paradox in Swiss Cinema —— 233

Hanna Prenzel
Individualization as a Shared Experience? —— 251
Precarious Conditions Negotiated in German Film: Individual Refusal and Collective Agency

Ewa Mazierska
Representation of Poverty and Precarity in Post-Communist Polish Cinema —— 271

Eva Näripea, Renata Šukaitytė, Zane Balčus
Economic and Social Precarity in Baltic Cinema —— 289

Anders Marklund
Screening Precarity Scenes —— 303
Precariousness and the Welfare State in Scandinavian Film

John Hill
Working-Class Precarity and the Social-Realist Tradition in British Cinema —— 325

Gert Jan Harkema
Relational Aesthetics of Precarity in Contemporary Dutch Documentary and Beyond —— 347

Contributors —— 365

Index —— 369

Drawing a Map of Precarity in European Film: Preface and Overview

We are writing this preface in November 2021 while the number of Covid-19 cases is—again—rising dramatically. Up to now, the virus has not only cost more than five million people their lives (1,650,000 in Europe alone, and with many more casualties to be expected), and permanently harmed many more. It has also thrown the economic well-being of an enormous number of people into disarray and worsened the already precarious situation of so many others. At the same time, the wealth of the rich and the super-rich still seems to be continually growing. Economic inequality is about to reach a new historic peak.

This volume is based on an international conference which was held at Film University Babelsberg in Potsdam from 30 January to 1 February 2020, just before Covid-19 became a major issue. We were lucky to be able to meet the thirteen invited scholars from all over Europe in person and to be able to listen to their presentations about the cinematic depiction of precarity in different regions and countries. The idea of the conference had been to draw an imaginary map of these representations and to compare film traditions, stylistic and narrative approaches, prevalent tendencies and recurring themes, and political implications.

In order to fill some gaps the conference had left, we asked other scholars to add their expertise. The aim was to avoid excluding any film producing country in (geographically defined) Europe and thus to draw the map as completely as possible. Thanks to our authors' efforts we have almost succeeded—with some regrettable exceptions the attentive reader will easily spot.

This volume's subtitle—"depictions and discourses"—is meant to specify what is meant by "precarity in European film" here. We do not treat precarious working conditions in film production—which would certainly merit a monograph or an anthology of its own. Instead, we have focused on questions of representation, which are divided into two subcategories. The question of how precarity is being *depicted* is connected to concrete systems of images: Who is represented as precarious in contemporary European film? What are their visual attributes and characteristics? Are we witnessing new iconographies (in comparison to those of 'classical' poverty)? While these questions concern filmic representations directly in terms of their features as audiovisual texts, questions regarding their *discursive* dimensions need to take larger structures and contexts into account: What do the films try to convince us of? Whom do they address and from which position do they formulate their implicit or explicit arguments? What do they (willingly or unknowingly) omit? How do they react to other (audiovisual) texts and the broader public discourse? Although most of the authors have not

Open Access. © 2022 Elisa Cuter, et al., published by De Gruyter. This work is licensed under the Creative Commons Attribution-NonCommercial-NoDerivatives 4.0 International License.
https://doi.org/10.1515/9783110707816-203

formulated these questions *as such*, inquiries into the nature of the films' representations are at the heart of all the chapters.

One advantage of speaking of depictions and discourse—instead of, for instance, of fictions and narratives—is that these concepts encompass a range of filmic forms and formats. We have deliberately included both fiction and documentary films, and some articles have even focused on more experimental forms or on TV series. Each contribution to this volume is the result of the authors' creative solutions to what was almost a mission impossible. We had asked them both to sketch general tendencies concerning the respective representations of precarity and to discuss prominent examples in a detailed fashion while also providing the necessary information on the economic and political context. The authors have employed different strategies to deal with this challenge. Some articles begin with sociological findings, others are more philosophical in nature; some highlight the importance of filmic traditions that bear on contemporary depictions of precarity, some put more emphasis on current political situations; some have organized their overviews by themes or motifs, others have chosen a more chronological approach.

The order of the articles can be thought of as an imaginary tour through the landscape of cinematic precarity discourses in Europe. Before we set off on the journey, Guido Kirsten introduces the concept of the *cinema of precarity* and suggests three main lines of inquiry to approach it: poetics, impact studies, and discourse analysis. Against auteurist notions of the cinema of precarity, Kirsten proposes a wider understanding of the term: He argues that it ought to be studied in all its formal and thematic heterogeneity. Precarity is itself a multi-faceted phenomenon that affects people differently, encompassing both *objective* aspects (such as the lack of permanent contracts, social security, work permits, health care, etc.) and *subjective* ones (feelings of anger, anxiety, anomie, and alienation). When studying the cinema of precarity we should consider how these aspects are being translated into filmic forms with different implications.

Kirsten's suggestion is perhaps confirmed by the variety of approaches that are included in our imaginary journey through Europe. It starts with Martin O'Shaughnessy's chapter, focusing on France and the Francophone part of Belgium. Besides convergences among the many recent films on precarity, O'Shaughnessy notes significant variations. In part, these concern the central characters, who can be seen as revealing the crisis of the mature male and the rise of other precarious figures. O'Shaughnessy reads this as a symptom of the exit from Fordism and the constitutive exclusions which used to accord that male figure his centrality. The political implications of this new phase are discussed, distinguishing between films that display moralism, an ethical yet individual framing, and a search for transnational solidarity.

Next, Manuel Garin's chapter takes us to Spain. Garin explores the audiovisual depiction of housing precarity in contemporary documentaries, positing that the class, gender, and race issues mobilized in them are symptomatically linked to modes and structures of Francoism, thus intertwining past and present inequalities that are deeply ingrained in Spain's social fabric. Instead of focusing solely on hegemonic power, however, his analyses delve into forms of resistance and bonding between precarious individuals and collectives that fight back in spite of the class, institutional, and corporate burdens they carry.

Turning to Portugal, Nino Klingler observes that this country's cinema has often found unconventional ways of dealing with social questions such as poverty and precarity. This tendency has become even stronger since the eurozone crisis, resulting in films that appear to balance seemingly mutually exclusive tendencies of formal realism, discursive criticism, and aesthetic experimentalism. Through a comparative examination of a number of emblematic scenes, the chapter argues that these films are characterized by an unlikely combination of a rather straightforward critical sociopolitical ethos and an essential interpretative openness. According to Klingler, it is precisely this lack of formal closure that engages the viewers in an ethical project of searching for appropriate ways to depict the economic hardships of the Portuguese people truthfully.

The next stop on the trip through European cinema's imaginary of poverty and precarity is Italy. Elisa Cuter's chapter analyzes Italian film production by comparing two strands: arthouse films aimed at the international festival circuit and comedies produced by major private companies for the domestic audience. Differentiating between these tendencies provides a conceptual framework that takes the parameters of production, reception, and discourse into account, as well as the consequences of the economic crisis on the film industry and independent filmmaking. Cuter discusses some examples of these two varieties and argues that the gap between them reflects the lack of a cohesive narrative on the problems of poverty and precarity. In addition, she presents some films that allow for a different discursive strategy.

Ursula-Helen Kassaveti then takes us to Greece. After an excursion looking at traditional depictions of precarity in Greek film history and the specific situation of Greece after the economic crisis, her chapter explores how the precariat is represented in Greek films produced between 2009 and 2019. In three sample films, she identifies three possible types of reactions to the condition of precarity experienced especially by young people.

Coming to Turkey, more specifically to the city of Istanbul, Özgür Çiçek focuses on what she calls the "precarious essence" of that city and its filmic depiction. Çiçek first discusses two films from the late *Yeşilçam* era before turning to more recent films that display an evolution of the precarious subject through gentrification processes. Comparing films from different decades, Çiçek indicates the variety of the precariat in Turkey, and tells us about a cinema that focuses on its impact on precarious subjectivities.

Turning to Romania and Bulgaria, Christian Ferencz-Flatz's chapter addresses two topics, which are frequently and rightfully seen as characteristic for Eastern-European societies: economic migration and the social and economic exclusion of the Roma populations. In discussing several Romanian films that illustrate the advantages of tackling these social issues with the instruments of cinema, he proposes to extend Axel Honneth's concept of mutual recognition as *social visibility* to cinematic representations and debates the possible consequences of applying such a framework to films depicting precarity in a transnational context.

Next on the route are the countries that used to form the multi-ethnic state of Yugoslavia. Aleksandra Miljković explores recent representations of precarity in post-Yugoslav cinema concentrating on depictions of the precarization of the working class, the double burden of women's work, and the inherited precarity of the youth. Through her film analyses, with special attention to the interplay between post-socialist legacy, social class, and post-transitional disorientation, she is able to detect how the characters' passivity, disaffection, and despair are mirrored by an environment that evokes the intricate processes of welfare state eradication and lack of individual self-assertion.

With the ensuing chapter by László Strausz we turn to Hungary. This chapter investigates the theme of precarity in terms of downward social mobility in Hungarian cinema between the mid-1980s and 2018. Through a quantitative method and a qualitative analysis, he shows how feature films imagine downward social mobility in distinct formations from the mid-1980s onward, ranging from the thematization of crisis due to larger social-historical forces to the result of the protagonists' own decisions.

Traveling further north on our imaginary map, we reach Slovakia. Katarína Mišíková's chapter deals with the trend of social documentary and social film drama in contemporary Slovak cinema. In particular, she analyzes motifs and figures of *social martyrs*, tracing their roots in a broader cultural tradition. Mišíková argues that many recent films that display this trope can be seen as critical reflections of the post-socialist version of capitalism, but also as more abstract and universal stories about the human condition that transcend the sheer observation of reality towards poetic meanings and cultural archetypes.

Coming to Austria, Melanie Letschnig opens her contribution with a reflection on the impact of Covid-19 on workers and examines the depiction of precarized work in four Austrian films whose protagonists earn their living in sectors that typically have bad working conditions: harvesting, seasonal work in the restaurant business, cleaning, sex work, and elder care. Letschnig argues that these films—by blurring and complicating the demarcation between documentary and fiction—witness the protagonists' everyday lives with the purpose of revealing and denouncing greater political and socioeconomic dynamics of exploitation.

As far as national stereotypes go, Switzerland, the next country on our route, is at first glance not likely to be associated with poverty or precarity—either in general terms or as a central theme for its artistic output. And yet, as Marcy Goldberg shows, the list of Swiss films about topics related to precarity is quite long. As she demonstrates, the case of Switzerland involves several layers of paradox: a wealthy nation with a film sector that is itself precariously funded; a country focused on itself even as it exerts geopolitical and international financial influence; and a preoccupation with national and regional identity that might be deemed provincial or narcissistic but is actually self-critical on a number of levels. All of these elements continue to shape the ways in which Swiss cinema engages with precarity, even as it evolves and expands to include new voices and points of view.

Hanna Prenzel's ensuing chapter explores how German films represent and negotiate dissent under precarious conditions, using two case studies: one film portraying individual refusal and one illustrating collective resistance. Prenzel argues that depictions of denial in film can be read as empowering since they unmask mechanisms of subjugation and the absurdity of the neoliberal reform of the welfare system in the early 2000s. But there are also films that focus on collective agency: Providing an overview of the political and cinematic landscape of documentary films dealing with Berlin's housing crisis and resulting processes of gentrification, Prenzel explores intersectional struggles and the possibility of collective agency even when precarized subjects are affected differently by structural inequality.

Turning to representations of poverty and precarity in Polish cinema, Ewa Mazierska draws on the political and economic history of Poland from the time it regained independence in 1918 to the present day. Her assumption is that cinema engages with social and political reality, although not through mirroring this reality, but rather by hiding or emphasizing some of its features. Poverty tends to be hidden, beautified, or dramatized, because by itself it is rather mundane and its existence reflects badly on the government, on the country's elites, and on its citizens. As Mazierska demonstrates, this is certainly the case with Polish cinema, which in different periods adopted different approaches to depicting poverty and precarity.

Moving further north, Eva Näripea, Renata Šukaitytė, and Zane Balčus take us to the three Baltic countries Lithuania, Latvia, and Estonia. The authors suggest that only a few filmmakers deal with the new precariat as a distinct social class, a theme that attracts a younger generation of documentary filmmakers rather than established fiction auteurs or popular filmmakers. Although no codified or universal representations and narratives of precarity and the precarious have been established in Baltic film, the study demonstrates that certain key tropes can be identified, for instance the systemic deprivation of the working class, domestic migration and emigration, and the underprivileged status of the Russophone minority.

In his chapter on Scandinavian film, Anders Marklund aims to see how different film practices articulate comparable situations, and to relate these to a wider social context. Introducing the concept of the *precarity scene*, he analyzes scenes that depict situations in which someone urgently depends on others and needs to ask for their help to survive or to get by. Marklund focuses on how those precarity scenes are constructed differently in different kinds of films from mainstream crime thrillers and realist dramas to arthouse films and transgressive narrations.

The next-to-last stop on our route is the United Kingdom. John Hill's chapter locates contemporary representations of precarity in relation to a lengthy social-realist tradition within British cinema stretching back to the 1930s when the documentary movement "honored" manual labor, but also associated the working class with poverty, poor housing, unemployment, and economic insecurity. In his analysis, Hill identifies the 1980s and 1990s as the key period for the emergence of a new kind of cinematic imagery and storytelling that has remained highly influential and explores the most recent examples of this tradition.

The Netherlands is the final stop on our imaginary journey through the map of filmic depictions and discourses of precarity in Europe. Gert-Jan Harkema's chapter contextualizes two documentary series within the post-millennial political discourse of *flexicurity* and reduced social security. Harkema argues that these documentaries present the viewer with a relational and interpersonal picture of precarious living which is, as a kind of cultural geography, mapped out over the city of Amsterdam and should be seen as an artistic-political strategy to involve the spectator physically, emotionally, and politically.

Thanks to the contributions of our authors and the kaleidoscope of their different approaches, we have been able to expand our horizons—both figuratively and literally. Our research project "Cinematic Discourse of Deprivation: Analyzing the Representation of Precarity and Exclusion in European Fiction Film and Documentary" is occupied with questions of the filmic representation of poverty and precarity in European cinema. This project is funded by the DFG (Deutsche Forschungsgemeinschaft), a foundation to which we owe our greatest thanks for enabling our research and for financing both the conference and this publication.

The present volume is the first in the newly created book series *Film, Class, Society* that we have founded together with Daniel Fairfax, whom we would like to thank for his support. We would also like to express our deep gratitude to the members of our advisory board as well as Anja-Simone Michalski and Myrto Aspioti from De Gruyter, who invited us to create this series and to publish this book at their prestigious publishing house. Working as a student assistant in our research project, Josefine Knuth-Pollok helped organize the conference and our first steps in producing this book, for which we thank her very much. Our other assistant and colleague, Aleksandra Miljković, has also helped in the preparation of the conference, contributed a chapter to this volume, and worked with us on editing every chapter. Thank you, Sasha!

Without the contributions of our authors, we would not have discovered many important European films and their negotiations of precarity. Their varied perspectives have enriched, broadened, and problematized our understanding of the phenomena we are concerned with. This virtual journey through European cinema has convinced us once again of the urgency of these questions and of the importance of adopting different approaches to what is in every sense a plural and collective issue.

Elisa Cuter
Guido Kirsten
Hanna Prenzel

Guido Kirsten
Studying the Cinema of Precarity
An Introduction

In his 1845 article "Rapid Progress of Communism in Germany," young Frederick Engels informs the readers of the English weekly *The New Moral World* about the latest political developments in Germany. He claims that "the rapidity with which Socialism has progressed in this country is quite miraculous," and discusses a painting by Carl Wilhelm Hübner (1814–1879), called *Die schlesischen Weber* (*The Silesian Weavers*, 1844, Fig. 1), which, according to Engels, "has made a more effectual Socialist agitation than a hundred pamphlets might have done."[1]

Remarkable is not only the enormous effect Engels attributes to the painting, but also his description of what is depicted. It is a genuine ekphrasis of the absent work, which he sought to vividly present to his readers. Moreover, besides meticulously and illustratively *describing* the picture, Engels in the same movement *interprets* it in order to explain the claimed political effect. According to him, the canvas not only shows "some Silesian weavers bringing woven linen to a factory owner" but also "very impressively contrasts cold-hearted wealth on the one side with desperate poverty on the other."[2]

Narrativizing the pictorial elements,[3] Engels reads the arrangement of the figures as a particular situation within a larger story:

> The well-fed manufacturer is represented with a face as red and unfeeling as brass, rejecting a piece of cloth which belongs to a woman; the woman, seeing no chance of selling the cloth, is sinking down and fainting, surrounded by her two little children, and hardly kept up by an old man [. . .]; and two men, each with a piece of rejected cloth on his back, are just leaving the room, one of whom is clenching his fist in rage, whilst the other, putting his hand on his neighbour's arm, points up towards heaven, as if saying: be quiet, there is a judge to punish him.[4]

Engels thus discerns several smaller scenes within the overall scene, several micro-narratives, which have as their common theme the exploitation of the Silesian weavers' families by rich linen factory merchants, embodied by the

---

1 Frederick Engels, "Rapid Progress of Communism in Germany" [1845], in *Collected Works, Volume 4, Marx and Engels, 1844–1845* (London: Lawrence & Wishart, 1975), 230.
2 Ibid.
3 "Narrativization" in the semio-pragmatic sense, cf. Roger Odin, *De la fiction* (Brussels: DeBoeck, 2000), 25–36; cf. Guido Kirsten, *Filmischer Realismus* (Marburg: Schüren, 2013), 153–157.
4 Engels, "Rapid Progress," 230–231.

Open Access. © 2022 Guido Kirsten, published by De Gruyter. This work is licensed under the Creative Commons Attribution-NonCommercial-NoDerivatives 4.0 International License.
https://doi.org/10.1515/9783110707816-001

Fig. 1: *Die schlesischen Weber* (*The Silesian Weavers*, Carl Wilhelm Hübner, 1844/1846).

patriarch centrally placed in the picture, his employees, and his son. Engels's reading is clearly informed by the broader media discourse of his time (including newspaper articles, political pamphlets, and poems), which had made the general public particularly sensitive to the suffering of the Silesian weavers after their uprising in June 1844.[5]

Engels's description and interpretation raises several questions that can be linked to our contemporary research on filmic representations of precarity.[6] In what follows, I will sketch three sets of research questions. The first is concerned with film production and aesthetic structures, the second with the filmic works' different kinds of impact, the third with the social discourse to which the works relate. After that I will discuss Lauren Berlant's concept of the "cinema of precarity" in an attempt to redefine it before engaging with the polysemic term "precarity" itself.

---

[5] Christina von Hodenberg, *Aufstand der Weber. Die Revolte von 1844 und ihr Aufstieg zum Mythos* (Bonn: Dietz, 1997); Heinrich Heine's famous poem "The Silesian Weavers" was first published under the title "Die armen Weber" on July 10, 1844 in the socialist daily *Vorwärts*, run by Karl Marx's. Engels translated it into English.

[6] For the term "precarity scene" see Anders Marklund's contribution to this volume.

Three Sets of Research Questions

1. Poetics

The first set of questions has to do with *poetics*, that is, with the relation between artworks and the circumstances of their production: What are the major principles of construction and composition of the work in question? What stylistic repertoires were at hand, what formal choices were common, what functions might those which were chosen fulfill? What kinds of (commercial, ideological, aesthetic) objectives were involved in the production? Who authored the work and under what economic, political and artistic conditions? And who can be supposed to be the public primarily targeted by it? The success of *The Silesian Weavers* can at least partially be explained by the timing of its creation and exhibition. Hübner completed the canvas in July 1844, immediately after the famous uprising of the weavers in the small Silesian towns of Peterswaldau and Langenbielau on June 3 and 4.[7] But he had begun work on it earlier, in the course of a major fundraising campaign in support of the weavers in the Rhenish press in the spring of the same year. The large-format painting, which bears traces of romantic painting but can also be seen as an early example of nineteenth-century realism, attracted public attention in Cologne, Berlin, and other places where it was exhibited from July onwards—under the immediate impression of the June events, which were much discussed, although or precisely because there were few established facts about them. Hübner did not thematize the uprising itself, but his painting could be understood as illustrating its causes, and also as clearly taking sides in favor of the weavers. (The unsympathetically drawn factory owner was easily identified as the particularly exploitative textile merchant Ernst Friedrich Zwanziger, whose house and warehouse became the target of the first attack by the Peterswaldau weavers.)

Hübner was not a socialist, however, and his main target audience was the bourgeoisie in the Rhineland. Historian Christina von Hodenberg explicitly discusses his painting not as part of the socialist line of interpretation of the events but as part of its "bourgeois myth."[8] The immediate intention of *The Silesian Weavers* was a charitable one: As part of the above-mentioned campaign, it sought to motivate wealthy donors to aid the impoverished weavers, in which

---

[7] The painting exists in three versions, two of which Hübner produced in 1844, one (in a smaller format) in 1846. Lilian Landes, *Carl Wilhelm Hübner (1814–1879): Genre und Zeitgeschichte im deutschen Vormärz* (Munich/Berlin: Deutscher Verlag, 2008), 64–65.
[8] Von Hodenberg, *Aufstand der Weber*, 115–136. All translations, if not otherwise stated in the bibliography, are by me, G.K.

it apparently succeeded.[9] Albeit clearly critical of the textile merchant's cold-heartedness and his supposed greed, the main impression the painting sought to elicit was *pity*.

Questions of authorship, address, contexts of production, and their bearing on the works' form are important for the cinema of precarity, as well. In the conclusion of his *Ghettos, Tramps, and Welfare Queens*, Stephen Pimpare introduces the concept of the "propertied gaze" in order to explain the problematic biases in cinematic representations of the poor in twentieth-century Hollywood cinema. Pimpare proposes the term "propertied gaze" in analogy to Laura Mulvey's famous feminist concept of the "male gaze": "I want to argue that American movies have also had a propertied gaze—the viewer is never assumed to be poor or homeless, and films are never meant for them, even when they are ostensibly about them."[10] As a reason for this bias, Pimpare states that poor people are much less likely to author cinematic works than they are to write books, for example, because of the high financial costs and organizational prerequisites involved in film production. Only in exceptional cases, therefore, are films about poverty informed by first-hand experiences.

Whether his diagnosis ought to be limited to twentieth-century Hollywood productions—at some moments in his books, Pimpare introduces European films such as *Major Barbara* (Gabriel Pascal, 1941) and *Entre les murs* (*The Class*, Laurent Cantet, 2008) as more progressive alternatives—is an open question.[11] What is certain, however, is that in the more recent cinema of precarity, the division between the depicted (the precarized) and those depicting them (directors, screenwriters, actors, cinematographers, etc.) is less clear-cut. There are two reasons for this: First, the means of film production have become more widely available. Access to cameras and editing devices is not limited to studios anymore. This allows for filmic self-representations of the precarized. A case in point is *A la deriva, por los circuitos de la precariedad feminina* (*Adrift in the Circuits of Women's Precarious Lives*, 2003) collaboratively produced by the Spanish activist group Precarias a la deriva, in which the female producers of the film tell the story of how and why they formed the group, how they approach the matter of precarity, and what they see as their political projects and forms of action.[12]

---

9 Ibid., 118.
10 Stephen Pimpare, *Ghettos, Tramps, and Welfare Queens: Down and Out on the Silver Screen* (New York: Oxford University Press, 2017), 288.
11 Ibid., 66–67 and 98.
12 Hanna Prenzel, "Feminist Perspectives on Precarization: Revisiting Gendered Strike in Collaboratively Produced Films," *Image [&] Narrative* 22, no. 3 (2021).

While *Adrift in the Circuits of Women's Precarious Lives* is an activist film at the margins of cinema, many of those working in the film business—as in the creative and cultural industries in general—experience precarity themselves and can talk about it from their own experience. Here, we can refer to Julian Radlmaier's comedy *Selbstkritik eines bürgerlichen Hundes* (*Self-Criticism of a Bourgeois Dog*, 2017), in which Radlmaier plays a precarious director who, unable to raise funding for his new film project, is forced to accept a job as a seasonal farmhand.

These examples should not suggest that the structural asymmetry between precarious subjects and filmmakers has entirely vanished. Even when the filmmakers come from proletarian or poor middle-class milieus themselves, and are thus informed by their own experiences and personal acquaintances—such as the Dardenne brothers from Seraing, the industrial suburb of Liège (Belgium), or Andrea Arnold from a working-class family in Dartford, Kent (UK)—the success and the prestige of their films have opened up a certain cultural distance between them and the underclass world they portray. We have to acknowledge, however, that the picture has become more complex and diverse. It would be wrong to apply Pimpare's concept of the "propertied gaze" indiscriminately to the cinema of precarity which includes films as diverse as the autobiographic art-film *Ray & Liz* (Richard Billingham, 2018), the "ethnographic" semi-documentary *Epizoda u životu berača željeza* (*Episode in the Life of an Iron Picker*, Danis Tanović, 2013), or the satirical comedy *Tutta la vita davanti* (*Her Whole Life Ahead*, Paolo Virzì, 2008). They all have different connections to reality (based on personal re-collections by the filmmaker, or by the non-professional actors who "play themselves" and re-enact past events, or by a more loose and general diagnostics of the emergence of a well-educated "cognitariat" in Italy). They use different devices and different genre formulae, and thus develop different perspectives on the phenomena of precarity, poverty, social exclusion, and exploitation. The challenge for a poetics of the cinema of precarity is precisely to study it in all its diversity.

2. Impact

This diversity is also important for the second set of questions inspired by Engels' reading of *The Silesian Weavers*. These questions deal with matters of *impact*: How do representations of precarity affect us? What short-term, mid-term, and long-term effects do they engender? How do they change the audience, how do they influence politics?

It is exactly the alleged impact that motivates Engels's discussion of the painting in his article: whatever its style, whatever Hübner's own background, whatever the circumstances and conditions of production, whatever the immediate intentions involved—what counts for Engels is that it "made a more effectual Socialist agitation than a hundred pamphlets might have done"; that it "prepared a good many minds for Social ideas."[13] Of course, it is quite impossible to prove the truth of these claims. What we do know is that the canvas was exhibited in several German cities and that it attracted an interested audience. Historian Karl Biedermann reported that onlookers at the exhibitions "murmured to each other the name of the hard man (a well-known rich factory owner in Silesia), whom the picture was thought to represent" and that they "made connections between the individual case and general reflections on the situation of the working-classes."[14]

The painting also had a remarkable mid- and long-term impact. Its motif soon circulated through many written testimonies about the fate of the Silesian weavers.[15] Apparently, Hübner's painting provided authors with vivid visual material, which they only had to dress up and embellish in words. As Christina von Hodenberg has described it:

> Hübner's impressive painting achieved a high degree of recognition and shaped the further reception of the material. Hübner was the first to focus on the striking juxtaposition of rich and poor, of despair and arrogance. This contrast became the most common motif in literature on the weavers. The scene Hübner devised—the delivery of the cloth to the merchant's house—also became a leitmotif of subsequent designs. The hard factory owner, who has no eye for the misery surrounding him, became a popular topos, as did the weaver's wife, who collapses from despair or hunger.[16]

This heritage is visible, for example, in Gerhart Hauptmann's famous play *Die Weber* (*The Weavers*, 1892). The description of the first act's scenery and its narrative development are quite obviously inspired by the scene depicted in the painting.[17]

The more narrowly *political* impact is, of course, difficult to assess: Did it truly convert anyone to socialism, did it have any measurable influence on

---

13 Engels, "Rapid Progress," 230–231.
14 Karl Biedermann, *Dreißig Jahre deutsche Geschichte*, Vol. 1 (Breslau: Schottlaender, 1881), 158.
15 "In the year of its creation and far beyond, countless picture descriptions appeared in newspapers, magazines, encyclopaedias and overview works." Landes, *Carl Wilhelm Hübner*, 64.
16 Von Hodenberg, *Aufstand der Weber*, 118.
17 Gerhart Hauptmann, "The Weavers", in *The Dramatic Works, Vol. 1: Social Dramas* (New York: Huebsch, 1923), 201–226. Its film adaptation *Die Weber* (*The Weavers*, Frederic [Friedrich] Zelnik, 1927) also opens with a similar scene, but visually it is not reminiscent of Hübner's canvas: Inspired by Russian montage cinema, Zelnik has split up the scene into a rapid sequence of medium shots and close-ups.

public opinion, did it help organize protest? This is not only due to the scarcity of historical sources but also to more general theoretical and methodological problems in studying media impact. While there is an overall agreement among filmmakers and researchers that films can contribute to changing political thought and action,[18] the specific influence of individual works is hard to prove. As Jens Eder argues, "film's political impacts, like any media effects, are mostly social, cumulative, indirect, and transactional."[19] Even a case like the Dardenne brothers' film *Rosetta* (1999) which allegedly led to a law in Belgium protecting teenage workers against precarity,[20] is less impressive when looked at more closely. In fact, the bill had already been in the works, and the minister simply seized the opportunity of the film's prestigious win of the Cannes Palme d'Or in 1999 to popularize his politics.[21] The social and political impact of filmic works is normally less concrete and specific, more diffuse and ephemeral, which makes it harder to grasp but no less real.

Engels's claim involves another aspect that is relevant here. His comparison of the power of the image to that of pamphlets can be read as a sort of political *paragone* in which the medium of painting appears to be superior to written text. What he appears to imply is that the canvas provokes a more immediate impression in its beholders, potentially engendering affects and emotions such as anger, hate, frustration, pity, and empathy, as well as political judgements concerning responsibilities and solutions to the intolerable situation.

This dimension is certainly also important for filmic works. One of the undeniable powers of the cinema lies in providing us with compelling, sometimes even haunting images of characters (or real persons) in specific situations. For a certain timespan, we accompany Rosetta or Daniel Blake, Vanda or Thierry

---

18 Jens Eder, "Political Impact: On the Social Vibrancy of Film," in *What Film is Good For: Varieties of Ethical Experience in Cinematic Spectatorship*, ed. Julian Hanich and Martin Roussow (Oakland: University of California Press [forthcoming]).
19 Eder, "Political Impact." Eder references Patti M. Valkenburg, Jochen Peter, and Joseph B. Walther, "Media Effects: Theory and Research," *Annual Review of Psychology* 67, no. 1 (2016).
20 Adrian Martin, "*Rosetta*," *Film Critic* (February 2001), http://www.filmcritic.com.au/reviews/r/rosetta.html; Janice Morgan, "The Social Realism of Body Language in *Rosetta*," *The French Review* 77, no. 3 (February, 2004): 534 (fn 4); Lauren Berlant, *Cruel Optimism* (Durham, NC: Duke University Press, 2011), 162–163 and 288 (fn1).
21 Xan Brooks, "We're the same: one person, four eyes," *The Guardian*, February 9, 2006, https://www.theguardian.com/film/2006/feb/09/features.xanbrooks; Sheila Johnson, "The secret of the Dardenne brothers' Palme d'Or success," *Independent*, March 17, 2006, https://www.independent.co.uk/arts-entertainment/films/features/the-secret-of-the-dardenne-brothers-palme-d-or-success-6106488.html.

Taugourdeau,[22] and experience vicariously what it means to be in their shoes. We can become aware of hardships, impasses, and injustices which we may have never experienced ourselves and thus come close to imaginary persons from social strata and cultural milieus other than our own. Or we may be reminded of problems we know all too well from our own lives and recognize our own situation—as single mothers, as unemployed, as addicts, as stressed-out temporary workers, etc.—mirrored on the screen.

Precarity is a social phenomenon which cannot be defined by objective data alone. An important component of it is the *feeling of insecurity*, which is subjectively experienced as, transformed into, or articulated through affects and emotions such as anxiety, depression, and fear of expulsion/extinction (the "three complex affective states that capture the dynamics of precarity" according to Francesco Sticchi), or anger, anomie, anxiety, and alienation (which Guy Standing sees as the four main emotional responses to precarity).[23] Films are not only able to make us sensitive for these different subjective states, they can also let us empathically experience them ourselves. Besides, they can let us understand their specific causes, and thereby enlighten us politically. Adopting such an attitude, we can learn, through and with Daniel Blake, how the recent changes in the UK social system regarding employment and support allowance cause suffering; we can learn, watching Nazif and Senada Mujić (from *Episode in the Life of an Iron Picker*) what the systemic discrimination of Roma effectively means for those affected; or, through Sandra (from *Deux jours, une nuit* [*Two Days, One Night*, Jean-Pierre and Luc Dardenne, 1999]), how management can pit employees against each other when there is no union representation to prevent it.

Films produce images that may feed into collective representations of social problems, providing us with concrete scenes and feelings of what otherwise remain mere news reports and statistics.[24] When reading or hearing of precarity, we normally do not know how to define the phenomenon either intensionally

---

22 From *Rosetta* (Jean-Pierre and Luc Dardenne, 1999), *I, Daniel Blake* (Ken Loach, 2016), *No Quarto da Vanda* (*In Vanda's Room*, Pedro Costa, 2000), and *La Loi du marché* (*The Measure of a Man*, Stéphane Brizé, 2015) respectively.
23 Francesco Sticchi, *Mapping Precarity in Contemporary Cinema and Television: Chronotopes of Anxiety, Depression, Expulsion/Extinction* (Cham, Switzerland: Springer & Palgrave Macmillan, 2021), 18; Guy Standing, *The Precariat: The New Dangerous Class* (London/New York: Bloomsbury, 2011), 19–24.
24 An empirical study has found that, under specific conditions, "non-news factual television programming offers spectators a more proximate, active and complex mediated experience of distant suffering than television news" (Martin Scott, "The Mediation of Distant Suffering: An Empirical Contribution beyond Television News Texts," *Media, Culture & Society* 36, no.1 [2014]: 4). As Scott concludes, "it seems reasonable to suggest that if we wish to see the media

(by its characteristics) or extensionally (by who we would have to include in the count). But we may remember Rosetta fighting to keep her job or lying in bed at night, comforting herself with the words "I have found a job, I have found a friend, I have a normal life, I'm not going to fall into the hole"; of Vanda drugging herself in her room in Fontainhas in the suburbs of Lisbon; or of Antoni, a Polish taxi driver in Hans-Christian Schmid's *Distant Lights (Lichter,* 2003), struggling to raise money for a communion dress for his daughter (a subplot that refers to a very similar storyline in Loach's 1993 film *Raining Stones*). We may think of Mia from *Fish Tank* (Andrea Arnold, 2011) growing up in dysfunctional surroundings in Essex, UK; of Daniel Blake despairing on the phone and in front of a computer monitor, trying in vain to get his social security allowance, and later on having to sell his furniture. These scenes and images may be stored in the backs of our minds, and they can be actualized when we hear or read about similar events. Instances of precarity can thus become personalized and connected to faces and bodies in particular situations. They enrich what Charles Taylor has called our "social imaginary," a "largely unstructured and inarticulate understanding of our whole situation," which feeds into a repertory of possible actions.[25] This kind of impact should not be underestimated.

3. Discourse

The third set of questions, which I believe to be most central to studying the cinema of precarity, is connected to the first two in multiple ways. While poetics relates the structure of the works back to their process of creation, and impact studies draw a line to their effects on the audience, the third set of questions aims at the core of the representations themselves. These questions concern the works in their *discursive* dimension: What are they actually about? What aspects of precarity do they address and in what way?[26] Do they have a specific political message, or are they ambiguous? How are they linked to other discourses, and

---

playing a role in promoting 'solidarity between humans' then the appearance of distant others in programming outside of the news should be a priority." (Ibid., 18).
25 Charles Taylor, *Modern Social Imaginaries* (Durham, NC: Duke University Press, 2004), 25; Christoph Büttner has also argued that films contribute to the repertory of social imaginaries described by Taylor by providing possible images, narratives and myths: Christoph Büttner, "'Das gute Leben': Räume und Imaginationen prä-moderner Zukunftsentwürfe im deutschen Gegenwartskino," in *Cosmopolitan Cinema: Kunst und Politik in der Zweiten Moderne*, ed. Matthias Christen and Kathrin Rothemund (Marburg: Schüren, 2019), 260–263.
26 "Aspect" both in its colloquial understanding and in Wittgenstein's sense; for the latter see Nino Klingler's chapter in this book.

where can we situate them in the wider discursive field (made up not only of other pictures, other films, and other audio-visual productions, but also of journalistic, academic, literary texts, radio-features, and every-day conversations concerning related topics)?

Engels's account of the *The Silesian Weavers* consists largely of a description of its pictorial content. But, as I wrote above, this description is not purely objective; it not only registers what is visible, but interprets the content of the picture in the same breath. It is an iconographic miniature, an explication of the painting's "subject matter or meaning."[27] In fact, without the explication, it would be difficult for a contemporary audience to understand the image at all: How could we grasp who the figures are supposed to embody, what their gestures and gazes allude to, what the whole scene is supposed to mean?

The same is true for cinematic representations of precarity when the context is not or no longer known. Less evidently (because as viewers we are embedded in the discourse of our times and have tacit knowledge of certain economic practices and political institutions), the same goes for the contemporary cinema of precarity: To grasp the meaning of a film like *Sorry We Missed You* (Ken Loach, 2019), it is vital to have at least some basic ideas about the so-called "gig economy," and about the practice of "zero-hour contracts." Just as we automatically discern basic elements while watching a film—such as characters and their traits, connections between characters, actions, and motivations for these actions—we are invited to also identify less concrete and less distinct *social phenomena*. Doing so, we depart from a mere "fictionalizing mode of reading" and begin to "read" the film as a discourse, in the terms of Roger Odin's semio-pragmatic approach.[28]

Generally speaking, to view films as discourses means, first of all, that they are not simply understood as reflections of social processes but as meaningful works that actively contribute to our understanding of reality. Second, "discourse" is an overarching term that comprises fiction and documentary film. The conditions of production, rhetorical strategies, and truth-claims may differ, but both fiction and documentary films can be fruitfully regarded as discourses on

---

[27] Erwin Panofsky, *Studies in Iconology: Humanistic Themes in the Art of the Renaissance* (New York: Oxford University Press, 1939), 3.

[28] Roger Odin, *Les Espaces de communication: Introduction à la sémio-pragmatique* (Grenoble: PUG, 2011), 112; Guido Kirsten, "Jean-Pierre Meunier's Modalities of the 'Filmic Attitude': Towards a Theory of Referentiality in Cinematic Discourse," in *The Structures of Film Experience by Jean-Pierre Meunier: Historical Assessments and Phenomenological Expansions*, ed. Julian Hanich and Daniel Fairfax (Amsterdam: Amsterdam University Press, 2019).

social events and structures. Third, the term is intended to open up a different perspective on the films: instead of paying attention to audio-visual style or to narration in themselves, the focus is on argumentative or quasi-argumentative structures (and on how these are supported by certain stylistic and narrative means). Questions are then: What is the film trying to convince us of? Can we identify implicit presuppositions? How does the film's dramaturgy suggest a particular argument? What does the film's structure reveal about who is primarily addressed by the discourse and in what way, and who is rhetorically excluded? Fourth, the discourse-theoretical approach enables us to examine filmic works in terms of what they absorb from the wider cultural discourse and how this context enriches the understanding of a film.

Odin defines every "mode of producing meaning and affect" as a series of articulated operations. Inspired by Odin, but also departing from his definition of the "discursive mode," I would claim the following operations to be necessary for this mode:

1. Reading a film as a discourse means to interrogate the relations of diegetic figurations to structures and institutions of the real world. We are not only interested in what is going on in the story world of *Sorry We Missed You*, for example, and what happens to the fictional beings inhabiting it (as in the fictionalizing mode), but we also construct a *reference* to concrete and abstract entities that we believe to be part of social reality, such as family structures, gender relations, political systems and decisions, etc.

2. The discursive reading implies the translation of narration into argumentation (or at least into some kind of suggestion or suasion): What happens to the family in *Sorry We Missed You* is then not only a *story*, but moreover a *demonstration*. While in our narrative reading, we are linking states and events into a chain of action (the connection of the elements is dynamically causal like in a complex domino track), the discursive syntagmatic has the form of loose syllogisms (albeit the logic applied need not be formally consistent; rather, it is a kind of "everyday logic," "common-sense," or "plausibility"). Read discursively, the presentation of the events in *Sorry We Missed You* is thus translated into premises which suggest a conclusion, such as: gig-economy and zero-hour contracts do not only lead to economic precarity and stress, they also tend to disintegrate families.

3. The second point implies a third one, already mentioned, but not really elaborated on by Odin: part of the discursive mode of meaning and affect is *rhetoric*. The connections between different filmic and narrative elements are not purely logical, but also suggestive, and they aim at creating a certain pathos (an emotional suasion accompanying the rational one). In the

discursive mode, "affects are used to persuade."[29] Here, the ordering of events is crucial, as are omissions and rhetorical figures such as metaphor, metonymy, paralipsis, hyperbole etc. When studying the presumed effects of filmic discourses, we therefore need to pay attention to the rhetoric involved.

Viewers normally do not perform the operations consciously but rather preconsciously and automatically (like most cognitive operations in our daily life). It is the researcher's task to explicate these operations and to scrutinize the filmic work's structures that invite them. Studying the cinema of precarity, we should do both—"read" the films "discursively," and analyze what in the film inclines us (and other viewers whose discursive readings we can reconstruct from reviews and criticism) to view them this way.

The Cinema of Precarity, Redefined

The term "cinema of precarity," which I have used without disambiguation or definition up to this point, was introduced by Lauren Berlant in her 2011 book *Cruel Optimism*.[30] It was then picked up by scholars like Alice Bardan, Ritu Vij, and others.[31] Berlant originally proposed it in relation to two films by the French filmmaker Laurent Cantet, *Ressources humaines* (*Human Resources*, 1999) and *L'Emploi du temps* (*Time Out*, 2001), and to the Dardenne brothers' *La Promesse* (*The Promise*, 1996) and *Rosetta*. Her understanding of the cinema of precarity (or "precarious cinema" as she synonymously calls it) combines formal and thematical aspects, relating it back to older forms of realist aesthetics in Hollywood melodrama and Italian neorealism, and to the more recent "French cinematic 'New Realism'" and the so-called Neo-neo-realism in US-independent filmmaking.[32] The films of the cinema of precarity, writes Berlant, "record the loneliness of collective singularity, the impacts of affective fraying, and the tiny optimism of recuperative gestures in the middle of it all"; also they attend to "the proprioceptive—to bodies moving in space performing affectively

---

29 Odin, *Les Espaces de communication*, 112.
30 Berlant, *Cruel Optimism*, 201.
31 Alice Bardan, "The New European Cinema of Precarity: A Transnational Perspective," in *Work in Cinema: Labor and The Human Condition*, ed. Ewa Mazierska (New York: Palgrave Macmillan, 2013); Ritu Vij, "Affective Fields of Precarity: Gendered Antinomies in Contemporary Japan," *Alternatives: Global, Local, Political* 38, no. 2 (May 2013).
32 Berlant, *Cruel Optimism*, 201 and 295 (fn 30).

laden gestures—to investigate new potential conditions of solidarity emerging from subjects not with similar historical identities or social locations but with similar adjustment styles to the pressures of the emergent new ordinariness."[33]

The cinema of precarity is thereby connected to "cruel optimism," the overarching concept of her book. "Cruel optimism" describes a situation in which something you desire (such as some kind of food, a love relationship, a fantasy of the good life, or a political project) becomes "an obstacle to your flourishing," so that "the object that draws your attachment actively impedes the aim that brought you to it initially."[34] In *Rosetta*, cruel optimism takes the form of "aspirational normativity," which persists even "in the project of life-building on the bottom of contemporary class society."[35] Rosetta's bedtime whispers to herself, quoted above, are most symptomatic of this longing for normalcy.[36] To attain this goal she almost goes so far as to kill her only friend Riquet—metaphorically, but nearly even physically—just to take his place.[37] Here, the "aspirational normativity" is indeed *cruel* in Berlant's sense not because it harms Riquet but because he appears to be Rosetta's only viable source of a potentially healthy relationship, a direly needed base of emotional support. Berlant sees the "aspirational normativity" impersonated by Rosetta (and by Igor in *The Promise*), as a sign of the widely shared "collective attachments to fundamentally stressful conventional lives" in late capitalism.[38]

While her discussion of *Rosetta* and *The Promise* binds the cinema of precarity back to the idea of cruel optimism through the concept of "aspirational normativity," she also diagnoses a new narrative form in these films, which she calls the "situation tragedy," defined as "the marriage between tragedy and situation comedy where people are fated to express their flaws episodically, over and over, without learning, being relieved, becoming better, or dying." In contrast to the sitcom where "*the world has the room for us that enables us to endure*" (with all our flaws, our ticks, our anxieties), "in the situation tragedy,

---

33 Ibid., 201–202.
34 Ibid., 1.
35 Ibid., 164.
36 Cf. Ruth Sonderegger, "Wie diszipliniert ist (Ideologie-)Kritik?: Zwischen Philosophie, Soziologie und Kunst," in *Was ist Kritik?*, ed. Rahel Jaeggi and Tilo Wesche (Frankfurt a.M.: Suhrkamp, 2009), 74–78.
37 Martin O'Shaughnessy discusses the recurrent motif of the ethical question whether to kill or to let live in the Dardenne brothers' films: Martin O'Shaughnessy, "Beyond Neoliberalism? Gift Economies in the Films of the Dardenne Brothers," in *Cinema of Crisis: Film and Contemporary Europe*, ed. Thomas Austin and Angelos Koutsourakis (Edinburgh: Edinburgh University Press, 2020).
38 Berlant, *Cruel Optimism*, 167.

one moves between having a little and being ejected from the social, where life is lived on the outside of value, in terrifying nonplaces where one is a squatter, trying to make an event in which one will matter to something or someone."[39]

As is typical of Berlant's critical work, her definition of the "new genre hybrid" intertwines formal (narrative and stylistic) and thematic aspects, with strong affective components. This is also true of another critical category, the "impasse" which replaces the situational tragedy in Berlant's reading of Cantet's films, a concept she offers "both as a formal term for encountering the duration of the present, and a specific term for tracking the circulation of precariousness through diverse locales and bodies."[40]

A question that remains open after reading Berlant's two chapters on the Dardennes' and Cantet's films is to what extent the conclusions she draws from her interpretations are valid for the cinema of precarity in general. Her discussion of *Human Resources*, for example, concludes with the following sentence: "In the cinema of precarity, the shift in the portrayal of immobility from a normative, conventional, habituated solidity to living paralysis, playful repetition, or animated still-life has become a convention of representing the impasse as a relief from the devastating pain of this unfinished class transition."[41] While this is certainly an appropriate and inspiring interpretation of the film (the "unfinished class transition" describing the situation of the film's protagonist who is caught up between his working-class background and his position as a management trainee), it remains questionable to what extend this is helpful to characterize the cinema of precarity more generally.

Another problematic point is Berlant's auteurist penchant; her list of "writer-directors of this heavily atmospheric witnessing mode of contemporary capitalist *fraying*" includes names like Ramin Bahrani, Christian Mungiu, Jia Zhangke, Kelly Reichardt, and others.[42] While all of these have certainly contributed relevant filmic works to the portrayal of precarity in different parts of the world, it remains questionable why someone like Ken Loach, who has devoted most of his

---

[39] Ibid., 176–177.
[40] More concretely, she speaks of three different kinds of impasse: The first is the one encountered after a dramatic loss (such as a broken heart, the sudden death of someone close, or any kind of social catastrophe), when one does not know how to live on. The second kind of impasse describes an uncertain situation in which one cannot navigate and for which one lacks "a name and procedures of managing it". The third kind of impasse appears to be a more positive situation "where managing the presence of a problem/event that dissolves the old sureties and forces improvisation and reflection on life-without-guarantees is a pleasure and a plus, not a loss." Ibid., 200.
[41] Ibid., 212.
[42] Ibid., 295, fn 30 (Berlant erroneously gives Bahrani the forename Hooman).

career to portraying the precarious life of the working class, is absent from the list. (One can only suspect that Loach's style and dramaturgy are too classical for Berlant's preference for *new* forms, which are supposed to capture the new affective situation.) Moreover, I wonder why the "cinema of precarity" should be bound to the notion of the *auteur* at all. It appears to make more sense to include *any work* that focuses on precarious lives—in *any style* and by *any filmmaker or group of filmmakers*. To my mind, the cinema of precarity denotes the whole of the corpus of filmic works that centrally engage with aspects of precarity in society.[43]

My re-definition thus differs in three aspects from Berlant's original ideas: First, I do not assume that relations of cruel optimism are an essential or necessary part of all films belonging to the cinema of precarity. Some characters in some of the films certainly do desire something that is counterproductive to their flourishing (be it in the form of "aspirational normativity" or in another form), but this need not be the case for all of them (at least if we do not wish to completely dilute this concept). Second, in my eyes, the cinema of precarity is not bound to the notion of *auteur*; it does not matter at all whether the makers of films that portray situations of precarity are considered "authors" in the cinephile sense, whether they dispose of a signature style or an original vision of the world. Third, and related to this last point, my understanding of the cinema of precarity is far more pluralistic in regard to matters of form, style, mood, and genre. *Los lunes al sol* (*Mondays in the Sun*, Fernando Léon de Aranoa, 2002), a mainstream tragicomedy about unemployment in a northern Spanish port town, is as much an example of the cinema of precarity as *9 Leben* (*9 Lives*, Maria Speth, 2011), an experimental black-and-white documentary about homelessness in Berlin. In fact, whether they explicitly refer to Berlant's term or not, film scholars who have studied the cinema of precarity such as Bardan, Vij, Tom Zaniello,[44]

---

43 Simply for the practical reason of reducing the scope of the endeavor, I suggest limiting the corpus to films that are intended to be shown in the cinema and excluding other audiovisual works such as television series, reports and TV documentaries, installations and VR works, web series and other internet content. I do not think that such works are less important socially and politically—surely they merit as much study as cinema films. But they need not necessarily be studied under the heading of the "cinema of precarity." Films that only marginally treat the subject (where, for example, a minor character is precarious, without playing a major role in the story) are also excluded by definition. Of course, there are many borderline cases, as with any corpus. On the other hand, no geographical or historical limitation is intended. The focus in this introduction on European films from the past 30 years owes itself to the context of its publication.
44 Tom Zaniello, *The Cinema of the Precariat, The Exploited, Underemployed, and Temp Workers of the World* (New York and London: Bloomsbury, 2020). Zaniello, however, does not relate

Gabriel Bortzmeyer,[45] Sticchi, the authors of *The Precarious in the Cinemas of the Americas*,[46] and those in the present volume appear all aware of the diversity of their object of study.[47]

If we apprehend that the cinema of precarity is necessarily broad and diverse—not limited to auteur films, not limited to a new realism, not limited to the specific variety of precarity that directly relates to cruel optimism—we can study its formal and thematic heterogeneity. We can ask what genres, forms, devices the filmmakers have chosen in order to portray, analyze, or criticize different kinds and aspects of precarity. But it is therefore crucial to have at least some basic ideas of what the term precarity relates to and which of its aspects are relevant to our aims.

The Concept of Precarity

The bibliography on "precarity," "precariousness," and "the precariat" is by now so enormous that it is not possible to attempt anything like a complete overview here. I can only sketch some of the concept's somewhat fuzzy outlines.

As a term to denote a new kind of social insecurity, *precarietà* came into use in Italy in the 1960s.[48] More influentially, the word *précarité* was used in French social sciences in the 1980s and '90s, most notably in Robert Castel's book on the history of wage labor and in Pierre Bourdieu's famous speech "La précarité est aujourd'hui partout."[49] From French and other Romance languages it was introduced

---

to Berlant's term at all. His study is very much based on Guy Standing's work on the "precariat," and he devotes the chapters of his book to what he sees as different sub-classes of the precariat such as internal migrants in China, the "women of the precariat," or the "cyberprecariat" (ibid., 1–15 and x–xiii).

45 Gabriel Bortzmeyer, *Le Peuple précaire du cinéma contemporain* (Paris: Hermann, 2020).
46 Constanza Burucúa and Carolina Sitnisky, eds.,*The Precarious in the Cinemas of the Americas* (Cham, Switzerland: Springer & Palgrave Macmillan, 2018).
47 For a more extensive reflection upon the heterogeneity of the "cinema of precarity," see Martin O'Shaughnessy's chapter in this book.
48 Arianna Bove, Annalisa Murgia, and Emiliana Armano, "Mapping Precariousness: Subjectivities and Resistance. An Introduction," in *Mapping Precariousness, Labour Insecurity and Uncertain Livelihoods: Subjectivities and Resistance,* ed. Emiliana Armano, Arianna Bove, and Annalisa Murgia (London/New York: Routledge, 2017), 1.
49 Robert Castel, *From Manual Workers to Wage Laborers: The Transformation of the Social Question* (New Brunswick/London: Transaction, 2003); Pierre Bourdieu, "Job Insecurity is Everywhere Now," in *Acts of Resistance: Against the New Myths of our Time,* trans. Richard Nice (Cambridge: Polity Press, 1998).

into English where the noun "precarity" is relatively new, whereas "precariousness" has a longer lineage.

Etymologically these terms date back to ancient Latin, where the words *precor* or *precari* were in common use. They signify "to beg," "to implore," or "to pray for;" the adjective *precarius* meant something obtained by entreaty or mere favor, something which could be taken back at any time and therefore remained uncertain. The word thus implies the need to ask favors of others, to be depended on their benevolence.[50] The French adjective *précaire*, originating in the seventeenth century,[51] diffused into other European languages. In the context of nineteenth-century industrialization and under the then new conditions of labor under an ever-expanding capitalism, the semantic layer of insecurity was reinforced and the term mostly used as an attribute to characterize volatile conditions of life and work. For Karl Marx this attribute is part of a "general law" of the capitalist economy, which says that "the higher the productiveness of labour [. . .] the more precarious, therefore, becomes their [i.e. the labourers'] condition of existence, viz., the sale of their own labour-power for the increasing of another's wealth, or for the self-expansion of capital."[52] After the experience of the Fordist regime of capitalism, based as it was on the social integration of the working classes through a relatively high level of consumption and economic well-being, the general truth of Marx's "law" must appear doubtful. To what degree Fordism was actually an exception in the history of capitalism, however, is still a matter of debate.[53]

In its contemporary acceptation, the term *precarity* has come to name a *new* form of social insecurity, which is generally seen as the consequence of a neoliberal policy regarding job market de-regulation and the dismantling of the Fordist welfare state, in times of an ever more dynamic globalization. Some commentators emphasize the financialization of capitalism as the cause of these recent developments, while others stress the growing tertiary sector of immaterial and digital production, and the influence of new media.[54]

---

50 Sieglinde Lemke, *Inequality, Poverty, and Precarity in Contemporary American Culture* (New York: Palgrave Macmillan, 2016), 14; Berlant, *Cruel Optimism*, 192.
51 Lemke, *Inequality, Poverty, and Precarity*, 14.
52 Karl Marx, *Capital: A Critique of Political Economy* [1867] (New York: The Modern Library, 1906), 708.
53 Brett Neilson and Ned Rossiter, "Precarity as a Political Concept, or, Fordism as Exception," *Theory, Culture & Society* 25, no. 7–8 (December 2008).
54 Klaus Dörre, "Prekarität im Finanzmarkt-Kapitalismus," in *Prekarität, Abstieg, Ausgrenzung: Die soziale Frage am Beginn des 21. Jahrhunderts*, ed. Robert Castel and Klaus Dörre (Frankfurt a.M.: Campus, 2009); Maurizio Lazzarato, "Immaterial Labor," in *Radical Thought in Italy: A Potential Politics*, ed. Michael Hardt and Paolo Virno (Minneapolis, MN: University

For some social scientists, such as Robert Castel, precarity describes the situation of those who neither belong to the well-off and securely employed nor to the unemployed and excluded. Castel uses the term *vulnerability* as a heuristic tool to characterize a specific zone of social cohesion, which he distinguishes from a zone of integration and a zone of "disaffiliation" or "detachment." The zone of integration is defined by a combination of "stable work and durable social relationships," whereas "the absence of any participation in productive activities and relative social isolation give way to the negative effects of 'exclusion,' or rather [. . .] of 'disaffiliation.' [. . .] The zone of vulnerability is thus located in between the two extremes as an intermediate, unstable zone that goes along with the precariousness of work and the fragility of proximate supports."[55]

Writing a history of the social question in France and focusing on different regimes of wage labor, Castel diagnoses a paradigm shift in the years after 1970 from relative security and thus a relative wide zone of integration to a widening of the zone of vulnerability: "[T]he essence of the social question today will be, once again, the existence of the 'useless of the world,' supernumeraries, and beyond them a nebulousness of conditions marked by insecurity and uncertainty about tomorrow that testifies to the return of mass vulnerability."[56] But this new rise of precarity is specific (at least in the developed capitalist countries of the west) in that it comes *after* a period of relative well-being, "a vulnerability that exists even after the rise of social protections."[57]

One problematic point in this account is that it takes the "standard employment" in Western countries of the second half of the twentieth century as an implicit norm and tends to overlook that this was historically connected to a male-centered model of wage-labor. As Brigitte Aulenbacher and others have criticized, "precarity" only became a major issue in the social sciences when more and more *men* had been affected, whereas women often had to work under sub-standard and precarious conditions long before.[58]

---

of Minnesota Press, 1996); Rosalind Gill and Andy Pratt, "Precarity and Cultural Work in the Social Factory? Immaterial Labour, Precariousness and Cultural Work," *Oncurating.org* 16/13 (2013); David Kergel and Birte Heidkamp, "Media Change—Precarity *Within* and Precarity *Through* the Internet," in *Precarity within the Digital Age: Media Change and Social Insecurity*, ed. Birte Heidkamp and David Kergel (Wiesbaden: Springer VS, 2017).
55 Castel, *From Manual Workers to Wage Laborers*, XV–XVI.
56 Ibid., 445.
57 Ibid.
58 Brigitte Aulenbacher, "Die soziale Frage neu gestellt – Gesellschaftsanalysen der Prekarisierungs- und Geschlechterforschung," in *Prekarität, Abstieg, Ausgrenzung: Die soziale Frage am Beginn des 21. Jahrhunderts*, ed. Robert Castel and Klaus Dörre (Frankfurt a.M.: Campus, 2009).

This directly relates to the question of who is regarded as precarious or as "the precariat" in theoretical and sociological accounts.[59] While in Castel's approach, vulnerability and precarity characterize an intermediate zone, and Andrew Ross has described the precariat as "a highly trained aristocracy of labor, intermittently employed in low-end jobs,"[60] German and British sociologists have used the terms in a quite different way. In a widely discussed study by the social democratic Friedrich-Ebert-Institut from 2006, the authors use the phrase "abgehängtes Prekariat" ("detached precariat") to denote a new underclass, defined by multiple problems such as unemployment or extremely low income, family issues, alcohol or drug abuse, and precarious housing conditions—a social group that is made up of people who have lost all hope of participating in society in any meaningful way.[61] Guy Standing calls the precariat the group of people who have underpaid and insecure jobs, and situates it between the "shrinking 'core' of manual employees, the essence of the old 'working class'" and "an army of unemployed and a detached group of socially ill misfits living off the dregs of society."[62] Compared to classical phenomena of poverty, precarity seems to mean on the one hand being slightly better off than the average poor, or being not actually poor yet but only "at risk of poverty"—and on the other hand being even worse off, largely excluded from society. Bortzmeyer has also stated this ambiguity: "Today, 'precarious' can refer as much to the ensemble of workers suffering from an erosion of their status as to the most disaffiliated groups."[63]

In European cinema, we encounter both types of precarity. On the one hand working-class and middle-class families trying, and eventually failing, to maintain their status in times of economic crisis—for example Elsa and Michele in the Italian tragicomedy *Giorni e nuvole* (*Days and Clouds*, Silvio Soldini, 2007).[64] On the other hand, there are examples like the already mentioned Rosetta, living with her alcoholic mother in a caravan on the margins of society and struggling every day to keep going and maintain a semblance of dignity.

---

59 Magdalena Freudenschuss, *Prekär ist wer? Der Prekarisierungsdiskurs als Arena sozialer Kämpfe* (Wuppertal: Dampfboot, 2013).
60 Andrew Ross, *Nice Work If You Can Get It: Life and Labor in Precarious Times* (New York/London: New York University Press, 2009), 6.
61 Rita Müller-Hilmer (Friedrich-Ebert-Stiftung & TNS Infratest), "Gesellschaft im Reformprozess" (Bonn: FES, 2006), https://www.nachdenkseiten.de/upload/pdf/080625%20Hinweise%20PDF%20Datei%20zur%20Infratest%20Studie.pdf.
62 Standing, *The Precariat*, 8.
63 Bortzmeyer, *Le Peuple précaire*, 84.
64 Bardan, "The New European Cinema of Precarity," 77–78.

The example of *Rosetta* can also be related to an important categorial distinction introduced by Judith Butler in 2009. Butler suggests that we distinguish between *precarity* and the more general notion of *precariousness* or "being precarious." While *precariousness* is a pervasive fact of human life because "lives are by definition precarious: they can be expunged at will or by accident; their persistence is in no sense guaranteed," *precarity* more specifically "designates that politically induced condition, in which certain populations suffer from failing social and economic networks of support and become differentially exposed to injury, violence, and death."[65] In extreme cases such as Rosetta's, the socio-political condition of precarity becomes inseparable from the socio-anthropological condition of being precarious in a very somatic sense.

This is obviously also the case for people who had to flee from a war, from state repression, or simply from situations of extreme poverty, and who have arrived in Europe with empty hands, looking for a place to stay and some possibility to earn an income. An impressive film on these matters is Fernand Melgar's *L'Abri* (*The Shelter*, 2014), a direct cinema style documentary that portrays a social shelter in Lausanne (Switzerland), offering a place to sleep and a warm meal, but not able to provide enough places to sleep for all the people in need. Time and again, the social workers have to turn people away and lock them out even in cold winter nights, which seems like quite a scandal in one of the richest countries in the world.

Observers agree that precarity has an *objective* side defined by deregulated social structures and neo-liberal politics and a *subjective* side articulated in feelings such as vulnerability, stress, a pervasive feeling of being dependent and insecure.[66] Lauren Berlant has even called the precariat "an affective class" (defined by the "fading of security and upward mobility" and the loss of "social democratic good-life fantasies").[67] In passing I have already mentioned Sticchi's and Standing's reflections on affects, emotions, and mental health issues, such as anger, anxiety, and depression, as elements of the experience of being precarized. Sticchi discusses them as affective states which

---

[65] Judith Butler, *Frames of War: When Is Life Grievable?* (London/New York: Verso, 2009), 25; cf. Isabell Lorey, *State of Insecurity: Government of the Precarious* [2012] (London: Verso, 2015), 11–13. A similar differentiation between an ontological precarity (*precarité vitale*) and a genuinely social precarity (*précarité sociale*) was introduced by Guillaume Le Blanc in his *Vies ordinaires, vies précaires* (Paris: Seuil, 2007).
[66] Oliver Marchart, "Auf dem Weg in die Prekarisierungsgesellschaft," in *Facetten der Prekarisierungsgesellschaft: Prekäre Verhältnisse. Sozialwissenschaftliche Perspektiven auf die Prekarisierung von Arbeit und Leben*, ed. Oliver Marchart (Bielefeld: Transcript, 2013), 13.
[67] Berlant, *Cruel Optimism*, 195.

relate to certain "cinematic chronotopes" that he attempts to map in his book: chronotopes of anxiety in films and TV series such as *I, Daniel Blake*, *The Measure of a Man*, or *Fish Tank*; chronotopes of depression in films by Kelly Reichardt, in *Two Days, One Night*, and others; and chronotopes of expulsion/extinction for instance in *Gisaengchung* (*Parasite*, Bong Joon Ho, 2019), *The Florida Project* (Sean Baker, 2017), *Orange Is the New Black* (Jenji Kohan, 2013–2019), or *Show Me a Hero* (Paul Haggis and David Simon, 2015).[68] Guy Standing, in his book, diagnoses a "precariatised mind" and sees anger (stemming "from frustration at the seemingly blocked avenues for advancing a meaningful life and from a sense of relative deprivation"), anomie ("from listlessness associated with sustained defeat"), anxiety ("chronic insecurity associated not only with teetering on the edge [. . .], but also with a fear of losing what they possess even while feeling cheated by not having more"), and alienation (arising "from knowing that what one is doing is not for one's own purpose or for what one could respect or appreciate") as the four typical accompaniments of being precarized.[69]

Standing has attempted to define the *objective* conditions of this experience as well. He proposes understanding precarity as the lack of seven forms of labor-related security that used to be common (or even taken for granted) in the era of industrial citizenship: 1. labor market security (adequate income-earning opportunities due to enough available jobs), 2. employment security (protection against arbitrary dismissal), 3. job security (ability and opportunity to retain a certain niche in employment including possible 'upward' mobility), 4. work security (protection against accidents and illness at work through effective regulations), 5. skill reproduction security (opportunity to gain skills, through apprenticeships, employment training etc.), 6. income security (adequate and stable income), and 7. representation security (for example through being organized in independent trade unions, with a right to strike). Precarity means to lack not only one or two of these basic securities, but all seven of them.[70] One good way of looking at films that represent job- or labor-centered precarity would certainly be to determine in which way the absence of these securities and the consequences of that absence are being narrativized.

Related to this is another point in Standing's argument. He makes a crucial distinction between labor and work, using the first to denote that kind of work which is regarded from the angle of its immediate exchange value and which is

---

68 Sticchi, *Mapping Precarity*.
69 Standing, *The Precariat*, 18–24.
70 Standing, *The Precariat*, 10.

being remunerated. "Work" on the other hand is defined by its use value and can take many different forms such as "cultural" or "political" or "care work." One specificity of a flexibilized labor market is precisely that people need to do a lot of work-for-labor, as Standing calls it. They have to spend a lot of time searching for jobs and dealing with the bureaucracy: "Queuing, commuting to queue, form filling, answering questions, answering more questions, obtaining certificates to prove something or other, all these are painfully time consuming yet are usually ignored."[71] Add to this the imperative to constantly improve the ability of selling yourself, which is expected from the precarious subjects on a flexible job market:

> Those in the precariat face a quandary. If they are uncertain about what they should do, they will soon find themselves under pressure to receive counselling, including 'employability training'. They can be depicted as abnormal in not knowing what to do or not being able to 'settle down' in a steady job, or they may be labelled 'virtually unemployable'.[72]

Reading these passages reminds me of moments in several German films such as *Die Bewerbung* (*Interview*, Harun Farocki, 1996), *Dunkler Lippenstift macht seriöser* (*Dark Lipstick Makes More Serious*, Kathrin Rothe, 2003), *In Dir muss brennen* (*Must Burn Within Yourself*, Kathrin Pethke, 2009), *Eine flexible Frau* (*The Drifter*, Tatjana Turanskyj, 2010), or *Reise nach Jerusalem* (*The Chairs Game*, Lucia Chiarla, 2018).[73] But first and foremost, I think of one scene from the French film *The Measure of a Man*, in which the unemployed factory worker Thierry Taugourdeau (played by Vincent Lindon) undergoes training in how to talk and to comport himself in future job interviews, or when speaking to a future superior. A simulation of such an interview has been filmed and the video is played back to Thierry and his co-trainees, who criticize him for being dressed too casually, for appearing too cold, or not smiling enough. For Thierry —and for the viewer who feels with him—this is yet another humiliating experience after a degrading job interview on skype with an employer who obviously has no intention of hiring him.[74] The training situation is one of the darkest moments of the film, a culmination of the victory of neo-liberalism where the subjects teach each other the rules of the new regime of capitalism which they have to internalize in order to survive on a job market structured by an oversupply

---

71 Ibid., 120.
72 Ibid., 126.
73 For an analysis of *Dunkler Lippenstift macht seriöser* and *In Dir muss brennen*, see Christoph Büttner, "'In dir muss brennen!' Self/Change-Management in Arbeitswelt und Dokumentarfilm," in *Opus und Labor: Arbeit in autobiographischen und biographischen Erzählungen*, ed. Iuditha Balint, Katharina Lammers, Kerstin Wilhelms, and Thomas Wortmann (Essen: Klartext, 2018); also see Hanna Prenzel's chapter in this book.
74 See Francesco Sticchi's discussion of the film in his *Mapping Precarity*, 49–62.

of cheap labor. Those who suffer from it appear not only to accept the system, they even train each other in adapting to it, based on a generalized fear of becoming precarious—precarity as the "new normal."[75] Sociologists and theoreticians have indeed diagnosed that precarization is gradually encompassing all of society:[76]

> The generalization, especially towards the middle class, shifts precarity from a question of the margins to a question relevant for society as a whole. The objective insecurity is supplemented by a subjective insecurity of all workers, even those who are not directly affected by precarity.[77]

For Bourdieu and for many after him, precarity is thus not only a certain condition that concerns a particular group of people but rather "part of a mode of domination of a new kind, based on the creation of a generalized and permanent state of insecurity aimed at forcing workers into submission, into the acceptance of exploitation."[78]

However, there is no reason to accept this condition as an unchangeable given, Bourdieu continues:

> Against this political system, political struggle is possible. In the form of charitable or militant activity, it can first aim to encourage the victims of exploitation, all the present and potential victims of insecurity, to work together against the destructive effects of insecurity [. . .] and above all to mobilize *on an international scale*, that is to say at the same level at which the policy of inducing insecurity exerts its effects, so as to combat this policy and neutralize the competition it seeks to create between the workers of different countries.[79]

Indeed, the struggles against them have always played an important role in processes of precarization. International movements such as the EuroMayDay have used the label of precarity long before it became a much-discussed topic in academia, and groups such as the above-mentioned Precarias a la deriva (or the *Gruppe kpD/kleines postfordistisches Drama* in Germany) have raised the question of how to react artistically and politically against a situation of individualization and social insecurity. Scholars agree that precarization and the politics

---

75 Berlant, *Cruel Optimism*, 206–211.
76 Neilson, Rossiter, "Precarity as a Political Concept," 68; Oliver Marchart, *Die Prekarisierungsgesellschaft: Prekäre Proteste. Politik und Ökonomie im Zeichen der Prekarisierung.* (Bielefeld: Transcript, 2013).
77 Freudenschuss, *Prekär ist wer?*, 38.
78 Bourdieu, "Job Insecurity is Everywhere Now," 85; Lorey, *State of Insecurity*, 17–39.
79 Ibid., 86.

against precarization cannot be separated from each other.[80] The question, however, to what degree precarity has formed or is forming a new political subject, and how the large social gaps between different groups struggling with precarity can be closed (or at least temporarily bridged) in order to effectively and efficiently work together, is still open.

Concluding Questions and Remarks

My discussion of the concept of precarity has hopefully indicated its complexity. It is not easy to give a simple definition. Rather, it can be associated with certain (overlapping) semantic fields such as "uncertainty" (which encompasses a temporal dimension, an unforeseeable and therefore unplannable future), "vulnerability," and "dependence." Studying the cinema of precarity, we can ask how these feelings, grounded as they are in structural realities, can be represented and recreated by narrative and stylistic means: How, for example, does a film make us sensitive to the subjective experience of time under the condition of permanent uncertainty? Which devices and narrative techniques are used to portray the feeling of stress, even, or especially, under the condition of unemployment?[81] Furthermore, we may analyze which factors the films represent as causes for precarity: Are they work-related (such as Standing's list of vanishing securities), or do they have to do with social geography (such as growing up in a deprived neighborhood), with oppressive gender relations, with a lacking residence permit status, or with other factors? How do films introduce these factors and how do they figure in the quasi-arguments of the filmic discourses? Or, if we take the governmental dimension into view, how is the new mode of domination (described by Bourdieu, Lorey, and others) articulated? And what sorts of protest, resistance, and solidarity in response to the precarization of our lives—from individual refusal to new forms of strike—are present on Europe's cinema screens; what claims are formulated or suggested?

These questions are central to the discursive dimension I have outlined above. But they can also be linked to the other two sets of questions, to poetics and impact studies: What tasks do filmmakers set themselves in relation to

---

80 Neilson, Rossiter, "Precarity as a Political Concept," 52–55; Marchart, *Die Prekarisierungsgesellschaft*, 171–188.
81 Thomas Keefe, "The Stresses of Unemployment," *Social Work* 29, no. 3 (May-June 1984).

their artistic and political engagement with precarity? What effects do those films have on their audience? Yet another group of questions relates to the typical and to stereotypes. Is it more progressive to try to paint an image of poverty and precarity that is as realistic as possible (and to run the risk of reproducing stereotypes) or is it more appropriate to break with widespread preconceptions (and to risk becoming disconnected from the actual problems)? How many clichés can be deconstructed without creating something completely unrecognizable and incomprehensible? Or, relating to ethics in documentary filmmaking: to what degree may the helplessness of the precarious be exposed? At what point does the filming become humiliating? At what point do restraint and caution turn into euphemism? So many questions—and probably many more—seem crucial to the study of the cinema of precarity. Andrea Grunert is right: The subject of poverty and precarity in film is rich indeed.[82]

As mentioned above, one of the affective consequences of precarity, according to Standing, is alienation. Working in academia, most of us who study the cinema of precarity have experienced precarious employment situations ourselves. Writing funding applications with limited prospects of success instead of effectively doing research can be an alienating experience, too (even though this is still a relatively luxurious situation compared to the more existential forms of precarity mentioned above). However, the possibility of a meaningful contribution to the emerging field of research on the relation between cinema and the social question can possibly counteract alienation. In contrast to matters of gender and race, matters of class (exploitation, housing, poverty, precarity etc.) have never enjoyed a high priority in film and media studies, not even in the heyday of Marxist film criticism in the 1970s (when the focus was mostly on ideology and form). Recently, though, the tide appears to have changed. Research in that rich field has begun.

---

[82] Andrea Grunert, "Introduction: De la construction de la pauvrété au cinéma," *CinémAction*, no. 149 (2013): 18–19.

Bibliography

Aulenbacher, Brigitte. "Die soziale Frage neu gestellt – Gesellschaftsanalysen der Prekarisierungs- und Geschlechterforschung." In *Prekarität, Abstieg, Ausgrenzung: Die soziale Frage am Beginn des 21. Jahrhunderts*, ed. Robert Castel and Klaus Dörre. Frankfurt a.M.: Campus, 2009, 65–77.

Bardan, Alice. "The New European Cinema of Precarity: A Transnational Perspective." In *Work in Cinema: Labor and The Human Condition*, ed. Ewa Mazierska. New York: Palgrave Macmillan, 2013, 69–90.

Berlant, Lauren. *Cruel Optimism*. Durham, NC: Duke University Press, 2011.

Biedermann, Karl. *Dreißig Jahre deutsche Geschichte*, Vol. 1. Breslau: Schottlaender, 1881.

Bortzmeyer, Gabriel. *Le Peuple précaire du cinéma contemporain*. Paris: Hermann, 2020.

Bove, Arianna, Annalisa Murgia, and Emiliana Armano. "Mapping Precariousness: Subjectivities and Resistance. An Introduction." In *Mapping Precariousness, Labour Insecurity and Uncertain Livelihoods: Subjectivities and Resistance*, ed. Emiliana Armano, Arianna Bove, and Annalisa Murgia. London/New York: Routledge, 2017, 1–12.

Bourdieu, Pierre. "Job Insecurity is Everywhere Now." In *Acts of Resistance: Against the New Myths of our Time*. Trans. Richard Nice. Cambridge: Polity Press, 1998, 81–87.

Brooks, Xan. "We're the same: one person, four eyes." *The Guardian*, February 9, 2006. https://www.theguardian.com/film/2006/feb/09/features.xanbrooks.

Burucúa, Constanza, and Carolina Sitnisky, eds. *The Precarious in the Cinemas of the Americas*. Cham, Switzerland: Palgrave Macmillan/Springer, 2018.

Butler, Judith. *Frames of War: When Is Life Grievable?* London/New York: Verso, 2009.

Büttner, Christoph. "'In dir muss brennen!' Self/Change-Management in Arbeitswelt und Dokumentarfilm." In *Opus und Labor: Arbeit in autobiographischen und biographischen Erzählungen.*, ed. Iuditha Balint, Katharina Lammers, Kerstin Wilhelms, and Thomas Wortmann. Essen: Klartext, 2018, 191–212.

––. "'Das gute Leben': Räume und Imaginationen prä-moderner Zukunftsentwürfe im deutschen Gegenwartskino." In *Cosmopolitan Cinema: Kunst und Politik in der Zweiten Moderne*, ed. Matthias Christen and Kathrin Rothemund. Marburg: Schüren, 2019, 247–265.

Castel, Robert. *From Manual Workers to Wage Laborers: The Transformation of the Social Question* [1995]. New Brunswick/London: Transaction, 2003.

Dörre, Klaus. "Prekarität im Finanzmarkt-Kapitalismus." In *Prekarität, Abstieg, Ausgrenzung: Die soziale Frage am Beginn des 21. Jahrhunderts*, ed. Robert Castel and Klaus Dörre. Frankfurt a.M.: Campus, 2009, 35–64.

Eder, Jens. "Political Impact: On the Social Vibrancy of Film." In *What Film is Good For: On the Ethics of Spectatorship*, ed. Julian Hanich, and Martin Roussow. Oakland: University of California Press [forthcoming].

Engels, Frederick. "Rapid Progress of Communism in Germany" [1845]. In *Collected Works, Volume 4, Marx and Engels, 1844–1845*. London: Lawrence & Wishart, 1975, 229–233.

Freudenschuss, Magdalena. *Prekär ist wer? Der Prekarisierungsdiskurs als Arena sozialer Kämpfe*. Wuppertal: Dampfboot, 2013.

Gill, Rosalind, and Andy Pratt. "Precarity and Cultural Work in the Social Factory? Immaterial labour, Precariousness and Cultural Work." *Oncurating.org* 16/13: 26–40. http://www.e-flux.com/wp-content/uploads/2013/05/Precarity_cultural.pdf.

Grunert, Andrea. "Introduction: De la construction de la pauvreté au cinéma." *CinémAction*, no. 149 (2013): 13–19.
Hauptmann, Gerhart. *The Weavers* [1892]. In *The Dramatic Works, Vol. 1: Social Dramas*. New York: Huebsch, 1923, 195–356.
Keefe, Thomas. "The Stresses of Unemployment." *Social Work* 29, no. 3 (May–June 1984), 264–268.
Kergel, David, and Birte Heidkamp. "Media Change—Precarity *Within* and Precarity *Through* the Internet." In *Precarity within the Digital Age: Media Change and Social Insecurity*, ed. Birte Heidkamp and David Kergel. Wiesbaden: Springer, 2017, 9–27.
Kirsten, Guido. *Filmischer Realismus*. Marburg: Schüren, 2013.
——. "Jean-Pierre Meunier's Modalities of the 'Filmic Attitude': Towards a Theory of Referentiality in Cinematic Discourse." In *The Structures of Film Experience by Jean-Pierre Meunier: Historical Assessments and Phenomenological Expansions*, ed. Julian Hanich and Daniel Fairfax. Amsterdam: Amsterdam University Press, 2019, 273–284. DOI: 10.5117/9789462986565_kirsten.
Landes, Lilian. *Carl Wilhelm Hübner (1814–1879): Genre und Zeitgeschichte im deutschen Vormärz*. Munich/Berlin: Deutscher Verlag, 2008.
Lazzarato, Maurizio. "Immaterial Labor." In *Radical Thought in Italy: A Potential Politics*, ed. Michael Hardt and Paolo Virno. Minneapolis: University of Minnesota Press, 1996, 133–147.
Le Blanc, Guillaume. *Vies ordinaires, vies précaires*. Paris: Seuil, 2007.
Lemke, Sieglinde. *Inequality, Poverty, and Precarity in Contemporary American Culture*. New York: Palgrave Macmillan, 2016.
Lorey, Isabell. *State of Insecurity: Government of the Precarious* [2012]. London: Verso, 2015.
Marchart, Oliver. "Auf dem Weg in die Prekarisierungsgesellschaft." In *Facetten der Prekarisierungsgesellschaft: Prekäre Verhältnisse. Sozialwissenschaftliche Perspektiven auf die Prekarisierung von Arbeit und Leben*, ed. Oliver Marchart. Bielefeld: Transcript, 2013, 7–20.
——. *Die Prekarisierungsgesellschaft: Prekäre Proteste. Politik und Ökonomie im Zeichen der Prekarisierung*. Bielefeld: Transcript, 2013.
Martin, Adrian. "*Rosetta*." *Film Critic*, February 2001. http://www.filmcritic.com.au/reviews/r/rosetta.html.
Marx, Karl. *Capital: A Critique of Political Economy* [1867]. New York: The Modern Library, 1906.
Morgan, Janice. "The Social Realism of Body Language in *Rosetta*." *The French Review* 77, no. 3 (February 2004): 526–535.
Müller-Hilmer, Rita. "Gesellschaft im Reformprozess." Bonn: Friedrich-Ebert-Stiftung & TNS Infratest, 2006. https://www.nachdenkseiten.de/upload/pdf/080625%20Hinweise%20PDF%20Datei%20zur%20Infratest%20Studie.pdf.
Neilson, Brett, and Ned Rossiter. "Precarity as a Political Concept, or, Fordism as Exception." *Theory, Culture & Society* 25, no. 7–8 (December 2008): 51–72.
O'Shaughnessy, Martin. "Beyond Neoliberalism? Gift Economies in the Films of the Dardenne Brothers." In *Cinema of Crisis: Film and Contemporary Europe*, ed. Thomas Austin and Angelos Koutsourakis. Edinburgh: Edinburgh University Press, 2020, 43–75.
Odin, Roger. *De la fiction*. Brussels: DeBoeck, 2000.
——. *Les Espaces de communication: Introduction à la sémio-pragmatique*. Grenoble: PUG, 2011.

Panofsky, Erwin. *Studies in Iconology: Humanistic Themes in the Art of the Renaissance.* New York: Oxford University Press, 1939.

Parchesky, Jennifer. "Lois Weber's *The Blot*: Rewriting Melodrama, Reproducing the Middle Class." *Cinema Journal* 39, no. 1 (1999): 25–53.

Pimpare, Stephen. *Ghettos, Tramps, and Welfare Queens: Down and Out on the Silver Screen.* New York: Oxford University Press, 2017.

Prenzel, Hanna. "Feminist Perspectives on Precarization: Revisiting Gendered Strike in Collaboratively Produced Films." *Image [&] Narrative* 22, no. 3 (2021): 50–70.

Ross, Andrew. *Nice Work If You Can Get It: Life and Labor in Precarious Times.* New York/London: New York University Press, 2009.

Scott, Martin. "The Mediation of Distant Suffering: An Empirical Contribution beyond Television News Texts." *Media, Culture & Society* 36, no.1 (2014): 3–19.

Sheila Johnson. "The secret of the Dardenne brothers' Palme d'Or success." *Independent*, March 17, 2006. https://www.independent.co.uk/arts-entertainment/films/features/the-secret-of-the-dardenne-brothers-palme-d-or-success-6106488.html.

Sonderegger, Ruth. "Wie diszipliniert ist (Ideologie-)Kritik?: Zwischen Philosophie, Soziologie und Kunst." In *Was ist Kritik?*, ed. Rahel Jaeggi and Tilo Wesche. Frankfurt a.M.: Suhrkamp, 2009, 55–80.

Stamp, Shelley. "Lois Weber, Progressive Cinema, and the Fate of 'The Work-a-Day Girls' in *Shoes*." *Camera Obscura* 19, no. 2 (September 2004): 140–169.

Standing, Guy. *The Precariat: The New Dangerous Class.* London/New York: Bloomsbury, 2011.

Sticchi, Francesco. *Mapping Precarity in Contemporary Cinema and Television: Chronotopes of Anxiety, Depression, Expulsion/Extinction.* Cham, Switzerland: Springer and Palgrave Macmillan, 2021.

Taylor, Charles. *Modern Social Imaginaries.* Durham, NC: Duke University Press, 2004.

Valkenburg, Patti M., Jochen Peter, and Joseph B. Walther. "Media Effects: Theory and Research." *Annual Review of Psychology* 67, no. 1 (2016): 315–338.

Vij, Ritu. "Affective Fields of Precarity: Gendered Antinomies in Contemporary Japan." *Alternatives: Global, Local, Political* 38, no. 2 (May 2013): 122–138.

Von Hodenberg, Christina. *Aufstand der Weber. Die Revolte von 1844 und ihr Aufstieg zum Mythos.* Bonn: Dietz, 1997.

Zaniello, Tom. *The Cinema of the Precariat: The Exploited, Underemployed, and Temp Workers of the World.* New York/London: Bloomsbury, 2020.

Filmography

9 Leben (*9 Lives*). Dir. Maria Speth. Germany, 2011.

A la deriva, por los circuitos de la precariedad feminina (*Adrift in the Circuits of Women's Precarious Lives*). Spain, 2003.

Deux jours, une nuit (*Two Days, One Night*). Dir. Jean-Pierre and Luc Dardenne. Belgium/France/Italy, 1999.

Die Bewerbung (*Interview*). Dir. Harun Farocki. Germany, 1996.

Distant Lights (*Lichter*). Hans-Christian Schmid. Germany, 2003.

Dunkler Lippenstift macht seriöser (*Dark Lipstick Makes More Serious*). Dir. Kathrin Rothe. Germany, 2003.
Eine flexible Frau (*The Drifter*). Dir. Tatjana Turanskyj. Germany, 2010.
Entre les murs (*The Class*). Dir. Laurent Cantet. France, 2008.
Epizoda u životu berača željeza (*Episode in the Life of an Iron Picker*). Dir. Danis Tanović., Bosnia and Herzegovina/France/Slovenia/Italy, 2013.
Fish Tank. Dir. Andrea Arnold. Netherlands/United Kingdom, 2011.
Giorni e nuvole (*Days and Clouds*). Dir. Silvio Soldini. Italy/Switzerland, 2007.
Gisaengchung (*Parasite*). Dir. Bong Joon Ho. South Korea, 2019.
I, Daniel Blake. Dir. Ken Loach and Laura Obiols. United Kingdom/France/Belgium, 2016.
In Dir muss brennen (*Must Burn Within Yourself*). Dir. Kathrin Pethke. Germany, 2009.
L'Abri (*The Shelter*). Dir. Fernand Melgar. Switzerland, 2014.
L'Emploi du temps (*Time Out*). Dir. Laurent Cantet. France, 2001.
La Loi du marché (*The Measure of a Man*). Dir. Stéphane Brizé. France, 2015.
La Promesse (*The Promise*). Dir. Jean-Pierre and Luc Dardenne. Belgium/France/Luxembourg/Tunisia, 1996.
Los lunes al sol (*Mondays in the Sun*). Dir. Fernando Léon de Aranoa. Spain/France/Italy, 2002.
Major Barbara. Dir. Gabriel Pascal. United Kingdom, 1941.
No Quarto da Vanda (*In Vanda's Room*). Dir. Pedro Costa, Portugal/Germany/Switzerland, 2000.
Orange Is the New Black. Dir. Jenji Kohan. United States, 2013–2019.
Raining Stones. Dir. Ken Loach. United Kingdom, 1993.
Ray & Liz. Dir. Richard Billingham. United Kingdom, 2018.
Reise nach Jerusalem (The Chairs Game). Dir. Lucia Chiarla. Germany, 2018.
Ressources humaines (*Human Resources*). Dir. Laurent Cantet. France/United Kingdom, 1999.
Rosetta. Dir. Jean-Pierre and Luc Dardenne. Belgium/France, 1999.
Selbstkritik eines bürgerlichen Hundes (*Self-Criticism of a Bourgeois Dog*). Dir. Julian Radlmaier. Germany/Italy, 2017.
Show Me a Hero. Dir. Paul Haggis and David Simon. United States, 2015.
Sorry We Missed You. Dir. Ken Loach. United Kingdom/France/Belgium, 2019.
The Florida Project. Dir. Sean Baker. United States, 2017.
Tutta la vita davanti (*Her Whole Life Ahead*). Dir. Paolo Virzì. Italy, 2008.

Martin O'Shaughnessy
Precarious Narratives in French and Francophone Belgian Cinema

How might we approach precarity in French and Francophone Belgian film? Should we begin with a surely necessary theorization of the term and seek cinematic examples to illustrate the theory? Or should we work out from films that figure elements of precarity and attempt to find stylistic or thematic commonalities between them? There being no automatically correct approach, and an inevitable element of circularity or self-confirmation in each, I will begin with some key films, or sequences from them, and explore patterns and divergences within them. I will ask to what extent it makes sense to talk about a French and Francophone Belgian cinema of precarity and whether the application of such a label risks erasing differences between groups of films, the social conditions they address and the politics of representation they embody. I will then place the films in dialogue with some key theorists of precariousness and precarity (Isabell Lorey, Maurizio Lazzarato, Ronaldo Munck, Judith Butler) as I seek to draw lessons from the patterns identified among them.

Precarious Fragments

Tracked by a handheld camera that struggles to avoid obstacles and keep up with her, a young woman rushes down a bare corridor to confront someone whom she considers responsible for her sacking. A manager tells her that she has finished her trial period and can be fired. She attacks him. The frenzy of her gestures is amplified by the proximity of the handheld camera, its rapid movement as it seeks to follow what is happening, and the blurring of the image that necessarily results. A cut moves us into a new situation where, again following the character from behind, we struggle to make sense of what is occurring. Security guards appear and the young woman is dragged out of the locker room in which she has sought refuge. As she is being carried away, she clings to a locker. We then see her catch a bus, enter a woodland and finally a caravan park. Belatedly, we deduce that she lives in a space of temporary accommodation symbolically separated from the town, but we still have insufficient narrative information to make complete sense of the situation. As the film proceeds, we see the young woman, who lives with her alcoholic mother, torn between a murderous desire to remove competitors for workplace inclusion from her path and a refusal of murder. The film ends with her

Open Access. © 2022 Martin O'Shaughnessy, published by De Gruyter. This work is licensed under the Creative Commons Attribution-NonCommercial-NoDerivatives 4.0 International License.
https://doi.org/10.1515/9783110707816-002

failed suicide attempt and acceptance of human interdependence. This is *Rosetta* (1999) by Jean-Pierre and Luc Dardenne.

A slowly backward-tracking shot frames a young man, a management trainee, as he approaches his father, an ageing machine operator, in the factory where the latter works. A series of relatively long takes with a static camera show the son with his father, the latter's repetitive gestures at his machine and the arrival of a foreman who stops and accuses the father of slowing production. A worker at the back of the shot makes barking noises at the management 'guard dog.' Introducing conflict into the world of the film, this relatively low-key sequence announces the drama to come. The son thinks his role is to consult the workforce about how precisely the thirty-five-hour working week will be introduced. It emerges, however, that management are using the consultation to distract from the layoffs they plan to impose. The father is on the list of those to go, but only joins the workers' defensive strike action with great reluctance. This is Laurent Cantet's *Ressources humaines* (*Human Resources*, 1999).

An older man is caught in close-up as he hammers away at a piece of wood. A voice is heard calling his name: Slimane. He slowly turns his head towards the source of the noise, his boss. A series of medium shots and close-ups capture their animated dialogue as the boss lambasts him for his slowness and failure to respect the work schedule. The camera pans to another figure, José, as he stares back at the boss, mutely supporting Slimane. Slimane, we will learn, has worked for many years as an undeclared migrant worker before acquiring proper employment status and the associated pension rights. The remainder of the film will see him as, supported by his extended family, he seeks to turn an old boat into a floating restaurant, reinventing himself as an aspiring small businessman in the process. The film is *La graine et le mulet* (*The Secret of the Grain*, 2007) by Abdellatif Kechiche.

An older worker sits at a desk explaining how, since a workplace accident, he has been disabled. The reverse shot shows his interlocutor, an angel-faced young man, sitting behind a computer screen, wearing smart business clothes. As the sequence continues, we see three similar interactions in classic shot/reverse-shot with small variations of camera proximity and angle. One involves a single mother with two children and a husband who will not pay the alimony. The young man asks her if she would be willing to work on Saturdays, to which her obvious reply is that, with two children to look after, she cannot. The sequence occurs in *Violence des échanges en milieu tempéré* (*Work Hard, Play Hard*, Jean-Marc Moutout, 2004). The young man, a management consultant, has to help companies shed workers if he is to safeguard his own career. The apparently friendly interviews were effectively asking workers to self-identify as being disposable according to the degree of flexibility and enthusiasm they were able to demonstrate.

A camera tracks forward into a close-up of the face of a young man who stands with his eyes shut, a large, overturned rubbish bin behind him. He opens his eyes and stares. We cut to a close-up of the back of his head as he looks at a line of riot police. As the sound of an airplane is heard, as if imitating its ability to fly, the camera rises up, and moves over the young man to bring the line of police defending a police station into clear view. A long, lateral tracking shot takes us along the police line as a police radio announces the arrest of a minor. The camera stops to show the same young man, no longer where we left him, writing graffiti on the back of a police vehicle. As Bob Marley's song, "Burnin' and Lootin" fades in, a succession of shots shows him finishing the graffiti with its message of "baise la police" ("fuck the police"), a reference to NWA's song, "Fuck tha police," and his name, Said. With its black and white photography, American cultural references, and self-consciously stylish shots, this is the start of *La haine* (*Hate*, Mathieu Kassovitz, 1995). The film famously follows Maghrebi-French Said, black Hubert, and Jewish Vinz, as they take stock of the aftermath of the riot that has followed the murderous police beating of another youth and make an abortive trip from their *banlieue* (outer city) into the center of Paris. The trip ends with the death of Vinz at the hands of the police and a stand-off between Hubert, holding a gun, and an armed policeman.

An extreme long shot of a container port shows the arabesques traced by container trucks as they weave their way towards a ferry. A succession of closer shots moves in on an individual truck as it approaches a checkpoint. Ominous music plays. The film cuts between the clandestine migrants inside the truck as they place plastic bags over their heads to prevent their breath being detected and the guards outside, one of whom inserts a device designed to detect carbon dioxide. One young man panics and pulls the bag off his head. Men with dogs enter the truck. The film is Philippe Lioret's *Welcome* (2009) and narrates the bond that arises between the young man and a world-weary French swimming instructor. The former is so desperate to reach the girl he loves in England that he learns to swim in order to undertake the perilous channel crossing.

Gathering the Fragments: Towards a Cinema of Precarity?

To what extent does it make sense to group these films and other similar ones under the overarching label of a *cinema of precarity* despite their stylistic, generic, and other differences? Certainly, some sort of precarity runs through them: the older workers evicted from secure labor, the younger person struggling for the stable employment that might signify social belonging, the marginalized youth of the banlieue confronted by police repression, the migrant threatened with expulsion and able to access only illicit, unstable labor: all these figures, and the trajectories associated with them, could be assembled as a cinema of precarity. Their shared sense of vulnerability is typically accentuated by the established or growing social isolation of their lead protagonists around whom the frame tightens (the Dardennes' cinema) or who find themselves as small figures in an epic space once occupied by a collective class protagonist—the empty steelmills of Seraing in *La promesse* (*The Promise*, 1996) by the Dardenne brothers or the deindustrialized Marseille or Nord regions in Robert Guédiguian's and Bruno Dumont's films respectively.

The films converge substantially in their temporality. They tend to show characters in a state of "impasse," as Lauren Berlant describes it, struggling to survive in an oppressive present and denied any meaningful sense of an alternative future.[1] They are marked by the general absence of any tradition of collective resistance unless it be expressed in the form of a doomed, terminal battle like in *En guerre* (*At War*, Stéphane Brizé, 2018) or given merely residual expression (Guédiguian's films being the outstanding examples here). Some of these broader transformations find concentrated expression in the worker suicide (or failed suicide) narratives that recur across a range of films like Brizé's *At War* and *La loi du marché* (*The Measure of a Man*, Stéphane Brizé, 2015) as well as the Dardennes' *Rosetta* and *Deux jours, une nuit* (*Two Days, One Night*, Jean-Pierre and Luc Dardenne, 2014). Whereas workers were once collectively seen as epic agents of historical transformation, they are now more likely to identify with their own disposability. In the suicide-centered works but also across the films in general, systemic violence impacts directly on bodies that are asked to speak of the harm done to them. In their mute expressivity, they compensate for the silencing or absence of a shared oppositional language. At the same time, and paradoxically, giving this focusing in on the body, ultimate narrative causality tends to move off-screen, into the space of a globalized economy or, in the case of migrant films, whatever factors trigger migration. In my previous work, I have used the notion of the "aesthetic of the fragment" to theorize the interconnected formal and thematic shifts that accompany this dismantling of an epic sense of class struggle and the focus on individuals or small groups deprived of a collective oppositional language able to name and locate the cause of what is happening to them.[2]

---

[1] Lauren Berlant, *Cruel Optimism* (Durham, NC: Duke University Press, 2011), 191–222.
[2] Martin O'Shaughnessy, *The New Face of Political Cinema: Commitment in French Film since 1995* (New York/Oxford: Berghahn, 2007), 99–130.

What of the differences between the films? Despite an unsurprising convergence on some form of social realism, they show substantial stylistic variety. The Dardennes' typically close framing and obsessive tracking with a handheld camera of their characters contrasts with Cantet's more self-effacing style, which is unlike Kassovitz's stylized rendition of the banlieue, which is unlike Kechiche's long takes and close attention to the sensuous vitality and exhaustion of bodies. Given that *most* of the films are broadly art-house works and that their directors would typically be presented as auteurs, we could argue that these stylistic differences are entirely expected, a necessary by-product of the sort of cinema under examination with its drive to directorial differentiation. Different budget sizes also clearly inform the casting, look, and desire to please of the films. Such contrasts do not disqualify a search for convergences between the films.

Other significant differences relating to the figures at the heart of the films, their narrative trajectories, and the questions their stories raise are harder to dismiss and problematize any sense of a *coherent* cinema of precarity. Certainly, labor is both the privileged route to social inclusion and dignity and associated with increased precarity and systemic violence in many of the films. But there are significant variations in narratives surrounding it relating to age, gender, class, ethnicity, the relationship to struggle, and spatio-temporal framing.

Fig. 1: The defeated figure of the older worker in *Ressources humaines* (*Human Resources*, Laurent Cantet, 1999).

Given the *relative* centrality of labor, it is unsurprising that expulsion from the security of Fordism is a recurrent theme. It is typically framed as a crisis of the mature or older male in films like *Human Resources* (Fig. 1), *At War*, or *The Secret of the Grain* and a good number of other films. *The Secret of the Grain* introduces a significant variation, however. Although the tired, ageing, and ultimately defeated body of its hero, Slimane (Habib Boufares), echoes the bowed bodies of characters like the defeated older worker in *Human Resources*, his trajectory problematizes a western-centric narrative of the movement from (Fordist) stability to precarity. While precarity is a *new* experience for Cantet's character, Slimane has only *belatedly* achieved stable employment. An initially undeclared immigrant worker, his journey moves out of precarity and then back into it. Similarly, while films focused on expulsion from Fordism, and thus with a longer historical memory, tend to bear at least a memory of resistance, the resistance takes different forms: belated and defensive in *Human Resources*, it is explosive but terminal in *At War*, residual and borne in individuals in Robert Guédiguian's *Marius et Jeannette* (*Marius and Jeannette*, 1997), and still active, but associated with young women rather than defeated older men in *The Secret of the Grain*. Where precarious labor is associated with entrapment in the present and lacks access to a memory of collective resistance, it is more likely to bear a younger, female face. The Dardennes' *Rosetta* is exemplary in this respect but their *Two Days, One Night* and Erick Zonka's *La vie rêvée des anges* (*The Dreamlife of Angels*, 1998) are also prominent examples.

Precarity is not simply associated with working-class figures. Increasingly, as in *Work Hard, Play Hard* and across a range of films—*La question humaine* (*Heartbeat Detector*, Nicolas Klotz, 2007); *L'emploi du temps* (*Time Out*, Laurent Cantet, 2001); *Corporate* (Nicolas Silhol, 2017); *Ceux qui travaillent* (*Those Who Work*, Antoine Russbach, 2018)—, it has been framed in relation to the middle-class employees of corporations or consultancy firms whose heroes can only maintain access to their privileged position if they are happy to participate in the elimination of others. The question of complicity in elimination is also raised by some working-class centered films including those of the Dardenne brothers and Brizé's *The Measure of a Man*, but it is more systematically present in the films about corporate and managerial work. The latter are also noteworthy for how they foreground, not simply labor, but also the requirement under neoliberalism to produce a competitive, high-performing self to survive in the workplace. The hero of *Work Hard, Play Hard*, for example, is obliged to produce a ruthless self even as he evaluates other people's commitment to the firm. The presence of precarity in middle-class focused films might encourage us to group them with the other works discussed but the way the films differ in terms of the issues they raise and the figures at their heart might make us hesitate to do so too quickly.

When we consider *banlieue films*, we might arrive at some similar conclusions: they have things in common with the other films, but their central figures and the dynamics within them are different. Work and its capacity to provide a sense of value and direction to a life is a structuring absence, part of a more general sense of an absent future. The claustrophobia generated by this temporal entrapment is exacerbated by the typical spatiality of banlieue films: the banlieue is a place from which, as in *Hate*, characters struggle to escape, their spatial enclosure suggesting a broader social marginalization. Characters in the films often collide with the police, as repressive agents of the state. These collisions typically have a racialized dimension, as again in *Hate*, and may lead to broader explosions of anger, as seen in the closing riots of *Ma 6-t va crack-er* (*My Suburbs Are Going to Crack*, Jean-François Richet, 1997) and *Les misérables* (Ladj Ly, 2019). There are also explosions of terminal violence in workplace-related films like *At War* or *Une minute de silence* (*A Minute of Silence*, Florent-Emilio Siri, 1998) but there is at least a residual politics in those films. There is nothing similar in the banlieue films: violence may be given a quasi-insurrectional quality but lacks any explicit politics. Of course, not all banlieue films are the same: some, like *L'esquive* (*Games of Love and Chance*, Abdellatif Kechiche, 2003), focus more on the creativity of the banlieue's inhabitants while others, like Céline Sciamma's *Bande de filles* (*Girlhood*, 2014) and Houda Benyamina's *Divines* (2016) challenge the predominantly male focus of this group of works. Collectively, however, in terms of their spatial economy, the tensions within them and the figures (the young men and women) around which they typically revolve, the banlieue films are significantly different to other films discussed here despite some convergence around precarity.

Similar comments might be made around the growing number of films about migrants and refugees. Despite their shared focus on undeniably precarized groups and individuals, they vary individually from each other and collectively from the other films discussed. Some, such as *Une saison en France* (*A Season in France*, Mahamat Saleh Haroun, 2017), *La faute à Voltaire* (*Poetical Refugee*, Abdellatif Kechiche, 2000), the Dardennes' *The Promise* or *Samba* (Olivier Nakache and Eric Toledano, 2015), focus on migrants' precarious status within France or Belgium. Some also center on the migrant or refugee's exploited employment, a situation obviously linked to the imminent risk of expulsion and the docility it can lead to. Some films, like *Welcome* but also, for example, Sylvain George's *Qu'ils reposent en révolte* (*May They Rest in Revolt*, 2011) foreground migrants' unstable or precarious living conditions in and around Calais. They are less about migrants' attempts to build lives in France than about their struggle to survive within it while seeking a better life elsewhere. Implicit in their mise-en-scène of activity around the port, of container lorries and ferries moving freely while migrants are pinned down, is a sense of the profoundly unequal distribution of mobility in a world of global flows. This focus on the specifically spatial dimension of migrant lives might seem to provide a bridge to the banlieue films within which social exclusion is also spatialized. But, while the spatial dynamics of banlieue films focus on distance from French urban centers, and implicitly confirm a national framing, those of at least some migrant films look beyond a national frame to a more global or transnational mobility.

The migrant films belong to very different categories and their politics diverge considerably. Some are arthouse, auteur works. George's films are experimental and low budget. Nakache and Toledano's *Samba* is a hybrid rom-com-drama star vehicle aimed at a mass national audience and an international arthouse one. The films all tend to be about some form of solidarity between Europeans and non-Europeans. In most cases, this solidarity is broadly humanist and may be expressed through a romance like in *Samba* and *A Season in France*, or a personal, ethical commitment that involves the European protagonist taking increasing risks to help the migrant as in *Welcome* and *The Promise*. In films such as *Welcome*, this commitment comes worryingly close to a perverse *white saviour* narrative through which a tired or burned-out European has their energy and hunger restored by them by helping the migrant. In George's films, particularly his *Vers Madrid* (*The Burning Bright*, 2012) and *Paris est une fête* (*Paris Is a Moveable Feast*, 2017), migration is positioned alongside political resistances to precarization in a way that invites us to imagine, as we will see, a post-national politics of precarity.

Precarious Politics?

The kind of political differences noted among the migrant films are reflected in the broader corpus where we find positions ranging from the nostalgic, through the conformist, to the ethical and the politically radical. Because we would expect any group of films to differ in terms of their politics, these divergences are to some extent unremarkable. But, in the specific set of variations they offer, they nonetheless cast light on the current moment and how films position themselves in relation to it.

As we have seen, there are traces of explicit or implicit nostalgia in a range of works, especially but not only those associated with the figure of the older, typically male figure and his eviction from stable employment. With their repeated references to memories of antifascist struggle and fading worker militancy and solidarity, the films of Robert Guédiguian—such as *Marius and Jeannette* and *La ville est tranquille* (*The Town is Quiet*, 2000)—embody this tendency. Although the films foreground neoliberalism's assault on the organized working class and cling to the remnants of an oppositional politics, the kind of critique they generate risks veering into a sterile left moralism. In her account of the phenomenon, Wendy Brown describes it as "a kind of moralizing *against* history" (her emphasis) which disavows history "as a productive or transformative force."[3] Guédiguian's films and others discussed here such as *At War* or *Work Hard, Play Hard* align with this description. They dramatize neoliberalism's production of precarity through the destruction of solidarity and communities but tend to frame examples of resistance, where they are seen at all, as residual reflexes rather than newly emergent possibilities.

The films of the Dardennes refuse this nostalgic temptation. Rather than clinging to the fading politics and solidarity of the Fordist era, they are founded on the recognition of the need to find alternative ways to live in the present. They use the collisions between precarious bodies to drive into view the murderous violence of a system that values the thing above the person, places all in competition with all, and demands labor as a condition of inclusion while rationing productive places. At the same time, by repeatedly confronting their characters with the vulnerability of the Other, in a way inspired by the ethical philosophy of Emanuel Levinas, they open a path away from murder.[4] Much mainstream cinema refuses to engage with the systemic and frames socio-economic violence in terms of individual conflicts and choices. In *partial* contrast, the Dardennes' films evidence a sustained if implicit awareness of the systemic roots of interpersonal violence. Yet, in their attachment to an interpersonal ethics based on the self-other diptych, it is not obvious that they are ready to move beyond the individualism of more obviously conventional films.

The political limits of their filmmaking are paradoxically most obvious in their *Two Days, One Night*, the film that comes nearest to recognizing the urgency of building new bonds of solidarity. Its heroine, Sandra (Marion Cotillard) has been off work with depression. Her fellow workers have been pressured to vote for a sometimes desperately needed €1,000 bonus rather than have Sandra back. They have effectively chosen self-preservation and gain over the vulnerable Other. The manager is persuaded to run a second vote. Over the course of a weekend, Sandra visits her sixteen colleagues individually to ask them to support her and persuades eight of them. The boss offers to retain her but says he will have to let a worker on a short-term contract go. Sandra refuses to accept this and walks away. The film shows an awareness that people have become atomized, and that solidarity needs to be knitted back together. But the way it does this through a bravura repetition of individual face-to-face encounters and ethical decisions points

---

[3] Wendy Brown, *Politics out of History* (Princeton, NJ/Oxford: Princeton University Press, 2001), 30.

[4] For an excellent Levinasian reading of the Dardennes' films, see Sarah Cooper, "Mortal Ethics: Reading Levinas with the Dardenne Brothers," *Film-Philosophy* 11, no. 2 (2007), http://www.film-philosophy.com/2007v11n2/cooper.pdf.

to the limits of its framing and unwillingness or inability to move back towards a mise-en-scène of collective political subjects.

Other films discussed here such as *The Measure of a Man* or *Work Hard, Play Hard* also stage the tension between competitive individualism and human vulnerability in humanist or ethical terms. But the same tension can lend itself to a far more conservative articulation, as Jacques Audiard's films show. Across a range of genres, ranging from melodrama, through the crime and prison film, to the western, the latter's heroes typically find themselves in vicious environments which they cannot control, where their bodies are exposed to danger, and where they often seem destined for subaltern or precarious labor. Although they seek to compete, they are obliged to recognize their vulnerability when confronted with more powerful others. *Un prophète* (*A Prophet*, Jacques Audiard, 2009) is typical in this respect. With its gangs fighting for power and money and state authorities unable or unwilling to protect its inmates, its prison world bears a striking resemblance to social life under conditions of neoliberalism. Its hero escapes the violence that threatens him and avoids the subaltern labor he is being trained for (making jeans, cleaning the prison, serving food) by forming networks that allow him to out-compete his rivals. The film foregrounds socio-economic and bodily precarity but recuperates it by inserting it into a feel-good story of entrepreneurial self-fashioning. This pattern is repeated with variations across Audiard's cinema. Precarity is a taken-for-granted context and justification for characters' actions in the films: they avoid it and open a better personal future within the status quo by remaking themselves as flexible, networked neoliberal subjects.

Audiard's films are among the most commercially mainstream discussed here. Different in almost every way, George's poetic works come from the experimental side of documentary, feature-filmmaking's poor cousin. They are significant in the context of this chapter for their very different framing of precarity and the temporalities associated with it. Unrestricted by mainstream narrative, the films rely on observational footage and montage. The footage is sometimes of individuals, typically migrants, but more typically of groups in their interaction with different built and natural environments in and around Calais, Madrid, or Paris. Locations and the objects within them (buildings, statues, abandoned consumer objects, political graffiti, and posters) receive considerable attention in their own right. The montage invites us to make connections between different groups, spaces, and objects, but in a way that leaves the nature of those connections open. There is also, frequently, a kind of montage in the shot, whereby people—rough sleepers, demonstrators—are framed next to shops, buildings, or statues in a way which invites us to ponder their combined resonance and how the histories embedded in the city's material fabric might align with present events. If this evokes Walter Benjamin's famous concept of the constellation whereby past and present line up to reactivate earlier aspirations and tear the present out of the predictable unfolding of time, this is unsurprising. George frequently evokes his debt to Benjamin.[5]

Fig. 2: Reactivating political traditions in *Paris est une fête* (*Paris is a Moveable Feast*, Sylvain George, 2017).

The way this plays out in a specific film, *Paris Is a Moveable Feast*, is worth exploring. Despite its apparently celebratory title, the film deliberately undermines consensual images of the French capital in the aftermath of the 2015 terror attacks. Assembled through montage, its Paris brings together the following: migrants trying to find places to sleep while being harassed by the police; performed reconstructions of the life of Mohamad, an individual migrant, surviving on the city's streets; demonstrations around the Place de la République in support of migrants and refugees and against austerity and the repressive security regime; the modest monument in the Clichy-sous-Bois banlieue to Zyed Benna and Bouna Traoré who died fleeing from the police. By bringing together different precarities, the film asks us to ponder potential connections between them. At the same time, by repeatedly showing contemporary mobilizations in the Place de la République, with its famous monument of Marianne, the archetypal symbol of the French republic (Fig. 2), the film asks us to rethink core French and European political traditions

---

5 See, for example: Sylvain George, interviewed by *Débordements*, "Sylvain George: ne pas savoir d'où cela vient, où cela va," *Débordements*, November 6, 2014, https://debordements.fr/Sylvain-George.

for new times. The past is not activated nostalgically as in some other films. It is reactivated and aligned with the present to point towards a potentially different future. The space of the international or global is evoked in some of the other films to suggest the migration of causality out of a national political and economic space. In migrant-centered films, it is often an unseen space whose dangers explain the migrants' presence. In George's film, however, it is given a crucial additional dimension. The montage of migrants and political demonstrations invites us to think a new politics beyond the national frame in which claims were typically enacted. Rather than simply being a space of absent causes, the global is re-signified as a locus of potential political agency. All this might seem too positive. But the need to assemble different precarities through montage underscores separation as much as potential convergence.

The pattern of discussion here might suggest an implicit hierarchy of films, from conformist mainstream works through the limited challenges of auteurist films to the more radical questioning offered by avant-garde works such as those of George. Such a hierarchy would risk blinding us to the capacity of more mainstream films to bring emergent political possibilities into view and should be avoided. The anarchic popular comedies of Kervern and Delépine are worth mentioning in this context. In films such as *Louise-Michel* (Benoît Delépine and Gustave Kervern, 2008), *Mammuth* (Benoît Delépine and Gustave Kervern, 2010), *Le grand soir* (Benoît Delépine and Gustave Kervern, 2012), they have repeatedly told stories about people who are rejected by the neoliberal economy and whose tired, aging, overweight, or rebellious bodies refuse neoliberal self-disciplining. But rather than focusing on the suffering of bodies, as other films often do, they use them to explore the pleasures and liberatory capacity of economically unproductive activity and sociabilities associated with it.

Making Sense of On-Screen Precarity

If we gather the lessons of what has been discussed so far, we might arrive at two broad conclusions: the first being that there is considerable evidence of the rise of a thematics of precarity across a wide range of contemporary French and Franco-Belgian cinema; the second being that these films are marked by a high level of heterogeneity both across their general range and within each sub-group of films. Some of this heterogeneity, a kind of intrinsic 'white noise,' can be explained by the 'natural' variation one expects from auteur cinema, generic specificity (where relevant), and positioning with respect to the mainstream. But some heterogeneity seems harder to explain away and relates more to the adequacy of precarity as a coherent label for a diverse body of films.

Reference to theories of precarity may help us here. Leaning towards an understanding of precarity in terms of its universal applicability, while recognizing the diversity of the social categories affected by it, Guy Standing famously suggested that contemporary capitalism was producing the 'precariat,' as a new global class.[6] Other analysts, like Maurizio Lazzarato, Isabell Lorey, and Ronaldo Munck takes a different line that prioritizes diversity over cohesion. Lazzarato notes how, moving away from the mass enclosure of workers within the disciplinary space of the factory, neoliberalism functions through a modulation of insecurity. Old measures of protection are not completely withdrawn but are tied to incentives and made conditional so that they produce precarity rather than stability. Work status differences are multiplied in a way that individualizes and renders fragile. There is no longer a clear divide between those included and excluded but an inclusive continuum of insecure positions whose stratified nature obstructs any clear political polarization.[7] Taking a similar line, drawing inspiration from the work of Judith Butler, Isabell Lorey makes the crucial distinction between precariousness, precarity, and governmental precarization. Precariousness, as she uses it, relates to the ontological vulnerability of all human life: we are born into a world in which our survival is dependent on others. Precarity refers to how our unequal positioning with respect to this precariousness is used as a governmental tool (in the Foucauldian sense) along the lines Lazzarato describes. Governmental precarization encapsulates not simply the deployment of precarity but also the way in which people internalize it and build subjectivities around it and the way in which the state security apparatus is deployed to secure compliance with it.[8]

In an article where he notes the massive incorporation into proletarianized labor that occurs in the non-Western world during the neoliberal period, Munck suggests that the notion of precarity and especially of the precariat as a global class derives from an overgeneralization to a global level of a phase of Europe's post-Fordist working-class history. He comments, "while the precariat discourse exudes a nostalgia for something which has passed (the Keynesian/Fordist/welfare state), it does not speak to a South which has never experienced welfare

---

[6] Guy Standing, *The Precariat: The New Dangerous Class* (London/New York: Bloomsbury, 2011), 1–25.
[7] Maurizio Lazzarato, *Le Gouvernement des inégalités: critique de l'insécurité néolibérale* (Paris: Editions Amsterdam, 2008).
[8] Isabell Lorey, *State of Insecurity: Government of the Precarious*, trans. Aileen Derieg (London: Verso, 2015), 17–22 and 63–71.

state capitalism."[9] He acknowledges, however, the political purchase of the discourse of precarity in Western Europe in the 2000s with its protest against the end of security for those entering the workforce in that region.[10] Also focusing on Occupy-style protests against precarization, Butler noted how, instead of allowing embodied vulnerability to be individualized and relegated to the private sphere, they brought bodies and their needs into public space as part of a collective demand for conditions under which a livable interdependence would become possible.[11]

Without providing some impossible totalizing explanation, this engagement with different accounts of precarity casts light on patterns and variations within the films discussed. To begin with, we might note that the notion of precarity not so much as a shared condition but as a differential continuum of precarized positions resonates with our observation that precarity can be found across a broad range of films but narrated in very different ways according to the group portrayed and the figures evoked. Looking across a similar array of films in a recently published book, Bortzmeyer seeks to identify what a cinematic figure of the precarized people might look like in neoliberal times. He concludes that the figure lacks any consistency, durability, or defined substance. While earlier periods generated more solid and stable cultural figures of the common people, precarity is unsurprisingly associated with precarious figures lacking group or class anchorage.[12] In his study of an international corpus of precarity films, Francesco Sticchi similarly notes the impossibility and undesirability of pinning down stable or singular figures embodying precarity.[13] In my own corpus, probably the most recurrent figure identified was the defeated older male, a figure which tellingly bore witness to the loss of both its own solidity and that of the broadly Fordist world that had sustained it. One could argue that, in their differences of age, gender, ethnicity, and nationality, the other figures also spoke not only of their own precarity but also of the constitutive exclusions that had endowed that older male figure with its once stable centrality. This was particularly the case for a film like *The Secret of the Grain* which implicitly problematized any Eurocentric framing of the history of the working class and nostalgia for a lost security that only ever applied to some. It

---

9 Ronaldo Munck, "The Precariat: a View from the South," *Third World Quarterly* 34, no. 5 (2013): 752.
10 Ibid., 753–754.
11 Judith Butler, *Notes Toward a Performative Theory of Assembly* (Cambridge, MA/London: Harvard University Press, 2015), 66–98.
12 Gabriel Bortzmeyer, *Le Peuple précaire du cinéma contemporain* (Paris: Hermann, 2020), 213–228.
13 Francesco Sticchi, *Mapping Precarity in Contemporary Cinema and Television: Chronotopes of Anxiety, Depression, Expulsion/Extinction* (Cham, Switzerland: Springer & Palgrave Macmillan, 2021), v–vi and 18–21.

was also the case for the migrant films within which the migrants' typically unseen histories spoke of insecurities in excess of any Eurocentric narrative of precarization.

The theory helps explain key aspects of the context to which the films are a response. But, in the diversity of their spatio-temporal economies, their uses of the body, and their ethical, political, or moral positionings, the films demonstrate that there is no mechanical link between socio-economic context and film form. We find a sense of stasis or impasse in many but not all of the works. Some, but not all, show evidence of nostalgia and draw critical purchase from what remains of the traditional politics of the left even at the risk of veering towards a left moralism. Refusing nostalgia, others take the absence of an available leftist project as a starting point and seek to find ethical or moral grounds to guide behaviors in the present. George's cinema takes a different route: positioning past values and aspirations alongside contemporary mobilizations, it seeks to open a potential future for both. Many of the films focus on bodily vulnerability in a way that responds to the mobilization of precarity as a governmental machinery and the weakening of collective and institutional protections. But the way in which they make the body speak of the violence done to it and compensate for the silencing of oppositional languages shows that film shapes the sensual and socio-economic material around it to find its own voice. The films use embodied interactions to probe how relations of care and interdependence might open alternatives to the violence of institutionalized competitiveness. Less focused on suffering and vulnerability, Delépine and Kervern use recalcitrant bodies to explore the liberatory capacity of unproductive time. More aligned with the politics of Occupy as analyzed by Butler, George explores how collective bodies refuse the privatization of vulnerability and make precarity not simply a socio-economic given, but a focus for mobilization. Collectively, and in their diversity, between the politics that was, the status quo, and a politics yet to be found, the films help us map and navigate the precarious terrain on which we find ourselves.

Bibliography

Berlant, Lauren. *Cruel Optimism*. Durham, NC: Duke University Press, 2011.
Bortzmeyer, Gabriel. *Le Peuple précaire du cinéma contemporain*. Paris: Hermann, 2020.
Brown, Wendy. *Politics out of History*. Princeton, NJ/Oxford: Princeton University Press, 2001.
Butler, Judith. *Notes Toward a Performative Theory of Assembly*. Cambridge, MA/London: Harvard University Press, 2015.
Cooper, Sarah. "Mortal Ethics: Reading Levinas with the Dardenne Brothers." *Film-Philosophy* 11, no. 2 (2007): 66–87. http://www.film-philosophy.com/2007v11n2/cooper.pdf.

George, Sylvain, interviewed by *Débordements*. "Sylvain George: ne pas savoir d'où cela vient, où cela va." *Débordements*, November 6, 2014. https://debordements.fr/Sylvain-George.

Lazzarato, Maurizio. *Le Gouvernement des inégalités: critique de l'insécurité néolibérale*. Paris: Editions Amsterdam, 2008.

Lorey, Isabell. *State of Insecurity: Government of the Precarious*. Trans. Aileen Derieg. London: Verso, 2015.

Munck, Ronaldo. "The Precariat: a View from the South." *Third World Quarterly* 34, no. 5 (2013): 747–762.

O'Shaughnessy, Martin. *The New Face of Political Cinema: Commitment in French Film since 1995*. New York/Oxford: Berghahn, 2007.

Standing, Guy. *The Precariat: The New Dangerous Class*. London/New York: Bloomsbury, 2011.

Sticchi, Francesco. *Mapping Precarity in Contemporary Cinema and Television: Chronotopes of Anxiety, Depression, Expulsion/Extinction*. Cham, Switzerland: Springer and Palgrave Macmillan, 2021.

Filmography

Bande de filles (*Girlhood*). Dir. Céline Sciamma. France, 2014.
Ceux qui travaillent (*Those Who Work*). Dir. Antoine Russbach. Switzerland/Belgium, 2018.
Corporate. Dir. Nicolas Silhol. France, 2017.
Deux jours, une nuit (*Two Days, One Night*). Dir. Jean-Pierre and Luc Dardenne. Belgium/France/Italy, 2014.
Divines. Dir. Houda Benyamina. France/Qatar, 2016.
En guerre (*At War*). Dir. Stéphane Brizé. France, 2018.
L'emploi du temps (*Time Out*). Dir. Laurent Cantet. France, 2001.
L'esquive (*Games of Love and Chance*). Dir. Abdellatif Kechiche. France, 2003.
La faute à Voltaire (*Poetical Refugee*). Dir. Abdellatif Kechiche. France, 2000.
La graine et le mulet (*The Secret of the Grain*). Dir. Abdellatif Kechiche. France, 2007.
La haine (*Hate*). Dir. Mathieu Kassovitz. France, 1995.
La loi du marché (*The Measure of a Man*). Dir. Stéphane Brizé. France, 2015.
La promesse (*The Promise*). Dir. Jean-Pierre and Luc Dardenne. Belgium/France/Luxembourg/Tunisia, 1996.
La question humaine (*Heartbeat Detector*). Dir. Nicolas Klotz. France, 2007.
La vie rêvée des anges (*The Dreamlife of Angels*). Dir. Erick Zonka. France, 1998.
La ville est tranquille (*The Town is Quiet*). Dir. Robert Guédiguian. France, 2000.
Le grand soir. Dir. Benoît Delépine and Gustave Kervern. France/Belgium/Germany, 2012.
Les misérables. Dir. Ladj Ly, France. France, 2019.
Louise-Michel. Dir. Benoît Delépine and Gustave Kervern. France, 2008.
Ma 6-t va crack-er (*My Suburbs are Going to Crack*). Dir. Jean-François Richet. France, 1997.
Mammuth. Dir. Benoît Delépine and Gustave Kervern. France, 2010.
Marius et Jeannette (*Marius and Jeannette*). Dir. Robert Guédiguian. France, 1997.
Paris est une fête (*Paris Is a Moveable Feast*). Dir. Sylvain George. France, 2017.
Qu'ils reposent en révolte (*May They Rest in Revolt*). Dir. Sylvain George. France, 2011.
Ressources humaines (*Human Resources*). Dir. Laurent Cantet. France/UK, 1999.

Rosetta. Dir. Jean-Pierre and Luc Dardenne. France/Belgium, 1999.
Samba. Dir. Olivier Nakache and Eric Toledano. France, 2015.
Un prophète (*A Prophet*). Dir. Jacques Audiard. France/Italy, 2009.
Une minute de silence (*A Minute of Silence*). Dir. Florent-Emilio Siri. France, 1998.
Une saison en France (*A Season in France*). Dir. Mahamat Saleh Haroun. France, 2017.
Vers Madrid (*The Burning Bright*). Dir. Sylvain George. Spain/France, 2012.
Violence des échanges en milieu tempéré (*Work Hard, Play Hard*). Dir. Jean-Marc Moutout. France/Belgium, 2004.
Welcome. Dir. Philippe Lioret. France, 2009.

Manuel Garin
Housing Precarity and Construction in Spanish Cinema
From Francoism to Contemporary Documentary

Tracing the images back to key precedents in Spanish film history, from Buñuel's *Las Hurdes* (*Land Without Bread*, 1933) to the films of José Antonio Nieves Conde in the 1950s, this chapter explores the audiovisual depiction of housing precarity and construction in the contemporary documentaries *En construcción* (*Work in Progress*, José Luis Guerín, 2001), *Edificio España* (*The Building*, Victor Moreno, 2012) and *Mercado de futuros* (*Futures Market*, Mercedes Álvarez, 2011). It also contextualizes them in relation to other relevant films focused on the so-called "economic crisis." Instead of reading such films as dealing with new or hypermodern forms of housing precarity, I will argue that the class, gender, and racial issues mobilized in them are symptomatically linked with the modes and structures of Francoism, intertwining past and present inequalities deeply ingrained in Spain's social fabric. If, as David Graeber demonstrates, the exploitative and globalized structures of the contemporary economy are historically rooted in earlier practices of colonialism, patriarchy, and violence,[1] the following pages aim to expose the critical divides of housing precarity in Spain (wealth vs. income, origin vs. citizenship, heritage vs. meritocracy, private vs. public) by looking back to its authoritarian and troubled past. But, instead of focusing on hegemonic power, I will delve into forms of resistance and bonding between precarious individuals and collectives that thrive and fight back in spite of the historical debts that still place class, institutional, and corporate burdens on them today.

With the hypothesis that housing precarity is tied to construction and real estate speculation just like inequality is tied to power, the following pages explore only a small sample of materials dealing with the topic: the aforementioned documentaries partake in a much larger ecosystem of audiovisual depictions of precariousness, crisis, and inequality in Spain. As discussed in the international symposium that inspired this book, multiple and deeply co-dependent spheres (geographies, bodies, languages) are involved when talking about precarity, so it is key to keep in mind what Lauren Berlant called the mutability of "that porous domain of hyperexploitive entrepreneurial atomism that has been variously dubbed globalization, liberal sovereignty, late capitalism,

---

[1] David Graeber, *Debt: The First 5,000 Years* (New York: Melville, 2011), 127–211.

post-Fordism, or neoliberalism,"[2] its multifaceted and all-consuming nature. That is why, before focusing on housing and construction, I want to briefly mention other films that deal with various contemporary forms of precarity in Spain, grouped here in six main thematic contexts.[3]

First, there are very significant films that portray racial prejudice, ethnic minorities, and labor migrants as layers of precarious life, such as Isaki Lacuesta's essential duology *La leyenda del tiempo* (*The Legend of Time*, 2006) and *Entre dos aguas* (*Between Two Waters*, 2018), or the strongly affective *La plaga* (*The Plague*, Neus Ballús, 2013). A second group deals with industrial labor, unemployment, and relocation, like another indispensable duology formed by Joaquim Jordà's *Numax presenta* (*Numax Presents*, 1980) and *Veinte años no es nada* (*Twenty Years Is Nothing*, 2005), drama-oriented fictions like *Los lunes al sol* (*Mondays in the Sun*, Fernando León, 2002), or the fascinating split-screen documentary *El año del descubrimiento* (*The Year of the Discovery*, Luis López Carrasco, 2020). Precarity has also been depicted, thirdly, as a contrast between rural depopulation and mass urban development, in titles like *El cielo gira* (*The Sky Turns*, Mercedes Álvarez, 2004), *La soledad* (*Solitary Fragments*, Jaime Rosales, 2007), and *Arraianos* (Eloy Enciso, 2012). Generational imbalances are depicted in a fourth group of films, including fictions such as *Hermosa juventud* (*Beautiful Youth*, Jaime Rosales, 2014), *Viaje al cuarto de una madre* (*Journey to a Mother's Room*, Celia Rico, 2018), or *La innocència* (*The Innocence*, Lucía Alemany, 2019), and various documentaries focused on the 15-M movement that explore aspects of the young precariat. Gender inequality and patriarchal rule lie at the core of a fifth group, comprised of different films directed by Icíar Bollaín and Benito Zambrano, or Almodóvar's *Volver* (2006), as well as other explorations of misogyny and precarity from the perspective of race (*Carmen y Lola, Carmen & Lola*, Arantxa Echeverría, 2018) and class (*Techo y comida, Roof and Food*, Juan Miguel del Castillo, 2015). Finally, there are symptomatic films that expose precarious lives in relation to social and mental stigmatization, from *De nens* (*Playing with Children*, Joaquim Jordà, 2004) and *Sobre la marxa* (*The Creator of the Jungle*, Jordi Morató, 2013) to *Sense sostre* (*Outside*, Pep Garrido, Xesc Cabot, 2019) or *Zauria(k): Eromena, Gorputza, Feminismoak* (*Wound[s]: Madness, Body and Feminisms*, Maier Irigoien, Isabel Sáez, Iker Oiz, 2019). Tellingly, many of these films contain scenes and

---

2 Lauren Berlant, *Cruel Optimism* (Durham, NC: Duke University Press, 2011), 167.
3 Like any other list of films, the following one is of course limited and subjective, especially since this chapter is not concerned with all-encompassing or panoramic views. For a monographic survey of Spanish films about the crisis: María José Hellín and Helena Talaya, eds., *El cine de la crisis. Respuestas cinematográficas a la crisis económica española en el siglo XXI* (Barcelona: UOC Press, 2018).

characters tied to the housing crisis or real estate speculation, which feed into all the other issues, intertwining various forms of precarity.

Precarity is Power: Francoism and the Structures of Precarious Housing

From a visual standpoint, the representation of precarity in Spanish film history has always been linked with the power mechanisms that sustain and perpetuate it, that is, with the various forms of imposed authority (royal, military, religious) ingrained in the country's social as well as economical structures.[4] Unlike other European countries, which either overthrew their kings or found middle ways to mitigate authoritarian power within democratic standards, Spain spent most of the twentieth century, that is, the century of cinema, under the rule of monarchs or dictators. One of the first state attempts to document and visualize precarity, the newsreels of Alfonso XIII's visit to the impoverished region of Las Hurdes in June 1922, is already testimony of that juxtaposition of extreme power with extreme poverty: the royal expedition across 150 km of rocky isolated land was organized as a news event, glorifying the king's adventurous spirit and charitable concerns in a twofold mixture of spectacle (for masses) and surveillance (for rulers), to use Susan Sontag's words about the ambivalent liaisons between photography and the news.[5] The silent footage documenting the precarious living conditions of the region's poor inhabitants is inseparable from the visual representation of royal power (the king), religious authority (the bishop), and biopolitical control (the doctor) which *made such images possible* in the first place. This is a key issue that will resurface throughout the chapter: the most symptomatic depictions of housing precarity, its geographies and faces, expose—and often certify—structures of power.

---

4 For a critical reading of the Spanish nation as anachronism: Stanley. G. Payne, "Nationalism, Regionalism and Micronationalism in Spain," *Journal of Contemporary History* 26 no. 3/4 (1991): 486; Angel. G. Loureiro, "Spanish Nationalism and the Ghost of Empire," *Journal of Spanish Cultural Studies* 4, no. 1 (2003): 65, https://doi.org/10.1080/1463620032000058686; Diego Muro and Alejandro Quiroga, "Spanish Nationalism: Ethnic or Civic?" *Ethnicities* 5, no. 1 (2005): 18, https://doi.org/10.1177/1468796805049922.
5 Susan Sontag, *On Photography* (London: Penguin, 1979), 178. For an analysis of Alfonso XIII's public representation in newsreels: Juli Montero, José Javier Sánchez, and María Paz, *La imagen pública de la monarquía* (Madrid: Akal, 2001).

That is, no doubt, why Luis Buñuel's *Las Hurdes, tierra sin pan* created such an immense controversy when it was released—and subsequently prohibited—in 1933, due to the indignant reaction of the state establishment (biopolitical in the figure of Dr. Gregorio Marañón, but also by the leftwing Republican alliance), because it was not only another denunciation of the poor living conditions of the region but of poverty and precarity as a whole, not an isolated but a *systemic* attack in the most radical surrealist terms. Beyond the multiple readings and legends concerning the film, I would like to underline Mercè Ibarz's point about how the shooting itself was based on an acknowledgment of the radical inequality between the film crew and the locals, since as Buñuel himself explained at a screening in New York, "all the shots that you see in the film had to be paid for."[6] Facts were not only manipulated but bought, acquired through an aberrant logic of transaction that gives the work its true documentary value, by inscribing the mechanisms of power that are inseparable from precarity in the film itself.

After years of sanctimonious paternalism towards the region, the scandal of poverty could only be properly denounced in a scandalous fashion. Not by chance, this antagonized the "good conscience" of all established powers, both in Spain and abroad. The fact that the film was censored in France and England, as well, cutting off the image of a map that highlighted similar regions in other European countries, is key because it confirms that there is a certain *degree* of precarity that exposes powers too much, that unmasks and visualizes too overtly, and therefore, has to be censored (a constant that will reemerge throughout the chapter). Furthermore, Buñuel himself finally decided not to include the movie in the screening program he curated for the Republican Pavilion at the 1937 Paris Exposition, given its volatile radicalism, which did not portray the most desirable image of a country so desperately in need of international aid because of the Civil War. As Jordana Mendelson has pointed out, the film was *too much* for that fragile moment in history; such backward precarity just could not be screened.[7]

This issue of what can and cannot be screened connects *Las Hurdes* with the Francoist context we will now focus on and, more importantly, it reappears in contemporary documentaries about housing precarity and real estate speculation (with cases of censorship when it comes to banks or hedge funds owning buildings, as we will see). In that sense, one might argue that the most *contemporary*

---

[6] Mercè Ibarz, *Buñuel documental. Las Hurdes, tierra sin pan i el seu temps* (Barcelona: UPF, 1997), 222. All translations, if not otherwise stated in the bibliography, are by me, M.G.
[7] Jordana Mendelson, *Documenting Spain* (University Park, PA: Pennsylvania State University Press, 2005), 162.

film about housing precarity ever made in Spain was shot in 1957 in Madrid, six decades before the crash of Lehman Brothers and the subprime mortgage crisis. *El inquilino* (*The Tenant*, J. A. Nieves Conde, 1958), a milestone of satirical critique under the dictatorship, tells the story of a housing eviction affecting a family of six, by juxtaposing the desperate attempts of the parents to find a place to live with the ongoing destruction of their building due to real estate speculation, all in light comedic terms. The topic of precarious living conditions and the lack of proper housing was treated in other films such as *Esa pareja feliz* (*That Happy Couple*, Juan Antonio Bardem and Luis García Berlanga, 1953), *Historias de Madrid* (*Madrid Stories*, Ramón Comas, 1958) or the terrifyingly hilarious *El pisito* (*The Little Apartment*, Marco Ferreri and Isidoro M. Ferry, 1958), and remained a central theme in many of the multi-faceted and clever movies made under Francoism that film historians Josetxo Cerdán and Castro de Paz labeled as being between *sainete y esperpento*, between farce and the grotesque.[8] But among them, *El inquilino* remains the most visually audacious, socially visionary, and fiercely critical fiction film dealing with the topic, because it foretold contemporary forms of housing precarity.

First of all, it is important to underline that the researchers and scholars who have analyzed the film, both from the perspective of cinema history[9] and of architecture and urban planning,[10] emphasize that it was conceived and shot like a documentary. The director himself stressed this approach in one of the last interviews he gave, literally calling it "otro documental madrileño"[11] ("another Madrid documentary") along with *Surcos* (*Furrows*, José Antonio Nieves Conde, 1951), a more tragic but still documentary-spirited film that focused on rural immigrants traveling to an overpopulated and precarious neighborhood in Madrid. Beyond the heated debate in Spanish film historiography about whether these films were influenced more by Italian neorealism or by the indigenous literary tradition of *realismo*,[12] both titles were shot in the impoverished quarter of Lavapiés and all the mise en scène elements point to a down-to-earth, uncondescending, and extremely material depiction of real characters in

---

[8] José Luis Castro de Paz and Josetxo Cerdán, *Del sainete al esperpento* (Madrid: Cátedra, 2011), 45.
[9] Luis Deltell, *Madrid en el cine de la década de los cincuenta* (Madrid: Ayuntamiento, 2007), 171.
[10] Alba Zarza, "La imagen social de la vivienda en el cine español de posguerra (1940–1960)," *TRIM*, no. 14 (2008); Ana Esteban, "La vivienda social española en la década de los 50," *Cuaderno de Notas*, no. 7 (1999).
[11] José Luis Castro de Paz and Julio Pérez Perucha, "Realismo(s), tragedia e ironía: José Antonio Nieves Conde," *L'Atalante*, no. 20 (2015).
[12] For a discussion between Spanish film scholars see the aforementioned issue of *L'Atalante*, no. 20, 76–90.

precarious spaces. This is particularly relevant in *El inquilino*, given its satirical but humanly close and humorous critique, because the images of the construction workers tearing apart the building where the evicted family is still living, a surreal countdown of precarity, transmit a sense of everydayness and it-could-happen-to-you proximity that can only be called documentary in style. And the issues it exposes are related to the contemporary documentaries we will later focus on.

The film exemplifies in its protagonists the ten characteristics analyzed by Lauren Berlant in her discussion of "Precarity: A Savage Journey to the Heart of Embodied Capitalism" by Vassilis Tsianos and Dimitris Papadopoulos.[13] It thus suggests that the weights of precarious life in contemporary Spain are rooted in its Francoist heritage. *Vulnerability* (1) is inscribed in the very structure of the film, with constant images of the workers demolishing the building where the family still lives. *Hyperactivity* (2) is what defines the father's part time job as a *practicante* (practitioner) who administers injections on call and is required to be ready any time. *Simultaneity* (3) is what the mother struggles with, because she has to take care of four kids *and* find a new place to live at the same time. *Recombination* (4) of antagonistic networks and social milieus is ever-present, with the father asking indiscriminately for help from a banker, a Rom, a bureaucrat, a prostitute, or a bullfighter among others. *Post-sexuality* (5) does not seem to be a *new* late-capitalist problem according to the running gag showing the father as unable to sleep in the same bed with his wife, in spite of efforts to the contrary. *Fluid intimacies* (6) are embodied in the cross-gendered role of one construction worker who covers for the precarious mom by feeding and taking care of the kids himself. *Restlessness* (7) is constantly present in the abundance of comments, laughs and critiques from the opinionated neighbors, especially in the nearby bar. *Unsettledness* (8) is transmitted by the perpetual flux of other families and tenants who are *also* seeking a room, competing with the protagonists; a pressure turned into harsh satire when, after the death of the previous tenant, dozens of characters amass in a landlord's house to beg for a rental. *Affective exhaustion* (9) erupts as a surrealist happy dream of living in an upper-class house and, more importantly, in the final attempt of the father to earn money by ridiculously gambling with his life in a third-rate bullfight spectacle. And, finally, *cunning* (10) is what the protagonist is most accused of lacking, as if not being a trickster or opportunistic enough was his own fault.

---

[13] Berlant, *Cruel Optimism*, 197; Vassilis Tsianos and Dimitris Papadopoulos, "Precarity: A Savage Journey to the Heart of Embodied Capitalism," *Transversal*, no. 10 (2006), https://transversal.at/transversal/1106/tsianos-papadopoulos/en.

What makes *El inquilino* unique is that these tremendously serious issues were filmed through the comedic veil of irony, or to quote Northrop Frye's memorable definition of satire, "militant irony."[14] Not in a gratuitous or ultimately cathartic way, not for comic relief, but in a truly critical and socially concerned way that triggered the immediate removal of the film from movie theaters and its subsequent ban. It is likely that the film's script was approved for shooting by the censors due to the director's prewar ties with Primo de Rivera's *falangismo*, which was the earlier version of Spanish fascism—more interested in class struggle and without the religious traditionalism of Franco's *nacionalcatolicismo*. But once the film was shot and screened, the recently created Ministerio de Vivienda, the top state authority dealing with housing, ordered the immediate seizure of all copies until proper cuts were made. It took three years to get a new exhibition license, after removing several scenes, adding an opening title that expresses the *concern of the regime with the housing problem*, and more importantly, changing the original ending (where the building is demolished and the family's furniture moved into the street as they become homeless) for a phony happy ending—nevertheless ironic— where they get a last-minute house in the brand-new *Barrio La Esperanza*. As Hannah Arendt pointed out, the deprivation of a house "to feel sheltered against the world" is mass society's most extreme and most antihuman sign,[15] something that *had to be* censored.

But beyond the symptomatology of the cuts, I want to highlight that the ten aforementioned precarious layers of the film were maximized by its comedic intelligence, which links it to Sianne Ngai's concept of the *zanni* character as an embodiment of contemporary precarity.[16] The full collapse of male agency in *El inquilino*, with the father behaving like a precarious clown (thanks to the inept comedic style mastered by the actor, Fernando Fernán Gómez), functions as a class mirror that exposes the *true powers* of Francoism as a whole. First, the property owner from Spanish nobility, a marquis living in a lavishly luxurious mansion who cannot remember which house is being demolished because "he has so many." Second, the real estate company, with a double satire of its privileged, moronic board of directors and of the inhumanly small and faulty new apartments they build. Third, the bankers, with one of them (cigar in hand) telling the poor father, "how can you ask me for a loan if you don't have any money?" And finally, the state apparatus, in a clever scene that mocks bureaucratization as well as the

---

14 Northrop Frye, *Anatomy of Criticism* (Princeton, NJ: Princeton University Press, 1957), 223.
15 Hannah Arendt, *The Human Condition* (Chicago: The University of Chicago Press, 1958), 59.
16 Sianne Ngai, *Our Aesthetic Categories* (Cambridge, MA: Harvard University Press, 2015), 174–232. Ngai traces the half-servant half-clown nature of the zanni from Commedia dell'Arte to Lucille Ball and sitcoms.

nepotistic DNA of Spain's social fabric, based on personal *favores* and hierarchical class-based recommendations. But, beyond the targets of such satire, what makes *El inquilino* such a contemporary film is that the precarious bodies of the characters are not only crushed by the wealth and salary inequalities of the system,[17] they also have to smile, run, and wear the various exploitative masks of the zanni, that is, serve their masters (and their affects) *happily*.

Worker's Solidarity vs. Real Estate Speculation, Behind the Façade

Perhaps the most telling aspect of *El inquilino*, and the one I want to highlight in relation to recent Spanish documentaries, is that the construction workers tearing down the house, the very same individuals who are getting paid to demolish and rebuild, are the ones that *care* for the evicted and precarious family. Through a series of simple yet touching scenes, the demolition crew decides to buy the poor family a little more time by moving their furniture down to the first floor and tearing the building down from the top. The shots of the rock and clay structure falling apart, blow by blow, function as a stopwatch for both: precarity and speculation. When the workers stop to eat or talk during the recesses, affective bonds are built and they find new ways of helping the family ("if we the poor don't help each other . . ."). The film's repeated image of the crew waiting outside the door to stop the official in charge of the eviction transforms this ever-present visual motif of housing precarity into a moment of class empowerment, shared resistance, and worker's solidarity, that proves that all evictions could be stopped if it depended not on armed force but on human decency. After all, how many times have we seen the image of police and judicial authorities in front of a closed door to enforce *desahucios* (evictions) in recent years? In that sense, the workers in *El inquilino* prefigure the communal bonding of the PAH association that, half a century later, stopped and still stops thousands of bank-mortgage evictions in Spain, as seen in the documentary film *Sí se puede* (*Seven Days at PAH Barcelona*, Pau Faus, 2014).

Not by chance, in his discussion of Habermas' concept of the public sphere from the perspective of documentary film, Alexander Kluge referred to evictions

---

[17] Even for scholars focused on statistics, the imbalances between wealth and income have been signaled as the biggest scandal of world economy: Thomas Piketty, *Le Capital au XXIe siècle* (Paris: Seuil, 2013).

(in his case from a house occupied by squatters) as a multifaceted and contested signifier of the tensions between activists, film crews, and society at large.[18] The kind of fragile equilibrium depicted in two indispensable contemporary documentaries that also visualize the strength of worker's solidarity—the ability to dialog and bond during construction—against the mute pressures of real estate speculation: *En construcción* and *Edificio España*. The former documents the *exterior* habitats of urban redevelopment and housing precarity in the Raval neighborhood of Barcelona (Fig. 1), and the latter focuses on the *interior* of a single building in Madrid while it is demolished to the core (an extremely iconic skyscraper, symbol of Francoist economic *desarrollismo*; Fig. 2).[19] In their own ways, both films succeed in capturing affinities between workers from multiple nationalities, and install an affective *hiatus* in the midst of real estate automatisms. The spaces and atmospheres differ, as well as the mise en scène strategies, but still it is very symptomatic how the two films share the need to situate the faces and rhythms of work (embodied in the construction workers) at the center of two of the most emblematic urban redevelopments of Spain's recent history. And they do so by tying the precarious—but also powerful and multifaceted—lives of the workers with those of the inhabitants who are being relocated or evicted due to the construction, just like *El inquilino* did.

In that sense, both films foster what Ilona Hongisto calls the viewer's awareness of the political potential of documentaries through "indeterminate forces of affection that 'insist' or 'subsist' in the moment."[20] Her discussion of Deleuze and Guattari's reinterpretation of Spinoza's ethics in relation to documentary is particularly useful in terms of the power/precarity binary we have been discussing so far, because it politicizes the clash between *potestas (pouvoir)* as the rule of dominance and *potentia (puissance)* as the force of life, or in our case, the tensions between real estate speculation and precarious bodies. Instead of indulging in Manichean divisions, the films juxtapose the monumental procedurality of the two construction sites in Barcelona and Madrid (heavy machinery, scientific rationales, official bureaucratization, sales pitches) with the down-to-earth exchanges and playful improvisations between workers and neighbors. In a natural and patient manner, both films emphasize random moments of empathy between the immigrant workers and the children playing

---

18 Alexander Kluge, "On Film and the Public Sphere," *New German Critique*, no. 24/25 (1981).
19 The term *desarrollismo* is used to name the second historical stage of Francoism (1959–1969), which preceded *tardofranquismo* (1969–1975) and was characterized by an economic boom and the regime's attempts to sell a modern image of the country abroad, while remaining politically backward.
20 Ilona Hongisto, *Soul of the Documentary* (Amsterdam: Amsterdam University Press, 2015), 113.

Fig. 1: En construcción (Work in Progress, José Luis Guerín, 2001).

Fig. 2: Edificio España (The Building, Victor Moreno, 2012).

among the rubble, or the tenants who are about to be evicted and the construction site guards, building bridges between various forms of precarity.[21]

---

[21] For Pierre Bourdieu, the cohabitation and social relations of different human groups, their *collectivism*, is exactly what neocon housing policies (try to) deactivate: *Contre-feux* (Paris: Éditions Raisons d'Agir, 1998), 18.

The two documentaries capture an ecosystem of shared potentialities and affects in the radical interruption of the construction work, that is, they create what Lauren Berlant calls an *impasse*,[22] in this case the delay of planned construction schedules. In Barcelona's Raval quarter it is due to archeological findings that halted the redevelopment for months, and in *Edificio España* due to a series of property shifts between banks and hedge funds (tied to the Spanish financial crisis) that stopped the building's renovation for several years. *En construcción* was shot in a moment when the construction bubble had not yet burst in Spain, the early 2000s, and thus offers a more optimistic take on housing precarity. Whereas *Edificio España*, being shot much later, during the economic crisis, documents the moral vacuum of an entire system through the radical emptiness of the giant building at the end, once the last tenant is evicted and the workers leave to join the ranks of unemployment (25 percent of the national workforce back then). Both films manage to *interrupt* the constant power/precarity transactions of late capitalism, the first one in an observational and humorous way, the second in a testimonial and metaphoric one, but more importantly, they do so in the most "human" way possible, inscribing little moments of chatter, boredom, and mockery that deactivate and boycott the quintessential structure of economic profit during urban redevelopments: construction schedules.

If, as proven by *El inquilino*, Spanish housing precarity is inextricably linked to structures of (royal, economic, biopolitical) power, the achievement of *En construcción* and *Edificio España* was to place the camera and the microphones where the codependence of real estate speculation and housing precarity most reveals itself, freezing the temporality of construction and economic profit, making things stop. On that note, it does not seem a coincidence that in her discussion of precarity, Berlant draws on the philosophy of Giorgio Agamben to vindicate the sociopolitical puissance of gestures as medial acts, signs of sociality, problem-events that generate an *impasse* in reality:

> I offer impasse both as a formal term for encountering the duration of the present, and a specific term for tracking the circulation of precariousness through diverse locales and bodies. The concept of the present as impasse opens up different ways that the interruption of norms of the reproduction of life can be adapted to, felt out, and lived.[23]

That is, precisely, what the two films achieve in their different ways, the suspension of construction schedules as a radical *opening* in the temporality of

---

[22] Berlant, *Cruel Optimism*, 199.
[23] Ibid.

capitalism, a fissure that thanks to the gazes, puns and silences of the characters becomes irresistibly appealing and strong.[24]

In the case of *Edificio España* the fissure was so deep and self-evident, so representative of the *state of affairs* in Spain due to the financial crisis that, immediately after being screened in a few festivals, the film was blocked by Banco Santander (the bank owning the building via one of its hedge funds), obstructing its release for fifteen months by threatening legal actions against the filmmakers. Only after the online newspaper *ElDiario.es* denounced such censorship in a public media campaign, could the movie finally be exhibited, and it was nominated for the Goya award for the best documentary. This is not only reminiscent of the Francoist censorship and release ban of *El inquilino* discussed above, it also confirms that the movie's true power, its denunciation of real estate speculation and housing precarity, was tied to the construction *impasse* it documented and made public. For one of the uppermost structures of power in the country, a major bank, the ghostly image of *that* building (called Spain), the redevelopment of which could not be completed because of financial difficulties, must have been so damaging, so contrary to the inner workings and needs of greedy extractive capitalism, that the film had to be barred. The documentary did not even need to name Banco Santander in its opening or closing titles (it never did), the visual representation and human refutation of the economies behind it, the black hole beneath the façade, was strong enough for the bank to try to prevent its release no matter what.

In that regard, *Edificio España* posits a variation of Bertolt Brecht's famous claim about the exterior view of the AEG building and the opacity of power, by literally filming the emptiness behind the façade:

> The situation has become so complicated because the simple 'reproduction of reality' says less than ever about that reality. A photograph of the Krupp works or AEG reveals almost nothing about these institutions. Reality as such has slipped into the domain of the functional.[25]

Quoted by Kluge and Sontag in their respective analyses of visual representation and the public sphere, the sentence resonates in the dozens of interior shots, off-screens, and silent traveling shots that populate *Edificio España*, both

---

[24] The use of direct sound, voices, and soundscapes is key to capturing such charismatic moments. For a text written by the sound recordist of *En construcción* and *Mercado de futuros*, Amanda Villavieja, see: Manuel Garin and Amanda Villavieja, "Willful voices: a/synchronic sound in Chantal Akerman's self-portrait films," *Feminist Media Studies* 16, no. 6 (2016), https://doi.org/10.1080/14680777.2016.1234236.

[25] Bertolt Brecht, *Brecht on Film and Radio*, trans. Marc Silberman (London: Methuen, 2000), 164.

in its literal and metaphoric sense: the film shows us the façade first, and then documents the speculative vacuum behind it. For five decades after its construction between 1948 and 1953, the building exemplified the heights of Francoist and post-Francoist commercial pride: 77,000 square meters, 32 elevators servicing 26 floors, a luxury hotel, shopping galleries . . . So when Banco Santander acquired it for 389 million euros, no one imagined that the reconstruction and interior demolition started in 2008 would lead to a complete halt for almost a decade, or that, miraculously, a documentary would capture its radical hollowness and *unproductivity* forever. That the property was later resold several times between a Chinese investment group, dubious property holdings, and a half-German, half-Majorcan tourist corporation, simply confirms what the film had previously testified: that precarious bodies are the only *real* thing behind the façade.

That is something that becomes even clearer in the documentary that brings this chapter to a close. Less polished and more intriguing than *En construcción* and *Edificio España*, *Mercado de Futuros* confronts the hollowness of the Spanish construction bubble with its inner anxieties, combining footage of a ridiculously self-therapeutic real estate fair (with its stands, commercial meetings, and coaching sessions) with the last images from Els Encants Vells flea market in Barcelona, before it was demolished and relocated. Aware of the spread of precarity to multiple layers of society, the film contrasts the failing efficiency of trade fairs and stock markets with the witty and contingent trade of an old man in the flea market, who does not want to sell anything. Thus, showing that the inhabitants of the former seem much more alienated by their own precarity (moving like zanni across halls and stands, selling someone else's lies through the telephone, pretending to know) than the good old man. The real estate agents and brokers are filmed as *dominants-dominés*, to use Bourdieu's term about the precarization of the managerial class: exhausted and stressed by excessive work, always on the verge of being fired, but still devoted to business with body and soul.[26] Hence, what Mercedes Álvarez and her crew compose is an intermittent parody of the economic system as a whole, which brings the issues discussed throughout the chapter to a zone of indistinction, a tragicomic standstill where it is increasingly difficult to decide where speculation ends and precarity begins, why houses are built or destroyed, and if markets have shares or fleas.

As a closing hypothesis, it is interesting to see *Mercado de futuros* as a calmer and ironic corollary of the Spanish economic crisis and the property bubble, that is, a film that not only confronts the inhuman vacuum of real estate speculation with the liveliness of precarious affects (like *En construcción*

---

[26] Pierre Bourdieu, *Contre-feux 2* (Paris: Éditions Raisons d'Agir, 2001), 48.

and *Edificio España* did focusing on the construction workers), but also mocks and satirizes the in/efficiency of late capitalism itself. Reminiscent of the sharp critique and the politicized sense of humor of *El inquilino*, and of Tati's patient way of letting *modernity* ridicule itself in *Playtime* (1967), this multifaceted documentary suggests that perhaps the best way to expose, deactivate, and repurpose the inequalities of power and precarity is satire: letting us laugh *and* think about the rigged hierarchies of the system by making power look ridiculous, and more importantly, vulnerable.

Under that light, the executives who obediently follow the motivational talk of some guru in a business convention are revealed as what they truly are: walking clichés. Just like the ridiculous multitasking brokers depicted in another scene, who do not seem to have a clue about what they are actually selling or buying. Compared to them, the old man at the flea market or the curious bystanders seem infinitely more interesting, alive, and bold. So, if late capitalism is morphing towards speculative and increasingly abstract modes of economic quantification, as David Graeber proposed in the title of *Debt*'s last chapter, "The Beginning of Something Yet to Be Determined (1971–present),"[27] what all these films ultimately capture and vindicate are forms of resistance based on closeness, humor, and solidarity that bring precarious bodies together instead of setting them apart, with little winks and smiles instead of big budgets. After all, wasn't the real trick of Commedia dell'Arte's servants, the zanni, to work together and make their masters look dumb and weak?

Bibliography

Agamben, Giorgio. *Means Without Ends*. Minneapolis: University of Minnesota Press, 2000.
Arendt, Hannah. *The Human Condition*. Chicago: The University of Chicago Press, 1958.
Berlant, Lauren. *Cruel Optimism*. Durham, NC: Duke University Press, 2011.
Bourdieu, Pierre. *Contre-feux*. Paris: Éditions Raisons d'Agir, 1998.
——. *Contre-feux 2*. Paris: Éditions Raisons d'Agir, 2001.
Brecht, Bertolt. *Brecht on Film and Radio*, trans. M. Silberman. London: Methuen, 2000.
Castro de Paz, José Luis, and Josetxo Cerdán. *Del sainete al esperpento*. Madrid: Cátedra, 2011.
Castro de Paz, José Luis, and Julio Pérez Perucha. "Realismo(s), tragedia e ironía: José Antonio Nieves Conde." *L'Atalante*, no. 20 (2015): 66–75.
Deltell, Luis. *Madrid en el cine de la década de los cincuenta*. Madrid: Ayuntamiento, 2007.
Esteban, Ana. "La vivienda social española en la década de los 50." *Cuaderno de notas*, no. 7 (1999): 55–80. http://oa.upm.es/6561/.
Frye, Northrop. *Anatomy of Criticism*. Princeton, NJ: Princeton University Press, 1957.

---

27 Graeber, *Debt*, 361.

Garin, Manuel, and Amanda Villavieja. "Willful voices: a/synchronic sound in Chantal Akerman's self-portrait films." *Feminist Media Studies* 16, no. 6 (September 2016): 1117–1120. https://doi.org/10.1080/14680777.2016.1234236.

Garin, Manuel, and Ana Aitana Fernández. "Images and visual motifs of Spanish economic power: the IBEX court and the banking crisis (2011–13)." *Communication & Society* 34, no. 2 (2021): 333–350.

Graeber, David. *Debt. The First 5,000 Years*. New York: Melville, 2011.

Hellín, María José, and Helena Talaya, eds. *El cine de la crisis. Respuestas cinematográficas a la crisis económica española en el siglo XXI*. Barcelona: UOC Press, 2018.

Hongisto, Ilona. *Soul of the Documentary*. Amsterdam: Amsterdam University Press, 2015.

Ibarz, Mercè. *Buñuel documental. Las Hurdes, tierra sin pan i el seu temps*. Barcelona: UPF, 1997.

Kluge, Alexander. "On Film and the Public Sphere." *New German Critique*, no. 24/25 (1981): 206–220.

Loureiro, Angel G. "Spanish Nationalism and the Ghost of Empire." *Journal of Cultural Studies* 4, no. 1 (2003): 65–76. https://doi.org/10.1080/1463620032000058686.

Mendelson, Jordana. *Documenting Spain*. University Park, PA: Pennsylvania State University Press, 2005.

Montero, Juli, José Javier Sánchez, and María Paz. *La imagen pública de la monarquía*. Madrid: Akal, 2001.

Muro, Diego, and Alejandro Quiroga. "Spanish Nationalism: Ethnic or Civic?" *Ethnicities* 5, no. 1 (2005): 9–29. https://doi.org/10.1177/1468796805049922.

Ngai, Sianne. *Our Aesthetic Categories*. Cambridge, MA: Harvard University Press, 2015.

Payne, Stanley G. "Nationalism, Regionalism and Micronationalism in Spain." *Journal of Contemporary History* 26, no. 3/4 (1991): 479–491.

Piketty, Thomas. *Le Capital au XXIe siècle*. Paris: Seuil, 2013.

Sontag, Susan. *On Photography*. London: Penguin, 1979.

Tsianos, Vassilis, and Dimitris Papadopoulos. "Precarity: A Savage Journey to the Heart of Embodied Capitalism." *Transversal*, no. 10 (2006). https://transversal.at/transversal/1106/tsianos-papadopoulos/en.

Zarza Arribas, Alba. "La imagen social de la Vivienda en el cine español de posguerra (1940–1960)." *TRIM*, no. 14 (2018): 61–78.

Filmography

Arraianos. Dir. Eloy Enciso. Spain, 2012.
Carmen y Lola (*Carmen & Lola*). Dir. Arantxa Echevarría. Spain, 2018.
De nens (*Playing with Children*). Dir. Joaquim Jordà. Spain, 2004.
Edificio España (*The Building*). Dir. Victor Moreno. Spain, 2012.
El año del descubrimiento (*The Year of the Discovery*). Dir. Luis López Carrasco. Spain/Switzerland, 2020.
El cielo gira (*The Sky Turns*). Dir. Mercedes Álvarez. Spain, 2004.
El inquilino (*The Tenant*). Dir. José Antonio Nieves Conde. Spain, 1958.
El pisito (*The Little Apartment*). Dir. Marco Ferreri and Isidoro M. Ferry. Spain, 1958.

En construcción (*Work in Progress*). Dir. José Luis Guerín. Spain, 2001.
Entre dos aguas (*Between Two Waters*). Dir. Isaki Lacuesta. Spain, 2018.
Esa pareja feliz (*That Happy Couple*). Dir. Juan Antonio Bardem and Luis García Berlanga. Spain, 1953.
Hermosa juventud (*Beautiful Youth*). Dir. Jaime Rosales. Spain/France, 2014.
Historias de Madrid (*Madrid Stories*). Dir. Ramón Comas. Spain, 1958.
Las Hurdes (*Land Without Bread*). Dir. Luis Buñuel. Spain, 1933.
La innocència (*The Innocence*). Dir. Lucía Alemany. Spain, 2019.
La leyenda del tiempo (*The Legend of Time*). Dir. Isaki Lacuesta. Spain, 2006.
La plaga (*The Plague*). Dir. Neus Ballús. Spain/France/Germany, 2013.
La soledad (*Solitary Fragments*). Dir. Jaime Rosales. Spain, 2007.
Los lunes al sol (*Mondays in the Sun*). Dir. Fernando León de Aranoa. Spain/France/Italy, 2002.
Mercado de futuros (*Futures Market*). Dir. Mercedes Álvarez. Spain, 2011.
Numax presenta (*Numax Presents*). Dir. Joaquim Jordà. Spain, 1980.
Playtime. Dir. Jacques Tati. France/Italy, 1967.
Sense sostre (*Outside*). Dir. Pep Garrido and Xesc Cabot. Spain, 2019.
Sí se puede (*Seven Days at PAH Barcelona*). Dir. Pau Faus. Spain, 2014.
Sobre la marxa (*The Creator of the Jungle*). Dir. Jordi Morató. Spain, 2013.
Surcos (*Furrows*). Dir. José Antonio Nieves Conde. Spain, 1951.
Techo y comida (*Roof and Food*). Dir. Juan Miguel del Castillo. Spain, 2015.
Veinte años no es nada (*Twenty Years Is Nothing*). Dir. Joaquim Jordà. Spain, 2005.
Viaje al cuarto de una madre (*Journey to a Mother's Room*). Dir. Celia Rico. Spain/France, 2018.
Volver. Dir. Pedro Almodóvar. Spain, 2006.
Zauria(k): Eromena, Gorputza, Feminismoak (*Wound[s]: Madness, Body and Feminism*). Dir. Maier Irigoien, Isabel Sáez, Iker Oiz. Spain, 2019.

Nino Klingler
Aspects of Poverty and Precarity
Puzzle-Pictures from Portugal

Fig. 1: Linha Vermelha (Red Line, José Filipe Costa, 2012).

The still above (Fig. 1) is an archival image from 1975. It appears at a decisive moment in the essayistic documentary *Linha Vermelha* (*Red Line*, José Filipe Costa, 2012). We see a group of bullock carts standing idly in the countryside. This type of carts was in use in agriculture in Portugal for a long time. When the animals pulling the cart are unyoked, the two-wheeled contraptions tilt over to the back, the front sticking out and pointing to the sky.

Working with these carts must have been exceptionally rough and exhausting labor. They remind us of the great level of poverty and underdevelopment of Portugal in the second half of the twentieth century, especially in the "anachronistic" agricultural sector,[1] with productivity rates of "half of the levels in Greece and Spain and a quarter of the EC average" until the mid-1980s.[2] Thus, the image

---

[1] Eric Solestan, *Portugal: A Country Study* (Washington, D.C.: Federal Research Division, Library of Congress, 1993), 116.
[2] Ibid.

of the bullock carts can be seen as a symbol of the poverty of a population that had to invest great efforts to produce basic goods.

This kind of vehicle was also in use on a large, aristocratically owned tree farming estate by the name of Torre Bela. *Red Line* reconstructs the tumultuous history of the place. The shot above was taken there, shortly after the revolution and the military coup that overthrew the dictatorship of the *Estado Novo* in 1974/ 75. In 1975, Torre Bela was occupied by peasants suffering under an archaic feudal system. They took control of the land they had been working for generations, but which up until then had remained the property of a cruel and greedy landlord. They formed a cooperative to transform private property into commons.

In *Red Line*, we learn that the military took aerial surveillance photographs of the area. But the soldiers got confused when they spotted the bullock carts. They thought they were seeing weapons. Cannons. Possibly flak artillery. There was the danger that the peasant cooperative had received weapons from abroad and trained "for Cuban style guerila warfare."[3] The military saw signs of a threat.

When soldiers arrived in Torre Bela to investigate, they found no weapons, only bullock carts. Nevertheless, some occupiers were taken into custody. One could say that they were imprisoned because of images, not because of facts. Images that had been printed on the title pages of big newspapers in Lisbon by that time. Images of imaginary weapons of an imaginary guerila force. "An image can change the world, after all," the voice-over in *Red Line* states dryly.

The image of the bullock carts/cannons can be understood as showing two things, and by that token two perspectives on the disenfranchised peasant population. It can be seen as a concrete symbol of poverty and exploitation, of a kind of manual labor people in Portugal had to perform in order to survive and to make their landlord wealthier. On the other hand, viewed from the aerial perspective of those in power, the image shows what they are afraid of: the possibility of a revolutionary proletariat.

This kind of complex treatment of political and social reality can be encountered in the works of many Portuguese filmmakers such as Manoel de Oliveira, Antonio Reis and Margarida Cordeiro, Teresa Villaverde, Roberto Rodrigues, Pedro Costa, Miguel Gomes, Marta Mateus, to name just a few.[4] Moreover, the layering of

---

[3] This is a quote from José Rodrigues, a former member of the cooperative, in *Red Line*, Min. 50:30.

[4] One reason for these similar approaches might be the country's complicated political heritage with a long fascist period and the resulting limitations and obstacles to freedom of artistic expression. See José Manuel Costa, "Questions About Documentary Making in Portugal," in *Portugal: um retrato cinematográfico*, ed. Nuno Figueiredo and Diniz Guarda (Lisbon: Número-Arte e Cultura, 2004), 122. Costa argues that because of the political and economic conditions, documentary

competing aspects of reality as in the case of the bullock carts/cannons often materializes in single images, or condensed passages dealing with topics like poverty, precariousness, and social exclusion. This article lists some examples of these kinds of images of poverty in Portuguese films and tries to reflect upon their possible political implications.[5]

Films from Portugal have for a long time—at least since the period of the Novo Cinema in the 1960s and 1970s—been socially aware, dealing with various facets of (often rural) poverty in manifold ways.[6] But in the wake of the recent economic crisis in Portugal, there has been a new surge of films dealing with issues of economic exclusion and precarity[7]—not least because the national cinema industry itself is in a precarious situation:

> One of the countries hit the hardest by the euro-zone debt crisis starting in 2008, Portugal saw its audiovisual market shrink dramatically ever since. 2012 was labelled the 'year zero' of Portuguese cinema, as for the first time since the 1970s zero funds were attributed to the film sector.[8]

---

and fiction have always been "impure" genres in Portugal, never clearly separated, always leaking into each other. His thoughts can therefore be taken as instructive for all the movies discussed in this text (ibid., 119–120).

5 It is important to note that this is not an argument for a possible defining trait of any kind of national cinematography. There are numerous examples of films shot in Portugal that tell stories about precarious lives which do not include the kind of ambivalent images discussed here; for example João Canijo's phenomenal family epos *Sangue do Meu Sangue* (*Blood of My Blood*, 2011), the rural elegy *Volta à Terra* (*[Be]longing*, João Pedro Plácido, 2014), or João Salaviza's dramatic shorts *Arena* (2009) and *Rafa* (2012), set in bleak high-rise blocks.

6 Cf. Costa, "Questions About Documentary Making in Portugal"; filmmakers one could mention as examples would be Manoel de Oliveira (*O Acto da Primavera*, *Rite of Spring*, 1963), Margarida Cordeiro and António Reis (*Trás-os-Montes*, 1973), Paulo Rocha (*Os verdes Anos*, *The Green Years*, 1966; *Murdar de vida*, *Change of Life*, 1966), or António Campos (*Falamos de Rio de Onor*, *We Talk About Rio de Onor*, 1973).

7 "In a generalised collective hysteria, the themes of debt, crisis and austerity permeated public discourse; and not surprisingly, artists and film-makers produced a wide body of work centring on these topics. In Portugal, many of the films and art projects that emerged during and in the aftermath of the financial bailout have in common the backdrop of the economic crisis and/or austerity." Patricia Sequeria Brás, "Post-Fordism in Active Life, Industrial Revolution and The Nothing Factory," in *Cinema of Crisis*, ed. Thomas Austin and Angelos Koutsourakis (Cambridge: Cambridge University Press, 2020), 76–77.

8 Mariana Liz, "Introduction: Framing the Global Appeal of Contemporary Portuguese Cinema," in *Portugal's Global Cinema*, ed. Mariana Liz (London: Bloomsbury Publishing, 2017), subheading "Portuguese cinema on the international stage" (last paragraph [quoted from Ebook]). Even though the GDP had been growing until the Coronavirus crisis, Portugal's economy is fragile, with a low level of productivity (60% of the EU average), an internationally uncompetitive agricultural sector, and a high level of unemployment (especially among younger

Wittgenstein's Puzzle-Pictures

Coming back to the question of multi-perspectivity in images of poverty (such as in the example of the bullock cart/cannon), there is a famous passage from Ludwig Wittgenstein's *Philosophical Investigations* dealing with the picture of the duck-rabbit.

Fig. 2: Wittgenstein's duck-rabbit.

Someone might see a rabbit, someone else a duck (Fig. 2). Once one becomes aware of the possible double reading, the effect is jarring. One sees the same, yet it's completely different. This experience could just as well happen when looking at a human face instead of an optical illusion: "I contemplate a face and then suddenly notice its likeness to another. I see that it has not changed; and yet I see it differently. I call this experience 'noticing an aspect'."[9] Here, Wittgenstein describes the possibility of a complex act of perception: seeing something as stable while at the same time having a new view of the thing. "The expression of a change of aspect is the expression of a new perception and at the same time of the perception's being unchanged."[10]

Shifting from one aspect to another, the perception never stabilizes into one single reading. This shift transforms an act of "looking at something" into a visual "experience" imbued with "thinking:" "the flashing of an aspect on us seems half visual experience, half thought." Wittgenstein's argument is that in these moments, the act of looking gets enmeshed with language, experience with concepts, image with words.

---

generations). In 2014, Portugal had one of the highest poverty rates in Western Europe (19% of the population). See: Walther L. Bernecker and Horst Pietschmann, *Geschichte Portugals* (Munich: Beck, 2014), 131.
9 Ludwig Wittgenstein, *Philosophical Investigations*, trans. Gertrude Elizabeth Margaret Anscombe, (Oxford: Basil Blackwell, 1958), 193.
10 Ibid., 196.

The "change [of aspect] produces a *surprise* not produced by the recognition."[11] In the German original Wittgenstein uses the term "Staunen"[12] (astonishment) which seems more fitting to me than *surprise* (which would translate as *Überraschung*).

Wittgenstein's reflections seem productive to understanding the poetics at work in the images of poverty and precarity in films from Portugal. Because they regularly trigger the sensation of something not dissimilar to *Staunen*, of being astonished by unconventional and complex depictions of precarious existences. One obviously needs to be very cautious here. It means straddling a fine line between appreciating inventive filmic techniques (and their possible emancipatory effects) and an aestheticizing exploitation of a movie's subjects. Tentatively, one might call the images at question with a term Wittgenstein uses to describe the duck-rabbit: "puzzle-pictures."[13] The images have the potential to puzzle because they challenge widespread assumptions on how poverty and precarity are depicted in cinema. They invite the viewer to engage with them.

Torre Bela and *Red Line*

The German director Thomas Harlan shot the documentary *Torre Bela* (1975) during the eponymous estate's occupation, the same year the two peasants were arrested by the soldiers because of the bullock carts. The film was to become one of the "most emblematic films ever made about the [revolutionary process] in Portugal."[14] This status is in part due to one famous and wildly discussed scene in which the peasants, together with political activists who joined them for the occupation, enter the residential mansion of the expelled landlord. They are, the movie tells us, in "the palace" for the first time.

---

11 Ibid., 199 (my italics, N.K.).
12 Ludwig Wittgenstein, *Philosophische Untersuchungen* (Frankfurt a.M.: Suhrkamp, 1967), 233.
13 David Lauer calls Wittgenstein's puzzle-pictures "Kippfiguren" which could be translated to "tilt-images." Like those children's collector cards that show different images when you move them in one direction or the other, you can never see both at the same time. David Lauer, "Anamorphotische Aspekte. Wittgenstein über Techniken des Sehens," in *Der entstellte Blick*, ed. Cha Kyung-Ho and Markus Rautzenberg (Munich: Fink, 2019).
14 Luís Trindade, "Filming Narratives Becoming Events: Documentary and the 'Emplotments' of the Carnation Revolution," in *Portugal's Global Cinema: Industry, History and Culture*, ed. Mariana Liz (London: Bloomsbury Publishing, 2017), subheading "Scenes from the class struggle in Portugal", first paragraph [quoted from Ebook].

The people stroll through the chambers. The camera is in their midst and highly mobile. The space is tight. Bodies flood narrow corridors and passages. Someone plays the piano. Others curiously open the drawers and find mementos, vases, religious figurines. They touch the finely embroidered lingerie, feel the weight of a smoking pipe, peek at photographs and pictures on sideboards and walls. One man tries on a velvet jacket: "I look like a duke." Another is dressing up like a priest and jokingly christens the group. It's a complexly layered, chaotic scene with a lot of simultaneous actions and no distanced point of observation.

Nothing gets destroyed, no anger breaks through. Every touch seems gentle and imbued with respect for a deeply unjust, yet very old social hierarchy that all of the "invaders" seem to have internalized. Even if the very fact of them being in the mansion makes manifest the disappearance of the power they had suffered from for so long, one cannot shake centuries of exploitation in one single act. Especially not in a single cinematographic act.

But this is not the only possible perception of the scene. Retrospectively, the passage in Harlan's film can also be seen as counterproductive to the occupation of Torre Bela and to the revolutionary project as a whole. The peasants were viewed as trespassers, intruders, looters, thieves. "Of course that was the image that stayed with many people . . . That things were stolen there . . ."[15] Private property is sacrosanct. Sympathy with a political movement quickly withers when things get taken illegitimately. In the scene in question, books are being taken out of a shelf, some people carry clothes out of the rooms, a woman shouts "do you need a rosary?" and the last shot of the scene shows a man leaving a room saying "we will all get arrested." Playful or criminal? Looting or visiting? "By maintaining the ambiguity of the event, *Torre Bela* was subjected to various political readings."[16]

To make matters worse—or more interesting—the scene was initiated by the movie director Harlan and was not a spontaneous act on the part of the occupiers. He thought his film needed "scenes of conflict," that it was lacking "a certain drama," as his producer José Pedro Dos Santos remembers in *Red Line*. The intrusion was staged. Or, at least, it was co-created by filmmakers and occupiers.

Red Line elaborately reconstructs the production of *Torre Bela* using audio tapes from the shooting, archival images, and interviews with some of the protagonists and crew members, as well as witnesses of the era. The scene of the peasants' visiting/looting of the mansion is central to this project. It gets read

---

[15] José Rodrigues in *Red Line*, Min 24:42.
[16] José Filipe Costa, "When Cinema Forges the Event: The Case of *Torre Bela*," *Third Text* 25, no. 1 (2011): 111.

and re-read multiple times in *Red Line*—as documentary, as staged reality, as political intervention. "Are we actors or are we occupiers?" one of the peasants asks in an audio tape of the shooting. We see the original footage again and again, see the film strip being rewound, and we listen to a school class discussing the right to revolt against exploitation versus the protection of private property. We get a catalogue of different readings, of different perspectives on one scene.

Costa's "deconstruction"[17] of Harlan's film is neither destructive nor reductive. *Red Line* acknowledges the legacy of *Torre Bela* while simultaneously questioning its "work procedures and ethos."[18] The film does not construct a simple fiction/reality divide.[19] Instead, it fans out multiple configurations, highlighting some aspects of the scene in question while obfuscating others. Different perceptions and readings of the scene are presented, all equally legitimate and equally wanting. Looting/visiting. Actors/occupiers. Bullock carts/cannons. Reality is treated generously in *Red Line*.

What is important is that one does not mistake one perception for the whole of reality. There is always another side. "At the end of the day, there is more than one truth, isn't there?"[20] The viewers are invited to challenge their own interpretation with competing or additional ones—to learn multi-perspectivity, so to speak. The films acknowledge the complexities of the real, and the possibility of sharing one's view or experience of reality with others. Something is shared, while something is kept. And in the act of viewing, we are capable of taking different viewpoints, highlighting different aspects of one problem.

The Mutants and *Arabian Nights*

In Teresa Villaverde's *Os Mutantes* (*The Mutants*, 1998), runaway street girl Andreia (Ana Moreia) is hospitalized after throwing herself down the stairs. Sitting next to her bed, a man—a social worker? her father?—lectures her. She was foolish, it was dangerous, she will face consequences. Andreia listens expressionlessly. The man leaves. Then something magical happens. A ghost-like, translucent

---
17 Trindade, "Filming Narratives Becoming Events," subheading "Scenes from the class struggle in Portugal", third paragraph [quoted from Ebook].
18 Ibid.
19 The closing voice-over of *Red Line* makes this point clear: "Sometimes one doesn't know what came first: reality or fiction. The characters in [Harlan's] film were occupiers and actors at the same time. [. . .] And what if the bullock carts had in fact been cannons? And if an occupier became a duke? And if another became a priest?".
20 Voice-over in *Red Line*, Min. 48:00.

version of Andreia extricates itself from her motionless body, pulls out the infusion needle, gets up and walks around in the hospital. The effect is produced via classical Meliès-style superimposition. The ghost-Andreia finds a pack of cigarettes on a counter, grabs and lights two, walks back to the bed, lies down next to herself, and gives the real Andreia one of the cigarettes. They lie there smoking, smiling at each other (Fig. 3).

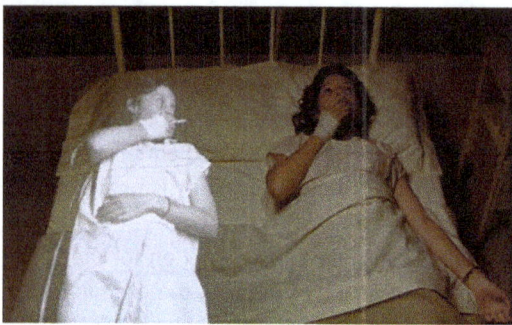

Fig. 3: Os Mutantes (The Mutants, Teresa Villaverde, 1998).

The scene subverts viewing expectations twice. First, the appearance of the ghost is unexpected because the movie's register up to that moment had been one of poetic, stylized, yet recognizable social realism. In more or less independent vignettes, *The Mutants* had shown some episodes in the lives of a group of homeless street children: how they sneak out of foster homes, how they are being exploited by shady movie directors, and how they are ignored by the society around them. But since we are used to apparitions in movies, one has little trouble shifting expectations to accommodate the appearance of the ghost. The scene can easily be read as a dream, maybe of escaping, of running away from authority. But when the ghost Andreia returns to bed and shares a smoke with herself, this reading gets shaken, too, and thus the experience of the entire movie becomes unstable. The cigarette is a magical object, transgressing the border between dream-logic and the fiction's reality. One can see it as real, or as imaginary. One is seeing a "problem child," both as fantasy and as reality. If it is a dream, it is not one of escaping, but of staying where you are. Smoking in the hospital bed, while being underage. Causing trouble. Choosing to live precariously.

Cristina Álvarez Lopez and Adrian Martin have argued against reading Teresa Villaverde's films as discourses on precarity—even though on a surface level, they often deal with subject matters such as homelessness,[21] prostitution,[22] or unemployment,[23] which would suggest such an approach:

> It would be easy to link [Villaverde's] films to the recent category of a 'cinema of precarity' [. . .] One needs to be careful [. . .] not to reduce films – especially as formally rich as Villaverde's – to their purely anecdotal, referential or sociological levels (as happens too often in discussions of depictions of precarity), a process which ends up flattening them (whatever the radical intention of the critical political discourse) into mirror reflections of topics outside cinema. If Villaverde's films teach us anything, it is that their fragile space of transformation – affective, imaginative and aesthetic – takes place within cinema and its particular powers.[24]

Yes and no. The smoking-scene in *The Mutants* obviously exceeds the register of what the authors dub "social issue cinema"—a cinema of transparency and intelligibility, of a straightforward transformation of social issues into a cinematic language that makes them accessible and their causes understandable. "A mode of representation which renders the situation of exploitation intelligible as the effect of specific causes and, further, which shows that situation to be the source of the forms of consciousness and affects that modify it."[25] None of the films discussed in this text satisfies these conditions.

But the alternative López and Martin offer is equally unsatisfactory. If a film is not "realist" in the narrowly defined terms of "social issue cinema" or "cinema of precarity,"[26] why then does it have to be purely cinematographic, "taking place within cinema"? Why would a director deal with the living existence of street children but choose an aesthetic that makes it impossible to think about the afilmic reality of their social life?[27] There seems to be a false dichotomy at work when the

---

21 *The Mutants.*
22 *Transe* (*Trance*, Teresa Villaverde, 2006).
23 *Colo* (Teresa Villaverde, 2017).
24 Cristina Álvarez Lopez and Adrian Martin, "Broken Links: The Cinema of Teresa Villaverde," in *Portugal's Global Cinema*, ed. Mariana Liz (London: Bloomsbury Publishing, 2017), subheading "Forms and transformations," second paragraph [quoted from Ebook].
25 Jacques Rancière, "The Politics of Pedro Costa" [2009], *Diagonal Thoughts* (July 13, 2012), https://www.diagonalthoughts.com/?p=1546.
26 The authors take the term from Lauren Berlant and name Agnès Varda, Laurent Cantet, and the Dardenne brothers as exemplary filmmakers of this mode of "anecdotal, referential" cinema. Álvarez Lopez and Martin, "Broken Links," subheading "Forms and transformations," first paragraph [quoted from Ebook].
27 "Afilmic" in the sense of Étienne Souriau: "the real and ordinary world, the one you and I live in every day, which exists independently of films and existed even before there were films." Souriau stresses the importance of this concept for films to be read as "realistic" or "documentary": "when speaking of realist films, one wants to say that they are either an exact image or, even more precisely, a sincere and accurate 'expression' of the afilmic universe."

authors go on to claim that Villaverde's cinema "militates against realism" and "escapes the realism of the social issue genre,"²⁸ as will become apparent when looking at Bertolt Brecht's concept of realism later on in this text.

It seems more fruitful to think of the puzzle-picture of Andreia as ghost and non-ghost as enriching the viewer's understanding of the reality of street children, of complicating it without destroying or denying it. Something changes, while something stays the same. Aspects that one might not have thought of become unveiled, the "inner life" (for lack of a better word) of Andreia is inhabiting the same shot as the depiction of her social existence.

Miguel Gomes' three-part *As mil e uma noites* (*Arabian Nights 1–3*, 2015)— mixing myths, costume play, documentary, fiction, and essay—offers more examples for a similar kind of unconventional depiction of precarious lives. The trilogy's overarching narrative—collecting a myriad of stories from Portugal during the Euro Crisis—explicitly refers to the fairytales of 1001 nights. Portugal is telling itself stories to delay extinction (by the Troika and its politics of austerity). The films have thus been criticized for having "nationalistic overtones" because they simplify capitalism's global dimension.²⁹

A more favorable reading understands Gomes's resorting to the structure of myths as a reaction to the hopelessness of the country's economic situation during the eurozone crisis, as Dominik Kamalzadeh suggests:

> Contemporary Europe and its disastrous economic politics—especially for the South—cannot [be countered] by realistic means alone. As if the rulebook of social realism had become too tight, [Gomes] resorts to the stockpile of folklore, fairytale, legendary traditions to expand the field of relationships and appropriations.³⁰

A long segment in *O Encantado* (*The Enchanted*), the last part of *Arabian Nights*, shows a popular pastime in a suburban area of Lisbon heavily affected by the economic crisis. A group of most likely unemployed, mostly middle-aged and

---

Étienne Souriau, "Die Struktur des filmischen Universums und das Vokabular der Filmologie," [1951], in *Das filmische Universum. Schriften zur Ästhetik des Kinos*, ed. and trans. Guido Kirsten (Munich: Fink, 2020), 56; upcoming is an English translation of the text in Vinzenz Hediger and Guido Kirsten, eds., *Filmology and the Invention of Film Studies: Selected Writings from the Revue internationale de Filmologie*.

28 Álvarez Lopez and Martin, "Broken Links," subheading "Forms and transformations" [quoted from Ebook].

29 Patricia Sequeria Brás, "Post-Fordism in Active Life, Industrial Revolution and The Nothing Factory," 77.

30 Dominik Kamalzadeh, "Mythen der Wirklichkeit. Volkskultur und Magie in Filmen von Alice Rohrwacher, Miguel Gomes und Pietro Marcello," *kolik.film*, Sonderheft 30 (October 2018): 7–8. All translations, if not otherwise stated in the bibliography, are by me, N.K.

elderly men patiently and diligently train chaffinches to sing. They are shown catching the birds, carrying around the cages wrapped in cloths, discussing the best training methods, and competing against each other to find out whose bird knows the most songs. The film takes a distant, observant perspective, one of a "respectful anthropologist."[31] Most takes are static; long and medium-long shots dominate. Not once does anybody mention the precarious economic situation they are living in. All conversations are about birds, and only about birds. Contextual information is only given through regular intertitles and sporadic found footage segments retelling the story of the neighborhood's economic downfall and its population's hardships. It is only because of these added pieces of information and through looking at the modest interiors of the men's homes, their washed-out clothes, and through contemplating the fact that they seem to have a lot of free time at their disposal that the viewer can speculate on the material situation of those depicted.

What is puzzling here is the discrepancy between what we expect unemployed characters in films to do—working for labor,[32] for instance—and what they actually *are doing*. We are used to associate a certain range of behavior with the social position of a film's character. *The Enchanted* challenges these expectations without annihilating them. The film does not paint the picture of a tranquil refuge from the permanent fight against precarity, but instead situates the strange and transfixing hobby of finch-breeding decisively within a concrete local, historical, social, and economic context.

Brecht's Concept of Montage and *A Fábrica de Nada*

Between 1937 and 1941, Bertolt Brecht wrote a number of texts on the question of realism.[33] He intervened at a decisive historic moment, when Stalinist realism was dominating leftist artistic production. Anything not adhering to a very limited tradition—which in the literary world included Balzac, Flaubert, and Dostoevsky, but not Pound or Joyce—was deemed antirealist, bourgeois, formalist, and

---

31 Ibid., 10.
32 A term coined by Guy Standing to signify the work needed to sustain a precarious existence, e.g. filling forms to apply for social welfare or jobs. See: Guy Standing, *The Precariat: The New Dangerous Class* (London: Bloomsbury, 2011).
33 For a selection of English translations, see Bertolt Brecht, *Brecht on Art and Politics*, ed. Steve Giles and Tom Kuhn (London: Bloomsbury, 2003), 205–270.

therefore anti-socialist. Brecht challenged this narrow view of admissible artistic styles to describe social problems and the truth of the proletariat's situation. Instead, he defended the technique of "montage,"[34] of an artistic "jumping from one kind of composition to another within the same artwork" without betraying the idea of a realist method.[35] His understanding of realism was not formal but political:

> Everybody who is not biased by formal arguments knows that the truth can be hushed up in many ways and must be told in many ways. That indignation by inhuman conditions can be kindled in various ways, through direct description in an impassioned and factual fashion, through the telling of fables and allegories, through jokes, through over- and understatement.[36]

Brecht insisted that art should be truthful about social reality and close to the poetics of the people. He drew from the experience of cooperating with workers on theater plays. He was struck by their aesthetic maturity and quick-wittedness. They would immediately detect any kind of patronizing attempt to be "folkloristic" or "approachable." Brecht concluded that being formally inventive does not necessarily mean being elitist or hard to understand. On the contrary, sticking to antiquated traditions of narration might show a disregard to the sensibilities of the people. "I am speaking from experience when I say: one need not be afraid to step in front of the proletariat with audacious and unexpected things, if only they refer to its reality."[37]

Brecht's statement should probably be taken with a grain of salt. It adheres to a jargon, an economic mode of production and a political frame of reference that stems from a past historical period. Still, Brecht's thoughts are far from anachronistic. Instead, they can be quite instructive about progressive political filmmaking, "audacious and unexpected" works of art that refer to the reality of capitalist production. *A Fábrica de Nada* (*The Nothing Factory*, 2017) by Pedro Pinho is a case in point.

After a long search for a fitting shooting location to turn a stage play by Dutch playwright Judith Herzbel[38] on an occupied factory into a movie, the team around Pinho discovered a factory producing lifts in Santa Póvoa de Iria, north of Lisbon. The factory named Fataleva had been run autonomously by the workers

---

34 Bertolt Brecht, "Über den formalistischen Charakter der Realismustheorie," in *Gesammelte Werke 19* (Frankfurt a.M.: Suhrkamp, 1967), 309.
35 Ibid., 306.
36 Bertolt Brecht, "Volkstümlichkeit und Realismus," in *Gesammelte Werke 19* (Frankfurt a.M.: Suhrkamp), 327.
37 Brecht, "Volkstümlichkeit und Realismus," 329.
38 Sequeria Brás, "Post-Fordism," 87.

since the revolution in 1975. When the factory went bankrupt and subsequently threatened to be dismantled, the workers took control of the means of production. Among the cast of *The Nothing Factory* were people working at Fataleva or at production sites close by. Sadly, the factory had to close down entirely during the post-production of the film.

Towards the end of the movie, when the workers finally receive a large order after struggling to keep the business running, they start singing and dancing. Their movements are carefully choreographed. The camera takes spectacular angles to arrange and re-arrange the blue-collared bodies in the factory space (Fig. 4). A guitar-driven, non-diegetic soundtrack underlines the scene's abstraction from concrete reality.

When the workers/performers form a circle on the floor of the production hall for a crescendo, a man starts talking from off-screen above. He harshly criticizes the workers' performance. It is the director (played by the "real" documentary director Danièle Incalcaterra)[39] who slowly descends from the ceiling, standing on an aerial work platform. He had already appeared in several scenes before, trying to gain access to the factory or discussing the idea of a self-managed factory in theoretical terms. He functions as a stand-in for a critical meta-reflection on the production of the film itself.[40]

The musical sequence is Brechtian in multiple ways: first, on the level of production, there is the cooperation between real factory workers and a film team. Then there is the "montage" of divergent styles and methods, mixing agitprop, a popular genre like the musical, and documentary methods. Lastly, there is the distancing effect produced by the self-reflexive appearance of the director. Patricia Sequeria Brás:

> On the one hand, the figure of the director serves self-reflexivity insofar as it problematises the way in which the cinematic medium often exploits the image of the worker. On the other hand, the musical sequence can be understood as a political moment in which the workers themselves withdraw from their social position.[41]

---

39 Danièle Incalcaterra directed the movie *Fasinpat* (2004) about a worker-controlled tile factory in Argentina. The title's acronym means "Fabrica sin patrones"—factory without bosses.
40 According to director Pedro Pinho, the character of the director was largely based on Thomas Harlan during the shooting of *Torre Bela*. *Red Line* was produced by Terratreme, a production company co-founded by Pinho. See: Pedro Pinho, interviewed by Luc Chessel, "Ce n'est pas le but qui compte, mais comment tu le fais," *Libération*, December 12, 2017, https://www.liberation.fr/cinema/2017/12/12/pedro-pinho-ce-n-est-pas-le-but-qui-compte-mais-comment-tu-le-fais_1616215/.
41 Sequeria Brás, "Post-Fordism," 88–89.

Fig. 4: A Fábrica de Nada (The Nothing Factory, Pedro Pinho, 2017).

Similarly to the chaffinch-breeders in *Arabian Nights*, the singing workers question our expectations of what a certain group of actors is supposed to do in a film. But in contrast to Gomes's documentary approach revealing the "hidden life" of unemployed men, Pinho opts for a constructivist interrogation of the workers' social positions. The musical sequence with its self-reflexive coda produces a puzzle-picture addressing two kinds of exploitation: It can be seen as showing both "the factory as a site of exploitation" (which is satirized by the workers performing non-productive acts like singing and dancing)[42] and "the exploitative capacities of the filmic medium" (which gets criticized by a long fight between the movie's main protagonist and the director about the hypocrisy of shooting an activist film).[43] Both readings are equally legitimate, yet also mutually exclusive. The scene, the entire movie even, could be seen as empowering, or as desperate.

Pedro Costa and Conclusion

The exploration of this possible dilemma—how to avoid exploiting the exploited through cinema?—arguably lies at the heart of the unique cinema of Pedro Costa. What follows are only some cursory remarks on the solemn, often

---

[42] The political function of the musical scene in *The Nothing Factory* is very different from the seemingly similar one in the factory in *Dancer in the Dark* (Lars von Trier, 2000). In *Dancer in the Dark*, the musical is just an imaginary escape from the harsh reality of capitalist exploitation in the factory. The individual cannot confront the system anymore. Art has no capacity to transform reality but instead reinforces unjust social hierarchies by offering false alternatives and numbing illusions.

[43] Sequeria Brás, "Post-Fordism," 78.

hermetic, opaque style of his movies, especially those following *No Quarto da Vanda* (*In Vanda's Room*, 2000).[44] Costa often works with the same amateur actors over a long period of time. He casts them in roles that are variations of their regular life. Almost all of them live precariously, struggling with substance abuse, unemployment, health issues, or unstable citizenship status. Costa films exclusively on location, mostly in very poor parts of Lisbon, using minimal light and a small production crew. But his movies are far from poverty porn. The stylized, boldly illuminated frames are reminiscent of paintings. They betray an incredible attention to the most minute details of life on the fringes of mainstream society.

Puzzle-pictures permeate Costa's whole cinematic style. Each frame, each face, and each object are full of latent aspects, of superimposed possible readings shifting the meaning of the shot in one direction or the other. One out of many possible examples is a bewildering section towards the middle of *Cavalo Dinheiro* (*Horse Money*, 2014)—a series of still shots of motionless people in humble, sometimes desolate environments. It is a pitch-black night, there is little light. We see alleyways and backyards full of rubble, bedrooms with moldy walls, crammed kitchens. The protagonists—mostly solitary, sometimes in groups, all of them black—pose as if for a photo shoot. They lie in bed smoking, peek out of windows and doorframes. They pray, sleep on the kitchen table, work at the sewing machine late at night. The shots are reminiscent of a series of black-and-white photographs by Jacob Riis at the beginning of the film, pictures of poor working-class life in New York around the end of the nineteenth century. Yet Costa's frames are not snapshots. In their carefully staged, minimally illuminated style they also have a vague resemblance to the works of someone like photographer Gregory Crewdson. They could be read as an *arte povera* response to Crewdson's big budget freeze-frame-dramas reminiscent of Hollywood. Every shot in the sequence is clearly taken on location, with real people in their own living environments. Yet due to the dramatic mise en scène there is a latent narrative potential in each frame; hidden, untold, and therefore important stories. This feeling gets reinforced by the soundtrack, playing the song "Alto Cuelo" by the Cape Verdean band Os Tubarões from 1976 almost in full length. The lyrics talk about lives ripped apart

---

44 For a good overview of Pedro Costa's production practices and the reception of his films, see: Nuno Barradas Jorge, *ReFocus: The Films of Pedro Costa. Producing and Consuming Contemporary Art and Cinema* (Edinburgh: University Press, 2020). For further reference on Pedro Costa's working methods see: Nuno Barradas Jorge, "Contextualizing Pedro Costa's Digital Filmmaking," in *Portugal's Global Cinema: Industry, History and Culture*, ed. Mariana Liz (London: Bloomsbury Publishing, 2017). For a study focusing on Costa's representation of poor neighborhoods in Lisbon, see: Igor Krstić, *Slums on Screen: World Cinema and the Planet of Slums* (Edinburgh: University Press, 2016), Chapter 7.

by poverty, of a wife waiting at home with hungry children, of a husband who migrated to Lisbon, to "work under contract/in rain and wind/shipyards, factories, scaffolds/[. . .] cheated by his white brother, exploited." The whole sequence is baffling, especially when compared to the hermetic, willfully mysterious, somnambulistic rest of the film. It is a music video, a series of documentary images, devoid of real narration, yet full of stories. It is arty and solemn, yet approachable due to the soundtrack. It is a scene portraying both very specific people and places and at the same time transcending them to tell something like "a universal history of poverty."[45]

The scene supports an argument by Jacques Rancière: "Pedro Costa does not film the 'misery of the world.' He films its wealth, the wealth that anyone at all can become master of: that of catching the splendor of a reflection of light, but also that of being able to speak in a way that is commensurate with one's fate."[46] Through the music, the harmonies from Cape Verde, the plain-spoken lyrics, one feels as if Costa tries to find an equilibrium between his stylistic predilections as an auteur-filmmaker and the sensibilities and poetics of the people he portrays. The film tries to translate—or better: to put into relation— the sensibilities of different social groups that are often sharply separated. His films get to the heart of the question why the cinematic treatment of precarity and poverty in films from Portugal seems politically relatable to an audience mostly comprised of people of a comparatively privileged social position.[47] Because even though the films described here have a limited exposure—mostly in festival runs and small cinema releases—an argument could be made that they actually *matter* because "Portuguese filmmakers not only capture political realities, but also make political films."[48]

The experiential openness of the puzzling pictures from Portugal stems not from them being vague, or overtly ambiguous, but rather being rich in meaning, generous in their realism. And this generosity carries in it the potential for a re-examination of established forms of the depiction and portrayal of lives that are normally shown as wanting. They hint at the possibility of other forms

---

45 Nick Pinkerton, "Film of the week: Horse Money," *Sight & Sound* (October 2015), https://www2.bfi.org.uk/news-opinion/sight-sound-magazine/reviews-recommendations/film-week-horse-money.
46 Rancière, "The Politics of Pedro Costa," *Diagonal Thoughts*, July 13, 2012, https://www.diagonalthoughts.com/?p=1546.
47 For further reference on the circulation of Costa's films on festivals and his appreciation by an advocate group of cinephiles, see Nuno Barradas Jorge, *ReFocus: The Films of Pedro Costa*, 69–89.
48 Liz, "Introduction," subheading "Key issues in contemporary Portuguese cinema", first paragraph [quoted from Ebook].

of visual politics, of distribution of wealth, of social action without losing sight of the real hardships, limitations, injustices, and impossibilities in our world. The images are part of a cinema that is "simultaneously a cinema of the possible and of the impossible."[49] The images and films are visually inventive, artistically attractive, accessible to a cinephile gaze, yet because of these strategies of aestheticization they keep their audience at a certain distance from what is portrayed. The "What" and the "How" of depiction never fully reconcile into one straightforward, coherent expression. One can enjoy the puzzle-pictures' inventiveness, yet be ashamed of this very enjoyment. They can make their viewers feel like they are more than observers, but that they could not become comrades. The pictures often remind us that their audience might be part of the problem, yet they invite us to think of possible solutions. Something changes while something stays the same.

Bibliography

Álvarez Lopez, Cristina, and Adrian Martin. "Broken Links: The Cinema of Teresa Villaverde." In *Portugal's Global Cinema: Industry, History and Culture*, ed. Mariana Liz. London: Bloomsbury, 2017, 151–166.
Barradas Jorge, Nuno. "Contextualizing Pedro Costa's Digital Filmmaking." In *Portugal's Global Cinema: Industry, History and Culture*, ed. Mariana Liz. London: Bloomsbury, 2017, 135–150.
——. *ReFocus: The Films of Pedro Costa. Producing and Consuming Contemporary Art and Cinema*. Edinburgh: Edinburgh University Press, 2020.
Bernecker, Walther L., and Horst Pietschmann. *Geschichte Portugals*. Munich: Beck, 2014.
Brecht, Bertolt. "Über den formalistischen Charakter der Realismustheorie." In *Gesammelte Werke 19*. Frankfurt a.M.: Suhrkamp, 1967, 298–300.
——. "Volkstümlichkeit und Realismus." In *Gesammelte Werke 19*. Frankfurt a.M.: Suhrkamp, 1967, 322–331.
——. *Brecht on Art and Politics*, ed. Steve Giles and Tom Kuhn. London: Bloomsbury, 2003.
Costa, José Filipe. "When Cinema Forges the Event: The Case of Torre Bela." *Third Text* 25, no. 1 (2011): 105–116. DOI: 10.1080/09528822.2011.545617.
Costa, José Manuel. "Questions About Documentary Making in Portugal." In *Portugal: um retrato cinematográfico*, ed. Nuno Figueiredo and Diniz Guarda. Lisbon: Número-Arte e Cultura, 2004, 118–144.
Kamalzadeh, Dominik. "Mythen der Wirklichkeit. Volkskultur und Magie in Filmen von Alice Rohrwacher, Miguel Gomes und Pietro Marcello." *kolik.film*, Special Issue 30 (October 2018): 7–18.
Krstić, Igor. *Slums on Screen: World Cinema and the Planet of Slums*. Edinburgh: University Press, 2016.

---

49 Rancière, "The Politics of Pedro Costa".

Lauer, David. "Anamorphotische Aspekte. Wittgenstein über Techniken des Sehens." In *Der entstellte Blick*, ed. Cha Kyung-Ho and Markus Rautzenberg. Munich: Fink, 2019, 230–244.

Liz, Mariana. "Introduction: Framing the Global Appeal of Contemporary Portuguese Cinema." In *Portugal's Global Cinema: Industry, History and Culture*, ed. Mariana Liz. London: Bloomsbury, 2017, Ebook.

Pinho, Pedro, interviewed by Luc Chessel. "Ce n'est pas le but qui compte, mais comment tu le fais." *Libération*, December 12, 2017. https://www.liberation.fr/cinema/2017/12/12/pedro-pinho-ce-n-est-pas-le-but-qui-compte-mais-comment-tu-le-fais_1616215/.

Pinkerton, Nick. "Film of the week: Horse Money." *Sight & Sound* 25, no. 10 (October 2015). https://www2.bfi.org.uk/news-opinion/sight-sound-magazine/reviews-recommendations/film-week-horse-money.

Rancière, Jacques. "The Politics of Pedro Costa" [2009]. *Diagonal Thoughts*, July 13, 2012. https://www.diagonalthoughts.com/?p=1546.

Sequeria Brás, Patricia. "Post-Fordism in Active Life, Industrial Revolution and The Nothing Factory." In *Cinema of Crisis*, ed. Thomas Austin and Angelos Koutsourakis. Cambridge: Cambridge University Press, 2020, 76–92.

Solestan, Eric. *Portugal: A Country Study*. Washington, D.C.: Federal Research Division, Library of Congress, 1993. https://www.loc.gov/resource/frdcstdy.portugalcountrys00sols_0/?sp=184.

Souriau, Étienne. "Die Struktur des filmischen Universums und das Vokabular der Filmologie" [1951]. In *Das filmische Universum. Schriften zur Ästhetik des Kinos*, ed. and trans. Guido Kirsten. Munich: Fink, 2020, 51–66.

Standing, Guy. *The Precariat. The New Dangerous Class*. London: Bloomsbury, 2011.

Trindade, Luís. "Filming Narratives Becoming Events: Documentary and the 'Emplotments' of the Carnation Revolution." In *Portugal's Global Cinema: Industry, History and Culture*, ed. Mariana Liz. London: Bloomsbury Publishing, 2017, 15–32.

Wittgenstein, Ludwig. *Philosophical Investigations*, trans. Gertrude Elizabeth Margaret Anscombe. Oxford: Basil Blackwell, 1958.

——. *Philosophische Untersuchungen*. Frankfurt a.M.: Suhrkamp, 1967.

Filmography

A Fábrica de Nada (*The Nothing Factory*). Dir. Pedro Pinho. Portugal, 2017.

Arena. Dir. João Salaviza. Portugal, 2009.

As mil e uma noites – Volume 1, O Inquieto (*Arabian Nights: Volume 1 – The Restless One*). Dir. Miguel Gomes. Portugal/France/Germany/Switzerland, 2015.

As Mil e Uma Noites – Volume 2, O Desolado (*Arabian Nights: Volume 2 – The Desolate One*). Dir. Miguel Gomes. Portugal/France/Germany/Switzerland, 2015.

As mil e uma noites – Volume 3, O Encantado (*Arabian Nights: Volume 3 – The Enchanted One*). Dir. Miguel Gomes. Portugal/France/Germany/Switzerland, 2015.

Cavalo Dinheiro (*Horse Money*). Dir. Pedro Costa. Portugal, 2014.

Colo. Dir. Teresa Villaverde. Portugal, 2017.

Dancer in the Dark. Dir. Lars von Trier. Denmark/Germany/Netherlands/Italy/United Kingdom/
France/Sweden/Finland/Iceland/Argentina/Norway/Taiwan/Belgium, 2000.
Falamos de Rio de Onor (*We Talk About Rio de Onor*). Dir. António Campos. Portugal, 1973.
Fasinpat (*Fábrica sin patrón*). Dir. Danièle Incalcaterra. Argentina, 2004.
Linha Vermelha (*Red Line*). Dir. José Filipe Costa. Portugal, 2012.
Murdar de vida (*Change of Life*). Dir. Paulo Rocha. Portugal, 1966.
No Quarto da Vanda (*In Vanda's Room*). Dir. Pedro Costa. Portugal, 2000.
O Acto da Primavera (*Rite of Spring*). Dir. Manoel de Oliveira. Portugal, 1963.
Os Mutantes (*The Mutants*). Dir. Teresa Villaverde. Portugal, 1998.
Os Verdes Anos (*The Green Years*). Dir. Paulo Rocha. Portugal, 1963.
Rafa. Dir. João Salaviza. Portugal, 2012.
Sangue do Meu Sangue (*Blood of My Blood*). João Canijo. Portugal, 2011.
Torre Bela. Dir. Thomas Harlan. France/Portugal/Italy/Switzerland, 1975.
Transe (*Trance*). Dir. Teresa Villaverde. Portugal, 2006.
Trás-os-Montes. Dir. Margarida Cordeiro, António Reis. Portugal, 1976.
Volta à Terra (*[Be]longing*). Dir. João Pedro Plácido. Portugal, 2014.

Elisa Cuter
From Poverty to Precarity
Bridging the Gap Between Arthouse Films and Domestic Blockbusters in Contemporary Italian Cinema

Depictions of poverty and precarity have been very prevalent in Italian cinema in the last twenty years. Countless films deal with social issues like unemployment, homelessness, migration, the precariat, deindustrialization, gentrification, petty crime, and so on. There are two reasons for this interest. First, it is connected to the Italian film tradition, since both neorealism and the ensuing popular genre of *commedia all'italiana* dealt with the topic extensively—each in its own way. Second, the interest in social problems is motivated by the circumstances the country currently has to face, as it has been heavily affected by the economic crisis and growing poverty rates. Considering these two factors together not only helps us to understand recent film production but also to grasp the country's sociocultural self-perception.

To do so, I propose to distinguish and compare two strands of Italian film production.[1] The first comprises arthouse films that are aimed at the international festival circuit and that pay tribute to neorealism in terms of style and self-branding. Critics and producers have labeled this new wave the *cinema del reale*. The young directors who are subsumed under this label present themselves at major festivals with works merging non-fiction and storytelling, depicting stories of social interest with relatively high (for arthouse films) production values and an aesthetically engaging approach. The second strain of production can be seen as an exaggerated version of *commedia all'italiana*. Compared to *cinema del reale*, this strand is much more profit-driven, has less of an artistic aura and value, and is produced by major private production companies for the domestic audience.

The differences between these two contrasting forms of production are reflected in the kind of poverty they tend to portray. While the first one focuses mainly on absolute poverty and extreme marginality, setting the films in deprived milieus (and sometimes being accused of "poverty porn" or of charitable and bourgeois pietism), the second illustrates relative poverty and the recently impoverished middle-class, resorting to stereotyped class disparities as a plot device.

---

[1] Please note that for the sake of the argument I will consider here the nationality of the directors and not of the production funding.

Differentiating these two prominent tendencies within contemporary Italian cinema provides a conceptual framework of analysis that takes the parameters of production, reception, and discourse[2] into account in order to map the national production in a historical phase in which the economic crisis impacts both the film industry and independent filmmaking.

In this article I will discuss some examples of these two varieties, arguing that the very gap between them reflects the country's lack of a cohesive narrative on the problems of poverty and precarity. In addition, I will mention examples of films that can instead be read as interesting attempts to challenge the political impasse caused by the widespread perception (reinforced by the previously outlined reception circuits) of an irreconcilable divide between a wealthy, educated, and progressive "elite" and an impoverished, reactionary "people."

Cinema del Reale

In the most iconic period of Italian cinema, poor and marginalized people found their way into the country's collective imagination as protagonists in neorealist films. Many critics and film historians identified the unifying feature of this period not in a coherent formal approach but rather in the humanist drive shared by all films and directors.[3] Their aim was to make the "subaltern social strata" of the country visible and "to comment on and denounce the evils of contemporary society."[4]

Alessia Cervini, in her careful reconstruction of Italian film history through the lens of its attention to the "poor, disinherited, and marginalized people,"[5]

---

2 See for the definition and the use of the term the introduction to this volume by Guido Kirsten, especially the questions: "What is the film trying to convince us of? Can we identify implicit presuppositions? How does the film dramaturgy suggest a particular argument? What does the film's structure reveal about who is primarily addressed by the discourse and in what way, and who is rhetorically excluded?"; the reading of films as "meaningful works which actively contribute to our understanding of reality;" and the "focus on argumentative or quasi-argumentative structures."
3 See Ernesto de Martino, "Realismo e folklore nel cinema italiano" [1952], in *Teorie del realismo*, ed. Edoardo Bruno (Rome: Bulzoni, 1977).
4 Masolino D'Amico, *La commedia all'italiana. Il cinema comico in Italia dal 1946 al 1975* (Milan: Il Saggiatore, 2008), 127. All translations, if not otherwise stated in the bibliography, are by me, E.C.
5 Alessia Cervini, "Ultimi," in *Lessico del cinema italiano*, Vol. III, ed. Roberto De Gaetano. (Milan/Udine: Minmesis, 2016), 291.

observes how Italian cinema, even before neorealism, tended to stage a conflict between the industrialized urban centers and the abandoned countryside when dealing with social problems, or between Northern Italy and the underdeveloped South: in short, a conflict between modernization and archaism. Such conflict, observes Cervini, did not hint at any possible trajectory for progress but was rather portrayed as destiny, an irreconcilable and tragic divide typical of what she calls the "dis-unitarian" history of Italy. "The absence of a common trait or of a shared condition, which forces one to think of the community in negative terms, as starting from something missing, is what characterizes the entire Italian culture most."[6]

In the absence of an actual community, the deprived are forced to try to master their own destiny in a struggle for life that knows little solidarity or collaboration. Many films from the neorealist phase signal these dynamics right at the beginning of the film. *Ladri di biciclette* (*Bicycle Thieves*, Vittorio De Sica, 1948), *Bellissima* (Luchino Visconti, 1951), and *Umberto D.* (Vittorio De Sica, 1952) open with scenes of a mass from which the protagonists break off, becoming the center of attention of the whole film. Cervini argues that rather than visually suggesting that their individual stories are to serve as typical examples, this symbolizes their desperate and unavoidable isolation, the impossibility that they can share the interests of the mass or be part of a group. This can be related to the remarkable lack of films on actual class struggle, except during a brief period in the 1970s.[7] Usually, in Italian cinema, the protagonists are not from the working class but rather from what Karl Marx called the *Lumpenproletariat*. Hence their dramatic and emotional narratives, marked by the impossibility of actual agency, mirrored by the structure of the realist form (low in action and therefore fully modern as Deleuze said).[8] The general lack of agency (and hope) is sometimes redeemed by an escape into fantasy, as in the well-known case of *Miracolo a Milano* (*Miracle in Milan*, Vittorio De Sica, 1951), which exemplifies the tendency of a fairy-tale, surreal turn of more classical realism.[9]

The oscillation between a fantastic register and a more crudely realistic one, together with a focus on stories of misery that offer little room for hope of an uprising of the subaltern, are elements that reappear in today's *cinema del reale*. The

---

[6] Ibid., 303.
[7] Carlo Testa, "The Working Class Goes to Hell: Economic Issues in Post-World War II in Italian Cinema," *Annali d'Italianistica*, 30 (2012), 345.
[8] See Gilles Deleuze, *Cinema 2: The Time Image* (London: Bloomsbury 2013), 1–13.
[9] Cervini identifies two strands, one of "dramatic realism" and one of "fairy-tale realism," held together more by the need to adhere to the point of view of the subaltern than by formal means. (See Cervini, "Ultimi," 312).

label applies to a generation of directors that came from documentary filmmaking, forced the limits of the genre, and hybridized its form by adding fiction and a strong authorial mark. Producer Dario Zonta, author of a book of interviews with some of the most prominent exponents of the wave, affirms that "its canon" is constituted by the

> hybridization between reality and fiction, between documentary and dramaturgy, between documental value and storytelling (. . .). These films, born outside the usual channels of production and distribution, have renewed Italian cinema in recent years, bringing a 'different cinema' to the attention of international festivals, critics, and now the public.[10]

A quick glance at the very different works of the authors grouped under this category shows that the label is more formal than thematic: The approach combining documentary and fiction can address individual memories as well as social issues. An example of a film interested in investigating the latter is *Louisiana/The Other Side*, presented at Un Certain Regard in Cannes in 2015, in which the director Roberto Minervini shows two supposedly complementary faces of the southern US state. The first part of the film follows the erratic life of Mark, a white drop-out crystal meth addict living on drug dealing and sporadic jobs. The second observes the rituals of right-wing militias who are arming themselves in the belief that then President Barack Obama is about to institute martial law. By juxtaposing the two sides loosely, Minervini appears to imply that both situations come from the same feeling of abandonment. However, while he is able to reach some discomforting closeness with Mark (often shown naked, shooting drugs, having sex, or in intimate moments with his family), in the second part he never achieves the same closeness to the other, even more disturbing reality of the militant far right —despite having shot the film with a very small team (only six persons).[11]

Similar to Giulio Andreotti's infamous quote about neorealist films ("dirty laundry that shouldn't be washed and hung to dry in the open"),[12] *Variety*'s

---

10 Dario Zonta, *L'invenzione del reale. Conversazioni su un altro cinema* (Rome: Contrasto, 2017), 7. he directors included in Zonta's book are Gianfranco Rosi, Roberto Minervini, Alina Marazzi, Pietro Marcello, Michelangelo Frammartino, Giovanni Columbu, Alessandro Comodin, Leonardo Di Costanzo, Alice Rohrwacher, and Matteo Garrone, but the label is also used to refer to works by Salvatore Mereu, Jonas Carpignano, Claudio Giovannesi, Irene Dionisio, and others.
11 See Maria Nadotti, "*Louisiana*, un film politico," *Doppiozero*, June 16, 2015, https://www.doppiozero.com/materiali/odeon/louisiana-un-film-politico.
12 Andreotti, one of the main exponents of the Catholic party Democrazia Cristiana and later prime minister, used to be the Undersecretary of Cultural Heritage with delegated authority for entertainment and head of the Central Office for Cinematography. As such he was responsible for the censorship of many neorealist films. The quoted phrase is not present in the open letter

critic Peter Debruge wrote in regard to *Louisiana/The Other Side*: "It's enough to make Americans feel ashamed of their countrymen (. . .) Meanwhile, foreign audiences will be free to confirm their worst assumptions about America's character."[13] Pietro Bianchi also complains that Minervini's observational approach ends up confirming all the broad public's prejudices and stereotyped views of American "white trash."[14]

Minervini's film is an instructive example of the *cinema del reale* because it is typical of the aim of having an international appeal that sometimes pushes filmmakers to focus on extreme situations, which are far removed from their own experience or from Italy's public sensibility.[15] There is a general tendency to describe underprivileged milieus that appear to be completely detached from the broader society that is also shown. One example is Matteo Garrone's *Gomorra* (2008)—although based on a report on Campania's mafia that exposed its entanglements with the economy and the government,[16] the film focuses solely on the degraded district of Scampia in Naples, running the risk of exoticizing its object.

While insisting that they are simply representing reality or giving voice to marginal subjectivities, many films of the *cinema del reale* seem to be overwhelmed and fascinated by it to the point of giving up on a political framing that might help interpret it. Apparently there is an interesting contradiction: despite the strong presence of the director both in the arrangement of the material in a narrative structure and in its aesthetic form, what is lacking is a directorial approach in terms of *discourse*.

Another example, *Lazzaro felice* (*Happy as Lazzaro*, 2018) by Alice Rohrwacher, may help explain this paradox better. The film is clearly a work of

---

he wrote to Vittorio De Sica ("Piaghe sociali e necessità di redenzione," *Libertas* 1, no. 7, February 28, 1952), but it neatly sums up the position expressed therein.

See Roberto Curti and Alessio Di Rocco, *Visioni proibite: I film vietati dalla censura italiana (1947–1968)* (Milan: Lindau, 2014) and Giovanni Sedita, "Giulio Andreotti e il neorealismo. De Sica, Rossellini, Visconti e la guerra fredda al cinema," *Nuova storia contemporanea: bimestrale di studi storici e politici sull'età contemporanea* 16, no. 1 (February 2012).

13 Peter Debruge, "Film Review: 'The Other Side'," *Variety*, June 24, 2015, https://variety.com/2015/film/festivals/the-other-side-review-cannes-film-festival-1201504388/.

14 Pietro Bianchi, *"La Louisiana dall'altro lato della storia,"* Doppiozero, May 29, 2015, https://www.doppiozero.com/materiali/odeon/la-louisiana-dall-altro-lato-della-storia.

15 See in this respect also *Below Sea Level* (Gianfranco Rosi, 2008), shot among the dropouts living in trailers in a desert area in southern California.

16 Roberto Saviano, *Gomorra. Viaggio nell'impero economico e nel sogno di dominio della camorra* (Milan: Mondadori, 2006).

fiction that contains both fantastic elements and bonds with reality. Along with the director's naturalist style (and her choice to shoot in Kodak Super16[17] and to cast a non-professional as main actor) there is the fact that the plot is inspired by a true story that took place in the 1980s in central Italy. The film tells the fairy-tale story of Lazzaro, an unceasingly kind, naive, and saint-like figure exploited as a peasant by a tobacco landowner baroness who keeps him and his coworkers completely unaware of the fact that the times of the métayage are over (as the director does with the viewer at the beginning of the film). Once freed by the police, Lazzaro and his peers must face the even more brutal reality of a contemporary northern city. Again, the narrative is split in two. The first part displays a fascination with idealized age-old traditions: the timeless simple costumes, the absence of private property among the peasants, their naive vitality, their relationship with nature, even their benign mischievousness. The second portrays how the former peasants are forced to adapt, living like aliens on the outskirts of the city in a container that looks like something between a Roma-settlement and a post-apocalyptic spaceship. While his coworkers were forced to find more or less legal ways to survive and to develop some cynicism, Lazzaro (Fig. 1)—who had fallen off a cliff just when the other were being freed and lain unconsciousness for decades—is still untainted by the modern world and believes that their former masters will help them. "In the balance between naturalism and abstraction," praised the film critic Daniela Persico, "lies the appeal of a cinema that is as 'pure' as the actions of its main character."[18] Nonetheless, among the Christological and hagiographic metaphors in the background there seems to be the same discourse that one discovers in Minervini's film: a preference for those victims whose desperation is linked with submissiveness. It is a recurring theme in Italian cinema, in which, observes Cervini, "those who are victims of injustice, whether social or judicial, are for that very reason closer to a pure and sinless origin."[19]

---

17 Cinematographer Hélène Louvart calls it "a medium that contributes something organic and artisanal and that corresponds to a different way of seeing the world." See Hélène Louvart, "Cinematographer Hélène Louvart, AFC, discusses her work on Alice Rohrwacher's *Lazzaro felice*," *Afcinema*, May 17, 2018, https://www.afcinema.com/Cinematographer-Helene-Louvart-AFC-discusses-her-work-on-Alice-Rohrwacher-s-Lazzaro-felice.html?lang=fr.
18 Daniela Persico, "Lazzaro Felice," *Filmidee*, no. 23, March 30, 2018, https://www.filmidee.it/2018/05/lazzaro-felice/.
19 Cervini, "Ultimi," 298. See also what screenwriter Giacomo Giubilini observes about the depiction of poor characters in Italian cinema and the application of petty bourgeois/catholic morality to them: "Among the most recurrent stylistic elements, here is in fact a jumble of aphasic characters pursued by filming the nape of their necks in decidedly ugly but exotic and sincere scenarios. Scenarios made of graffiti, rusty nets, mopeds without helmets, monkey grunts and social

Fig. 1: Lazzaro felice (Happy as Lazzaro, Alice Rohrwacher, 2018).

This is connected to a view of the past that is quite common in many of these films. In Italy, the process of modernization started later than in other European countries and remained a violent and regionally disparate phenomenon. The idea that poor people represent the strongholds of traditions and values at risk of disappearing because of urbanization and industrialization emerged in Italian cinema during fascism[20] and is still present in the Italian political debate. "Italian cinema of the last ten years," writes critic Gabriele Niola in his review of Rohrwacher's film, "tells only one great story, that of resistance to modernity. It is a trait that unites commercial and art films, films for huge audiences and niche ones, successful films and failed ones: The best of ourselves is in our past, every element of modernity is a symbol of decadence."[21]

This claim refers to the narratives, but it could also be useful to talk about the production conditions: In order to advertise the new wave, critics,[22] producers, and the general press insist on *cinema del reale*'s alleged continuation of neorealism. This is a clear symptom of a longing for the cultural grandeur and

---

petrification, seasoned, however, with banality and bourgeois afterthoughts. In short: you are poor, but you still have love, beauty and sincerity. Never revolt." Giacomo Giubilini, "Il cinema reazionario di stato," *Le parole e le cose*, June 11, 2017, https://www.leparoleelecose.it/?p=27930.
20 Cervini, "Ultimi," 296.
21 Gabriele Niola, "Lazzaro stava meglio quando stava peggio," *Esquire*, May 31, 2018, https://www.esquire.com/it/cultura/film/a20973116/lazzaro-felice-recensione/.
22 See Goffredo Fofi, "*Fuocoammare* racconta Lampedusa con pudore e rispetto," *Internazionale*, February 22, 2016, https://www.internazionale.it/opinione/goffredo-fofi/2016/02/22/fuocoammare-rosi-lampedusa-recensione, and Hanna Pilarczyk, "Die bodenständige Zauberin," *Der Spiegel*, September 10, 2018, https://www.spiegel.de/kultur/kino/regisseurin-alice-rohrwacher-die-bodenstaendige-zauberin-a-1226866.html.

international recognition Italian cinema was able to achieve in the 1950s. There are nonetheless some important differences between *cinema del reale*'s and neorealism's respective depiction of poverty as well as between their conditions of production. While neorealism consisted of fictional film that necessarily turned to realism because of its object of interest (poverty), *cinema del reale* is dominantly documentary cinema that has opened itself up to fiction and narration as a formal method moved by imperatives of production and reception.[23] Neorealism was born from a film industry in the strict sense of the word, while *cinema del reale* comes from independent filmmakers, working in a neoliberal context of self-entrepreneurship.[24]

Comedies of Inequality

The theme of the relationship with its past is an important aspect of the Italian situation when it comes to economic data, as well. In a situation of stagnation, the survival of the economy seems to rely on previous phases and generations: employment is decreasing, education has been commodified and is now based on titles that no longer provide for a career, the youth have to rely on their parents or grandparents and are generally forced into a crippling precarity. According to Oxfam one in four Italians is at risk of poverty.[25] Inequality is growing at record levels. Another report by the national statistics bureau ISTAT[26] from 2018

---

[23] Critic and director Maurizio Fantoni Minnella, (editor of *Film documentario d'autore*, Bologna: Odoya, 2018), states that reality meant "a linguistic and ethical resource for fictional filmmakers who, at a certain time [. . .] felt the urgency of a cinema that was more in keeping with the instances of reality [. . .]. Today, however, the opposite seems to be happening: are the filmmakers of reality looking at possible contaminations with fiction in order to enrich their language or to find greater public consensus?"

See Cinemonitor, "'Film documentario d'autore'. Un saggio Odoya mette ordine nel cinema del reale," *Cinemonitor*, April 3, 2018, https://cinemonitor.it/film-documentario-dautore-un-saggio-odoya-mette-ordine-nel-cinema-del-reale/.

[24] That these authors started out with documentary filmmaking was in fact also partially caused by the scarcity of public and private investments in arthouse cinema. Director Pietro Marcello observes: "There are always difficulties, from an economic point of view. Documentary is made with what you have." Quoted in Arianna Finos, "Cinema del reale: tradizione e nuova creatività, l'Italia riparte dai docufilm," *La Repubblica*, March 3, 2016, https://www.repubblica.it/spettacoli/cinema/2016/03/03/news/cinema_documentario-134711474/.

[25] AdnKronos, "Oxfam. 1 italiano su 4 a rischio povertà," *AdnKronos*, May 5, 2017, https://www.adnkronos.com/poverta-oxfam-una-persona-su-quattro-in-italia-a-rischio_4mBrB5ALXJXk21BDz7smV4.

[26] Istituto Nazionale di Statistica (ISTAT), *Le statistiche dell'ISTAT sulla povertà /Anno 2018* (2019), https://www.istat.it/it/files//2019/06/La-povert%C3%A0-in-Italia-2018.pdf.

explains how five percent of the population own the same amount of wealth as the poorest 90 percent. The GINI index ranked Italy 23rd among 28 European countries.[27] The ISTAT report shows how the situation has worsened over the past decade due to the economic crisis that hit Europe in 2008, and this does not even take into account the hardships faced because of the Covid-19 pandemic. The country relies more on private means and inheritance than on labor, exploiting almost three million people (mostly migrants) in jobs ranging from seasonal work in agriculture to undeclared care labor.[28] A third of all workers under 30 years old has a gross income below 800 euros per month,[29] and youth unemployment reached the 33.8 percent in January 2021.[30]

In such a problematic situation, every other day newspapers report the collapse of the cultural sector. When it comes to cinema, the only films that manage to make a profit at the box office are so-called "*cinepanettoni.*"[31] The term refers to a series of farcical comedies, traditionally directed and written by the Vanzina brothers and interpreted by actors Massimo Boldi and Christian De Sica (son of director Vittorio), released annually during the Christmas season. The debt of these films to the *commedia all'italiana* is explicit: the first example (*Vacanze di Natale* [*Christmas Vacations,* Carlo Vanzina, 1983]) was a remake of *Vacanze d'inverno* (*Winter Vacations,* Camillo Mastrocinque, 1959), in which a poor provincial father and his daughter win a week in a luxury alpine hotel in a radio contest.

In order to reach the widest possible audience, *commedia all'italiana* was often based on staging class disparities, understood in terms of different sociocultural capital. The main aim was to achieve a comic effect and the films were not always empathetic to the underlings. Yet the films managed to offer a fairly varied and truthful representation of society. *Commedia all'italiana* was itself a genre that stemmed from neorealism. During the 1950s the rhetoric of the economic miracle (made possible by the Marshall plan) infected neorealism, turning it into its so-called "pink" version, in which the plots revolved around romance and successful

---

[27] Barbara Ardù, "Oxfam, le disuguaglianze si accentuano. Duemila Paperoni più ricchi di 4,6 miliardi di persone," *La Repubblica,* January 20, 2020, https://www.repubblica.it/economia/2020/01/20/news/oxfam_le_diseguaglianze_persistono_anzi_si_accentuano-246134799/.
[28] Luca Ricolfi, *La società signorile di massa* (Milan: La Nave di Teseo, 2019).
[29] Ardù, "Oxfam, le disuguaglianze si accentuano."
[30] ANSA, "Ocse: allarme su disoccupazione giovanile Italia," *Ansa,* July 7, 2021, https://www.ansa.it/sito/notizie/economia/2021/07/07/ocse-allarme-su-disoccupazione-giovanile-italia_f92e4f79-e523-488b-8cdd-baa3f699ece6.html.
[31] On "cinepanettoni" in general see Alan O'Leary, *Fenomenologia del cinepanettone* (Catanzaro: Rubbettino, 2013).

upward mobility. The 1960s were then characterized by the success of the *commedia all'italiana*, in which a comic tone was used to satirize the vices of the upper middle class (and sometimes to denounce the dramatic social inequality that still plagued the country). From the 1980s on, comedy became the most commonly produced genre in Italy, accounting for more than 40 percent of the whole production in 2007.[32] Among those, the most successful were cinepanettoni, which tended to exaggerate the features of *commedia all'italiana* in vulgar and gross ways, both in dialogue and action.

A recent film ascribable to this tradition (the main role is even played by Christian De Sica) is *Poveri ma ricchi* (*Poor but Rich*, Fausto Brizzi, 2016).[33] The plot revolves around a lower-class family living in a small town in the region outside Rome, who wins an outstanding sum at the lotto, and then moves to Milan, in order to mingle with the "rich people." Once there they realize that their aspirations are doomed to fail, because their social and cultural background prevents them from being recognized as rich by the actual rich, who instead lead an understated life and do not show off (nor even seem to enjoy) their wealth. The narrative gimmick of sudden and unexpected upward mobility is a classical trope of cinepanettoni, but there are some interesting aspects. The first is the extreme aesthetic standardization of the film. The over-saturated color correction, the flat cinematography, the direction, the soundtrack, the acting: everything is stylized and blatantly fake, obeying the logic of production rather than of storytelling. This is demonstrated by the fact that there are no significant differences between the parts shot in the town and in Milan. This aesthetic standardization also bears on the representation, or rather non-representation, of poverty: even the "poor" town that the family comes from resembles a tourist postcard of an idealized Italian country burg (Fig. 2).[34]

It is therefore very interesting to realize that the family in the film is not actually poor, they just live in the countryside—from which, nonetheless, they cannot wait to escape to a fancier, more modern, urban life. It looks like a telling contrast with the tradition of Italian cinema that tends to glorify the simpler

---

[32] Francesco Casetti and Saverio Salvemini, eds., *È tutto un altro film. Più coraggio e più idee per il cinema italiano* (Milan: Egea, 2007), 39.

[33] "The most watched film in Italian theaters on Christmas day [. . .] also wins the competition among 2016's Cinepanettoni." See ComingSoon, "Poveri ma ricchi vince la sfida di Natale tra le commedie italiane," *Coming Soon*, December 27, 2016, https://www.comingsoon.it/cinema/news/poveri-ma-ricchi-vince-la-sfida-di-natale-tra-le-commedie-italiane/n62676/.

[34] It might be interesting to read the film in the light of John Urry's reflections on the tourist gaze, see for example *Tourist Gaze: Leisure and Travel in Contemporary Societies* (London: SAGE, 1990).

Fig. 2: Poveri ma ricchi (Poor but Rich, Fausto Brizzi, 2016).

rural lifestyle still rooted in those real values that modernity has allegedly forgotten. Yet the film does not really contradict this tradition: In the film's epilogue, ironically enough, the family's youngest, book-smart kid eventually decides to let the family think they had lost their fortune in a scam investment, so that they return to their hometown. There he administers their money, letting them enjoy little improvements over their previous daily life, dignified by labor, and rooted in a small and traditional community.

The kid, who is also the film's voice-over-narrator, channels the audience's gaze and perspective. Interestingly, the character resembles the youngest daughter of Alberto Sordi and Silvana Mangano in Lo scopone scientifico (The Scientific Cardplayer, Luigi Comencini, 1972), a film which revolves around the trope (quite common in Italian comedy) of social climbing through gambling. However, there is a telling difference: At the end of The Scientific Cardplayer the smartest kid tries to kill the rich American woman with whom the couple had been playing cards—obviously a metaphor for more radical strategies for the subproletarian class. In Brizzi's film, instead, we find both a patronizing message, inviting characters and viewers not to dream too big and to find pride in their modest situation, and an opposition between modernity and tradition, favoring the latter.

Comedies of Precarity

Film comedy in Italy did not necessarily or only reinforce this patronizing and nostalgic narrative, however. There are some films that lend themselves to different readings and address different audiences, proposing another discursive position.

Cases in point are the films that Paola Cortellesi, a TV stand-up comedian, wrote and played in. She tried to do something more daring and more socially engaging in her comedies. In Scusate se esisto! (Do You See Me?, Riccardo Milani,

2014) she plays an architect who comes back to Italy and struggles to find a job. She is forced to pretend to be a male architect (and when seen in person to claim that she is just his secretary) in order to obtain a project devoted to the improvement of Rome's poor district Corviale. While searching for a job, and later in her work on the project, she meets several characters from different precarious backgrounds and starts bonding with her gay boss at the restaurant where she works to make up for her low wages. The plot makes very clear how her calamities force her to build up a net of solidarity and make her aware of other struggles, in a real intersectional perspective.

In *Nessuno mi può giudicare* (*Escort in Love*, Massimiliano Bruno, 2011), Cortellesi overturns the stereotypical representation of social classes in comedy. The film is a riches-to-rags story, in which an affluent woman has to adjust to living in a multicultural, underclass neighborhood in Rome and becomes a sex-worker. The theme of prostitution had been a constant of Italian cinema in the 1950s and 1960s, e.g. *Le notti di Cabiria* (*The Nights of Cabiria*, Federico Fellini, 1952), *Adua e le compagne* (*Adua and her Friends*, Antonio Pietrangeli, 1960), *La ragazza in vetrina* (*Girl in the Window*, Luciano Emmer, 1961), or *La commare secca* (*The Grim Reaper*, Bernardo Bertolucci, 1962). Bruno's film, writes scholar Alice Bardan, "shows that economic hardship can lead even a 'proper' Italian girl to prostitute herself—a fresh change, given the recurrence of pitiful Eastern prostitutes in recent European cinema."[35] The film has an miraculous happy ending, in which the community gets together, the small business of a local Internet provider is saved from eviction, and the outspoken local fascist discovers himself attracted to a Senegalese woman, thus "negotiating, through film, fantasies of salvation, and possibilities of living together in today's Europe."[36]

Besides the politically progressive films starring Paola Cortellesi, there is a series of films released in the wake of the 2008 crisis which deal with the theme of youth precarity.[37] This little wave mixed comedy and realism in an attempt to bring attention to the precarious conditions faced particularly by those working in the intellectual, academic, creative, or artistic branches, and it addressed a

---

[35] Alice Bardan, "The New European Cinema of Precarity: A Transnational Perspective," in *Work in Cinema: Labor and the Human Condition*, ed. Ewa Mazierska (New York: Palgrave Macmillan, 2013), 87–88.

[36] Ibid., 87.

[37] Also worth mentioning are the romantic comedy *Generazione 1000 euro* (*Generation 1000 Euros*, Massimo Venier, 2009), the surreal/grotesque comedy *Fuga dal call center* (*Escape from the Call Center*, Federico Rizzo, 2009), the participative fiction film *Il Vangelo secondo Precario* (*The Gospel according to Precario*, Stefano Obino, 2005), and the documentary *Parole sante* (*Holy Words*, Ascanio Celestini, 2007).

public which would probably recognize itself in the films. Among these *Riprendimi* (*Good Morning Heartache*, 2008) by Anna Negri (daughter of philosopher Toni) stands out, a dramedy/mockumentary about a couple working in film production (she as an editor, he as an actor). The film's main theme is how the uncertainties they face due to financial restrictions affect their private relationship. The plot and the self-reflexivity of this film—at one point a camera operator enters the frame to confess his love for the protagonist—openly quotes a canonic example of participatory documentary: *Anna* (1975) by Alberto Grifi, the attempt to portray the life of an underaged addict that became a profound reflection on the practice of filming disadvantaged subjects.

Tutta la vita davanti (*Her Whole Life Ahead*, Paolo Virzì, 2008), a comedy about the struggles of an aspiring academic who ends up working in a call center, has the merit of highlighting how hard it is for a whole generation to resort to traditional forms of political representation (like parties and unions). Due to the very nature of their atypical employment they are not able to identify themselves as part of the traditional working class. The cinematic form is that of a contemporary *commedia all'italiana*, but the ironic and conscious use of stereotypes and genres, combined with grotesque exaggeration, make it a remarkable film that also found great resonance in the public debate.

The small selection of comedies presented here shows one important common trait: the shift of focus from an apparently timeless concept of *poverty* to the more contemporary one of *precarity*. In fact, the very term, which in most European languages has remained largely confined to academic circles, is used widely in the Italian public debate, referring specifically to the consequences of neoliberal labor policies. The films I have mentioned allude in various ways[38] to this awareness of the political causes of the recent impoverishment of large sections of the population who, during the first twenty years after World War II, had felt safe from this risk. It is perhaps this adherence to contemporaneity, and the will to talk about precarity in an accessible way, that allows these films to create characters with whom the audience they refer to can identify themselves. By offering moments of self-reflection and opening their narratives to

---

[38] In some cases, there is even a sort of critique of the uncritical adoption of the term and the risk that it might normalize the concept. In *Her Whole Life Ahead*, for instance, during a cultural evening organized by the unions, the protagonist introduces herself to everyone as a "precaria," bitterly alluding to her role as a potential new cause that they should take care of, but with little confidence that this can happen in a society in which even the unions seem to belong to a system based on a balance from which the new precarious workers have always been excluded.

multiple levels of reading, they not only represent but also address different segments of the population.

The Return of the Grotesque

Reading the previous paragraph, one might think that the only way to create a cohesive narrative in Italian cinema is to focus on precarity and relative poverty rather than on more extreme forms of absolute poverty, but that is not the case. A few films manage to pay attention to cases of marginalization, exclusion, and extreme poverty without falling into the traps of a nostalgic, exoticizing, or idealizing discourse. I am referring to films that belong to a relatively small but fundamental tradition in Italian cinema, namely that of the grotesque. These films take up the humanistic preoccupation of neorealism and its interest in the marginalized strata of society, but depict them in a stylized and exaggerated manner stemming from *commedia all'italiana* but twisted towards less reassuring and more decidedly grotesque forms. Central examples are *Brutti, sporchi e cattivi* (*Down and Dirty*, Ettore Scola, 1976), which brought the abject brutality of Rome's slums to Cannes, and Sergio Citti's films, which followed a tendency already present in the work of his mentor Pier Paolo Pasolini. In *Ostia* (1970), Citti offers images of queer solidarity among the neglected that was rarely shown in Italian cinema. *Ostia* tells the story of two brothers whose life in the slums of Rome (the *borgate*) is disrupted by the arrival of a woman. At first the three manage to build a sort of family of choice, but the petty bourgeois dream of a nuclear family destroys their relationship and leads to a fratricide. The film's epilogue seems to be a prefiguration of the "cruel optimism" Lauren Berlant speaks of in relation to the contemporary "cinema of precarity:" the attachment to forms of normativity that fuels competition and prevents possible solidarity between subordinates.[39]

One recent example that resembles Citti's films in many ways is also set in Ostia and revolves around two young men: *Non essere cattivo* (*Don't Be Bad*, 2015) by Claudio Caligari. In this film, set in the 1990s, Cesare and Vittorio are two friends addicted to synthetic drugs (Fig. 3). After risking his life, Vittorio (whose name is an explicit reference to Pasolini's *Accattone* from 1961),[40]

---

[39] Lauren Berlant, *Cruel Optimism* (Durham, NC: Duke University Press, 2011).
[40] Gianmaria Tammaro, "*Non essere cattivo* è il cinema di cui abbiamo bisogno," *Wired*, September 9, 2015, https://www.wired.it/play/cinema/2015/09/09/non-essere-cattivo-cinema-abbiamo-bisogno/.

decides to change things and takes on a job at a construction site. His attempt to convince his friend to do the same appears to be successful at first, but Cesare soon realizes that he will not be able to support his newborn child through work and he eventually dies during a robbery. The film relies mainly on the expressive yet realistic acting of its two main actors, and the stylization of the two characters makes the film an apologue on the "failure of the ideology of work," according to its screenwriter.[41] It should be noted that Claudio Caligari is one of the rare examples of Italian directors actually coming from the urban subproletariat: living in destitution until the end of his days, he was only able to shoot three feature films.

Fig. 3: Non essere cattivo (Don't Be Bad, Claudio Caligari, 2015).

Another example of this self-conscious recovery of the grotesque tradition is a documentary by Federica Di Giacomo, which is indeed called *Il lato grottesco della vita* (*The Grotesque Side of Life*, 2006). The title is a play on words, since the film is set in Matera's Sassi, two districts famous for their ancient cave dwellings (*grotte* in Italian) inhabited since the Paleolithic. Di Giacomo shows the life of some unemployed men who reinvent themselves as tour guides, often with hilarious (although tragic) results. The film is both a (self-)portrait of these figures and a reflection on the touristification of entire areas of the country that used to be deserted.

The theme of the marginalization of the South returns in *Liberami* (*Libera Nos*, 2016) by the same director, a documentary on the rebirth of exorcism in Sicily as a response to contemporary difficulties. Far from any aestheticization or idealization of archaic forms of life, Di Giacomo's cinema proves itself capable of

---

41 Francesca Serafini quoted in Silvana Silvestri, "Non essere cattivo, se puoi," *Il Manifesto*, September 8, 2015, https://ilmanifesto.it/non-essere-cattivo-se-puoi/.

discursively identifying what links the archaic past to the modern present: the poverty, impotence, and subjugation to which people are forced.

The use of the grotesque seems particularly useful for this kind of discourse. As observed by Roberto De Gaetano, the grotesque is neither a genre nor a style but rather characterizes a worldview that oscillates between comic and tragic spheres, laughter and horror, affirmation and negation, life and death.[42] It is precisely because of this ambivalence that the grotesque exemplified by these films seems to enable a specific reading of reality that combines satiric elements with an empathetic approach to the point of view of those who suffer. The films offer the potential to depict the horrors of poverty frankly and to avoiding any idealization, while at the same time refusing the normalization or domestication of the subaltern. They reject both archaism and unwarranted optimism.

Conclusions

Differentiating the two prominent strands of contemporary cinema has allowed me to sketch a conceptual framework of analysis that tied together production, reception, and discourse. The scenario that emerges is that of a filmmaking that reacts to the crisis by bowing to the logic of the market, even when it aspires to create innovative forms. Despite their radical formal differences, it is possible to identify some discursive similarities between arthouse films and domestic mainstream comedies in that both tend to present exclusion, backwardness, and poverty either as something inescapable (a destiny) or as something in some ways desirable (a mark of moral purity and tradition). At the same time, the fact that there are two separate reception circuits confirms the existence of a gap between the broader populace and an educated elite. While the latter appears to be concerned about the fate of the weakest, it is actually far from the reality of the country. This in turn reinforces a general suspicion against the elite that right-wing populist propaganda can easily exploit.

Against the background of these two strands with their conventions and recursive discourses we can identify films that lend themselves to an alternative reading. The provisional and incomplete corpus identified in the third and fourth sections is made up of films that hint at the possibility of seizing the dialectical possibilities of a phase in which precarity has become a widespread

---

[42] Roberto De Gaetano, *Il corpo e la maschera. Il grottesco nel cinema italiano* (Rome: Bulzoni, 1999).

phenomenon,[43] no longer linked exclusively to easily identifiable subjects (stereotyped in various ways by cinematic representation). Films that neither simply show reality nor betray it but rather inhabit it and find a situated space that allows them to take a political stance towards it as well.

Perhaps the formal heterogeneity of these films can be seen as a strength, as it is not incompatible with a unity of purpose that goes beyond a common ground based on identity. The heterogeneity of the films listed in the second half of this chapter is paradigmatic of the contemporary period. These films are, in short, just like the precariat, that "class in the making" identified by Guy Standing:[44] heterogeneous and without a shared identity, but virtually capable of attempting a collective narrative that might entice subordinates to claim what is due to them.

Bibliography

AdnKronos. "Oxfam. 1 italiano su 4 a rischio povertà." *AdnKronos*, May 5, 2017. https://www.adnkronos.com/poverta-oxfam-una-persona-su-quattro-in-italia-a-rischio_4mBrB5ALXJXk21BDz7smV4.

Andreotti, Giulio. "Piaghe sociali e necessità di redenzione." *Libertas* 1, no. 7, February 28, 1952.

Ardù, Barbara. "Oxfam, le disuguaglianze si accentuano. Duemila Paperoni più ricchi di 4,6 miliardi di persone." *La Repubblica*, January 1, 2020. https://www.repubblica.it/economia/2020/01/20/news/oxfam_le_diseguaglianze_persistono_anzi_si_accentuano-246134799/.

Bardan, Alice. "The New European Cinema of Precarity: A Transnational Perspective." In *Work in Cinema: Labor and the Human Condition*, ed. Ewa Mazierska. New York: Palgrave Macmillan, 2013, 69–90.

Berlant, Lauren. *Cruel Optimism*. Durham, NC: Duke University Press, 2011.

Bianchi, Pietro. "La Louisiana dall'altro lato della storia." *Doppiozero*, May 29, 2015. https://www.doppiozero.com/materiali/odeon/la-louisiana-dall-altro-lato-della-storia.

Bourdieu, Pierre. "Job Insecurity is Everywhere Now." In *Pierre Bourdieu, Acts of Resistance: Against the New Myths of Our Time*. Cambridge: Polity Press, 1998, 81–87.

Casetti, Francesco, and Saverio Salvemini, eds. *È tutto un altro film. Più coraggio e più idee per il cinema italiano*. Milan: Egea, 2007.

Cervini, Alessia. "Ultimi." In *Lessico del cinema italiano*, Vol. III, ed. Roberto de Gaetano. Milan/Udine: Mimesis, 2016, 291–358.

Curti, Roberto, and Alessio Di Rocco. *Visioni proibite: I film vietati dalla censura italiana (1947–1968)*. Milan: Lindau, 2014.

---

43 Pierre Bourdieu, "Job Insecurity is Everywhere Now," in *Acts of Resistance: Against the New Myths of Our Time* (Cambridge: Polity Press, 1998).
44 Guy Standing, *The Precariat: The New Dangerous Class* (London/New York: Bloomsbury, 2011).

D'Amico, Masolino. *La commedia all'italiana. Il cinema comico in Italia dal 1945 al 1975*. Milan: Il Saggiatore, 2008.

De Gaetano, Roberto. *Il soggetto e la maschera. Il grottesco nel cinema italiano*. Rome: Bulzoni, 1999.

De Martino, Ernesto. "Realismo e folklore nel cinema italiano." [1952]. In *Teorie del realismo*, ed. Edoardo Bruno. Rome: Bulzoni, 1977, 99–103.

Debruge, Peter. "Film Review: 'The Other Side'." *Variety*, May 24, 2015. https://variety.com/2015/film/festivals/the-other-side-review-cannes-film-festival-1201504388/.

Deleuze, Gilles. *Cinema 2: The Time Image*. London: Bloomsbury, 2013, 1–13.

Fantoni Minnella, Maurizio, ed. *Film documentario d'autore*. Bologna: Odoya, 2018.

Finos, Arianna. "Cinema del reale: tradizione e nuova creatività, l'Italia riparte dai docufilm." *La Repubblica*, March 3, 2016. https://www.repubblica.it/spettacoli/cinema/2016/03/03/news/cinema_documentario-134711474/.

Fofi, Goffredo. "*Fuocoammare* racconta Lampedusa con pudore e rispetto." *Internazionale*, February 22, 2016. https://www.internazionale.it/opinione/goffredo-fofi/2016/02/22/fuocoammare-rosi-lampedusa-recensione.

Giubilini, Giacomo. "Il cinema reazionario di Stato. *Cuori puri*, *Fortunata* e l'interesse culturale." *Le parole e le cose*, June 11, 2017. https://www.leparoleelecose.it/?p=27930.

Istituto Nazionale di Statistica (ISTAT). *Le statistiche dell'ISTAT sulla povertà /Anno 2018* (2019). https://www.istat.it/it/files//2019/06/La-povert%C3%A0-in-Italia-2018.pdf.

Louvart, Hélène. "Cinematographer Hélène Louvart, AFC, discusses her work on Alice Rohrwacher's *Lazzaro felice*." *Afcinema*, May 17, 2018. https://www.afcinema.com/Cinematographer-Helene-Louvart-AFC-discusses-her-work-on-Alice-Rohrwacher-s-Lazzaro-felice.html?lang=fr.

Nadotti, Maria. "*Louisiana*, un film politico." *Doppiozero*, June 16, 2015. https://www.doppiozero.com/materiali/odeon/louisiana-un-film-politico.

Niola, Gabriele. "Lazzaro stava meglio quando stava peggio." *Esquire*, May 31, 2018. https://www.esquire.com/it/cultura/film/a20973116/lazzaro-felice-recensione/.

O'Leary, Alan. *Fenomenologia del cinepanettone*. Catanzaro: Rubbettino, 2013.

Persico, Daniela. "*Lazzaro felice*." *Filmidee*, no. 23, March 30, 2018. https://www.filmidee.it/2018/05/lazzaro-felice/.

Pilarczyk, Hanna. "Die bodenständige Zauberin." *Der Spiegel*, September 10, 2018. https://www.spiegel.de/kultur/kino/regisseurin-alice-rohrwacher-die-bodenstaendige-zauberin-a-1226866.html.

ANSA. "Ocse: allarme su disoccupazione giovanile Italia." *Ansa*, July 7, 2021. https://www.ansa.it/sito/notizie/economia/2021/07/07/ocse-allarme-su-disoccupazione-giovanile-italia_f92e4f79-e523-488b-8cdd-baa3f699ece6.html.

Cinemonitor. "'Film documentario d'autore'. Un saggio Odoya mette ordine nel cinema del reale." *Cinemonitor*, April 3, 2018. https://cinemonitor.it/film-documentario-dautore-un-saggio-odoya-mette-ordine-nel-cinema-del-reale/.

Coming Soon, "Poveri ma ricchi vince la sfida di Natale tra le commedie italiane." *Coming Soon*, December 27, 2016. https://www.comingsoon.it/cinema/news/poveri-ma-ricchi-vince-la-sfida-di-natale-tra-le-commedie-italiane/n62676/.

Ricolfi, Luca. *La società signorile di massa*. Milan: La nave di Teseo, 2019.

Saviano, Roberto. *Gomorra. Viaggio nell'impero economico e nel sogno di dominio della camorra*. Milan: Mondadori, 2006.

Sedita, Giovanni. "Giulio Andreotti e il neorealismo. De Sica, Rossellini, Visconti e la guerra fredda al cinema." *Nuova storia contemporanea: bimestrale di studi storici e politici sull'età contemporanea*. 16, no. 1 (February 2012): 51–70.
Silvestri, Silvana. "Non essere cattivo, se puoi." *Il Manifesto*, September 9, 2015. https://ilmanifesto.it/non-essere-cattivo-se-puoi/.
Standing, Guy. *The Precariat: The New Dangerous Class*. London/New York: Bloomsbury, 2011.
Tammaro, Gianmaria. "*Non essere cattivo* è il cinema di cui abbiamo bisogno." *Wired*, September 9, 2015. https://www.wired.it/play/cinema/2015/09/09/non-essere-cattivo-cinema-abbiamo-bisogno/.
Testa, Carlo. "The Working Class Goes to Hell: Economic Issues in Post-World War II Italian Cinema." *Annali d'italianistica*, 30 (2012): 343–354.
Urry, John. *Tourist Gaze: Leisure and Travel in Contemporary Societies*. London: SAGE, 1990.
Zonta, Dario. *L'invenzione del reale. Conversazioni su un altro cinema*. Rome: Contrasti, 2017.

Filmography

Accattone. Dir. Pier Paolo Pasolini. Italy, 1961.
Adua e le compagne (Adua and her Friends). Dir. Antonio Pietrangeli. Italy, 1960.
Anna. Dir. Alberto Grifi. Italy, 1975.
Bellissima. Dir. Luchino Visconti. Italy, 1951.
Below Sea Level. Dir. Gianfranco Rosi. USA/Italy, 2008.
Brutti, sporchi e cattivi (Down and Dirty). Dir. Ettore Scola. Italy, 1976.
Fuga dal call center (Escape from the Call Center). Dir. Federico Rizzo. Italy, 2009.
Generazione 1000 euro (Generation 1000 Euros). Dir. Massimo Venier. Italy, 2009.
Gomorra. Dir. Matteo Garrone. Italy/Belgium, 2008.
Il lato grottesco della vita (The Grotesque Side of Life). Dir. Federica di Giacomo. Italy, 2006.
Il Vangelo secondo Precario (The Gospel according to Precario). Dir. Stefano Obino. Italy, 2005.
La commare secca (The Grim Reaper). Dir. Bernardo Bertolucci. Italy, 1962.
La ragazza in vetrina (Girl in the Window). Dir. Luciano Emmer. Italy, 1961.
Ladri di Biciclette (Bicycle Thieves). Dir. Vittorio De Sica. Italy, 1948.
Lazzaro felice (Happy as Lazzaro). Dir. Alice Rohrwacher. Italy/Switzerland/France/Germany, 2018.
Le notti di Cabiria (The Nights of Cabiria). Dir. Federico Fellini. Italy, 1952.
Liberami (Libera Nos). Dir. Federica di Giacomo. Italy/France, 2016.
Lo scopone scientifico (The Scientific Cardplayer). Dir. Luigi Comencini. Italy, 1972.
Louisiana/The Other Side. Dir. Roberto Minervini. Italy/France, 2015.
Miracolo a Milano (Miracle in Milan). Dir. Vittorio De Sica. Italy, 1951.
Nessuno mi può giudicare (Escort in Love). Dir. Massimiliano Bruno. Italy, 2011.
Non essere cattivo (Don't Be Bad). Dir. Claudio Caligari. Italy, 2015.
Ostia. Dir. Sergio Citti. Italy, 1970.
Parole sante (Holy Words). Dir. Ascanio Celestini. Italy, 2007.

Poveri ma ricchi (*Poor but Rich*). Dir. Fausto Brizzi. Italy, 2016.
Riprendimi (*Good Morning Heartache*). Dir. Anna Negri. 2008.
Scusate se esisto! (*Do You See Me?*). Dir. Riccardo Milani. Italy, 2014.
Tutta la vita davanti (*Her Whole Life Ahead*). Dir. Paolo Virzì. Italy, 2008.
Umberto D. Dir. Vittorio De Sica. Italy, 1952.
Vacanze d'inverno (*Winter Vacations*). Dir. Camillo Mastrocinque. Italy, 1959.
Vacanze di Natale (*Christmas Vacations*). Dir. Carlo Vanzina. Italy, 1983.

Ursula-Helen Kassaveti
Varieties of the Precariat in Contemporary Greek Cinema

As the French sociologist Pierre Bourdieu noted, precarity is now everywhere.[1] While there is a large amount of literature on working relations and precarity,[2] Bourdieu offers a useful starting point for an understanding of the term, which "pervades both the conscious and the unconscious mind":[3] Precarity is not an "economic inevitability" in the realm of post-industrial society and globalization but rather the product of a "political will."[4] This affects different professions, institutionalizes fear, poverty, and an all-encompassing insecurity, as it is inscribed through the "domination mode" of *flexploitation*, the exploitation resulting from wage flexibility and short-term contracts.[5] Precarity is therefore a quasi "political regime" that dramatically challenges and to a large extent reshapes the entire set of social premises—producing, under these circumstances, what Guy Standing has called the "precariat,"[6] a term that describes a new category of people who, educated or not, find themselves in insecure living and working conditions, resulting in in-work poverty and alienation.

The phenomenon can be observed in Greece too, especially in the urban context, in the increase in the financially inactive part of the Athenian population, shrinking full-time employment, insecure or flexible forms of work, and, finally, underemployment.[7] With such a backdrop, narratives of the

---

[1] Pierre Bourdieu, "Job Insecurity is Everywhere Now," in *Acts of Resistance: Against the New Myths of our Time*, trans. Richard Nice (Cambridge: Polity Press, 1998).
[2] To name a few: Guy Standing, *The Precariat: The New Dangerous Class* (London: Bloomsbury, 2011); Guy Standing, *A Precariat Charter. From Denizens to Citizens* (London/New York: Bloomsbury, 2014); Sanford F. Schram, *The Return of Ordinary Capitalism: Neoliberalism, Precarity, Occupy* (Oxford/New York: Oxford University Press, 2015); Stephen Campbell, *Border Capitalism, Disrupted: Precarity and Struggle in a Southeast Asian Industrial Zone* (Ithaca, NY: ILR Press, 2018); Nick Bernards, *The Global Governance of Precarity: Primitive Accumulation and the Politics of Irregular Work* (Abingdon: Routledge, 2018).
[3] Bourdieu, "Job Insecurity is Everywhere Now," 82.
[4] Ibid., 84.
[5] Ibid., 85.
[6] Guy Standing, "The Precariat and Class Struggle," *RCCS Annual Review*, no. 7 (2015), http://journals.openedition.org/rccsar/585.
[7] Aliki Mouriki, "Ston Vomo tis 'Antagonistikotitas' I Aporrythmisi tis Agoras Ergasias ke ton Ergasiakon Sheseon tin Periodo 2010–2012 ke oi Epiptoseis tis stis Prooptikes Anakampsis," in

crisis[8] and the subsequent recession became an explicit inspiration for the arts in Greece. A sympathetic depiction of the precariat and its struggles developed in Greek media[9] as an alternative or implicit way to comment on its gradual social emergence. In this chapter I will explore and comment on the ways the precariat is represented in Greek films produced between 2009 and 2019, both inscribing them in a previous tradition and highlighting their novelties. After an excursus on traditional depictions of precarity in Greek film history and on the specific situation of Greece after the economic crisis, I will demonstrate that current film narratives allow us to witness the birth of a Greek youth precariat, which will be analyzed using three categories identified by Standing (the *nostalgists*, the *atavists*, and the *progressives*) exemplified in three films: *Park* (Sofia Exarchou, 2016), *45m²* (Stratos Tzitzis, 2010), and *Na kathesai kai na koitas* (*Standing Aside, Watching*, Giorgos Servetas, 2013). I will analyze these films in terms of characters, plot and iconography, and the strategies deployed to illustrate precarity, its victims, and their life.

The Birth of the Precariat in Greece

Before focusing on recent films, it is necessary to understand the specifics of the recent situation in Greece and its genesis involving both global and national factors. An examination of the advent of the Greek precariat is vital to understanding the aftermath of the global crisis of 2007–2008 and its effects on the Greek economy and society, in order to assess the place that relevant media representations occupy in the public sphere.

The outbreak of the global financial crisis of 2007–2008 took the whole world by storm, involving it in a situation comparable to the one following the

---

To Koinoniko Portraito tis Elladas. Opseis tis Krisis, ed. Aliki Mouriki, Dionysis Balourdos, Olga Papaliou, Natalia Spyropoulou, Evi Fagadaki and Emmy Fronimou (Athens: EKKE, 2012), 12.

8 Betty Kaklamanidou and Ana Corbalán, eds., *European Film and Television: Crisis Narratives and Narratives in Crisis* (London: Routledge, 2018).

9 In the first years of the 2010s, there had been television shows aiming clearly at the underpaid or those trying to make ends meet: for example, in the everyday cooking series *Mageirevo Oikonomika/I Cook Affordably* (SKAI, 2010–2014), the chef Vissarionas Parthenis cooked the meals of a 4-member-family for a span of 5 days with only 50 euros. See also Vassilis Vamvakas, "To Tileoptiko Apotipoma tis Ellinikis Krisis (2009–2013)," *Nea Estia* 1876 (2018). Television fiction provided another outlet for study: e.g., the cases of the weekly series *Piso sto spiti/Back at Home* (MEGA CHANNEL, 2011–2013) or *I genia ton 592 Euro/Generation 592 Euros* (MEGA CHANNEL, 2010–2011) revolved around a persistent discourse of the Greek media aiming towards the precariat.

Wall Street Crash in 1929.[10] Europe was highly affected, and Mediterranean countries such as Spain, Portugal, and Greece in particular. As far as the latter is concerned, the immediate sociopolitical and cultural output of the Greek sovereign crisis[11] points at two aspects at once. First, it is embedded in the global neoliberalist spectrum and the worldwide recession and can thus be characterized by a "common-sense neoliberalism" with specific negative structural and affective consequences in everyday life.[12] Second, the Greek crisis could be attributed to specific domestic factors, such as underestimating older debts caused by previous governments (from the 1980s onwards), as well as the inequality by which the Eurozone framework operates.[13] Undoubtedly the Greek debt crisis affected the domestic labor market, as the European Union had begun to suffer short-time effects of unemployment, mainly on atypical jobs.[14] Due to the fact that the Greek economy was weakened in terms of its international competitiveness right after the country joined the Eurozone (2001), institutional changes and reversals took place within the wage payment system's structure during 2010–2012. However, the downward spiral of the Greek labor market soon started to make itself evident: The Greek Labor Employment Organization's (OAED) data on unemployment rates from the beginning of 2010 to the end of 2011 showed a rise of 18.28 percent in unemployment with 80 percent of the affected seeking a job. By employing statistical data from the European Union, the International

---

10 Ramón Peña-Casas, "Europe's Employment and Social Inclusion Policies amidst the Crisis: An Opportunity for the Future?" in *Social Developments in the European Union 2009*, ed. Christophe Degryse (Brussels: European Trade Union Institute and Observatoire Social Européen, 2010), 91.
11 See Nicholas Sevastakis and Yannis Stavrakakis, *Laikismos, Antilaikismos ke Krisi* (Athens: Nefeli, 2012); Petros Papasarantopoulos, *Mythoi ke Stereotypa tis Ellinikis Krisis* (Thessaloniki: Epikentro, 2012); Vassilis Vamvakas, *O Logos tis Krisis. Polosi, Via, Anastochasmos stin Politiki ke Dimofili Koultoura* (Thessaloniki: Epikentro).
12 Stuart Hall and Alan O'Shea, "Common-sense Neoliberalism," *Soundings*, no. 55 (2013): 8–9, 12. Drawing upon Gramscian theory, Hall and O'Shea argue that politics gains the consent of the public when it appears "common-sense," i.e. pragmatic, empirical with a reference to everyday life and thinking. "Common-sense" has a particular conservative content and acts as a self-fulfilling prophecy. Its effects include that "the individualization of everyone, the privatization of public troubles and the requirement to make competitive choices at every turn— has been paralleled by an upsurge in feelings of insecurity, anxiety, stress and depression."
13 Nikos Mouzelis, "Interview," in *To Koinoniko Portraito tis Elladas. Opseis tis Krisis*, ed. Aliki Mouriki, Dionysis Balourdos, Olga Papaliou, Natalia Spyropoulou, Evi Fagadaki and Emmy Fronimou (Athens: EKKE, 2012), 12.
14 Ramón Peña-Casas, "Europe's Employment and Social Inclusion Policies amidst the Crisis," 103. The European Employment Rate faced a sharp decline (from 2009 and onwards) as approx. 4.5 million jobs were lost and demand for the labor force dropped 30 percent.

Labor Organization (ILO) revealed that among the Greek unemployed are people who suffer from a total lack of income.[15] Mainly in Athens, unemployment rates have tripled,[16] and more than 1,045,000 jobs were lost from 2009 until two years ago.

Moreover, Greek clientelism has resulted in the recession in the country. Despite a series of reforms, tax increases, and spending cuts, with which the Greek government tried to confront the new financial landscape, Greece appealed to the Eurogroup, the International Monetary Fund, and the European Central Bank to secure bailout loans (memoranda of 2010, 2012, 2015). After the implementation of the memoranda, a distinctive precariat became visible. According to Zaimakis this includes

> underemployed in undeclared work, armies of unemployed, impoverished farmers, bankrupt merchants, small and medium-sized businesses and other members of the middle class, dismissed civil servants, young people and women excluded from working life and the majority of immigrants, with or without residence permits.[17]

In this light, the Greek precariat is subordinated to a regime of underemployment, flexible employment, as well as "pseudo-employment."[18]

Particular importance should be attached to young people and the youth precariat, as they could be held to be among the most direct victims of the crisis.[19] Youth unemployment has been tenacious since the mid-2000s and reached high levels since the Greek financial crisis.[20] A vicious circle of *flexploitation* began to

---

[15] Dimitris Karantinos, "Agora Ergasias, Egegrammeni Anergia ke Roes Ergatikou Dynamikou kata ti Diarkeia tis Trehousas Oikonomikis Yfesis," in *To Koinoniko Portraito tis Elladas. Opseis tis Krisis*, ed. Aliki Mouriki, Dionysis Balourdos, Olga Papaliou, Natalia Spyropoulou, Evi Fagadaki and Emmy Fronimou (Athens: EKKE, 2012), 98.

[16] Aliki Mouriki, "Ston Vomo tis' Antagonistikotitas'," 11.

[17] Yannis Zaimakis, "I Elastikopoiisii tis Ergasias ke to Neo 'Prekariat' stis Synthikes toy Eveliktou Kapitalismou," *O Kosmos tis Ergasias*, no. 2 (2015): 37.

[18] Indicative of such tensions is Zaimakis' observation that in the audits of the Corps of Labor Inspectors of 2012 in 19,083 businesses "36% of employees were undeclared and uninsured, while the respective audits in the period between 2010 and 2011 revealed percentages of 25% and 30% accordingly" Zaimakis, "I Elastikopoiisi tis Ergasias," 38.

[19] Athanassios Gouglas, "The Young Precariat in Greece: What Happened to 'Generation 700 Euros'?" *European Perspectives – Journal on European Perspectives of the Western Balkans* 5, no. 1 (2013).

[20] "Between 2008 and 2014 Greece recorded both the highest youth unemployment, but also the steepest rise within that period among its EU counterparts (from around 23% in 2008 to over 53% in 2014). In addition, Greece displayed one of the highest and sharply amplified long-term unemployment rates among the OECD countries, from 49% in Q4 2007 to 71% in Q1 2014 (OECD, 2014, 1)." Spyros Themelis, "Degrees of Precariousness: The Problematic Transition

take shape and involved especially the unemployed or underemployed youth. Notwithstanding their educational qualifications, young people are forced to take on undeclared and underpaid employment. If highly educated, they tend to be involved in a constant struggle to enrich their CVs with funded training programs, which do not fit their real needs. Their last gasp is migrating to other European countries, which offer better working and living opportunities. It is what the media has called the "generation 700 euros," which might best be seen as a "generational unit among other antagonistic units, fighting for generational justice and reform, within the 'young precariat'."[21] The analysis of Chiotaki-Poulou and Sakellariou shows that those belonging to the "generation 700 euros" are between 25 and 35 years old.[22] It consists of usually qualified but underpaid young people, whose youth has been extended, as they are still dependent on their families. This potentially makes them an oppositional force, stemming from a generational gap and the shared situation of a generation. Their discontent results from their inability to consume: "the material present seems to be their main concern and not a better future."[23]

The Greek Cinema of Precarity Before the Crisis

Precarity has always been present as a motif in Greek cinema, because work and unemployment have been two central themes in building a country that had already suffered the devastating consequences of WWII and a Civil War (1945–1949) and their impact on the socio-economic conditions. During that time, Greece, a country with a tenuous post-war industry and slow mechanization,[24] was struggling to overcome poverty and desolation in rural areas; from 1952, the Greek rural population started to decrease,[25] relocating to Greek

---

into the Labour Market of Greek Higher Education Graduates," *Forum Sociológico*, no. 31 (2017), http://journals.openedition.org/sociologico/1811.
21 Athanassios Gouglas, "The Young Precariat in Greece," 35–36.
22 Note that in their research of the daily Press between 2007–2008, Chiotaki-Poulou and Sakellariou demonstrate that the term "generation" is rather problematic or vague and best understood as a social construction, not as a social category. Chiotaki-Poulou and Sakellariou, "I Koinoniki Kataskevi," 25.
23 Chiotaki-Poulou and Sakellariou, "I Koinoniki Kataskevi," 3–32.
24 Nikos Mouzelis, *Neoelliniki Koinonia: Opseis Ypoanaptyksis* (Athens: Exantas, 1978), 27–28.
25 Grigoris Gizelis, Roxani Kaftantzoglou, Afroditi Teperoglou, and Vassilis Filias, *Paradosi kai Neoterikotita stis Politistikes drastiriotites tis Ellinikis Oikogeneias: Metavallomena Shimata* (Athens: EKKE, 1984), 18–24.

urban centers[26] or emigrating to the USA or to European countries to find better working and living conditions.[27] Migration was a direct and visible effect of unemployment in the primary sector, which led people to seek alternatives in atypical multi jobbing in the rural areas.[28] This also had implications for the Greek economy, whose characteristics from the 1950s on could be summarized as its transformation to a country oriented to an ever-growing tertiary sector.

In contexts such as these, representations of precarity have always found a place in various film fiction narratives, even in the early period of Greek film history. In the protest film *Koinoniki sapila* (*Social Decay*, Stelios Tatassopoulos, 1932), the filmmaker criticized various issues such as youth unemployment, which leads to their corruption, and the deplorable working conditions and exploitation of tobacco workers. During the 1950s, films in the neo-realist vein, such as *Pikro psomi* (*Bitter Bread*, Grigoris Grigoriou, 1951), *Mavri gi* (*Black Earth*, Stelios Tatasopoulos, 1952), or *Magiki polis* (*Magic City*, Nikos Koundouros, 1954), conveyed social commentary on the hardships of work, absolute poverty, and child labor.[29]

The mainstream Greek cinema that was highly popular in the 1960s provided several film narratives that revolve around precarity. In popular film genres, such as comedy[30] and melodrama,[31] the pursuit of a job or a better position and lack thereof are frequent themes. While the process of urbanization was beginning, popular comedies usually reflected the advent of consumerism, the social mobility of young working-class characters,[32] or the troubles of underdogs.[33]

---

26 Ibid., 274–277; Konstantinos Tsoukalas, *Kratos, Koinonia, Ergasia sti Metapolemiki Ellada* (Athens: Themelio, 1987), 32.
27 Vassilis Karapostolis, *I Katanalotiki Syberifora stin Elliniki Koinonia (1960–1975)* (Athens: EKKE, 1984), 109–112; Loukia M. Mousourou, *Metanastefsi ke Metanasteftiki Politiki stin Ellada ke tin Evropi* (Athens: Gutenberg, 2003), 25–50.
28 Paris Tsartas, *Erevna gia ta Koinonika Haraktiristika tis Apasholisis (Meleti III). Tourismos ke Agrotiki Polydrastiriotita* (Athens: EKKE, 1991), 15.
29 Maria Paradeisi, "O Neorealismos ston Elliniko Kinimatografo," *Ta Istorika*, no. 20 (1994).
30 Unfortunately, there is not enough space to address other genres or to scrutinize the already mentioned ones. Still, film musicals or dramas by Nikos Foskolos also reflect on such themes.
31 Orsalia-Eleni Kassaveti, "To Elliniko Melodrama. I Ekseliksi enos Dimofilous Kinimatografikou Eidous," in *Apo ton Proimo ston Syghrono Elliniko Kinimatografo. Zitimata Methodologias, Theorias, Istorias*, ed. Maria Paradeisi and Afroditi Nikolaidou (Athens: Gutenberg, 2017); Orsalia-Eleni Kassaveti, *Antestrammena Kosmoeidola. Dikastiko Drama, Melodrama, Malakos Erotikos Kinimatografos (1965–1974)* (Thessaloniki: Epikentro, 2017), 73–114.
32 Ioanna Athanassatou, *Ellinikos Kinimatografos (1950–1967). Laiki Mnimi ke Ideologia* (Athens: Finatec, 2001), 348; Eliza-Anna Delveroudi, *Oi Neoi stis Komodies tou Ellinikou Kinimatografou (1948–1974)* (Athens: IAEN, 2004), 57.
33 See *O ilias tou 16ou* (*The Policeman of the 16th Precinct*, Alekos Sakellarios, 1959). The actor Thanassis Veggos played a series of characters who are dismissed from their jobs and become

New Greek cinema, which arose in the late 1960s and the early 1970s, was mainly interested in representing the major shift that took place in the sociopolitical arena, especially under the Colonels' Junta beginning 1967, before which a few films had paved the way towards the emergence of this new direction.[34] During the 1970s, New Greek Cinema provided narratives of precarity, especially focusing on women's work or on the life of young internal immigrants coming to Athens to find a job, featuring contemporary criticism on both issues and subverting older film narratives and styles. Dramas, such as *To proxenio tis Annas* (*The Engagement of Anna*, Pantelis Voulgaris, 1972) or *Oi tembelides tis eforis koiladas* (*The Idlers of the Fertile Valley*, Nikos Panayotopoulos, 1978) represent the divide between the working class and the upper-middle-class, which is shown to suppress the former. In this context, filmmaker Pavlos Tasios in his film *To vary . . . peponi* (*The Heavy Melon*, 1977), highlights the difficulties of young internal immigrants, who come to Athens for a better life and cannot endure the harsh working conditions imposed in the capital.

During the 1980s, Greek popular comedies, as well as the comedies of the short-lived video-circuit of the era,[35] were highly interested in young blue-collar underdogs trying to find a job,[36] with such stories used to create comic tension. Also part of popular cinema in that decade, the social dramas of Giannis Dalianidis addressed youth unemployment: in *Ta tsakalia: Ena koinoniko provlima* (*The Jackals*, 1981) and *Oi epikindynoi (Mia diamartyria)* (*The Dangerous*, 1983), the young characters are unemployed and drift into juvenile delinquency to make ends meet.[37] Another example of the popular dramas of the era is *Pires ptyhio?*

---

unemployed, i.e., in the film *Polytehnitis kai erimospitis* (*Jack of All Trades, Master of None*, Alekos Sakellarios, 1963) or *O katafertzis* (*The Hustler*, Kostas Strantzalis, 1964). Furthermore, the actor Kostas Hatzichristos personified the role of the internal immigrant ("Vlahos") with a distinct accent and a temperament who tries to adhere to the ever-changing landscape of the Athenian center in comedy films, such as *O Thymios takane thalassa* (*Thymios Screws up*, Alekos Sakellarios, 1959). See also Delveroudi, *Oi Neoi*, 56.

34 For example *I 7i imera tis dimiourgias* (*The 7th Day of Creation*, Vassilis Georgiadis, 1968). Based on playwright Iakovos Kampanellis's play, the film reflects the shattered dreams of the 1950s generation and the lack of realism regarding the struggling pursuit for employment. The young main character (Giorgos Tzortzis) is unemployed because he and his father believe that his technical degree and his wit will secure him a desirable job position. He escapes in an imaginary world, believing in the lies he tells himself, involving in it his conceited wife, and he unwillingly returns to reality with a tragic ending.

35 Orsalia-Eleni Kassaveti, *I Elliniki Videotainia (1985–1990). Eidologikes, Koinonikes ke Politismikes Diastaseis* (Athens: Asini, 2014).

36 *Ta sainia* (*The Crackerjacks*, Christos Kyriakopoulos, 1982), *Trelos eimai o, ti thelo kano* (*I am Crazy and Do Whatever I Want*, Giannis Hartomatzidis, 1985).

37 Kassaveti, *I Elliniki Videotainia*, 57–59.

(*Did You Get a Degree?*, Grigoris Noulelis, 1985). The main protagonist (Vassilis Kailas) plays the role of an islander coming to Athens to study at a private technical college. Unable to find a steady job, he becomes a freelance bookseller, tries to get a job at a small swimsuit sewing business, and eventually fails all subsequent job interviews. Half-starved and facing eviction, his only resort is going back to the island he came from.

In the following decades, the 1990s Athens stock exchange boom and its subsequent crash in 1999 and various forms of financial support from the EC raised new questions about precarity in Greek cinema. Attempts to escape precarity were often represented, taking various forms such as petty crime and exploiting immigrants from former Eastern Bloc countries while boasting of being a European.[38] The image of "pseudo-prosperity" that was apparent in everyday life and its representations until the Olympic Games of 2004, was soon shattered and criticized in the following years, as we will see in the films selected here.

The Contemporary Greek Cinema of Precarity: Visions of Doom in Three Films

The everyday and almost inescapable effects of the recession made up a context in which Greek cinema began to internalize, process, and include narratives of the youth precariat. As mentioned earlier, it is clear that visual and narrative discourses on general precarity and its discontents have not been atypical in Greek film industry; quite the contrary: they have permeated the whole course of its history, aligning themselves with general anxieties in Greek society and audiences as well. Interestingly, though, the recent Greek cinema of precarity produced right after the recession operates in a somewhat different way, as it partially breaks with the inherited film tradition of precarity. It is preoccupied not only with national or self-reflexive imagery,[39] but also becomes more socially and politically aware, providing a discernible and recognizable portrait of those living in precarity. Its characters provide a set of typecasts, representing Standing's different varieties of the precariat, their connection to work, and

---

38 *Valkanizater* (Sotiris Gkoritsas, 1997), *Apo Tin akri tis polis (From the Edge of the City*, Konstantinos Giannaris, 1998).
39 Ursula-Helen Kassaveti and Afroditi Nikolaidou, "The Greek New Wave: Representing Work and Unemployment," in *European Film and Television: Crisis Narratives and Narratives in Crisis*, ed. Betty Kaklamanidou and Ana Corbalán (London: Routledge, 2018), 171–172.

their feelings towards the uncertainty of their future, and it makes use of a realistic iconography.

In light of this discussion, it is essential to remember that 72.3 percent of a corpus of 47 Greek films, produced between 2007–2017 and presented in ten of the most high-profile international festivals (Cannes, Berlinale, Venice, etc.), use work and unemployment as their central themes[40] and that they establish a set of representations that either operate as "allegories of work" or focus on small businesses and self-employed workers, the laboring poor, and youth unemployment.[41]

In theorizing the concept of the precariat, Standing attributes three distinct characteristics to it: the precariat's subject is a "supplicant, a beggar," it operates within "insecure labor relations," and it bears "class consciousness."[42] In a time of "Global Transformation," the precariat is still a "class-in-the-making," comprised of particular varieties: the *atavists* (old, uneducated, deprived, and frustrated working-class communities and families who delve into a glorious and prosperous past), the *nostalgists* (passive immigrants and minorities who have no present and no home), and the *progressives* (educated, or maybe bohemians, who hold no sense of future but could possibly act as a transformative agent).[43] Following Standing's categories, three film case-studies have been selected, which showcase the different varieties of the Greek youth precariat as represented on screen.

Park

Sofia Exarchou's *Park* (2016) offers a stunning portrait of the *nostalgist* young precariat living in Attica's Olympic Village, where the Greek Worker's Housing Organization built houses to accommodate the athletes of the 2004 Olympic Games. After the end of the Games, the housing complexes were given randomly to non-privileged people of low income. Anna (Dimitra Vlagopoulou), a young former athlete whose successful career came to an end after an accident, and the idle and totally disoriented teenager Dimitris (Dimitris Kitsos) are two of them.

---

40 Ibid., 164.
41 Ibid., 164–165. However, not all these films refer to the precariat. Besides, by limiting the number of films through the criterion of film festivals and "self-exported image," we lose vital information about precarity by excluding movies that may have participated in local or peripheral film festivals (see Stratos Tzitzis' film *45m²*).
42 Standing, "The Precariat and Class Struggle," 7.
43 Ibid., 7–8.

They form a doomed relationship while trying to escape from the stagnant pool (both literally and metaphorically) of the Olympic Village (Fig. 1). The children and early teenagers living there are shown to be driven by brutal and dark instincts. The viewer does not know whether they go to school or whether they work. They are filmed with a handheld camera in constant motion or wandering endlessly. The protagonists get their pocket money from dog breeding or odd jobs. Dimitris has already quit the manual work he did for his mother's boyfriend; Anna seeks a prince in every young boy on a motorcycle she wishes might take her away from the Village. The two of them take refuge in seaside hotels, where they try to get involved with tourists and act as if they were their friends in order to benefit from them—not very successfully, however, because of their social awkwardness. In the end, it all seems to grind to a halt with no exit for anyone.

Fig. 1: Park (Sofia Exarchou, 2016).

Exarchou translates the despair into harsh visual terms (the abandoned place, the wrecked facilities, etc.) and a rather minimalistic narration interspersed with a succession of slower or faster actions. Dialogues are scarce and moments of silence prevail. A hand-held camera dictates a rather documentary-like style with lots of awkward close-ups of the dirtiness, the poverty, the despair in the characters' faces. Their clothing is also old and dirty—or new but cheap and tasteless. Enclosed spaces are limited to the athletic complexes, and some aspects of the characters' uncared-for homes show a kind of underclass kitsch. On the other hand, open spaces, such as the beach where a hotel is located or the abandoned sports arenas, are documented in rather melancholic establishing shots.

The small, filthy children and teenagers, who are dressed in rags and seem like orphans, are just one step before entering adulthood, but that will not bring their integration in society, instead they will remain denizens in Standing's sense of the word. Entirely alienated, Anna and Dimitris are trapped in an endless void: with no or only inadequate social and work skills, they are doomed to unemployment and poverty. Finally, without any apparent motive, Dimitris tries to kill a friendly Scandinavian tourist in a high-key scene giving the viewers a full view of the action. In a sudden moment of clarity, he stops that and then goes back to where he belongs, but immerses himself further in his self-pity.

Both Anna and Dimitris represent the *nostalgic* variety of the precariat consisting of

> migrants and minorities, who have a strong sense of relative deprivation by virtue of having no present, no home [. . .] Politically, they tend to be relatively passive or disengaged, except for occasional days of rage when something that appears to be a direct threat to them sparks collective anger.[44]

As part of a small minority living in the outskirts of Athens, they seem to delve into the old days of glory of the Olympic Games, a time when Greece's economy was still functioning. A visual juxtaposition seems to be vital to understand these older, and most glorious, times. Anna is continuously asked to do sets of exercises she used to perform when she was an athlete. She opens her legs gracefully and performs quasi acrobatic tricks. But when she takes a bath, the scars from her operation are visible. Dimitris, for his part, tries to make easy money as he grew up believing that the world owed him something. Their nostalgia triggers nothing but a sense of absence: they have no home, and they have no future. Like refugees and other minorities, they, too, belong to the underdogs of the Olympic Village.

45m2

45m² begins with Christina (Efi Logginou) attending an interview for a job guarding antiquities at the Acropolis Museum and the camera focuses on her reactions, which culminate in anger. She breaks off the interview as soon as she realizes that there is no point to it, especially after persistent questions about any "special favors" and her consequent quarrel with the interviewer. She works as a salesperson at a posh leather store in Kolonaki, one of the oldest and upper-middle-class districts in Athens. With this job, she can hardly make ends meet, especially after renting a 45m² apartment for herself alone—her

---

[44] Standing, "The Precariat and Class Struggle," 8.

ticket to freedom. In a linear narrative that unfolds in just a few months (early summer to early autumn), Christina is shown leaving her two lovers and her mother behind, enjoying her single life in a small lower-class suburban neighborhood mostly populated by immigrants. However, she does not have enough money. To save some cash, she stops drinking alcohol and quits smoking. She works at a second job as a waitress at a bar and also applies for a call girl job. After arguing with her employer about a raise in her monthly salary, she leaves the job and her small apartment, and decides to search for employment on the island of Kos in the Dodecanese.

In his film, Tzitzis discusses issues of self-respect and dignity—a theme already examined by the filmmaker in his *Sose me* (*Save Me*, 2001)—and comments on the "generation 700 euros," a generation that is caught in a struggle between the need to survive and attempts to escape dependency on the parents. Personal value is not always associated with money, but it provides the employee or worker with dignity and promotes self-realization.[45] Christina, who blames herself for not being the type of "good student" who could attend university (instead she went to a private vocational training school), cannot survive without a job: she chooses to work during the vibrant Greek holiday season—a choice for non-qualified people who work in various odd, and sometimes atypical, holiday jobs to get extra money—as a final resort to keep the last pieces of her personal value intact.

Christina belongs to the "generation 700 euros" and her "material present seems to be her main concern and not a better future."[46] Her attitude echoes the *atavist* variety, "of those dropping out of old working-class communities and families. Mostly uneducated, they tend to relate their sense of deprivation and frustration to a lost past, real or imagined," and listen "to reactionary populist voices of the far right and blame the second and even third variety of precariat for their problems."[47] Likewise, Christina has few qualifications and comes from a poor single-parent family, as represented by her home's props and decoration. Her mother represents a relatively conservative part of Greek society; she wants her daughter to marry and live a conventional, stable life. Although Christina pursues her rebellious goals, she has no way of achieving them. She acts in a rush, as though everything will turn out fine without the protective cluster of her family. She gains happiness from small things (by observing

---

[45] Elisa Veronesi, *Cinema e lavoro. La rappresentazione dell'identità adulta fra miti, successo e precarietà* (Turin: Effatà, 2004).
[46] Chiotaki-Poulou and Sakellariou, "I Koinoniki Kataskevi," 25.
[47] Standing, "The Precariat and Class Struggle," 7.

her new low-class neighborhood or acquiring new furniture from the rubbish), but she does not change her attitude. She gradually sinks into a fantasy world about the former tenant, who supposedly acted in a revolutionary way and worked as a season worker at the islands to fund his artistic career. When she meets him and discovers that he went back to work at his father's business, she is shocked. Still, she decides to find a better job in Kos. Notwithstanding her honest and adventurist starting point, she is still a member of the precariat, as such occupations are often insecure, temporary, underpaid, and undeclared. Her job's precarious nature under crisis, which is not implied, but represented through her downward spiral, could only lead to another precarious venture.

Tzitzis' film meticulously portrays the habitus of the characters. This is enhanced by his shot-on-location realistic style: small neighborhoods near the center of Athens, inhabited by older Athenians and immigrants, are in stark contrast to the luminous historical center of Athens and Kolonaki. Christina's empty 45m^2 apartment becomes filled with furniture she finds on the street but also bought from expensive stores until it ends up empty again, just before her moving out. Outdoor spaces denote a middle-class milieu: big suburban cafes, ideal for men watching football, reveal the patriarchal environment in which Christina has to live and work.

Standing Aside, Watching

Precarity is said to have a transformative power for the educated who see no future, because they have to create it from scratch. Standing argues that this precariat variety

> consists of the educated, who experience in their irregular labour and in the lack of opportunity to construct a narrative for their lives a sense of relative deprivation and status frustration, because they have no sense of future. One might call them bohemians, but as they are the potentially transformative part of the precariat, the new vanguard, they are open to becoming the *progressives*.[48]

Such a "progressive" precariat may be found in Giorgos Servetas' film *Standing Aside, Watching* (Fig. 2). Marina Symeou plays the leading role of Antigoni, who left her village to study philology at the university. For as long as she can remember, Greece's prosperous financial past helped her parents to support her. During her studies and inasmuch as her pocket money allowed her, she took acting lessons and participated in an acting group, living on odd jobs. However, the crisis

---

48 Ibid., 8.

forced her to return to her hometown. This loss of perspective for many in the well-educated younger generation seems to be a predominant problem in Greek society after the crisis,[49] while others flee abroad to study further and pursue a more positive walk of life, contributing to the brain-drain phenomenon of the late 2000s and early 2010s.

Fig. 2: Na kathesai kai na koitas (Standing Aside, Watching, Giorgos Servetas, 2013).

Antigoni feels trapped in the small town. Her father holds her responsible, accusing her of laziness and an inability to rule her life, without acknowledging the crisis's broader context. She is forced to work undeclared and underpaid as a private teacher for small children. She represents one of the million Greek NEETs,[50] the

> more often than not female, between 20–24 years old, of Greek origin, medium to high educational attainment (including HE graduates), with some work experience, from low-income families, without prior training program attainment, supported by their family and often without social insurance.[51]

In this spirit, Antigoni begins to explore the dark side of the small town, run by a local mobster who offers her undeclared employment. Her higher education does not serve her needs, and she must learn to survive in such a hostile environment. The portrayal of precarity is reinforced by some small details: we see Pakistani immigrants walking next to the main road, probably working in the

---

[49] Nick Malkoutzis, *Young Greeks and the Crisis. The Danger of Losing a Generation* (Athens: Friedrich Ebert Stiftung, 2011), 3, http://library.fes.de/pdf-files/id/ipa/08465.pdf.
[50] The Acronym stands for "Not in Education, Employment, or Training."
[51] Themelis, "Degrees of Precariousness," 58.

village's fields. Besides, Antigoni's boyfriend (Giorgos Kafetzopoulos) works for the mob. He has to live on a small budget, as he is unpaid for two months. In this situation, Antigoni's sense of justice and order leads her to take action to help her brother and her mistreated childhood friend Eleni—she is becoming a *progressive*. Servetas renders Antigoni's precarity realistically, closely documenting her route towards self-realization and the need to protest—one should not stay aside and simply watch.

Although the film is relatively stylized with geometrical shots constructing prison-like worlds, moments of tension are shot with a hand-held camera to create a more realistic effect. In the film's opening, Antigoni's monologue about Greece's prosperous past in the 1980s and 1990s is juxtaposed with long shots of her miserable village; it is where her journey ends. Ominous electronic music plays, accompanying shots of containers, abandoned wagons, and solar panels (a way of making easy money, as the EU has subsidized them). Antigoni continues her voice-over about all those people who during and after the Greek Junta (1967–1973) seemed to have taken advantage of everything available to drive "big jeeps." Trapped in her village, she has to make do with what there is: a tacky local bar, where all the village's inhabitants entertain themselves. Like the homes, its interior pinpoints the lack of taste of people with a sudden but short-run income. Shots of nature, which has become a new refuge for Antigoni, are juxtaposed with her village's artificial universe: a universe of corruption, poverty, and despair.

Conclusions: Beyond the Greek Cinematic Youth Precarity

Precarity as a discursive and representational theme has been depicted on the big screen in Greece since the 1950s, even if the films often were limited in their characterization and criticism of Greece's actual problems in various periods. Breaking free from such continuities, a new representational emphasis can be discerned in contemporary Greek cinema after 2007–2008—a focus that pinpoints the subject of crisis. We have encountered different "varieties" of the precariat and various degrees of precariousness represented in the films, located in the Greek society and defined by the antithesis between secure and stable and insecure and unstable employment. This juxtaposition helps the viewers and the film characters understand the regime of precarity they live and work in. In the films mentioned above, though, precarity is not always associated with a previous social or cultural habitus: it pertains to the protagonists, secondary characters, the overall visual imagery, and the narrative. Despite having different stylistic approaches, all use filming strategies that articulate an almost documentary look with varying degrees of resolution, thanks to hand-held camera shooting. All three films deviate from the previous tradition, which frequently followed the golden rule of "happy endings." Here, no character seems to have achieved the crucial resolution of their conflicts, and if so, the end is open, vague, and with particular consequences for them. It is implied that the characters, although in a relatively unconscious way, are struggling not only with their problems but also against the neoliberal structure that provoked their precarity.

Despite their difference in traits, all three varieties of the precariat identified by Standing are born and come of age in what he calls the neoliberal inferno. He retains a belief in their transformative ability to rebel against it. As soon as the precariat recognizes itself, it can represent itself and participate in class struggle, demanding a new system of distribution and dignity. This self-recognition can aspire to become transnational, and these films could help in this direction. In that sense, by encapsulating critical social and cultural meanings, new Greek films on the precariat may perhaps allow foreign audiences to undertake cross-cultural readings of precarity and locate its frustrating global power, the same for all people.

Bibliography

Athanassatou, Ioanna. *Ellinikos Kinimatografos (1950–1967). Laiki Mnimi ke Ideologia.* Athens: Finatec, 2001.

Bernards, Nick. *The Global Governance of Precarity: Primitive Accumulation and the Politics of Irregular Work.* Abingdon: Routledge, 2018.

Bourdieu, Pierre. "Job Insecurity is Everywhere Now." In *Acts of Resistance. Against the New Myths of Our Time*, trans. Richard Nice. Cambridge/Oxford: Polity Press, 1998, 81–87.

Campbell, Stephen. *Border Capitalism, Disrupted: Precarity and Struggle in a Southeast Asian Industrial Zone.* Ithaca, NY: ILR Press, 2018.

Chiotaki-Poulou, Eirini, and Alexandros Sakellariou. "I Koinoniki Kataskevi tis 'Genias ton 700 Euros' ke I Anadysi tis ston Imerisio Typo: Mia Koinoniologiki Proseggisi." *Epitheorisi Koinonikon Erevnon* 131 (2010): 3–32.

Delveroudi, Eliza-Anna. *Oi Neoi stis Komodies tou Ellinikou Kinimatografou (1948–1974).* Athens: IAEN, 2004.

Gizelis, Grigoris, Roxani Kaftantzoglou, Afroditi Teperoglou, and Vassilis Filias. *Paradosi kai Neoterikotita stis Politistikes drastiriotites tis Ellinikis Oikogeneias: Metavallomena Shimata.* Athens: EKKE, 1984.

Gouglas, Athanassios. "The Young Precariat in Greece: What Happened to 'Generation 700 Euros'?" *European Perspectives – Journal on European Perspectives of the Western Balkans* 5, no. 1 (2013): 30–49.

Hall, Stuart, and Alan O'Shea. "Common-sense Neoliberalism." *Soundings*, no. 55 (2013): 9–25.

Kaklamanidou, Betty, and Ana Corbalán, eds. *European Film and Television: Crisis Narratives and Narratives in Crisis*. London: Routledge, 2018.

Karantinos, Dimitris. "Agora Ergasias, Egegrammeni Anergia ke Roes Ergatikou Dynamikou kata ti Diarkeia tis Trehousas Oikonomikis Yfesis." In *To Koinoniko Portraito tis Elladas. Opseis tis Krisis*, ed. Aliki Mouriki, Dionysis Balourdos, Olga Papaliou, Natalia Spyropoulou, Evi Fagadaki, and Emmy Fronimou. Athens: EKKE, 2012, 89–108.

Karapostolis, Vassilis. *I Katanalotiki Syberifora stin Elliniki Koinonia (1960–1975)*. Athens: EKKE, 1984.

Kassaveti, Orsalia-Eleni. *I Elliniki Videotainia (1985–1990). Eidologikes, Koinonikes ke Politismikes Diastaseis*. Athens: Asini, 2014.

——. "To Elliniko Melodrama. I Ekseliksi enos Dimofilous Kinimatografikou Eidous." In *Apo ton Proimo ston Syghrono Elliniko* Kinimatografo. Zitimata Methodologias, *Theorias, Istorias*, ed. Maria Paradeisi and Afroditi Nikolaidou. Athens: Gutenberg, 2017, 45–75.

——. *Antestrammena Kosmoeidola. Dikastiko Drama, Melodrama, Malakos Erotikos Kinimatografos (1965–1974)*. Thessaloniki: Epikentro, 2017.

Kassaveti, Ursula-Helen, and Afroditi Nikolaidou. "The Greek New Wave: Representing Work and Unemployment." In *European* Film *and* Television: *Crisis* Narratives *and* Narratives in *Crisis*, ed. Betty Kaklamanidou and Ana Corbalán. London: Routledge, 2018, 160–177.

Malkoutzis, Nick. *Young Greeks and the Crisis. The Danger of Losing a Generation*. Athens: Friedrich Ebert Stiftung, 2011. http://library.fes.de/pdf-files/id/ipa/08465.pdf.

Mouriki, Aliki. "Ston Vomo tis' Antagonistikotitas': I Aporrythmisi tis Agoras Ergasias ke ton Ergasiakon Sheseon tin Periodo 2010–2012 ke oi Epiptoseis tis stis Prooptikes Anakampsis." In *To Koinoniko Portraito tis Elladas. Opseis tis Krisis*, ed. Aliki Mouriki, Dionysis Balourdos, Olga Papaliou, Natalia Spyropoulou, Evi Fagadaki, and Emmy Fronimou. Athens: EKKE, 2012, 55–88.

Mousourou, Loukia M. *Metanastefsi ke Metanasteftiki Politiki stin Ellada ke tin Evropi*. Athens: Gutenberg, 2003.

Mouzelis, Nikos. "Interview." In *To Koinoniko Portraito tis Elladas. Opseis tis Krisis*, ed. Aliki Mouriki, Dionysis Balourdos, Olga Papaliou, Natalia Spyropoulou, Evi Fagadaki, and Emmy Fronimou. Athens: EKKE, 2012, 7–12.

——. *Neoelliniki Koinonia: Opseis Ypoanaptyksis*. Athens: Exantas, 1978.

Paradeisi, Maria. "O Neorealismos ston Elliniko Kinimatografo." *Ta Istorika*, no. 20 (1994): 123–146.

Peña-Casas, Ramón. "Europe's Employment and Social Inclusion Policies amidst the Crisis: An Opportunity for the Future?" In *Social Developments in the European* Union *2009*, ed. Christophe Degryse. Brussels: European Trade Union Institute and Observatoire Social Européen, 2010, 91–118.

Papasarantopoulos, Petros. *Mythoi ke Stereotypa tis Ellinikis Krisis*. Thessaloniki: Epikentro, 2012.

Schram, Sanford F. *The Return of Ordinary Capitalism: Neoliberalism, Precarity, Occupy*. Oxford/New York: Oxford University Press, 2015.

Sevastakis, Nicholas, and Yannis Stavrakakis. *Laikismos, Antilaikismos ke Krisi*. Athens: Nefeli, 2012.

Standing, Guy. *The Precariat: The New Dangerous Class*. London: Bloomsbury, 2011.
——. *A Precariat Charter. From Denizens to Citizens*. London/New York: Bloomsbury, 2014.
——. "The Precariat and Class Struggle." *RCCS Annual Review*, no. 7 (2015). http://journals.openedition.org/rccsar/585.
Themelis, Spyros. "Degrees of Precariousness: The Problematic Transition into the Labour Market of Greek Higher Education Graduates." *Forum Sociológico*, no. 31 (2017): 53–62. http://journals.openedition.org/sociologico/1811.
Tsartas, Paris. *Erevna gia ta Koinonika Haraktiristika tis Apasholisis (Meleti III). Tourismos ke Agrotiki Polydrastiriotita*. Athens: EKKE, 1991.
Tsoukalas, Konstantinos. *Kratos, Koinonia, Ergasia sti Metapolemiki Ellada*. Athens: Themelio, 1987.
Vamvakas, Vassilis. *O Logos tis Krisis. Polosi, Via, Anastochasmos stin Politiki ke Dimofili Koultoura*. Thessaloniki: Epikentro, 2014.
——. "To Tileoptiko Apotipoma tis Elliniis Krisis (2009–2013)." *Nea Estia* 1876 (2018): 184–232.
Veronesi, Elisa. *Cinema e lavoro. La rappresentazione dell'identità adulta fra miti, successo e precarietà*. Turin: Effatà, 2004.
Zaimakis, Yannis. "I Elastikopoiisi tis Ergasias ke to Neo 'Prekariat' stis Synthikes toy Eveliktou Kapitalismou." *O Kosmos tis Ergasias*, no. 2 (2015): 27–42.

Filmography

45m^2. Dir. Stratos Tzitzis. Greece, 2010.
Apo tin akri tis polis (From the Edge of the City). Dir. Konstantinos Giannaris. Greece, 1998.
I 7i imera tis dimiourgias (The 7th Day of Creation). Dir. Vassilis Georgiadis. Greece, 1968.
I genia ton 592 Euro (Generation 592 Euros). MEGA CHANNEL. Greece, 2010–2011.
Koinoniki sapila (Social Decay). Dir. Stelios Tatassopoulos. Greece, 1932.
Mageirevo Oikonomika (I Cook Affordably). SKAI. Greece, 2010–2014.
Magiki polis (Magic City). Dir. Nikos Koundouros. Greece, 1954.
Mavri gi (Black Earth). Dir. Stelios Tatasopoulos. Greece, 1952.
Na kathesai kai na koitas (Standing Aside, Watching). Dir. Giorgos Servetas. Greece, 2013.
O ilias tou 16ou (The Policeman of the 16th Precinct). Dir. Alekos Sakellarios. Greece, 1959.
O katafertzis (The Hustler). Dir. Kostas Strantzalis. Greece, 1964.
O Thymios takane thalassa (Thymios Screws Up). Dir. Alekos Sakellarios. Greece, 1959.
Oi epikindynoi (Mia diamartyria) (The Dangerous: A Protest). Dir. Giannis Dalianidis. Greece, 1983.
Oi tembelides tis eforis koiladas (The Idlers of the Fertile Valley). Dir. Nikos Panayotopoulos. Greece, 1978.
Park. Dir. Sofia Exarchou. Greece/Poland, 2016.
Pikro psomi (Bitter Bread). Dir. Grigoris Grigoriou. Greece, 1951.
Pires ptyhio? (Did You Get a Degree?). Dir. Grigoris Noulelis. Greece, 1985.
Piso sto spiti (Back at Home). MEGA CHANNEL. Greece, 2011–2013.
Polytehnitis kai erimospitis (Jack of All Trades, Master of None). Dir. Alekos Sakellarios. Greece, 1963.

Sose me (*Save Me*). Dir. Stratos Tzitzis. Greece, 2001.
Ta sainia (*The Crackerjacks*). Dir. Christos Kyriakopoulos. Greece, 1982.
Ta tsakalia: Ena koinoniko provlima (*The Jackals*). Dir. Giannis Dalianidis. Greece, 1981.
To proxenio tis Annas (*The Engagement of Anna*). Dir. Pantelis Voulgaris. Greece, 1972.
To vary . . . peponi (*The Heavy Melon*). Dir. Pavlos Tassios. Greece, 1977.
Trelos eimai o, ti thelo kano (*I Am Crazy and Do Whatever I Want*). Dir. Giannis Hartomatzidis. Greece, 1985.
Valkanizater. Dir. Sotiris Gkoritsas. France/Greece/Bulgaria/Switzerland, 1997.

Özgür Çiçek
Transformation of the Precariat in Istanbul
Naivete, Idealism, and Corruption with and within the City

Istanbul has always been a significant location where people from Europe and the Middle East with all their cultural and social baggage encountered each other. As the economic capital of Turkey, historically it has always promised a potential for moving up in social class, as workers have often hoped that they could make money easily in Istanbul. It is a fast city, a place for making dreams come true in a short time, but it can also be a setting where dreams evolve into nightmares. The city is constantly destroying and reconstructing itself, amidst the rising flux of people from inside and outside Turkey. Particularly for many working in uncertain, undocumented, or exploitative jobs or living in areas threatened by gentrification, and with the problem of battling Covid-19 without much economical support from the government, precarity is at the core of Istanbul.

This circulation of people in Istanbul has naturally influenced movies that portrayed migrants, as well as working-class people, and their survival in the city and their neighborhoods. The precarious living conditions have led to a particular survival mindset to cope with never-ending conditions of change and de/formation. Based on this, in this chapter I will discuss films from the late 1970s to 2018 that center on characters who are initially naive, who are deceived or cheated easily, or who deliberately refrain from adapting to the metropolis Istanbul even at the cost of being and staying poor. Thus I will focus on how the precarious essence of Istanbul—the insecure working conditions and the ongoing flow of people into the city—is expressed in a peculiar cinema of the working class in which the pressure on people is shown through the transformation of naive, pure, or pristine characters into either more self-centered or self-sacrificing ones. I will start with *Çöpçüler Kralı* (*The King of the Street Cleaners*, Zeki Ökten, 1977). Later I will look at how good-heartedness and virtue transform into insanity, and how even insanity is turned into a commodity in *Çıplak Vatandaş* (*Naked Citizen*, Başar Sabuncu, 1985). I will then refer to more recent films to look at precarious subjects transformed through gentrification processes in Ali Vatansever's *Saf* (2018), Kıvanç Sezer's *Babamın Kanatları* (*My Father's Wings*, 2016), and Ahu Öztürk's *Toz Bezi* (*Dust Cloth*, 2015). These films from different decades indicate the variety of the naive characters representing the precariat in Turkey as well as their desire and often their inability to fit in, both culturally and economically.

Before I move on to a critical look at the films mentioned above, I would like to introduce a project report titled "Poverty and Social Exclusion in Slum areas of Large Cities in Turkey" (2006) conducted by professors Çağlar Keyder and Fikret Adaman, as I believe their findings will help to analyze the films.[1] Their in-depth field research on the six largest cities of Turkey reveals the scope of social exclusion, especially in *gecekondu* inner-city neighborhoods.[2] They define social exclusion as "the process of excluding individuals from society—due to poverty, deprivation of basic education/skills, or discrimination—and preventing them from participating in social life as they wish."[3] Further, the authors emphasize that the people who are socially excluded have very limited power to take part actively in decision-making processes, as they face many obstacles for constructing social networks, and thus they mostly feel powerless.

In their detailed report, Keyder and Adaman define various forms of social exclusion. They start with (1) *economical exclusion* which refers to short or long-term processes of unemployment or of not being able to get funding or loans, and due to this being excluded from life. The most extreme point of economical exclusion would be hunger. Their next theoretical paradigm for exclusion (2) is *spatial exclusion* which refers to the obstacles for accessing certain spaces, institutions, or parts of the city. Spatial exclusion functions in two ways: the first is that certain people are socially excluded by the majority of society, due to the place and geography they live in. The second is the inability of a person to fully experience the social life of the city due to the inadequate levels of public services provided to where they live in. (3) *Cultural exclusion* means being unable to take part in social and cultural life, regardless of economic reasons. When the majority is taken into account as the base, cultural exclusion marks out the people coming from a different ethnic or racial background or having a different religious belief. Furthermore, those who cannot speak the language of the majority, or who speak with an accent, those who wear different clothes or who embody a minority sexual identity have to face different kinds of obstacles, are excluded from certain activities, and are often ostracized. Finally, (4) *political exclusion* refers to not being able to use the rights of citizenship, especially political and legal ones.[4]

---

[1] Fikret Adaman and Çağlar Keyder, "Türkiye'de büyük kentlerin gecekondu ve çöküntü mahallelerinde yaşanan yoksulluk ve sosyal dışlanma," (2006) ec.europa.eu/employment_social/social_inclusion/docs/2006/study_turkey_tr.pdf.
[2] Gecekondu can be translated as a "slum-house that was built in one night."
[3] Ibid., iii.
[4] Ibid., 9–10.

Poor and the King of the Streets

The history of cinema in Turkey includes many films that dealt with class differences and the kinds of exclusions referred to above. These include many love story plots and family romances that used class difference as a mechanism in melodramatic plot lines,[5] but also social realist films that revealed the circumstances of the poorer classes as well as how migration from the village to the city leads to social and cultural dichotomies.[6] The migrants are portrayed as characters with heavy accents, mostly with a lower economic status, who could lose their chance of surviving or succeeding in the city at any time if they cannot adapt to the urban mentality.

The King of the Street Cleaners is a film from the Yeşilçam era,[7] a time when many melodramatic films were produced that reflected cultural clashes in Turkish society. There were also comedies and family romances that ridiculed or played down class difference by emphasizing the emotional bonds in extended families who fought against poverty with a feeling of togetherness, in a sense of 'one for all or all for one.' The Yeşilçam Film industry was a star-based cinema, and the protagonist of *The King of the Street Cleaners*, Abdi, is played by a very popular actor in Turkey, Kemal Sunal. He was a star who mostly played poor, funny, and migrant characters, and Perin Gürel refers to the character Sunal embodied as the "wise fool," a simple, uneducated, but lovable countryman. "Like Charlie Chaplin in his late films, Sunal carries a well-established, downtrodden, simple bumpkin to a left-wing political conclusion."[8] Savas Arslan states that

> Sunal's characters search for a true path, purity, friendship, and love . . . Furthermore, Sunal's comedies also rehash Yeşilçam's melodramatic conflicts between good and evil, rich and poor, and rural and urban and augment the virtuous common man's morality and innocence, despite the clumsy, foulmouthed, and disorderly aspects of Sunal's characters.[9]

---

5 Other film examples are *Fakir Gencin Romanı* (*The Story of a Poor Young Man*, Nuri Ergün, 1965), *Seninle Ölmek Istiyorum* (*I Want to Die with You*, Lütfi Akad, 1969), *Bizim Aile* (*Our Family*, Ergin Orbey, 1975), *Aile Şerefi* (*Family Honor*, Orhan Aksoy, 1976) or *Kırık Bir Aşk Hikayesi* (*A Broken Love Story*, Ömer Kavur, 1981).
6 *Umut* (*The Hope*, Yilmaz Güney, 1970), *Zavallılar* (*The Poor Ones*, Yilmaz Guney and Atif Yilmaz, 1976), *Yusuf ile Kenan* (*Yusuf and Kenan*, Ömer Kavur, 1979), *Züğürt Ağa* (*The Broken Landlord*, Yavuz Turgul, 1985).
7 Yesilcam refers to the film industry in Turkey between the 1950s and early 1980s.
8 Perin Gürel, "America the Oppressively Funny: Humor and Anti-Americanisms in Modern Turkish Cinema," in *Humor in Middle Eastern Cinema*, ed. Gayatri Devi and Najat Rahman (Detroit, MI: Wayne State University Press, 2014), 191.
9 Savas Arslan, *Cinema in Turkey: A New Critical History* (New York/Oxford: Oxford University Press, 2011), 217–218.

Yeşilçam cinema typically utilizes dramatic love stories between the poor and the rich, and this class difference defines the major dramatic tension in the films. In Kemal Sunal's films there is always a love story plot, but there is never a heavy emotional side to it. This is due to the element of humor, but also because his characters are mostly immune to the disappointments of love stories, since their main motivation is merely to survive amid economic hardships. The social and political circumstances are always present, as they influence the economy, job market, and demand on the labor market.

Abdi lives and works in the heart of Istanbul as a street cleaner. From his accent it is easy to understand that he is a migrant, like many of the shop owners in his neighborhood. He sweeps the streets while also collecting information about the residents. At the same time, he picks up old shoes or household items from the street to sell to the junk dealers and recycling workers. He also keeps track of the shop owners and other service providers and is well informed about what people generally do, when and where they go every day, what they want, or what they dislike. He has close ties with the grocery store, and he sleeps at the *kahvehane*, the coffeehouse, where mostly unemployed men hang out during the day.

In the first twelve minutes, the film does not show any interior space, and the camera is mostly outside on the streets, just like the street cleaner Abdi. In this way, it gives us insights about the people around him, as well as about the impact of the political context on the people's lives. The camera situated on the street shows that people are waiting in bread, gas, and water lines due to the shortage of goods on the market. There are many street vendors as well, bringing the goods to their customers' doorsteps. The economic conditions are severe, yet life on the street reveals a neighborhood that enjoys close ties among both the residents and the shop owners. Abdi functions as a link between them all, since through his labor of fetching goods from the *bakkal* (store) and the butcher, he ties the shop owners to the residents and vice versa. Due to his constant and active position on the street he has information about everyone.

And Abdi uses his position on the street to impress his love, the cleaning lady Hacer, in as much as he tries to cut the lines for bread and gas and shows how he can do anything he wants in his neighborhood. He does not possess any material wealth to make an impression, but he has the neighborhood in the palm of his hand. Yet this does not impress Hacer, as all of her brothers are street vendors and they had to create their own work on the street despite the risk of getting caught by the city police. They are still in the process of finding their way in this big city, as they recently migrated to Istanbul. In this sense, they are trying to make up for leaving their hometown by earning quick and easy money as soon as they can. Due to this precarious state, Hacer's father wants his daughter to marry someone more prosperous than Abdi, someone who has a stable job, like the city police officer Şakir. Hacer never takes Abdi seriously as he cannot provide for her desires. Eventually, as a street worker *flaneur,* Abdi moves on to fall for another cleaning lady right after Hacer marries Şakir. Seeing another domestic worker cleaning the windows on his street, he starts singing while sweeping the streets for this new lady, revealing how his unfulfilled love story has not left any lasting trace on him and how he can quickly move on.

Poor, Naked, and Nuts: Becoming Visible Through Nudity

Moving on from *The King of Street Cleaners* from 1977 I will now turn to *Naked Citizen* from 1985. The early 1980s were a time when the economy in Turkey tried to decrease inflation rates amidst a post-coup economic crisis, as well as adapt itself to global capitalism. The film opens with a shot showing Ibrahim running naked on the street at night. He is running down the road along with the cars, barefoot, and the people around are staring at him while a vivid soundtrack accompanies this scene and the film's titles. Cut to the office of a newspaper where the boss is yelling at his workers that they need to find a catchy story to increase sales and advertisements because the numbers are so low and the paper will soon go bankrupt. Afterwards, the photographer comes excitedly in and shows the boss his new shots, mainly the negatives of this man running naked on the streets. The boss enthusiastically instructs his team to find this person and his story.

The film tells the naked citizen's story through documentary style interviews conducted with his wife, his friends, and his colleagues. The jumps in time and points of view build up an image of Ibrahim told by his friends and colleagues, all of whom create a consistent image of a worker who is obedient to his managers, respectful to his colleagues, always smiling and contented. He is an example of a low-income citizen who keeps being thankful for what he earns and never questions whether he should be paid better. We also learn that he has four children and that his wife is pregnant, again. All his children are craving for more, they always want things like new shoes or a new dress for a school ceremony. When he understands that his income is not enough to meet the needs of his family, he takes on side jobs in a Chaplinesque, clumsy way.

He starts working as a street vendor in the evenings and on weekends and also as a dishwasher on some days. He sells lemons and milk on the streets after work. Furthermore, he sells clothes on the ferries, or paper hats and flags during football matches. While doing all these side jobs, he risks getting caught by the city police many times. In total, he ends up working at eight different jobs, and still cannot meet the needs of his family. The fragmented points of view in the film's narration emphasize his multiple and fragmented ways of earning money as well. Yet despite all his efforts he loses his apartment when he cannot pay the rent and he moves into the apartment of one of his friends. Then begins to lose his mind, starts mixing up the various jobs he works at, utters words that do not fit his multiple jobs, and in the end, goes out naked on the streets, running relentlessly in the night, which takes us back to the beginning of the film.

As film scholars Sevcan Sönmez and Deniz Bilge indicate, Ibrahim is willing to try every option, but would never consider burglary or fraud, nor any other indecent or corrupt way of earning money. Also, he does not show any signs of revolt against his living conditions or the government, he never questions why the prices keep rising, why his children are so demanding, etc.[10] He is a selfless and naive person without any political consciousness, and he tries all the ways of earning money that he sees around or hears from his friends. His poverty and his never-ending struggles only become visible through his nudity as an external sign of his material incapacity (Fig. 1). Being stripped of the means to meet his primary needs, he goes physically naked as well, and hits the bottom that he had been trying hard to avoid.

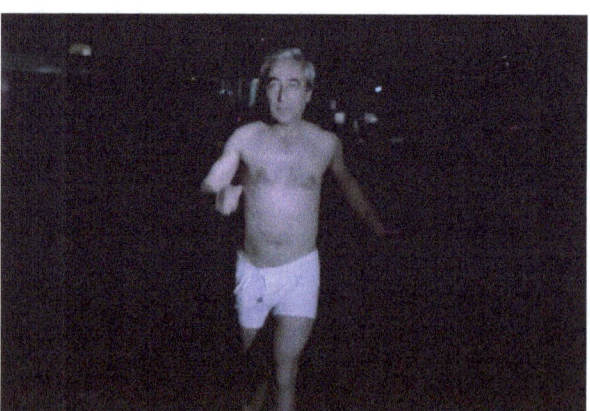

Fig. 1: Çıplak Vatandaş (Naked Citizen, Başar Sabuncu, 1985).

---

10 Sevcan Sönmez and Deniz Bilge, "Türkiye Sinemasında Aklın Sınırlarını Belirlemek: Çıplak Vatandaş ve Gişe Memuru Filmlerinde Delilik Temsilleri," *Ileti-s-im*, no. 20 (June 2014): 41–42.

For the journalists, Ibrahim's madness and its nudist consequences make a juicy story that can be manipulated and attracts public attention, as well as advertisers, to their newspaper. Made into a public hero for his supposed bravery, he becomes a celebrity and earns more than he could ever do as a state official. From the low point where he lost his apartment and moved into his neighbor's home, he ends up earning so much that he rents a new, comfortable apartment, buys a new car, as well as whatever his children and wife want. But when other people from his class see that nudity brings prosperity, everyone starts going onto the streets naked, and this turns into a social movement. Then, when his news value and advertisement value are lost or become a threat to the system, he is caught and sent back to the mental hospital. With the cycle of closeness and distance between the film's narrative and the mainstream media's narrative, the film points out the shifting sides the media take by heroizing and later abandoning the Naked Citizen.

These two films reveal two different types of precarity that evolved during the 1970s and 1980s in Turkey. There had been no consistency in the economy or in political institutions as the country went through the harsh political climates of the coups d'état in 1971 and 1980. In both films, severe economic circumstances are lightened by tragicomical narratives that transform hardships into humorous and tragic cinematic forms. However, while Abdi is a migrant character, *Naked Citizen* does not provide us any insight into Ibrahim's origins, but given that he is a state employee his precarity is different from Abdi's. Abdi's precarious condition is motivated by his migrant identity, in as much as he does not have a heritage in Istanbul, all he has is his labor, and it is being threatened by his boss. Ibrahim's precarious condition, however, is motivated by not being able to meet the needs of his family and the purchasing power of the post-coup d'état government and economy, and not being shrewd or cunning enough to move up at all.

Is It the City that Changes, or the People?: *Saf*

From the 1980s I will now move on to the 2010s to reveal how this romantic neighborhood atmosphere energized with humor has drastically changed due to gentrification processes that led to different visual aesthetics of the city. While the political instability caused by multiple coups d'état influenced the economy and motivated migration to Istanbul from Kurdistan and Anatolia before the 2000s, during the 2010s the Erdogan regime aimed mainly at expanding construction projects all over Turkey and Istanbul. Concurrently, there have been increasing flows of migration to Istanbul not just from inside Turkey but from many countries including Armenia, Georgia, Turkmenistan, Uzbekistan, Ukraine, Moldova, and Syria.

Furthermore, neighborhood solidarity has shifted either into a much more self-centered network of relationships or into a more political and organized one to win back what was lost during gentrification. In these thirty years, the increasingly fast-changing city reached a point where immigrants find work mostly in domestic labor and care services, textiles and clothing, and the construction industry.[11] Tragicomic narratives are no longer an adequate way to depict the circulation of documented or undocumented migrants in the labor market now that xenophobic and racist attitudes and behaviors represent the major source of conflicts between Turkish employers and workers, and migrants and refugees. Thus, during the last decade films started to reveal the living conditions of such workers in highly critical and social realist rather than humorous narratives.

To illustrate these points and the findings of the poverty and social exclusion report, I will start with Ali Vatansever's film *Saf* (Turkish for *naïve* or *pure*). The film reflects the changing conditions in Istanbul, focusing on a small *gecekondu* neighborhood in Fikirtepe that faces huge gentrification projects. The people construct small houses for themselves that lack proper infrastructure and are in poor condition. However, most of them have a garden, which you can hardly find in apartment life. The protagonists Kamil and his wife Remziye live in such a house, which is endangered by gentrification.

Çağlar Keyder notes that "Istanbul regularly scores at the top of lists of third world metropolises in terms of the proportion of 'illegal' housing. Exact figures vary depending on the count but usually exceed 50 percent."[12] In this sense, once at the periphery, locations like Fikirtepe served as cheap accommodation options for immigrants. The state ignored these *gecekondu* housings as they seemed to provide a solution for the problem of accommodation for immigrants. It even provided temporary registration for those houses so that they could gain access to water and electricity. However, those areas became valuable when the centers of Istanbul grew and spread, so that the peripheries of the city have also been gentrified. The land those *gecekondu* buildings were on was taken away from their residents by the municipality and the state. Still, the

---

[11] Gülay Toksöz, Seyhan Erdoğdu, and Selim Kaşka, *Irregular labour migration in Turkey and situation of migrant workers in the labour market* (Ankara: International Organization for Migration, 2012), 83–85.

[12] Çağlar Keyder, "The housing market from informal to global," in *Istanbul: Between the global and the local*, ed. Çağlar Keyder (Lanham, MD: Rowman & Littlefield, 1999), 143.

conflict between the contractors and the *gecekondu* owners is just one side of the conflict in *Saf*.

The film starts with a shot showing a group of men waiting in a line. A huge construction zone is in the background and the sound of construction equipment accompanies the scene. A worker wearing a helmet and work clothes asks everyone in the line for their name. When he comes to the one standing in front of Kamil, the worker notices that he is Syrian, not Turkish. At that moment he attacks him and blames him for taking the jobs of the Turkish people. He claims that Syrian workers agree to work for lower wages to the disadvantage of Turkish workers. Kamil intervenes and tries to break up the fight. Afterwards, Kamil is blamed for protecting the Syrian worker and he decides to leave the site without taking the job. At that point the camera starts following Kamil and we get into his perspective.

Not giving up on his ethical values, Kamil decides not to apply for certain masonry jobs at the construction projects in Fikirtepe, because the same construction projects have taken away his friends' houses. He refuses to work for such firms, or those that discriminate between Turkish and Syrian workers. Yet he soon finds himself in a position where these values prevent him from finding a job; he is portrayed as selfless to the point of stupidity. The film then opens up various ethical junctures where Kamil is forced to make compromises. The first step is when he decides to work for the construction firm that causes gentrification, after all. Now that Remziye thinks that he succeeded in getting the job, she starts planning ahead, as she wants to get pregnant as soon as she can leave her cleaning worker position. That is when Kamil really finds work. Abandoning his ethical values for this reason, he walks into the construction zone secretly and looks for the person responsible for recruiting workers. He finds out that there is a job available during the night shift, but only the position of the digger operator, which means that he has to apply for a digger license in order to get the work. In addition to this, the digger operator Ammar is a Syrian worker who got injured during work. He can only have Ammar's job if he agrees to work for the same low wage.

He has no choice but to accept, but due to this, Kamil is excluded from the group of Turkish workers at the construction site. He is at the same time bullied by Ammar. In addition, he needs to find the money to apply for the digger license, and he asks for a loan from his close friend Fatih, who just sold his *gecekondu* to a construction company. When Fatih refuses and his boss tells Kamil to get the license immediately, he finds himself under huge pressure between the obligation to find money to keep the work and the fear of facing Ammar. Worse still, while looking for objects to sell in his house he finds out that Remziye is secretly saving money and not sharing it with him although he drastically needs it. It is primarily this falling-out between Kamil and Remziye that corners both characters (Fig. 2).

Fig. 2: Saf (Ali Vatansever, 2018).

Thus, *Saf* reveals how the precarious positions of Remziye and Kamil push them apart unknowingly, how they start keeping secrets from each other. Kamil is under huge stress because of the double risk of losing their house to gentrification projects and of losing the job he just found if he cannot get the digger license. Learning that Remziye keeps some money for herself, Kamil loses what he had thought was the secure basis of his life. Already heavy-hearted about taking Ammar's job and under all this pressure, during a fight with Ammar he falls from the building under construction and dies.

The precarious position of the protagonist influences the chain of events as well as the spectator's experience of the film. With the main character's unexpected death, we are suddenly left feeling groundless, and we are now given Remziye's perspective. The change Remziye goes through after Kamil dies is the reverse of his. She was always blaming Kamil for being naive and acting like a fool, since he always put the rights of the others before himself. Kamil had rejected the mentality of finding work at all costs, but then could find no other way to fulfill Remziye's desires. Changing in the opposite direction, Remziye gradually becomes a more moral character while trying to find out how he died. In the house where she works as a cleaner, a Moldavian woman is also working as a babysitter while missing her own child whom she had to leave behind in Moldavia. In the beginning, Remziye was thinking about getting the Moldavian babysitter's position by informing the police about her illegal immigration status, thinking that childcare would be easier than cleaning, and that she could even do it while pregnant. But in the end, when she finds the key to the locked drawer where the boss and the mother of the house keep the Moldavian woman's passport, she gives the key to her, helping her to be able to go back and be with her daughter. Freeing the Moldovian domestic worker from the agency she works for, Remziye also begins to think about other people around her. With Kamil's death, his loss motivates her to internalize his motives, she transforms herself to come closer to Kamil's ethical values and reaches out to him in that way.

At the beginning of the film, neither Kamil nor Remziye had any class consciousness. Kamil only once attends a meeting in the coffeehouse where *gecekondu* residents get together to convince others not to sell their houses. But he stops going there when he starts working *for* the construction firm. The film ends with Remziye going to one of those meetings. Hence the film also criticizes being cut off from these networks or civil society organizations. Remziye attends the meetings because her *gecekondu* also risks being gentrified, and her house embodies the time, effort, and labor she shared with Kamil. It is the only thing that is left after Kamil died, and she does not want it to be taken away from her.

The Body of the Construction Worker: *My Father's Wings*

While *Saf* revolves around a plot of finding and keeping a construction site job, *My Father's Wings* by Kıvanç Sezer is about the lives of a group of construction workers in Beylikdüzü Istanbul. The film opens in a doctor's room where the physician tells the main character, Ibrahim, that he has come too late and that his coughs are due to a tumor in his lungs. He has cancer. He cannot have an operation at this stage, but should stop working and start chemotherapy immediately. Ibrahim is shocked by this news, but he has no chance to stop working as his family in Van in northern Kurdistan/eastern Turkey lives in temporary housing after the Van earthquake.[13] They applied for an apartment from the Ministry of Housing, but to get that new apartment, he will need to pay a monthly amount for the next twenty years. His income from the construction work and later on from his pension are the only means for his family in Van to get and keep the housing after the earthquake and to move from living in a temporary container into a proper apartment.

---

13 The 2011 Van earthquakes occurred in eastern Turkey around the city of Van. At least 11,232 buildings were damaged and 6,017 of them were found to be uninhabitable.

The film revolves around one main setting, which is the construction site. The construction company does not pay the workers properly. Their food is bad, and they have to work with too few workers and without any safety measures. When a group of workers try to get organized, to protest and demand their rights, they lose their jobs the next day. With many unemployed, any kind of revolt or asking for more is punished by being fired. Worse still, a young worker falls off the building and dies, and *blood money* is paid to his family, so that they will not file a court case. In this way, their legal rights are purchased. After experiencing the death of the young worker and its aftermath, Ibrahim thinks that he could throw himself from the construction site and thus make his death into a way for his family to get the money they need for their housing and future. While he is under this extreme stress to find a solution for his family's future, his young nephew Yusuf thinks that Ibrahim is not skillful and clever enough as a worker, since despite working at construction for over thirty years, he was unable to work his way up to a better position. He did not become a contractor, for instance, but has merely been working under them for his whole life.

Yet after Ibrahim dies, young Yusuf learns that the system is so corrupt that Ibrahim had decided to do whatever he could to stay ethically untainted and to avoid being corrupted by the system. If he had chosen to become a contractor, he would have had to lie to the workers, give them false hopes, hush up work crimes and erase them from the worklogs, and become part of the system. He did not become a contractor, he did not give up on his honesty and labor ethics or cause the death or injury of any worker just to keep the work going as fast as possible. Instead, he chose to instrumentalize his fatal illness so that his family would receive some money after his death. That is how he is affected by this system—by taking advantage of it, the money would be the *wings* that would take his family out the container to a new earthquake-resistant apartment. Yet after his death, his wife Hatice does not sign the contract to receive the blood money, which would also entail that she could not sue the firm about Ibrahim's death. The ending is left open: we do not know whether Hatice sues the company or not.

Kıvanç Sezer, the director, notes that he wanted to make this film to reveal that at least three workers die every day in Turkey, the workers are mostly reduced to a nonentity, and only individual salvation seems possible.[14] In this sense, by showing how construction work functions by abusing workers' rights, how buildings are constructed costing the lives of the workers, *My Father's Wings* reflects a city that is getting bigger and higher at the cost of paying blood money for work crimes.

---

14 Kıvanç Sezer, "İlk Film, İlk Yolculuk . . .," *SineFilozofi* 2, no. 3 (June 2017): 174–176.

Never-Ending Domestic Labor: *Dust Cloth*

I will conclude with Ahu Öztürk's *Dust Cloth*, a film about two Kurdish domestic workers[15] coming from the city Kars: Hatun and Nesrin. Hatun is married and has a son going to high school; her husband works at the neighborhood *kahvehane*. Nesrin and her daughter Asmine live together; after a fight between Nesrin and her husband (Cefo), whom we never actually see in the film, Nesrin is the sole bread winner. Working at a couple of houses as a cleaner, it becomes extremely hard for her to pay the rent and the bills.

Their linkage is again through space, they live in the same *gecekondu* apartment building, and although their family backgrounds are different, Hatun and Nesrin depend on each other to keep on working (Fig. 3). Working undocumented and without any job security, they are dependent on having good relations with the owners of the apartments they clean. Thus, they constantly support and motivate each other, and while they share their stories, the details of the houses they clean, they relax and find energy to go on. Nesrin cries over Cefo's absence, whereas Hatun complains about her husband Sero's laziness. Thus, while Nesrin is trying to find her missing husband, Hatun's husband Sero is non-functional and no help to her when he comes home. Hatun and Nesrin not only have to clean the houses they work in, but their work goes on at home, as well. Hatun keeps reminding Sero of the dripping tap he has to fix. Although he says he will, he never actually does so, and in the end, Hatun fixes the tap herself with the help of her son. Hence both Nesrin and Hatun are dealing with two precarious institutions: Their domestic work that could end at any time, as well as the—effective or real—absence of their husbands, on whom they feel dependent.

The film also reveals two different neighborhoods, the posh districts where they work and the poor infrastructure where they live. Nesrin and Hatun's neighborhood has steep hills, mostly composed of *gecekondu* houses. Their neighborhood is more socially interactive—the tenants wash their carpets on the street together, sweep the streets, and the neighbors all know each other—than the districts where they work. Gizem Çınar states that coming from the peripheries of the city and reaching the center where they work, the film positions Hatun and Nesrin "at the outskirts of life. Being pushed to the outskirts of the city would mean being pushed to the outskirts of life itself."[16] In this sense,

---

15 Other examples for cinematic depictions of female workers are *Zerre* (Erdem Tepegöz, 2012), *Nefesim Kesilene Kadar* (*Until I Lose My Breath*, Emine Emel Balcı, 2015) and *Kor* (*Ember*, Zeki Demirkubuz, 2016).
16 Gizem Çınar, "Çözümleme: Toz Bezi," *Sekans: Sinema Kültür Dergisi*, no. 9 (December 2018): 25–26.

Fig. 3: Toz Bezi (Dust Cloth, Ahu Öztürk, 2015).

while they live at the edge of the city, their social relations function though a kind of closeness like in rural districts. The film shows two highly contrasting neighborhoods and also reflects the class difference between the domestic workers and the residents and owners of the apartments they clean. Lacking any social and political consciousness and completely unaware of the living conditions of the precarious working class, the employers and apartment owners merely aim at getting the most from their labor, without ever thinking of providing social security.

Yet Hatun and Nesrin have different desires. Hatun dreams of owning an apartment in Moda, a trendy neighborhood close to the sea, where most of the houses she cleans are located. She keeps buying lottery tickets and prays in churches in Moda to own an apartment in that neighborhood. Thus, the houses she cleans make her want the kind of life found in that neighborhood. In Nesrin's case, one of the house owners suggests that she should find a job with social security and insurance. Taking this as a goal, she applies to the Worker Placement Agency, but only having elementary schooling, she lacks qualifications for the jobs offered there. She would first need to finish high school, but does not have time for that, constantly having to struggle to pay the rent and electricity bills. In the end her apartment's electricity is cut off and she loses hope of Cefo returning home, as well as of earning enough money for herself and her daughter. With another breadwinner in her home, Hatun's position seems more solid than Nesrin's. Exhausted from all her efforts, Nesrin loses all hope and when she understands that she is not able to cope alone, she leaves her daughter Asmina to Hatun and drifts away into the city, just like her husband had.

Conclusion

The films I have discussed show characters who are exploited physically, culturally, and emotionally. They are not only overburdened but excluded as well. Abdi and the naked citizen Ibrahim are both economically excluded because Abdi does not qualify for a prosperous marriage due to his low-level job and the food Ibrahim brings home is just enough for his children. Similarly, Kamil in *Saf* wears a borrowed jacket when he applies for construction work, trying to hide his economic exclusion. The construction worker Ibrahim does not have the time and money to take care of his illness; thus, he ignores his cancer and finds a way to instrumentalize it. Nesrin is in dire need of a steady income to be able to pay her rent and bills without her husband's income.

All these characters are spatially excluded as well. Abdi sleeps at the *kahvehane* and he can never enter the apartments on the street he cleans. Ibrahim loses his apartment when he cannot pay the constantly increasing rent. Nesrin and Hatun live in a *gecekondu* neighborhood far from the posh district where they go for cleaning work. Kamil and Remziye risk losing their *gecekondu* as gentrification projects have reached their community as well. The construction workers in *My Father's Wings* will never have a possibility of living in the apartments they construct.

All are also culturally and politically excluded. *Saf* reveals the exclusion of Syrians even from *gecekondu* neighborhoods and shows how they have no choice but to work for lower wages or how they are barred from working due to their national identity. Similarly, Hatun tries to conceal her Kurdish identity. When she is asked if she is Circassian, she replies yes, and later she tries to convince herself that maybe she could indeed be Circassian. The construction workers who decide to protest against severe working conditions will lose their jobs at the end in *My Father's Wings*.

These films also reveal characters who wanted to stay *saf*, not to get corrupted and contaminated by the harsh system they are in, like Kamil and the construction worker Ibrahim. These films never raise the possibility that these protagonists could evolve and develop into characters who could naturally adopt the culture and mentality of city life without becoming corrupted. On the contrary, they are pushed away and excluded in the many ways referred to above. So, they have no choice but to either continue being naive or to end up corrupt and part of the system. What keeps them all going is the impossibility of giving up, because they cannot exist if they stop working. They only have their labor power to depend on and nothing else. The risk of losing everything anytime influences their fate as well. We witness the loss of Kamil in *Saf*, and Ibrahim in *My Father's Wings*, and Nesrin's disappearance in *Dust Cloth*.

These films also depict the settings where all different *assemblages* of precarious work take place. The streets of 1970s and 1980s Istanbul reveal how it all started in a fast-changing city, and through the continuous visual presence of the never-ending construction work, the more recent films expose how massive construction projects have engulfed the city. The presence of the metropolis, Istanbul, and its changing forms are as crucial as the presence of the main characters. Their mutual and simultaneous deformation ties the space and the people together and discloses the intrinsic relationship between where they live and who they become in time.

Bibliography

Adaman, Fikret, and Çağlar Keyder. "Türkiye'de büyük kentlerin *gecekondu* ve çöküntü mahallelerinde yaşanan yoksulluk ve sosyal dışlanma." 2006. ec.europa.eu/employment_social/social_inclusion/docs/2006/study_turkey_tr.pdf.
Arslan, Savas. *Cinema in Turkey: A New Critical History*. New York/Oxford: Oxford University Press, 2011.
Cinar, Gizem. "Cözümleme: Toz Bezi." *Sekans: Sinema Kültür Dergisi*, no. 9 (December 2018): 22–30. http://sekans.org/tr/arsiv/e-sayilar/260-aralik-2018-sayi-e9.
Gürel, Perin. "America the Oppressively Funny: Humor and Anti-Americanisms in Modern Turkish Cinema." In *Humor in Middle Eastern Cinema*, ed. Gayatri Devi and Najat Rahman. Detroit, MI: Wayne State University Press, 2014, 188–213.
Keyder, Çağlar. "The housing market from informal to global." In *Istanbul: Between the Global and the Local*, ed. Çağlar Keyder. Lanham, MD: Rowman & Littlefield, 1999, 143–159.
Sezer, Kıvanç. "İlk Film, İlk Yolculuk . . ." *SineFilozofi* 2, no. 3 (June 2017): 174–176.
Sönmez, Sevcan, and Deniz Bilge. "Türkiye Sinemasında Aklın Sınırlarını Belirlemek: Çıplak Vatandaş ve Gişe Memuru Filmlerinde Delilik Temsilleri." *Ileti-s-im*, no. 20 (June 2014): 33–51.
Toksöz, Gülay, Seyhan Erdoğdu, and Selim Kaşka. *Irregular labour migration in Turkey and situation of migrant workers in the labour market*. Ankara: International Organization for Migration, 2012.

Filmography

Aile Şerefi (Family Honor). Dir. Orhan Aksoy. Turkey, 1976.
Babamın Kanatları (My Father's Wings). Dir. Kıvanç Sezer. Turkey, 2016.
Bizim Aile (Our Family). Dir. Ergin Orbey. Turkey, 1975.
Çıplak Vatandaş (Naked Citizen). Dir. Başar Sabuncu. Turkey, 1985.
Çöpçüler Kralı (The King of the Street Cleaners). Dir. Zeki Ökten. Turkey, 1977.
Fakir Gencin Romanı (The Story of a Poor Young Man). Dir. Nuri Ergün. Turkey, 1965.

Kırık Bir Aşk Hikayesi (*A Broken Love Story*). Dir. Ömer Kavur. Turkey, 1981.
Kor (*Ember*). Dir. Zeki Demirkubuz. Turkey, 2016.
Nefesim Kesilene Kadar (*Until I Lose My Breath*). Dir. Emine Emel Balci. Turkey, 2015.
Saf. Dir. Ali Vatansever. Turkey, 2018.
Seninle Ölmek İstiyorum (*I Want to Die with You*). Dir. Lütfi Akad. Turkey, 1969.
Toz Bezi (*Dust Cloth*). Dir. Ahu Öztürk. Turkey, 2015.
Umut (*The Hope*). Dir. Yilmaz Güney. Turkey, 1970.
Yusuf ile Kenan (*Yusuf and Kenan*). Dir. Ömer Kavur. Turkey, 1979.
Zavallılar (*The Poor Ones*). Dir. Yilmaz Guney and Atif Yilmaz. Turkey, 1976.
Zerre (*The Particle*). Dir. Erdem Tepegöz. Turkey, 2012.
Züğürt Ağa (*The Broken Landlord*). Dir. Yavuz Turgul. Turkey, 1985.

Christian Ferencz-Flatz
Film as Social Visibility
Two Forms of Precarity in Romanian (and Bulgarian) Cinema

One cannot properly assess discourses on social misery in recent Eastern European cinema without first taking note of the fact that filmic depictions of them are disproportionately scarce compared to the extent of the phenomenon itself. Keeping in mind that countries like Romania and Bulgaria constantly topped European statistics on poverty risk throughout the past two decades, it is striking how few of the local films directly tackle social issues as their central concern. At least in regard to Romania, this certainly applies to the earlier cinematic productions of the communist period, as well as to the hazy decade of transition and the more recent post-transition period, both for fiction films and documentaries.

Under the circumstances of the communist regime, this is easily understandable, since its official status as a "classless society" did not allow for societal discrepancies to be acknowledged openly. Consequently, these issues only came to view in contorted ways, for instance in an allegoric guise meant to bypass censorship. It suffices to think of a Romanian film like *O lacrimă de fată* (*A Maiden Tear*, Iosif Demian, 1980), which courageously delves into an almost overt criticism of the disastrous consequences of the planned economy in communist agriculture, while ultimately still prudently laying the blame on the feudal heritage. Documentaries of the period, which were in principle expected to keep track of the living conditions of the working class, were perhaps even less free in their choice of subject matters, since their mandatory commitment to reflect the triumphant construction of socialism only left room for criticism of those who resisted it.[1]

Interestingly, however, this lack of engagement with concrete social issues went on throughout the 1990s, when documentary filmmakers saw it as their main task to make up for the lost time by amply reflecting on the hardships of the communist period, while completely neglecting dramatic contemporary upheavals like the collapse of the industrial system, shady privatizations, or even social unrest leading to the brink of civil war. At the same time, fiction films achieved at best mere caricatures or grotesque extrapolations of societal

---

[1] Thus, several Romanian documentaries of the time took interest in bohemian youngsters, who were officially branded as social parasites; see, for instance, *Iarna unor pierde-vară* (*The Winter of Some Good-for-Nothings*, Iancu Moscu, 1974).

problems.[2] Moreover, the immediate post-transition period, which followed the European integration, did not fare decisively better, since the most important films of the period have widely favored more universal, moral, and existential conflicts over the direct representation of social conditions. Consequently, critics from the Left often accused contemporary Romanian cinema of catering exclusively to the ailments of the middle class, while taking note of poverty only as an object for the moral tribulations of the well-off.[3] It suffices to think of films like *Poziția copilului* (*The Child's Pose*, Călin Peter Netzer, 2013) or *Fixeur* (Adrian Sitaru, 2016), in which a poor child victim of a car accident (respectively an adolescent girl from the countryside forced into sex traffic) offers a mere pretext for elaborate ethical contortions of the middle class family (respectively the Bucharest journalist).

There are no doubt various possible explanations for this, ranging from the undisputed predominance of anti-communist, conservative discourses within the mainstream intellectual scene in Romania to the dominant *cinéma vérité* ethos in recent local cinema, driving middle class directors to prefer depicting life circumstances they are personally acquainted with rather than broader social questions deemed as abstract. Be that as it may, however, it is important to stress that *there is* a deficit in cinematic representations of social issues in contemporary Romanian—and also, to a large extent, in Bulgarian—cinema. This helps one see, when sifting through the productions of the past fifteen years in this region, that even films which include overt social motifs as their main topic of interest often fail to take those motifs at face value, only using them as means for dramatic or symbolic purposes.

This is precisely why one could be tempted, when dealing with questions of poverty and precarity in Eastern European cinema, to shift the focus from the direct treatment of such issues to the question of how the films elude them, even when they seem to engage them explicitly. One good point in case, which clearly illustrates how social themes are often hijacked for entirely different purposes in these films, is their representation of dismal, low-status professions. To give two quick examples: the Romanian film *Filantropica* (Nae Caranfil, 2002) features a teacher who owes money to a local mobster; to pay his debt, he becomes a professional beggar for an organized beggar's syndicate led by a charming impresario,

---

[2] A first more thorough overview of the Romanian cinema of this period is now available in Romanian: Andrei Gorzo and Gabriela Filippi, eds., *Filmul tranziției. Contribuții la interpretarea cinemaului românesc "nouăzecist"* (Cluj-Napoca: Tact, 2017).

[3] See for instance Costi Rogozanu, "Muntean. Cronicarul României middle class," in *Politicile filmului. Contribuții la interpretarea cinemaului românesc contemporan*, ed. Andrei Gorzo and Andrei State (Cluj-Napoca: Tact, 2014).

who conceives all of the beggars' stories and writes their texts. The Bulgarian film *Bezbog* (*Godless*, Ralitsa Petrova, 2016) features a nurse in a remote and extremely desolate small town, working as a caretaker for elderly people; the extreme sordidness of her work is used as a sheer mood-setting device for a discussion of religious faith against the backdrop of unrealistically total moral corruption. What these films—and one could easily refer to many more similar examples—have in common, is that they show no interest in addressing miserable working conditions as a problem *per se*, but instead simply use them as a means for (often comic) exoticization. Similar techniques are at work in the treatment of numerous other motifs. It suffices to think about the cliché narrative of visitors from the West (or in a slightly different version: from the big city) arriving at some remote rural part of Romania or Bulgaria only to be shocked, amazed, or bemused by the striking signs of deprivation around—again a motif treated with no intention of tackling underdevelopment, inequalities, or the wretchedness of rural life *per se*, but only for facile gags or to add atmospheric bleakness to genre narratives.[4] The same is true for most depictions of institutional failure and corruption in the region, where for instance dire accounts of the health care system are not tackled per se, but only serve to carry some symbolic religious connotations. To be sure, an exhaustive inventory of such motifs would by far exceed the possibilities of the present chapter. However, while I will pursue an entirely different path in what follows, this short overview nonetheless proves useful for noting that, against the backdrop of a long unwillingness to engage questions of social criticism in film, the past few years have witnessed the emergence of a new social awareness in Eastern European cinema.

In what follows, I would like to illustrate this change with a special emphasis on Romanian cinema by first running through two particular topics, which are highly relevant for contemporary Eastern European societies and which are lately beginning to benefit from a growingly consistent cinematographic treatment, namely: *economic migration* and the social and economic *exclusion of the Roma*. No doubt, none of these issues directly involves the core notion of precarity, as it is used by contemporary theorists like Guy Standing or Arne Kalleberg to designate a widespread deterioration of employment conditions in Western societies following the gradual dismantling of the welfare state.[5] In this context the "precariat" came to designate a growing category of employees

---

4 See, for example, *Ryna* (Ruxandra Zenide, 2005) or *Câini* (*Dogs*, Bogdan Mirică, 2016).
5 See for this Guy Standing, *The Precariat: The New Dangerous Class* (London: Bloomsbury, 2011) and Arne Kalleberg, *Precarious Lives: Job Insecurity and Well-Being in Rich Democracies* (Medford, MA: Polity, 2018).

facing high job insecurity, with all its associated material and psychological implications. While neither economic migration from Eastern countries, nor issues of racial exclusion within them are directly triggered by those social and economic processes, be it only because post-communist countries never had a similar form of welfare state to begin with, one might nonetheless claim that they are not entirely unrelated to those developments either. On the one hand, guest workers from Eastern Europe have themselves essentially partaken in the aforementioned transformations of Western economies and societies. This is the case insofar as their already precarious condition within these societies now became all the more insecure with the growing neoliberal deregulation of the job market. Indeed, as various scandals during the current coronavirus crisis have amply shown, they are the most disposable, worst-paid, and most vulnerable category of precarious workers in Western societies. At the same time, immigrant workers were constantly demonized by far-right rhetoric, for instance during the recent Brexit campaign, as one of the main causes behind growing unemployment and job insecurity in Western societies, which further heightened their social distress. On the other hand, it may be true that Eastern European societies never shared anything like the Western model of the welfare state, but they nonetheless experienced an analogous decay of their social security services following the disintegration of the communist state system, and this situation is indeed at least partially to blame for the contemporary acute marginalization of the Roma and their growing social misery as well. Following these considerations, I will conclude with some regional generalizations and some theoretical reflections, which will further pursue these issues along the lines of Axel Honneth's concept of recognition and its possible application to film.

Economic Migration

The question of economic migration has no doubt been on the Romanian public agenda for over two decades. However, the magnitude of the phenomenon only clearly came to view in 2019, when a United Nations report, which circulated in the local press, ranked the country second to Syria in this regard in recent statistics.[6] Of course, it was no mystery that Romania faced a massive wave of migration

---

[6] A brief international account of this can be found here: Craig Turp-Balasz, "Romania's Demographic New Statistics Confirm Catastrophe," *Emerging Europe*, March 2, 2018, https://emerging-europe.com/news/new-statistics-confirm-romanias-demographic-catastrophe/.

and one certainly finds innumerable references to this demographic fact in Romanian films ever since the early 2000s. Cristian Mungiu's debut film, *Occident*, already tackled the issue as early as 2002. The film tells the story of a young couple forced by unemployment to consider resettling, but, for the time being, their sole option is having the girl marry a French citizen, since work permits abroad are still virtually unattainable. Similarly, Cristi Puiu's debut film as a screenwriter—*Niki Ardelean, colonel în rezervă* (*Niki and Flo*, Lucian Pintilie, 2003)—featured a young couple preparing to migrate to the USA with the "visa lottery" program, while the story focused on the relationships between their in-laws. In fact, once you start looking, references emerge literally everywhere: in *Moartea domnului Lăzărescu* (*The Death of Dante Lazarescu*, Cristi Puiu, 2005), the main protagonist's daughter migrated to Canada leaving the old widower with no relative in town, while in *Polițist, adjectiv* (*Police, Adjective*, Corneliu Porumboiu, 2009), the youngster under investigation had a brother who migrated to the Netherlands. Ultimately, one might even say there is hardly any character in the New Romanian Cinema who does not have at least some emigrant among their relatives or friends. However, if there is indeed an undeniable public awareness of the phenomenon ever since the early 2000s, the focus in the first depictions of this issue was never on the life and plight of the migrants proper. It is precisely in this regard that the last ten years seem to have made up leeway cinematographically.

Thus, one might argue, the disturbing association with Syria, a country devastated by war, perhaps only raised such discussions recently because it came at a point when the public had already begun to be more sensitized towards the distressful fate of Romanians living abroad. Their cinematic depictions are both a symptom of this new awareness and have contributed to it. To be sure, the comparison itself ultimately proved to be fake news, since Romania was never second to Syria in absolute figures as was suggested—it constantly lagged somewhere around position 17 (after Italy or Germany)—even if the growth rate for migration was indeed particularly high immediately after accession to the European Union in 2008 and even if the percentage of migrants is still quite high against the backdrop of the remaining population. However, what makes the issue particularly relevant in the present context is not its sheer size, but rather the migrants' intricate economic and social situation. The issue was not completely ignored in earlier cinematographic accounts either. At least implicitly it came to view in the ostensive treatment of sexual trafficking, which indeed closely relates to questions of work migration insofar as the local trafficking networks notoriously lured their victims, mostly vulnerable girls from rural areas, with the promise of decent workplaces abroad, only to then sequestrate them, leave them without papers, and force them into prostitution. Instead, if this is probably the darkest aspect of the entire complex social phenomenon of mass migration in Eastern Europe, its extensive cinematic and televisual dramatization ever since the 1990s largely overshadowed not only various other forms of abuse by local and international networks of intermediaries—reflected in numerous press accounts decrying the contemporary persistence of "slave labor" in various places in Europe[7]—but it also clouded the more subtle and far more widespread form of precarity that came with this particular blend of economic migration even in absence of such graphic abuse. This is the case primarily because, in contrast to say Germans, who most frequently migrate for career opportunities in neighboring states like Switzerland or Austria, Romanians most frequently migrated by abandoning their careers, often leaving behind their families. Moreover, they accepted poor living conditions and unattractive jobs[8] in the hope of someday returning with their savings, and it is precisely the destitution of this in-between, provisional state, that several contemporary films began addressing in Romania.

An early example is *Acasă* (*Home*, Paul Negoescu, 2006), a short film that focuses on a migrant worker returning to Bucharest to spend Christmas with his family. Depicting his cab ride home from the international bus station in real time, the film tries to follow his bits of conversation with the cab driver. As such, it certainly does not delve any deeper than the usual clichés about migrant workers, but it gains in interest retrospectively in that it evokes details pertaining to the local atmosphere just months before accession to the EU. The worker is returning from Spain, where he only has a renewable work permit for nine months. The cab driver is also planning to leave, he even submitted the papers, but the procedure is still lagging. In and of itself the case presented here is not particularly representative. The worker had been doing this on and off since the 1990s; he had prior contracts in Israel and Germany. Moreover, his wife is a partial invalid, so it would have been difficult for her to accompany him in his extensive work trips anyhow. He is the sole provider for the family

---

[7] For some recent accounts in this respect, see: Bogdan Neagu, "Bucharest – Seasonal workers complain about working conditions in Germany," *Euractiv*, April 22, 2020, https://www.euractiv.com/section/all/short_news/bucharest-seasonal-workers-complain-about-working-conditions-in-germany/1457669/; Iulia Badea Guéritée, "The Romanian 'slaves' behind the Sicilian tomatoes," *Voxeurope_English*, May 5, 2018, https://voxeurop.eu/en/the-romanian-slaves-behind-the-sicilian-tomatoes/; Ana Maria Dima, "The other side of Europe: the exploitation of Romanian workers in the EU," *Open Democracy*, May 18, 2017, https://www.opendemocracy.net/en/other-side-of-europe-exploitation-of-romanian-workers-in-eu/.

[8] In Romania, they are frequently referred to generically as "strawberry pickers" (*căpșunari*) precisely because many indeed started working as field laborers on farms despite being, for example, trained engineers.

and his children are conveniently already grown-ups with children of their own that he misses at times. In other words: everything in this scenario seems to fit perfectly, so that only his personal, individual burden and exhaustion comes to view. Most often, however, the situation of migrant workers has been far more contorted, and one begins to get a good glimpse at that in several more recent Romanian films, which specifically engage the issue of Romanian families separated by economic migration.

Aici . . . adică acolo (*Here . . . I mean there*, Laura Căpățână-Juller, 2012) is a documentary that follows a year in the life of two preadolescent girls from Northern Romania, whose parents are working in Spain. Their grandparents in the countryside raise them and they are constantly in touch with their parents on the phone or on skype, and visit each other extensively during vacations. To be sure, this is not simply a story about lack and deprivation, for the children have everything they need materially. In a way, it is perhaps even rather about the local dream of prosperity, though analyzing such fantasies could itself offer valuable clues for discussing local "discourses of precarity." The parents started building a house in the village and they keep working abroad for the money required to finish it. Whoever has visited villages in northern Romania, where a great part of the younger population migrated to Italy or Spain and one sees such houses under construction everywhere, knows how widespread this situation actually is. The drama results not from migration itself, but from the fact that, in many cases, migrants are economically constrained to work abroad at an age and under circumstances where simply starting a new life is no longer deemed possible. Therefore, many of them accept this only as a temporary solution, often leaving their children behind in order to save more by living in very poor conditions. However, these provisional situations nonetheless often tend to prolong indefinitely, which is precisely what happens here as well. The parents in the film first left eleven years ago when the children were still in nursery school and nobody knows when they will finally return, so that the children virtually grow up as orphans. While most of the time they are not particularly wrought up about this, they obviously miss their parents, and the film ends on a more pathetic note with a direct expression of their frustration.

A short feature film, *Granițe* (*Borders*, Andra Chiriac, 2017), delves a bit deeper into the psychological tensions that develop under these distressing circumstances. This time, the main focus is on the relationship between the two partners: the husband (Fig. 1) remained at home with the children, while the wife left for work as a cleaning lady in France. Now he comes over for a brief visit and they have a tense discussion about when she will finally return. At this point, however, it becomes pretty clear how deeply the woman has settled into her new life. She has befriended the local community of Romanians and gained some comfort and independence there, while this—rather than the ever-present house under construction, which seems to be brought up here only as a pretext—makes her reluctant to give up everything and return immediately, as the husband demands. Therefore, she postpones indefinitely and in the end, nothing changes, while the family keeps waiting in vain for her return.

Fig. 1: Granițe (Borders, Andra Chiriac, 2017).

Roma Exclusion

These are not things one normally has in mind when considering Romanian migrant workers. In fact, economic migrants are only seldom associated with precarity at all, since they are often better off than their peers at home, while their remittances have even been considered a key for sustaining the Romanian economy during the economic crisis.[9] This is not the case with the social and economic exclusion of the Roma, which indeed involves the most patent and extreme forms of destitution in contemporary Romania. Despite this notable difference, however, the two phenomena are similar in that both involve forms of social and economic distress which we normally tend to ignore and which were rarely reflected in the cinema before.

In the case of the Roma, this primarily relates to the question of systemic racism, which is still alarmingly present in contemporary Romanian society. While Romania has a national office for fighting and preventing discrimination in

---

9 These views were certainly shaken by the recent parliamentary elections in Romania, where the frustrations of the *diaspora* became palpable with their overwhelming vote for a new far right party (AUR).

accordance with EU norms and overtly racist speech is banned from mainstream media, the local press is nevertheless flooded with news of overtly racist administrative initiatives all over the country: the mayor of Târgu Mures recently proposed that Roma be denied the right to have children under certain conditions; in Cluj, a large part of the Roma population was relocated in the vicinity of the local waste dump; civic militias are patrolling busses and violently ejecting Roma in several towns in Transylvania, while a legislative project in the city council of Timișoara last year forbid playing Roma music in public.[10]

Romanian cinema was until recently remarkably reluctant to address the issue, particularly considering the sheer extent of this alarming phenomenon, which has deep historic roots.[11] A survey by a local film magazine on representations of Roma in Romanian cinema showed that, with the exception of several recent films, Roma were exclusively depicted either as exotic figures, in their remote and highly fictionalized traditional communities, living in tents and obeying their own laws, or as minor stereotypical characters in genre films, for instance pocket thieves, restaurant musicians, or police informers in the classic cop flicks made by Sergiu Nicolaescu.[12] Among other things, the dossier is interesting in that it picks up a statistic inquiry made with regard to the general perception of Roma among Romanian citizens, wherein the negative view shared by a vast majority of Romanians is usually justified not by reference to race *per se*, but to lack of education, hygiene, civilization, laziness, or high criminality rates. This is, of course, a well-known vicious circle in racist discourse, as it is ultimately prejudice that leads to a lack of access to education, just as the latter reinforces prejudice; similarly, unemployment leads to poverty and neglect of hygiene, which makes getting a job difficult, just like social marginalization leads to criminality, which then motivates marginalization, and so on. While these discussions may seem tedious, it is precisely in considering them that one can fully appreciate the merits of several recent Romanian films which began not only to engage with the living conditions of Roma in contemporary Romania more seriously, but also sought out ways to break the aforementioned vicious circle and thus assist their viewers to overcome prejudice.

---

10 The debate was about the so-called "manele": not the traditional Roma music, but its contemporary party versions, which are quite popular among youngsters. They are generally regarded by the cultural elite with a sort of contempt that involves some racist undertones.
11 It suffices to consider how thoroughly racial prejudice is sedimented linguistically in expressions like *a se țigăni* ("to act like a gipsy"), which is a verb in its own right with negative connotations. Racist jokes have a lengthy tradition and are still widely accepted among people who otherwise hold themselves free of prejudice.
12 Mihai Fulger, ed., "Cu romii la cinema," *Film*, no. 2 (2019).

Aferim! (Radu Jude, 2015), awarded the Silver Bear in Berlin, is probably the best known among the three films I will discuss. On first appearance, the film deals with present day social issues only indirectly, by taking a detour through the distant past: it tells the story of a local boyar's captain at the beginning of the nineteenth century pursuing a fugitive Roma slave, accused of raping his mistress. As it turns out, the rape was not really rape, but the captured Rom is nonetheless punished in the end with utmost cruelty by castration. Instead, this historic detour is highly relevant in at least three respects precisely when viewed in a contemporary, rather than in a historic perspective. First of all, the entire issue of Roma slavery in the region, which continued until the mid-nineteenth century, is completely ignored in contemporary views of national history, while the fierce resistance with which the film was met showed that evoking this neglected past hit a sensitive spot. Secondly, *Aferim!* also serves the purpose of putting contemporary debates about the exclusion of Roma in an enlightening perspective. Thus, for instance, the still widespread belief about the innate laziness of the Roma, proffered ostentatiously throughout the film, visibly communicates, against the backdrop of its historic setting, with the cinematically far more familiar discourses about the "innate laziness of the negro," which were frequently used during the eighteenth and nineteenth centuries as a justification for slavery and abuse. Thirdly, there is also another reason why the historic detour as such is particularly apt at vexing contemporary viewers. For it is fair to presume that the average Romanian viewers of the film are neither militant racists, nor minority rights activists. Instead, they are most probably in between, people who watch their language and are theoretically supportive of Roma inclusion, while they would nonetheless still, for instance, prefer their child not to have Roma classmates. Such viewers, however, would easily become morally outraged when seeing some local contemporary form of racism at work. Instead, when presented with the experience of a world wherein overt and extreme racism are the socially accepted norm, proffered openly, they may get some abashed sense of the large shadow still looming today over one's own more cushioned, polite, and hypocritical form of prejudice.

The documentary *Toto și surorile lui* (*Toto and His Sisters*, Alexander Nanau, 2014) was actually shot before *Aferim!*, but its reception benefited widely from the awareness raised by the latter. The film tells the story of a family of Roma in the Ferentari ghetto (Fig. 2). This is already remarkable *per se*, since even the inhabitants of Bucharest only seldom get a glimpse of that place, which is of course considered unsafe and rarely ever benefits from media reflections (aside from brief scenes of horror in the evening news). The film deals with three Roma children—two adolescent girls and an elementary school boy—who struggle to take care of themselves, while their single mother is waiting to be released from prison for drug-dealing.[13] As such, the film is noteworthy on the one hand for how it minutely and representatively tracks down the well-known vicious circle determining these people's fate: the older girl visits a local NGO to help her get a job, but she has no papers and they require signatures from her absent parents in order to be able to provide her with a job. She finally sees no other option than to take up selling (and using) drugs again, ultimately discovering she is HIV positive. The younger girl and Toto take refuge at an orphanage, where things seem to lighten up for a while. They feel sheltered and we follow them as they attend a school led by another charitable NGO while the boy finds alleviation in break dance classes. These episodes show that they lack elementary prerequisites (the girl has difficulties even reading a plain sentence), while we also see how their stressful life before hardly allowed them to attend school regularly. Finally, the mother is released from prison, and they return home. The gloomy atmosphere on the train back to Ferentari suggests that this is probably not the best outcome for the children.

Fig. 2: Toto și surorile lui (Toto and His Sisters, Alexander Nanau, 2014).

Aside from this careful and sensitive depiction of how the individual's fate is ultimately governed by structural deficiencies, however, I would argue that the film is perhaps even more significant in that it places the viewer in the position of empathizing with the real day-to-day misery of Roma life in the ghetto. This may not seem much *in abstracto*. It is however something that Romanian spectators seldom get the chance to do in the cinema or in real life, and this is certainly at

---

13 Ferentari is, of course, also the main drug scene in Bucharest and generally figures as the neighborhood with the highest crime rate in the city.

least part of what makes such issues almost impossible to address administratively and politically as well.

Ivana Mladenović's debut feature film *Soldații: Poveste din Ferentari* (*Soldiers: Story from Ferentari*, 2017), finally, is also set in the Ferentari ghetto, although it follows a different path in challenging social prejudice. The protagonist—interpreted by Adi Schiop, the writer of both the initial novel and its film adaptation—is an anthropologist, who moves to Ferentari to complete his PhD research on *manele* culture. It is worth mentioning that the novel is itself an autofiction and Adi Schiop, whose research into the social universe of manele was recently published,[14] is part of a larger wave of young social scientists currently investigating contemporary Roma culture as a way of challenging cultural prejudice. The film seems to mock this kind of research—there is a brief scene, when a fellow anthropologist from Germany arrives in the neighborhood and she is rudely rejected by the locals, who ridicule her interest—while the narrative soon takes a surprising turn when the protagonist becomes involved in a homoerotic relationship with Alberto, a massive Rom recently out of prison. This is anything but a love story. On the one hand, because neither of the two characters overtly defines himself as homosexual. Both seem to have been drawn into the affair as a mere substitute for heterosexual relationships. On the other hand, because their entire liaison is charged with social implications throughout. It is in fact a "social gesture" as famously defined by Brecht:[15] Alberto depends on the main protagonist financially, but the latter does not earn enough for both. Thus, Alberto wants to get a job and the aforementioned vicious circle sets in: he cannot get a job, because he has no papers, and he needs money to have his papers done. Finally, they have a quarrel over money and the anthropologist takes off to his parents, leaving Alberto to his misery, as he ends up at a social shelter. The entire development, of course, looks like a handbook illustration of "intersectionality," wherein the discrimination suffered by the character as a Rom is multiplied by his identification as a homosexual, leading to his exclusion from the highly machist and homophobic Roma community as well. What makes the film important, however—and I think this is something that applies to all three films equally—is that it does not simply speak *about* intersectionality, or racism for that matter. Instead, it allows the standard

---

14 Adi Schiop, *Șmecherie și lumea rea. Universul social al manelelor* (Chișinău: Cartier, 2017).
15 "Not every gesture is a social gesture. Our gesture of chasing a fly is primarily not a social gesture, but being chased by a dog may be one, if this for instance expresses the struggles a poorly dressed person has to endure. [. . .] A social gesture is a gesture relevant for society, a gesture that allows one to draw consequences with regard to the social states of affairs." Bertolt Brecht, "Über gestische Musik" [1932], in *Schriften 1920–1956* (Frankfurt a.M.: Suhrkamp, 1998), 282.

viewers to phenomenologically process deep-rooted and intricate forms of social prejudice, which play a key role in perpetuating social discrimination and economic misery, by forcing them to empathically unscramble their own mixed reactions to the films.

Social Visibility

This is not just a question of whether or not viewers are drawn to privately experience empathy, or to sympathize with the characters while watching such films. In drawing on Axel Honneth's reflections on the mutual relationships between perception and social recognition,[16] one could make the case that, in engendering this, those films also perform an overt political function.

In his considerations, Honneth takes a common enough experience as his starting point: that of "looking through" someone as a way of demonstratively showing that the other does not exist for oneself. While this is a behavior one frequently encounters in racist contexts, Honneth is primarily interested in showing that social invisibility is not at all similar to simply overlooking someone. It is not just a failed perception, but instead a visible display, a performative stance, which builds on readable expressive gestures and often triggers overt provocation from its victims in response. In other words, social invisibility is not simply about whether one sees the other or not, but about how one expressively demonstrates and stages seeing or not seeing them, and this is precisely why its opposite, social visibility, requires far more than just visually registering someone as present.

In Honneth's view, social visibility also involves at least two further features. First, it requires epistemic identification, that is: expressive proof that one acknowledges the other for who they really are, without mistaking them for something else. Second, it should at the same time go beyond a mere cognitive acknowledgement and actually signal benevolence, thus serving as a symbolic promise of corresponding behavior, which practically validates the other. In view of these two features, Honneth terms expressive gestures of recognition, by means of which the other is made socially visible, "meta-actions."[17] He finds

---

16 For the following, see especially Axel Honneth, *Unsichtbarkeit. Stationen einer Theorie der Intersubjektivität* (Frankfurt a.M.: Suhrkamp, 2003) and Axel Honneth, *The Struggle for Recognition: The Moral Grammar of Social Conflicts* [1992], trans. Joel Anderson (Cambridge: Polity Press, 1995).
17 Honneth, *Unsichtbarkeit*, 21.

their original genetic prototype in the warm and encompassing gestures and regards by which the mother first introduces her infant to social interaction—an argument which, in his view, helps prove that social validation in fact predates a mere epistemic relationship to the social other.

Be this as it may, Honneth's theory poses some interesting questions with regard to the *filmic* treatment of social issues. According to Honneth's own definition, "social recognition is, in contrast to mere cognition, which is a private epistemic act, dependent on a medium able to express the validation of the other."[18] In his view, this medium is, to be sure, identified on its most elementary level with direct bodily gestures and expressions in face-to-face interaction. However, one could make the case for considering films, within this framework, as a higher-degree medium for engendering social validation.

Films indeed resemble expressive bodily behaviors in that they are not merely able to help us visualize forms of social otherness *per se*, but instead expressively demonstrate that vision as well. Secondly, they obviously combine the ability for a precise epistemic identification of contorted social issues and categories with a penchant for their empathic valorization and validation. While filmic expressions of such issues may well appear to be more abstract than direct face-to-face behavior, one may nonetheless claim, thirdly, that the emergence of the "invisible others" in the films of a specific society, their medial visibility, is far more telling as an index for their struggle for social validation than any concrete particular situation of perception and interaction could be. If this is indeed the case, then the medial acknowledgement of contemporary forms of social and economic precarity like the ones discussed in the present paper could be seen as more than just aesthetic facilitators of empathic experiences. They would appear instead as political actions—or rather meta-actions—which indeed contribute to actively shaping social visibility.

Transnational Perspectives

These issues are no doubt not unique to Romania and they are by no means only of local concern. Thus, Bulgaria grapples with similarly high emigration rates as well, while the failed integration of the Roma is a story that transcends borders and defines the entire region. An international production like the documentary *Welcome Nowhere* (Kate Ryan, 2013) lays proof of this. In dealing with a Roma ghetto at the outskirts of Sofia and the daily life of its inhabitants,

---

[18] Ibid., 15.

it pinpoints a combination of factors like unemployment, administrative and political disinterest, and local prejudice, which are certainly shared features throughout Eastern Europe, as causes for their destitute condition. Nonetheless, the treatment of these issues in the various national cinemas of the region is quite distinct. In contrast to the ever-growing presence of Roma stories in Romanian cinema, where the local festival scene has even witnessed the emergence of a Roma film festival featuring numerous recent productions, Bulgarian cinema hardly shows a similar upsurge of interest in the topic, which is only marginally dealt with in minor documentaries like *Paradise Hotel* (Sophia Tzavella, 2010) or *Cambridge* (Eldora Traykova, 2015). Significantly, both only address Roma in exotic offbeat places: the first focuses on a Roma tower block with an interesting history during the communist regime, the second features a Roma village with a remarkably good schooling system, both located in deep provincial Bulgaria. At the same time, questions related to economic migrants in the West are hardly addressed in recent Bulgarian films,[19] which still seem largely reluctant to engage in consistent social criticism despite the apparent persistence of social topics, for instance, in the socio-moral fables of Kristina Grozeva and Petar Valchanov.

One interesting aspect, nonetheless, pertaining to one of the aforementioned Bulgarian documentaries, *Cambridge*, could help take us push a step further. While the film focuses mostly on the school of a small Roma community in northern Bulgaria, its idealist teachers and the daily life of the children, one also learns that most of their parents are working in the West to support them. Of course, Roma are also among the local migrant workers, but while the issue itself, which seems fairly obvious, is not addressed in any more detail here, the coincidence of the two topics treated in this paper can prompt us to realize how deeply they are indeed interwoven. In fact, in Romanian public discourse Roma beggars have frequently been accused of spoiling the country's image abroad,[20] with the symbolic story of Roma hunting and eating a swan in Vienna sometimes during the 1990s repeated *ad nauseam*. At the same time, this also brought out some racist undertones in the Romanian economic migrants' complaints about being unjustly stereotyped as Roma in the West. Since this obviously involves a

---

19 One could probably only cite as exceptions the comedy *Mission London* (Dimitiar Mitovski, 2010), dealing with Bulgarian diplomats in the UK, or the documentary *Immigrants* (Andrey Altaparmakov, 2009), which portrays a small community of Bulgarians living in Spain.
20 On this, see Alina Dolea, "The Impact of Migration on the Construction of Romania's Country Image: Two Intersecting Public Problems," in *Debating Migration as a Public Problem: National Publics and Transnational Fields*, ed. Camelia Beciu, Mălina Ciocea, Irina Diana Mădroane, and Alexandru I. Cârlan (Bern/New York: Peter Lang, 2018).

conflation of rhetoric marking both Eastern and Western European discourses, it might be worthwhile to take a look at how it impacts cinematographic discourses both in Eastern and Western Europe.

If one indeed takes this path, one immediately observes that, while Romanian and Bulgarian emigrant workers were hardly visible in Western films until recently, these films nonetheless often featured Eastern European Roma, frequently stereotyped as either beggars or derelicts. One still finds this motif, for instance, in two recent Swedish productions, *The Square* (Ruben Östlund, 2017) and *Amatörer* (*Amateurs*, Gabriela Pichler, 2018), neither of which considers the particular situations and stories of such characters in a more nuanced way. A more sophisticated cinematographic account of these contorted issues can be found in Michael Haneke's *Code inconnu* (*Code Unknown*, 2000). One of the film's secondary story lines focuses on a Romanian emigrant worker interpreted by Luminița Gheorghiu, whom we first see sitting as a beggar on an elegant street in Paris. Following an altercation in which she is unwillingly involved, she is deported back to Romania, and returns to her village, where her family is busy building the sempiternal house. In fact, the entire village looks like an immense construction site, with all her neighbors engaged in intense discussions about work opportunities in the West. We soon learn that she was working in France illegally under a false permit, which she can now no longer use. Finally, while preparing to return to France, where she will probably only be able to beg for the money her family needs to continue the construction works, she recounts a small story of racism. It is a recollection of her feelings of aversion when a gipsy beggar once touched her, which torments her now, when she believes that passersby in France view her in precisely the same way.

Now, this was, to be sure, before the EU integration of Romania and Bulgaria, and things have changed in the meanwhile. However, the example nonetheless suggests a possible follow-up for our present reflections. For both economic migration and the fate of the Roma communities are from the onset—and even more so in the context of the EU—strikingly transnational phenomena. As such, a comparative approach, which confronts their depiction in the Romanian or Bulgarian national cinema with that in Western European films, might prove to be more fruitful than a strictly national or regional treatment. This is all the more the case since recent Eastern European films are in fact to an overwhelming extent co-productions with Western partners, while issues like Roma resettlement or economic migration, which involve transnational mobility between the East and the West as their defining feature, indeed suit such modes of production perfectly. Thus, it is certain, for instance, that our understanding of the complicated fate of economic migrants torn between a here and a there (neither here, neither there), would widely benefit from a comparison between the ways Romanian migrant workers are beginning to be reflected in recent Romanian films, on the one hand, and in various Western productions like *Edificio España* (*The Building*, Victor Moreno, 2014) or *In Blue* (Jaap van Heusden, 2017), on the other. To be sure, economic migrants define themselves from the onset in relation to two distinct social and economic frames of reference, insofar as they are at the same time part of the precariat in the West and part of a displaced diaspora in relation to the East, playing an important part in the political rhetoric of both regions. One could perhaps even say that their need for social visibility is from the onset dual and transnational as well, begging the question of how an increasingly transnational European cinema could help provide this.[21]

Bibliography

Badea Guéritée, Iulia. "The Romanian 'slaves' behind the Sicilian tomatoes." *Voxeurope_English*, May 5, 2018. https://voxeurop.eu/en/the-romanian-slaves-behind-the-sicilian-tomatoes/.

Brecht, Bertolt. "Über gestische Musik" [1932]. In *Schriften 1920–1956*. Frankfurt a.M.: Suhrkamp, 1998, 281–285.

Dima, Ana Maria. "The other side of Europe: the exploitation of Romanian workers in the EU." *Open Democracy*, May 18, 2017. https://www.opendemocracy.net/en/other-side-of-europe-exploitation-of-romanian-workers-in-eu/.

Dolea, Alina. "The Impact of Migration on the Construction of Romania's Country Image: Two Intersecting Public Problems." In *Debating Migration as a Public Problem: National Publics and Transnational Fields*, ed. Camelia Beciu, Mălina Ciocea, Irina Diana Mădroane, and Alexandru I. Cârlan. Bern/New York: Peter Lang, 2018, 83–111.

Fulger, Mihai, ed. "Cu romii la cinema." *Film*, no. 2 (2019): 28–39.

Gorzo, Andrei, and Gabriela Filippi, eds. *Filmul tranziției. Contribuții la interpretarea cinemaului românesc "nouăzecist."* Cluj-Napoca: Tact, 2017.

Honneth, Axel. *The Struggle for Recognition: The Moral Grammar of Social Conflicts* [1992], trans. Joel Anderson. Cambridge: Polity Press, 1995.

———. *Unsichtbarkeit. Stationen einer Theorie der Intersubjektivität*. Frankfurt a.M.: Suhrkamp, 2003.

Kalleberg, Arne. *Precarious Lives: Job Insecurity and Well-Being in Rich Democracies*. Medford, MA: Polity, 2018.

Neagu, Bogdan. "Bucharest – Seasonal workers complain about working conditions in Germany." *Euractiv*, April 22, 2020. https://www.euractiv.com/section/all/short_news/bucharest-seasonal-workers-complain-about-working-conditions-in-germany/1457669/.

Rogozanu, Costi. "Muntean. Cronicarul României middle class." In *Politicile filmului. Contribuții la interpretarea cinemaului românesc contemporan*, ed. Andrei Gorzo and Andrei State. Cluj-Napoca: Tact, 2014, 89–98.

---

21 I am grateful to Nina Yakimova, Manuel Garin, and Guido Kirsten for their helpful suggestions.

Schiop, Adi. *Șmecherie și lumea rea. Universul social al manelelor*. Chișinău: Cartier, 2017.
Standing, Guy. *The Precariat: The New Dangerous Class*. London: Bloomsbury, 2011.
Turp-Balasz, Craig. "Romania's Demographic New Statistics Confirm Catastrophe." *Emerging Europe*, March 2, 2018. https://emerging-europe.com/news/new-statistics-confirm-romanias-demographic-catastrophe/.

Filmography

Acasă (*Home*). Dir. Paul Negoescu. Romania, 2006.
Aferim!. Dir. Radu Jude. Romania/Bulgaria/Czech Republic/ France,2015.
Aici . . . adică acolo (*Here . . . I mean there*). Dir. Laura Căpățână-Juller. Romania, 2012.
Amatörer (*Amateurs*). Dir. Gabriela Pichler. Sweden, 2018.
Bezbog (*Godless*). Dir. Ralitsa Petrova. Bulgaria/Denmark/France, 2016.
Câini (*Dogs*). Dir. Bogdan Mirică. Romania/France/Bulgaria/Qatar, 2016.
Cambridge. Dir. Eldora Traykova. Bulgaria, 2015.
Code inconnu (*Code Unknown*). Dir. Michael Haneke. France/Austria/Romania/Germany, 2000.
Edificio España (*The Building*). Dir. Victor Moreno. Spain, 2014.
Filantropica. Dir. Nae Caranfil. Romania/France, 2002.
Fixeur. Dir. Adrian Sitaru. Romania/France, 2016.
Granițe (*Borders*). Dir. Andra Chiriac. Romania/France,2017.
Immigrants. Dir. Andrey Altaparmakov. Bulgaria, 2008.
In Blue. Dir. Jaap van Heusden. Netherlands/Belgium/Romania, 2017.
Mission London. Dir. Dimitiar Mitovski. Bulgaria/UK/Hungary/Republic of North Macedonia/ Sweden, 2010.
Moartea domnului Lăzărescu (*The Death of Dante Lazarescu*). Dir. Cristi Puiu. Romania, 2005.
Niki Ardelean, colonel în rezervă (*Niki and Flo*). Dir. Lucian Pintilie. France/Romania,2003.
O lacrimă de fată (*A Maiden Tear*). Dir. Iosif Demian. Romania, 1980.
Occident. Dir. Cristian Mungiu. Romania, 2002.
Paradise Hotel. Dir. Sophia Tzavella. Bulgaria, 2010.
Polițist, adjectiv (*Police, Adjective*). Dir. Corneliu Porumboiu. Romania, 2009.
Poziția copilului (*Child's Pose*). Dir. Călin Peter Netzer. Romania, 2013.
Ryna. Dir. Ruxandra Zenide. Switzerland/Romania, 2005.
Soldații: Poveste din Ferentari (*Soldiers: Story from Ferentari*). Dir. Ivana Mladenović. Romania/Serbia/Belgium, 2017.
The Square. Dir. Ruben Östlund. Sweden/Germany/France/Denmark/USA, 2017.
Toto și surorile lui (*Toto and His Sisters*). Dir. Alexander Nanau. Romania/Hungary/ Switzerland/Canada, 2014.
Welcome Nowhere. Dir. Kate Ryan. USA/Bulgaria, 2013.

Aleksandra Miljković
Precarity in Post-Yugoslav Cinema
Everyday Life in Post-Socialist, Post-War, and Transition Societies

When the Yugoslav director Goran Paskaljević called the Balkans a *powder keg* in his film collage *Bure baruta* (*The Powder Keg*, 1998),[1] he summed up all the calamities in this part of Europe with this metaphor. The Balkans are often referred to as the "Other of Europe,"[2] and are generally considered unstable, conflictual, and underdeveloped compared to the West. Furthermore, the Western Balkan—the usual political phrase for the post-Yugoslav region—seems to be responsible for a great deal of this image. *The Powder Keg* depicts, in a nutshell, the image of the post-war society torn by aggression, ethnic hatred, criminality, and economic decline, while at the same time anticipating the trauma, poverty, and insecurity that the turn of the century will bring.

Various transitions mark the period around the year 2000 in post-Yugoslav countries: from socialism to liberal democracy, from self-management to neoliberal capitalism, and from a multi-cultural and multi-ethnic society to the building of nation-states and a redefining of national cultural identities. The global financial crisis in 2008 did not come as a surprise because it was just a continuation of the ongoing crisis from the 1990s. However, it increased the overall insecurity by permanently dismantling parts of the economy. Bankruptcy or restructuring—these were two prospects for the war-ravaged or lagging industries. Neoliberal capitalism displaced the socialist dream and offered a future based on economic modernization, development of the labor market, and privatization of public corporations. The economic modernization of this region proved to be slow and expensive, while labor markets had low employment rates by European standards. This is observable particularly among the

---

[1] The metaphor *Balkan powder keg*, also known as *powder keg of Europe*, refers to the tensions and conflicts in the Balkan peninsula in the early twentieth century and has also established itself as a defamatory metaphor in the representation and comprehension of the Balkans. Tomislav Longinović mentions that "its World War I designation as the 'powder keg' of Europe owes this reputation to the way in which film footage was used to reproduce the violence of the area for the Western viewer." Tomislav Z. Longinović, "Playing the Western Eye: Balkan Masculinity and Post-Yugoslav War Cinema," in *Eastern European Cinemas*, ed. Anikó Imre (New York/London: Routledge, 2005), 38.

[2] Maria Todorova, *Imaginarni Balkan* [*Imagining the Balkans*, 1997], trans. Dragana Starčević and Aleksandra Bajazetov-Vučen (Belgrade: Biblioteka XX Vek, 2006), 47.

Open Access. © 2022 Aleksandra Miljković, published by De Gruyter. This work is licensed under the Creative Commons Attribution-NonCommercial-NoDerivatives 4.0 International License.
https://doi.org/10.1515/9783110707816-009

young population and women, who are more likely to suffer unemployment and lower payment.[3] Privatization was seen as a perfect solution and was executed quickly and without formal control, thus permanently shutting down insolvent industries. The results were a decline in standards of living and a rise in poverty and unemployment, all contributing to the ever-growing precarity in society. Although the official unemployment rate has decreased, this is due to temporary and part-time employment, inconsistent registration of unemployed people as well as rising economic migration. Taking all this into consideration, we may ask: What is the role of culture, and specifically of film culture, in a society marked by all these difficulties? And if precarity is no stranger to this part of Europe, in which ways is this harsh social situation reflected and narrated in cinema?

To answer these questions, I aim to map cinematic representations of precarity in post-Yugoslav cinema and outline related political discourses. To avoid the already extensively discussed war cinema of the 1990s, I have decided to focus on documentaries and feature films made in the post-2008 era. In opposition to the 1990s "cinema of self-balkanization,"[4] the Croatian film theorist Jurica Pavičić defines the post-2000 cinema as "the cinema of normalization (consolidation),"[5] which adopts more moderate non-nationalist (or rather post-nationalist) narratives. Along these lines, I will analyze the notion of precarity in neoliberal post-Yugoslav society[6] by concentrating on cinematic representations of (1) precarity of the working class, (2) the double burden of women's work, and (3) the inherited precarity of youth. First I will focus on films showing the group referred to by the Marxist term *proletariat* or *working class* and their struggle in neoliberal economy. What happens when the working class undergoes such a difficult change, as happened after the Yugoslav transitions, where it collectively started to erode and gradually slid into the precariat[7]? And what are the consequences of this

---

[3] Michael Pugh, "Precarity in Post-Conflict Yugoslavia: What About the Workers?" *Civil Wars* 20, no. 2 (2018): 158.
[4] Longinović, "Playing the Western Eye," 46.
[5] Jurica Pavičić, "'Cinema of Normalization': Changes of Stylistic Model in Post-Yugoslav Cinema After the 1990s" [2010], *Studies in Eastern European Cinema* 1, no. 1 (2014): 48.
[6] Nevertheless, it is important not to diminish the effects of war and trauma as the important factors affecting the economic prosperity of these countries as well as financial and psychological vulnerability of their citizens many years after. Michael Pugh argues that "the Balkan peace has been disfigured by a political economy of precarity." Pugh, "Precarity in Post-Conflict Yugoslavia," 151.
[7] Blending the two terms *precarity* and *proletariat*, Guy Standing defines the precariat as a "new dangerous class-in-the-making." Standing points out that the precariat cannot be part of the working class because the working class consists of "workers in long-term, stable, fixed-hour jobs with established routes of advancement, subject to unionization and collective

precarization of the working class for the workers and their families? Second, I will draw attention to the representation of working women in post-Yugoslav society, focusing on women's double burden and the inheritance of female precarization through generations. And third, I will address the precarity of the younger generation by looking at films that depict the life of the post-Yugoslav youth-in-crisis and examine the effects of the parents' precarization on their children. In which way is the transgenerational transfer of precarity depicted and what consequences does it have for the young generation? To trace the potential tradition of cinematic representations of precarity, I will first take a short detour through Yugoslav film history.

The Hidden Side of Socialism: Images of Deprivation in Yugoslav Film

After the rift between Tito and the Soviet Union in 1948, Yugoslav politics experienced a radical shift, founding the so-called "third way" between the two blocks. While seeking means for legitimization, the government recognized the potential of film as the art for the masses, thus prompting the development of Yugoslav filmmaking, thought of as the plurality of ideological and aesthetic expressions.

One of the main tasks of films made in the 1950s was to promote self-management as the main asset of a new socialist state by depicting the "heroic task of rebuilding a war-ravaged country, restoring agricultural production, and establishing the infrastructure for the industrialization and urbanization of Yugoslavia."[8] However, there was one particular film that dared topoint out the "rude and simple conditions in which the workers lived and toiled"[9] — *Priča o fabrici* (*Story of a Factory*, Vladimir Pogačić, 1949). At the same time, the film also continued to perpetuate the mythology about the workers, showing the determination of female textile workers who are willing to work on several machines simultaneously to optimize production. In contrast, new tendencies in films gradually started to deconstruct the socialist narratives throughout the 1960s and 1970s. Films from Krsto Škanata, for example, involved a searing look at Yugoslav marginalized spaces. His short documentary *Prvi padež – čovek* (*The First Case – Human*, 1964) juxtaposes images of school children learning

---

agreements [. . .]." Guy Standing, *The Precariat: The New Dangerous Class* (London/New York: Bloomsbury, 2011), 1.
8 Daniel J. Goulding, *Liberated Cinema: The Yugoslav Experience, 1945–2001* (Bloomington: Indiana University Press, 1985), 23.
9 Ibid., 25.

about what is "human" with cases of the alienation and injustice of the state bureaucracy towards workers.

Similarly, the *Black Wave films* intended to show social inequalities and class stratification and shape critical discourse about socialism. They responded to optimistic and triumphant heroes of socialism with cynical and self-aware antiheroes resigned to the periphery. These films were considered controversial and were often banned, censored, or officially attacked as useless, pessimistic, and anarchistic. Tomislav Longinović argues that this "view of proletarian life and working-class struggles was not glorious enough for the ... officials [...]."[10] In 1968 Želimir Žilnik made the short documentary *Nezaposleni ljudi* (*Unemployed*) that comments on the anger and confusion of workers whom the economic reform had left jobless, and who were forced to search for work in Western Europe. Krsto Papić addresses the same subject in his film *Specijalni vlakovi* (*Special Trains*, 1972). The legacy of the Black Wave films, according to the Serbian art historian Branislav Dimitrijević, "confronted the ideal image of the working class with the 'heterology' of mere existence and its social and cultural manifestations [...] [thus] depicting the process of the 'defetishization' of workers to make them visible and tangible again."[11]

Women's emancipation was acknowledged by socialist authorities and the 1946 Yugoslav Constitution recognized women's equal role as citizens and workers, and their right to equal pay.[12] Although depicting working women was not common, some films drew attention to the tough situation of women in the still patriarchal society. In the short documentary *Od 3 do 22* (*From 3 to 22*, 1966), Krešo Golik depicts the day of a young mother and textile worker, emphasizing the double burden that women often had to carry in socialist countries. This motif of the textile worker will become one of the dominant tropes in the cinematic representation of working women. That is the case in the documentary *Vera i Eržika* (*Vera and Eržika*, Želimir Žilnik, 1981) which follows two textile workers fighting for their right to retire. The 1980s brought the notion of women's independence as a struggle against patriarchy. The short documentary *Nezaposlena žena sa decom* (*Unemployed Woman with Children*, Krsto Papić, 1986) shows the difficulties highly educated women face competing for

---

10 Longinović, "Playing the Western Eye," 36.
11 Branislav Dimitrijević, "In-between Utopia and Nostalgia or: How the Worker Became Invisible on the Path from Shock-Worker to Consumer," in *Nostalgia on the Move*, ed. Mirjana Slavković and Marija Đorgović (Belgrade: Museum of Yugoslavia, 2017), 37.
12 See for this Chiara Bonfiglioli, "A Working Day That Has No End. The Double Burden in Socialist Yugoslavia," *Themenportal Europäische Geschichte* (2017), https://www.europa.clio-online.de/essay/id/fdae-1705.

traditionally male jobs. Films like *Petrijin venac* (*Petria's Wreath*, Srđan Karanović, 1980) and *Lepota poroka* (*The Beauty of Vice*, Živko Nikolić, 1986) contributed images of the liberation of rural women.[13]

The cinematic representation of Yugoslav socialist youth started almost simultaneously with the 1950s fabled depiction of the working class. However, the Black Wave directors were again those who looked behind the socialist ideological setting to find a more fitting image of the Yugoslav youth. In the short documentary *Pioniri maleni [. . .]* (*Little Pioneers*, 1968), Žilnik juxtaposes the idealized image of pioneers, expressed through the famous socialist children's song cited in the film title, with the pictures of poor and hampered children playing in ruins. Goran Marković's *Specijalno Vaspitanje* (*Special Education*, 1977) and Darko Bajić's films *Sivi dom* (*Gray Home*, 1984) and *Zaboravljeni* (*Forgotten*, 1988) brought images of adolescents residing in the juvenile detention centers.

From *Shock Worker* to *Shock Therapy*: The Precarization of Post-Yugoslav Working Class

The neoliberal transition in former Yugoslavia, usually located around 1989–1990, supplanted the socialist, Marxist-based workers' utopia. The governments of the newly formed post-Yugoslav states put forward a profit-driven privatization and liquidation scheme, thus disregarding the self-management tradition. Some of the new owners wanted to make a short-term profit out of the liquidation process. Others started optimizing production by pursuing labor market flexibility and labor re-commodification. The workers were transformed from being subjects with equal rights into *flexible laborers* without a say in decision-making. The new assets of the neoliberal agenda such as market flexibility, privatization, restructuring, and modernization proved to be just a code for de-industrialization, the looting of social and state property, and precarization of workers and society.

Within the precarity debate, *precarization* and *precarity* are often discussed as different but correlating perspectives. According to Guy Standing, to be precarized means to "be subject to pressures and experiences that lead to a precariat existence, of living in the present, without a secure identity or sense of development achieved through work and lifestyle."[14] Similarly, Mona Motakef notes that

---
13 See for this Dijana Jelača, "Cinematic Images of Women at a Time of National(ist) Crisis: The Case of Three Yugoslav Films," in *Storytelling in World Cinemas: Contexts*, ed. Lina Khatib (New York: Columbia University Press, 2012).
14 Standing, *The Precariat*, 16.

precarization is a process of becoming insecure (*Entsicherungsprozess*), while precarity represents the status quo of deprivation.[15] Regarding these differences, I will focus first on films that depict the precarization process and workers' struggles. Second, I will present examples that deal with everyday life precarity as a specific consequence of the workers' precarization. The films I will take into consideration focus on workers' collectives, uniting men and women in one social body. Examples are: *Rudarska opera* (*Miner's Opera*, Oleg Novković, 2006), *Stara škola kapitalizma* (*Old School Capitalism*, Želimir Žilnik, 2009), *Tvornica je naša!* (*The Factory is ours!*, Vedrana Pribačić, 2017), *Radnička klasa odlazi u raj* (*The Working Class is Off to Paradise*, Marko Cvejić, 2017) and *Na vodi* (*On the Water*, Goran Dević 2018).

As one of the first and the best-known examples, Žilnik's hybrid docu-drama *Old School Capitalism* follows the struggle of worker-shareholders in the privatized factories Šinvoz and BEK in Zrenjanin (Serbia) in 2009. This film reflects upon the consequences of the implementation of neoliberal principles and the transition from the *shock workers* of the socialist self-management to the *redundant workers* of the shock therapy. Self-management gave workers the power of political and economic decision-making, by transferring the management of the companies from the state to the workers. The liberal market economy started to affect Yugoslav self-management as early as the 1970s, a process which was accelerated by the neoliberal agenda in the 1990s. The workers slowly lost their rights without noticing it—a process Goran Musić has named *the boiling frog*[16]—and in this way gradually *slid* into precarity.

Žilnik starts his film with the workers apprehending their situation after they have been cut out of their factory shares and were forbidden to enter the now private factory ground. They then decide to take the matter into their own hands and go on strike. The first part of the film focuses on the efforts to self-organize and defend their rights, thus revealing "the absolute 'silence' of the workers as political protagonists in contemporary Serbian society."[17] To quote Dimitrijević, "strike was the greatest taboo of socialist self-management, for there was actually no discourse within which one could ponder the possibility

---

[15] Mona Motakef, *Prekarisierung* (Bielefeld: Transcript, 2015), 10.
[16] Goran Musić, *Serbia's Working Class in Transition, 1988–2013* (Belgrade: Rosa Luxemburg Foundation, 2013), 20, https://arhiv.rosalux.rs/userfiles/files/Goran_Music_Working_Class_Serbia.pdf.
[17] Branka Ćurčić, "The Paradigm of Fragility of the Workers' Issue in (Post-) Socialist Yugoslavia," *ŽŽ – Želimir Žilnik Web Site* (2009), https://www.zilnikzelimir.net/essay/paradigm-fragility-workers-issue-post-socialist-yugoslavia.

of workers striking against themselves."[18] In former Yugoslavia, the state had the institutional monopoly over workers' organizations, and, therefore had suppressed independent unions. Independent unionism, self-organization, the equal position of female employees, the right to strike, and the right to a public gathering is something that the workers would have to learn through the forthcoming battle.[19] Nevertheless, the workers continued to distrust the unions, which, even upon their creation, "were fragmented, ethnically divided or undermined by illegal employment and accused of compromises with bosses."[20] This failure of the workers' organization occupies the first part of the film, bringing up further disparities like the lack of education of the workers, their nationalistic versus Yugoslav adherence, as well as the discrepancy between the intellectual elite and the working class.

To create an alternative space for workers' political agendas, Žilnik dedicates the second part of the film to the re-enactment of the occupation of the factory. He shows the workers demolishing the factory gates and discovering that the bosses are gone, along with the entire means of production and materials. Incited by a group of young anarcho-syndicalists, they take their bosses hostage and pressure them to return the stolen property. Žilnik developed the story in his recognizable docu-drama style by documenting (a demonstration in Belgrade), reenacting (the breaking in and reconquering of the factory), and fictionalizing (the hostage-taking) the struggle of the workers. However, the film plays with the whole range of stereotypes by showing the workers as a disorganized and primitive bunch that is pliable and easy to manipulate. When offered the opportunity to take over and self-manage their factory, they respond: "We don't know how to manage the factory! We only know how to work." In this way they declare their incapability to redirect the situation to their advantage.[21] In one of the interviews, Žilnik points out that the tragic ending of the film is the symbol of the actual lack of hope for any radical change and political engagement.[22] Referring to the Marxist notion of *Lumpenproletariat*, Ewa Mazierska has

---

18 Dimitrijević, "In-between Utopia and Nostalgia," 38.
19 Musić, *Serbia's Working Class in Transition*, 55.
20 Pugh, "Precarity in Post-Conflict Yugoslavia," 162.
21 The film *The Factory is Ours!* (2017) from documentary filmmaker Vedrana Pribačić offers a completely different outcome. The film shows the metalworkers from the ITAS Prvomajska factory in Croatia, who, after eleven years of struggle, managed to regain ownership and management of their factory.
22 Želimir Žilnik, interviewed by Greg DeCuir, Jr., "Old School Capitalism: An Interview with Želimir Žilnik," *Cineaste* 35, no. 4 (Fall 2010), https://www.cineaste.com/fall2010/old-school-capitalism-an-interview-with-zelimir-zilnik.

remarked that Žilnik "suggests that under postcommunist neoliberalism, at least its Serbian version, the lumpenproletariat expanded – practically the whole old communist industrial working class 'lumpen-proletariased'."[23] Alternatively, we may say that the proletariat was actually precarized—transformed into the *precariat*.

Following Žilnik's story, Marko Cvejić's film *The Working Class is Off to Paradise* shows the workers from Zrenjanin eight years after their struggle and job loss. The film shows the everyday lives of five protagonists who talk about the actual process of falling into precarity. They all belong to the same generation (born in 1958–59), come from the same locality (Zrenjanin), and are co-workers (they used to work at the before-mentioned BEK and Šinvoz factories). In this way, Cvejić gives a profile of the average blue-collar worker who was most affected by neoliberal reform. The camera zooms into their private spaces, at moments when they are bathing, cleaning their houses, or eating, thus disclosing the extent of their poverty and the lack of decent living conditions. The post-Yugoslav working-class dwells in unfinished houses, shacks, and sometimes even abandoned buildings. They lack running water and electricity, and they obtain their food from food banks. We see them strolling pointlessly through the city in search of opportunities, visiting their old workplace, or just sitting in their candlelit rooms. What Cvejić summons here is a very bleak image of unemployment and insufficient social benefits. He shows the social exclusion of these people as a result of their lack of qualification and their age. They are too young to retire and too old for any of the few newly opened companies to hire them. Being considered unemployable, they are left at the mercy of the unregistered job markets or often on the streets. The images of precarized workers we see in this film could be defined by the term *detached precariat* ("abgehängtes Prekariat")[24]—a new *underclass* characterized by financial insecurity, social exclusion, and disorientation.

The second group of, mostly fiction films, contemplate the consequences of precarity such as family dysfunction, suicidal tendencies, depression, and an overall feeling of futility, these films depict precarity as a ubiquitous state of being and a familiar trope of everyday life. Characters, often represented as desperate and depressed, are placed in an environment characterized by decayed and old-fashioned homes, ruinous high-rise neighborhoods, and polluted

---

[23] Ewa Mazierska, "Želimir Žilnik and Eastern European Independent Cinema," *Images* 13, no. 22 (2013): 145.
[24] Rita Müller-Hilmer, *Gesellschaft im Reformprozess* (Bonn: Friedrich-Ebert-Foundation, 2006), 2.

industrial cities. As the family breadwinners, men are mostly depicted in a struggle to justify or retain their patriarchal position. These films include works such as *Hadersfild* (Ivan Živković, 2007), *Inferno* (Vinko Möderndorfer 2014), *Beli, beli svet (White, White World,* Oleg Novković, 2010), and *Otac (Father,* Srdan Golubović, 2020).

In *White, White World,* Serbian director Oleg Novković follows a family living and working in the eastern Serbian industrial town of Bor, home to one of the largest copper mines in Europe. The big pit in which metal is mined and which is currently for sale has become a symbol of the economic standstill of an entire region. Polluted and run down, the town is troubled by the job cuts and emigration. Novković focuses on the life of a former miner and boxer named Kralj, who returns from abroad and opens a local bar. The story becomes complicated when his ex-lover Ružica, who was in prison for murdering her husband, returns to his life. Kralj meets her daughter Rosa, who becomes his current mistress, thus committing incest and bringing a bitter Shakespearean ending to the whole story. Using the form of Greek tragedy, Novković depicts the disorientation of the post-Yugoslav *lost generation*—those born in the mid-1960s—whose hopes got buried under the emotional and material ruins of the wars and transitions. The characters, utterly passive and confused with their futile lives, oscillate between self-destruction and inflicting pain on their loved ones. Depicting a familiar kind of stereotypical representation of the dirty, wild, and troubled Balkans, Novković walks the fine line between self-balkanizing *manière* and its new, critical, and self-assertive counterpart. Tragic moments from the characters' lives are staged in relation to the city's slummy neighborhoods and polluted landscapes, thus making the town of Bor a tacit protagonist of this tragedy. As a part of the social *mise-en-scène* we can observe the miners gathering on the streets, standing in groups, smoking and waiting, taking part in something that resembles a silent, passive demonstration. We do not hear their collective voice until the end of the film when, standing at the edge of the mining pit as a huge chorus, they sing about their unfortunate, precarious lives, thus back-lighting the tragic fates of the characters.

"Women, Worker, Mother": The Representation of Working Women's *Double Burden*

As mentioned above, films about working women as central figures were not very common in Yugoslav Film. Nevertheless, with the debut of younger filmmakers, cinematic representations of motherhood and/or *double precarity* (economic precarity and patriarchal repression) experienced by women are appearing more often. Films reflecting these circumstances include: *Jas sum od Titov Veles* (*I Am from Titov Veles*, Teona Strugar Mitevska, 2007), *Majka asfalta* (*Mother of Asphalt*, Dalibor Matanić, 2010), *Rekvijem za gospođu J.* (*Requiem for Mrs. J.*, Bojan Vuletić, 2017) and *Gospod postoi, imeto i' e Petrunija* (*God Exists, Her Name Is Petrunya*, Teona Strugar Mitevska, 2019).

The situation of post-Yugoslav female workers is represented in a generational range of characters in the film *Requiem for Mrs. J.* The film focuses on middle-aged Jelena living with her two daughters and her mother-in-law in Belgrade. She has recently lost her husband and her job, leaving her utterly passive and deeply depressed. The story begins when Mrs. J., finding her late husband's pistol and deciding to put an end to her futile life, sets out on the quest of finally solving a couple of formal things. Mrs. J.'s journey shows all the difficulties unemployed people face if they dare to claim some of the elemental state benefits in Serbia's convoluted and corrupt bureaucratic system. In a gloomy Kafkaesque atmosphere, the film takes us from an overrun health center to an outdated employment agency office and finally to the decaying factory. In a sequence in which Ms. J. visits her former factory, now an empty ruin inhabited by pigeons, Vuletić combines a reminiscence of the *golden age* of workers' Yugoslavia with the devastation brought about by neoliberal privatization where workers, mostly women, became redundant overnight. Back home, Mrs. J. cleans the house, prepares her daughter's school meal, and puts her best dress on. In the next scene, we see her sitting at the table. In front of her the pistol, some cigarettes, and a glass of beer. Vuletić underscores her femininity here by dwelling on the woman's working hands and also by putting male symbols—pistol, cigarettes, and alcohol—into the shaky and clumsy hands of a woman who has decided to put an end to her life (Fig. 1).

Two aspects of female precarity are present in this film. The first one is the gendered precarity that was passed on from one generation to the other, shown in the harsh living conditions of all four women. Jelena, as well as her mother-in-law, are depicted as lonely, passive, and somewhat superfluous characters. However, Jelena's daughters—Ana as the family's sole breadwinner and rebellious Koviljka as a school outsider—announce not only a generational but also a gender shift. The second aspect concerns the representation of suicidal and depressed working women, not uncommon in Yugoslav film history rich with the images of self-sacrificing women.[25] Jelena, however, will decide not to kill

---

[25] See for example Vesi Vuković, "Cinematic Suicide: Representations of Working Women in Yugoslav New Film," *Apparatus. Film, Media and Digital Cultures in Central and Eastern Europe*, no. 9 (2019), http://dx.doi.org/10.17892/app.2019.0009.156.

Fig. 1: Rekvijem za gospođu J. (Requiem for Mrs. J., Bojan Vuletić, 2017).

herself. At the end she is shown singing and liberating her (folk)voice in a kind of stereotypical demonstration of women's resistance and life will.

Precarity as a Legacy: The Case of Post-Yugoslav Youth

The last decade in post-Yugoslav cinematography has seen the advent of a generation of young filmmakers who, wanting to share their feelings and experiences, actively focus on the life of young people. Dijana Jelača points out that the coming-of-age narratives are frequently used to express a "critique of the social, cultural and economic circumstances of precarity rooted in the post-socialist transition."[26] The youth depicted in these films is growing up in a frail society, with unemployed parents, in broken families, and with limited opportunities.

In her book *Frames of War*, Judith Butler distinguishes between the more general notion of *precariousness* as a universal condition of human life, and that of *precarity*, which—seen as a more individual and specifically social experience—can become the starting point of political action. Precariousness lies in the fact that we are born vulnerable and dependent. Precarity, on the other side, "designates that politically induced condition in which certain populations suffer from failing social and economic networks of support and become differentially exposed to injury, violence, and death."[27] Butler acknowledges the importance of political orders, including economic and social institutions,

---

26 Jelača, "Sex and Uncivil Disobedience," 121.
27 Judith Butler, *Frames of War: When is Life Grievable?* (London/New York: Verso, 2009), 25.

as a means of surpassing the initial state of precariousness. These institutions are "designed to address those very needs without which the risk of mortality is heightened."[28] Taking into consideration that post-Yugoslav youth was born into a society lacking these political orders and institutions, we can see the young generations as already born into precarity.

Elaborating on youth precarity, Standing argues that "the experience of a precariatized existence by one generation will also transmit attitudes and behavioral norms to the next."[29] Furthermore, he adds that seeing "parents lose status, income, pride, and stability," results in children losing the role models they could otherwise emulate.[30] Finally, this youth also loses educational opportunities that could allow them to move up the class ladder. They have to accept a worse-paid, temporary, or dead-end position, gradually falling into precarity, thus perpetuating the legacy of their parents. Precisely these issues are treated in the following films: *Armin* (Ognjen Sviličić, 2007), *Tilva roš* (*Tilva Ros*, Nikola Ležaić, 2010), *Šišanje* (*Skinning*, Stevan Filipović, 2010), *Djeca* (*Children of Sarajevo*, Aida Begić, 2012), *Klip* (*Clip*, Maja Miloš, 2012), *Varvari* (*The Barbarians*, Ivan Ikić, 2014), *Ne gledaj mi u pijat* (*Quit Staring at My Plate*, Hana Jušić, 2016), *Lijenština* (*Lazy Guy*, Aleksa Stefan Radunović, 2018), and *Ne bom več luzerka* (*My Last Year as a Loser*, Ursa Menart, 2018).

The motif of *youth-in-crisis* appears in several recently written texts dedicated to this group of films. Dijana Jelača employs the term *parent culture*, which she defines as a "set of complicated assemblages that entail the specificity of the historical moment within which youth subcultures are operating, and their ideological/hegemonic, political, and also economic/material domains, rather than simply in the youth's literal relations to their parents."[31] She further argues that, even though not materially present, parent culture is omnipresent in a form of "dislocated memory."[32] This means that trauma is being transmitted in a transgenerational way. Jelača notices that one of the ways to position oneself toward this inherited memory, especially for the youth from materially deprived families, is to approach it within a subcultural activity that helps them deal with inherited pain through acts of anger and aggression. In their text "La jeunesse désaffectée in contemporary Serbian cinema," Nevena Daković and Maša Seničić have used the term *disaffected youth*, established by the French

---

28 Ibid.
29 Standing, *The Precariat*, 67.
30 Ibid.
31 Dijana Jelača, "The Genealogy of Dislocated Memory: Yugoslav Cinema after the Break," (PhD diss., University of Massachusetts Amherst 2014), 208.
32 Ibid., 258.

philosopher Bernard Stiegler, to denote the detachment, disorientation, and passivity that the young generation experiences when growing up in poverty and with no future perspectives. What makes them disaffected is the lack of an established social position, the impossibility of acting within the given political framework, as well as an identity that is fluid, adaptable, and apolitical.[33]

Nikola Ležajić's debut film *Tilva Ros* shows one summer in the life of teenagers in the provincial town Bor, the same mining town as in *White, White World*. Inspired by an amateur *Jackass*-like film made by two best friends and skaters-for-life—Toda and Stefke—Ležajić decides to return to Bor, where he too was born, and to film a story about young people of his hometown. The film features Toda and Stefke, playing themselves and recreating some of their dangerous subcultural ventures. By juxtaposing different dichotomies—fiction/documentary, professional actors/amateurs, and video/film—Ležajić created a distinct *cinéma vérité* feeling. Similarly, the film features two dichotomies that shed light on the precarious living situation of provincial youth. The first one consists of the representation of youth subculture versus parent culture and the second one zooms deeper into the relationship of two friends and their different class backgrounds. Following the skater group strolling the streets and seeing their parents taking part in the workers' union strikes, Ležajić keeps his young protagonists disinterested and passive toward the social turmoil. They take over abandoned mine pits and make skating rinks out of them, thus living out their frustration and pain. Dijana Jelača argues that through this re-appropriation "the skaters rupture the veneer of seamlessness that conceals the traumatic passage from past economic prosperity to present precarity to uncertain future."[34] With the second dichotomy, Ležajić introduces the main protagonists' different class backgrounds, thus showing the class stratification that precarious parents pass on to their children. Stefke is the son of a manager, preparing to leave Bor for his studies in the capital. Toda is a miner's son and his family cannot afford to send him to college. He has to stay in Bor and search for a job. Ležajić elaborates this situation in a sequence showing Toda attending CV-workshops and fictive job applications. This never-ending circle of job-search, job-training, filling out forms, and queuing in benefit-offices—doing *work-for-labor*[35]—is here shown as something that makes young people utterly passive and even detached. In Toda's case, this disaffection

---

33 Nevena Daković and Maša Seničić, "*La jeunesse désaffectée* in Contemporary Serbian Cinema," in *Contemporary European Cinema: Crisis of Narratives and Narratives in Crisis*, ed. Betty Kaklamanidou and Ana Corbalán (London/New York: Routledge, 2019), 149.
34 Dijana Jelača, "Youth after Yugoslavia: Subcultures and Phantom Pain," *Studies in Eastern European Cinema* 5, no. 2 (July 2014): 149.
35 Standing, *The Precariat*, 48.

is articulated through pain-inflicting games that give him adrenaline rushes and ease his frustration.

Another instance of youth precarity is shown in Hana Jušić's film *Quit Staring at my Plate*. In a mix of social and psychological realism, Jušić tells the story of Marijana, a young girl from the coastal town Šibenik (Croatia), who lives in a small, dirty, and cluttered apartment with an aggressive paterfamilias, a deeply cynical and almost catatonic mother, and a mentally disabled older brother. She works as a laboratory technician at a health center, continually fearing the rumors about layoffs. At home, sitting at family lunch and listening to her parents gossiping about people who are better off, she acts hunched and absent, not daring to contradict her father's criticism (Fig. 2).

Fig. 2: Ne gledaj mi u pijat (Quit Staring at My Plate, Hana Jušić, 2016).

When her father suffers a stroke and remains bedridden, Marijana takes responsibility for feeding the whole family. After the first shock, an unexpected feeling of freedom is born. Her slowly growing sense of independence also includes sexual freedom, and she engages in sexual relations with strangers. For Marijana these encounters seem to be liberating, even escapist forms of dealing with her unbearable family situation and her material deprivation. And even though these sex scenes create an awkward feeling and strike a wave of "moral panic," they also show Marijana, otherwise passive and wistful, as a kind of poker-faced, decisive girl who dares to break out of the patriarchal boundaries. Jelača points out that "patriarchal conservativism has shifted in the post-socialist, post-conflict context of the former Yugoslavia into a mechanism by which moral panics about youth delinquency and female sexuality further mask the roots of social precarity."[36] Jušić's film adds to the ever-growing list of

---

36 Jelača, "Sex and Uncivil Disobedience," 137.

stories about the effort and possibilities of post-Yugoslav women and girls' social and sexual liberation.

Conclusion: More Work to Be Done

Precarity is a global, all-encompassing tendency, but in the post-Yugoslav states it is buried under nationalist and post-war narratives. The state of relative security and stability in which previous generations lived seems today like a distant dream. The neoliberal agenda came together with the development of new national identities and liberal social systems, distancing itself from the communist legacy. Terms such as self-management, collective work, social order have been supplanted by the terms precariousness, labor market, labor flexibility, and precariat. These notions, even if familiar, are still relatively rarely found in the media and academic discourse in post-Yugoslav states. Their absence shows that the problems of unemployment, poverty, the position of workers, and job insecurity are being systematically ignored.

Unlike the general public and the mainstream, it seems that film art has increasingly focused on the subject of precarity, especially if we take the productions of younger directors into account. The national cinemas of the 1990s focused on the war and on nationalist subjects. This has changed in the 2000s when films became stylistically and thematically more coherent and more socio-politically oriented. Many of the films I have presented in this article were created as co-productions of several post-Yugoslav states. Therefore, Pavličić's definition of the "cinema of consolidation" could be used to point out the unification of powers to speak about precarity and poverty as general border-crossing problems.

The films I have discussed approach precarity from different points of view, but in a similar way. From the representation of the working class, with special emphasis on collective efforts, to the individual destinies of the workers and their families and children, these films focus on ordinary people. They sometimes reflect a feeling of longing for the Yugoslav welfare state and at the same time debate how to proceed onward and save the socialist legacies of workers' solidarity and cooperation. Some films also present the difficulties of long term precarity by showing the consequences that this hard social situation has on the psychological and physical health of the worker. Questions about the uncertain future are particularly present in the films about youth precarity, a corpus which is growing from year to year, showing the interest of the younger generations in openly and collectively discussing their problems. These films are defining discourses that were censored or ignored for years. Among them are female sexuality and the fight against patriarchal oppression and the assertion of male vulnerability and the refusal of the *homo balcanicus* stereotype.

However, the broader forms of precarization and marginalization including homelessness, queer and gender issues, as well as migration still need to be addressed more closely. Another important topic, which I did not have the space to discuss here, is the cinematic representation of the Roma minority that, unlike in Yugoslav times, has taken a turn toward less clichéd representation of their particularly precarious life situation.[37] Precarity is affecting the majority of people in post-Yugoslav states, but to what extent are they aware of their situation, and if they cannot define it with words, are they able to recognize the feelings connected with it? One thing is sure, many of the films presented here endeavor and manage to show the precarious conditions in people's lives with the aim of producing knowledge and inspiring actions.

Bibliography

Bonfiglioli, Chiara. "A Working Day That Has No End. The Double Burden in Socialist Yugoslavia." *Themenportal Europäische Geschichte* (2017). https://www.europa.clio-online.de/essay/id/fdae-1705.

Butler, Judith. *Frames of War: When is Life Grievable?* London/New York: Verso, 2009.

Ćurčić, Branka. "The Paradigm of Fragility of the Workers' Issue in (Post-) Socialist Yugoslavia." *ŽŽ – Želimir Žilnik Web Site* (2009). https://www.zilnikzelimir.net/essay/paradigm-fragility-workers-issue-post-socialist-yugoslavia.

Daković, Nevena, and Maša Seničić. "*La jeunesse désaffectée* in Contemporary Serbian Cinema." In *Contemporary European Cinema: Crisis of Narratives and Narratives in Crisis*, ed. Betty Kaklamanidou and Ana Corbalán. London/New York: Routledge, 2019, 147–159.

Dimitrijević, Branislav. "In-between Utopia and Nostalgia or: How the Worker Became Invisible on the Path from Shock-Worker to Consumer." In *Nostalgia on the Move*, ed. Mirjana Slavković and Marija Đorgović. Belgrade: The Museum of Yugoslavia, 2017, 30–41.

Goulding, Daniel J. *Liberated Cinema: The Yugoslav Experience*, 1945–2001. Bloomington: Indiana University Press, 1985.

Hadziavdic, Habiba, and Hilde Hoffmann. "Moving Images of Exclusion: Persisting Tropes in the Filmic Representation of European Roma." *Identities* 24, no. 6 (November 2017): 701–719. https://doi.org/10.1080/1070289X.2017.1380269.

---

[37] As shown in *Epizoda u životu berača željeza* (*An Episode in the Life of an Iron Picker*, Danis Tanović, 2013) and *Margina* (*Margin*, Ljupčo Temelkovski, 2015). More about in Habiba Hadziavdic and Hilde Hoffmann, "Moving Images of Exclusion: Persisting Tropes in the Filmic Representation of European Roma," *Identities* 24, no. 6 (2017). https://doi.org/10.1080/1070289X.2017.1380269.

Jelača, Dijana. "Cinematic Images of Women at a Time of National(ist) Crisis: The Case of Three Yugoslav Films." In *Storytelling in World Cinemas: Contexts*, ed. Lina Khatib. New York: Columbia University Press, 2012, 133–143.

——. "The Genealogy of Dislocated Memory: Yugoslav Cinema after the Break." PhD diss., University of Massachusetts Amherst, 2014. https://doi.org/10.7275/vztj-0y40 https://scholarworks.umass.edu/dissertations_2/10.

——. "Youth after Yugoslavia: Subcultures and Phantom Pain." *Studies in Eastern European Cinema* 5, no. 2 (July 2014): 139–154.

——. "Sex and Uncivil Disobedience: Girlhood and Social Class in Transitional Post-Yugoslav Cinema." *Contemporary Southeastern Europe* 4, no. 2 (2017): 121–140.

Longinović, Tomislav Z. "Playing the Western Eye: Balkan Masculinity and Post-Yugoslav War Cinema." *Eastern European Cinemas*, ed. Anikó Imre. New York/London: Routledge, 2005, 35–47.

Müller-Hilmer, Rita. *Gesellschaft im Reformprozess*. Bonn: Friedrich-Ebert-Foundation, 2006.

Mazierska, Ewa. "Želimir Žilnik and Eastern European Independent Cinema." *Images* 13, no. 22 (2013): 133–149.

Motakef, Mona. *Prekarisierung*. Bielefeld: Transcript, 2015.

Musić, Goran. *Serbia's Working Class in Transition 1988–2013*. Belgrade: Rosa Luxemburg Foundation, 2013. https://arhiv.rosalux.rs/userfiles/files/Goran_Music_Working_Class_Serbia.pdf.

Pavičić, Jurica. "'Cinema of Normalization': Changes of Stylistic Model in Post-Yugoslav Cinema After the 1990s" [2010]. *Studies in Eastern European Cinema* 1, no. 1 (January 2014): 43–56.

Pugh, Michael. "Precarity in Post-Conflict Yugoslavia: What About the Workers?" *Civil Wars* 20, no. 2 (August 2018): 151–170.

Standing, Guy. *The Precariat: The New Dangerous Class*. London/New York: Bloomsbury Academic, 2011.

Todorova, Marija. *Imaginarni Balkan [Imagining the Balkans, 1997]*. Trans. Dragana Starčević and Aleksandra Bajazetov-Vučen. Beograd: Biblioteka XX Vek, 2006.

Vuković, Vesi. "Cinematic Suicide: Representations of Working Women in Yugoslav New Film." *Apparatus. Film, Media and Digital Cultures in Central and Eastern Europe*, no. 9, (2019). http://dx.doi.org/10.17892/app.2019.0009.156.

Žilnik, Želimir, interviewed by Greg DeCuir, Jr. "Old School Capitalism: An Interview with Želimir Žilnik." *Cineaste* 35, no. 4 (Fall 2010). https://www.cineaste.com/fall2010/old-school-capitalism-an-interview-with-zelimir-zilni.

Filmography

Armin. Dir. Ognjen Sviličić. Croatia/Bosnia and Herzegovina/Germany, 2007.
Beli, beli svet (White, White World). Dir. Oleg Novković. Serbia/Germany/Sweden, 2010.
Bure baruta (The Powder Keg). Dir. Goran Paskaljević. Federal Republic of Yugoslavia/Republic of North Macedonia/France/Greece/Turkey, 1998.
Djeca (Children of Sarajevo). Dir. Aida Begić. Bosnia and Herzegovina/Germany/France/Turkey, 2012.

Epizoda u životu berača željeza (*An Episode in the Life of an Iron Picker*). Dir. Danis Tanović. Bosnia and Herzegovina/France/Slovenia/Italy, 2013.
Gospod postoi, imeto i' e Petrunija (*God Exists, Her Name Is Petrunya*). Dir. Teona Strugar Mitevska. Republic of North Macedonia/Belgium/France/Croatia/Slovenia, 2019.
Hadersfild. Dir. Ivan Živković. Serbia, 2007.
Inferno. Dir. Vinko Moderndorfer. Slovenia/Croatia/Republic of North Macedonia/Serbia, 2014.
Jas sum od Titov Veles (*I Am from Titov Veles*). Dir. Teona Strugar Mitevska. Republic of North Macedonia/Belgium/France/Slovenia, 2007.
Klip (*Clip*). Dir. Maja Miloš. Serbia, 2012.
Lepota poroka (*The Beauty of Vice*). Živko Nikolić. Yugoslavia, 1986.
Lijenština (*Lazy Guy*). Dir. Aleksa Stefan Radunović. Montenegro, 2018.
Majka asfalta (*Mother of Asphalt*). Dir. Dalibor Matanić. Croatia, 2010.
Margina (*Margin*). Dir. Ljupčo Temelkovski. Germany/Republic of North Macedonia, 2015.
Na vodi (*On the water*). Dir. Goran Dević. Croatia, 2018.
Ne bom več luzerka (*My Last Year as a Loser*). Dir. Ursa Menart. Slovenia, 2018.
Ne gledaj mi u pijat (*Quit Staring at My Plate*). Dir. Hana Jušić. Croatia/Denmark, 2016.
Nezaposlena žena sa decom (*Unemployed Woman with Children*). Dir. Krsto Papić. Yugoslavia, 1986.
Nezaposleni ljudi (*Unemployed*). Dir. Želimir Žilnik. Yugoslavia, 1968.
Od 3 do 22 (*From 3 to 22*). Dir. Krešo Golik. Yugoslavia, 1966.
Otac (*Father*). Dir. Srdan Golubović. Serbia/France/Germany/Slovenia/Croatia/Bosnia and Herzegovina, 2019.
Petrijin venac (*Petria's Wreath*). Dir. Srđan Karanovi. Yugoslavia, 1980.
Pioniri maleni mi smo vojska prava, svakog dana ničemu ko zelena trava (*Little Pioneers*). Dir. Želimir Žilnik. Yugoslavia, 1968.
Priča o fabrici (*Story of a Factory*). Dir. Vladimir Pogačić. Yugoslavia, 1949.
Prvi padež – čovek (*The First Case – Human*). Dir. Krsto Škanata. Yugoslavia, 1964.
Radnička klasa odlazi u raj (*The Working Class is Off to Paradise*). Dir. Marko Cvejić. Serbia, 2017.
Rekvijem za gospođu J. (*Requiem for Mrs. J.*). Dir. Bojan Vuletić. Serbia/Bulgaria/Republic of North Macedonia, 2017.
Rudarska opera (*Miners Opera*). Dir. Oleg Novković. Serbia, 2006.
Sivi dom (*Gray Home*). Dir. Darko Bajić. Yugoslavia, 1986.
Specijalni vlakovi (*Special Trains*). Dir. Krsto Papić.Yugoslavia, 1972.
Specijalno vaspitanje (*Special Education*). Dir. Goran Marković. Yugoslavia, 1977.
Stara škola kapitalizma (*Old School Capitalism*). Dir. Želimir Žilnik. Serbia, 2009.
Šišanje (*Skinning*). Dir. Stevan Filipović. Serbia, 2010.
Tilva roš (*Tilva Ros*). Dir. Nikola Ležaić. Serbia, 2010.
Tvornica je naša! (*The Factory is Ours!*). Dir. Vedrana Pribačić. Croatia, 2017.
Varvari (*The Barbarians*). Dir. Ivan Ikić. Serbia/Montenegro/Slovenia/Bosnia and Herzegovina, 2014.
Vera i Erzika (*Vera and Eržika*). Dir. Želimir Žilnik. Yugoslavia, 1981.
Zaboravljeni (*Forgotten*). Dir. Darko Bajić. Yugoslavia, 1988.

László Strausz
Move on Down
Precarity and Downward Mobility in Contemporary Hungarian Feature Films

A young woman's naked body rolls down a dusty, indistinct hillside in the dark. She attempts to grab ahold of anything she can as she helplessly tumbles, but her hands only clasp dirt. The camera captures her movements in slow motion, which accentuates her desperate efforts. Highlighting the contours of her body with sparse, high contrast light, the shots emphasize the pain resulting from her bare skin grinding against the rough surface. Eventually, the long shots give way to close-ups, and we see that she is making the screaming sounds that could be heard from the beginning of the scene. With scared eyes and her mouth wide open, the defenseless, shrieking figure rolls out of the frame at the bottom. After a quick cut, we see the same woman suddenly waking and sitting up in her bed, hyperventilating, letting the viewer realize that the dark scenario was just a bad dream. Nonetheless, the haunting opening scene of the film *Édes Emma, drága Böbe* (*Sweet Emma, Dear Böbe*, István Szabó, 1992) functions as an alarming foreshadowing of events to come for the protagonists Emma and her friend Böbe, who experience the bottomless instability of post-regime-change Hungary throughout the story.

The dream scene hints at a crucial theme that preoccupied contemporary Hungarian cinema even before the regime change that launched tectonic social transformations leading to widespread instability. Precarity will be discussed here as downward intragenerational mobility from an economic (protagonists loses material wealth) *and* social perspective (protagonist's social network, such as family, friends, and workplace disintegrates) from the final years of state socialism until the present.[1] In this essay, I will show that fiction films imagine precarity and downward social mobility in three distinct formations or phases from the mid-1980s onward.[2] While the thematization of crisis due to

---

[1] Precarity in contemporary Eastern Europe shows distinct formations due to the region's abrupt shift from state socialism to neoliberal capitalism, which are mainly attributable to the dual crisis of marketization/privatization and deindustrialization. See Ivan Szelenyi, "Pathways from and Crises after Communism: the Case of Central Eastern Europe," *Belvedere Meridionale* 26, no. 4 (2014): 10.

[2] While the 1989 regime change represented a crucial social break and signalled the start of the so-called contemporary period of Hungary's history, the same year does not appear as a fundamental break in the (social) history of cinema. The trends visible in the year 1989 started

---

Open Access. © 2022 László Strausz, published by De Gruyter. This work is licensed under the Creative Commons Attribution-NonCommercial-NoDerivatives 4.0 International License.
https://doi.org/10.1515/9783110707816-010

larger social-historical forces appears to be the principal mode in films until about 1995, downward mobility is almost exclusively the result of the protagonists' own decisions in the second phase. This trend continues in a less extreme form throughout the third phase as protagonists with situational precarity reappear during the early 2000s in larger numbers.

Analyzing Downward Mobility in Contemporary Hungarian Cinema

Social histories of cinema are traditionally based on qualitative methods, which has at times led to the formation and proliferation of critical-evaluative concepts that often lack a scholarly basis.[3] One such conception divided state socialist era Hungarian cinema into politically committed auteur films and entertaining genre pictures devoid of socially relevant topics.[4] Among other things, my article attempts to show that at least in the case of downward mobility, this categorization fails to hold up. As part of the project 'The social history of Hungarian cinema'[5] conducted by the research collective at the Department of Film Studies at Eötvös Loránd University (ELTE) in Budapest, a database was created that categorizes all Hungarian feature films using variables such as production information, genre markers, conflict types, locations, and detailed information about the films' characters. This quantitative method allows film historians to run queries in the database and identify, for example, how the fates of characters in feature films change throughout the course of the narrative. Subsequently, the quantitatively identified trends can be dissected using the qualitative methodology of textual analysis. Here I will adopt this briefly described method in order to identify the main trends in the representation of precarity and downward mobility in contemporary Hungarian cinema.

---

several years earlier, around 1985, and continued until the mid-1990s. In the closing section of my article, I will briefly attempt to unpack the factors that explain this disparity between social and cinematic periodization.
3 See András Bálint Kovács, "Műfajok a magyar filmtörténetben," *Apertúra*, 3 April, 2018, https://uj.apertura.hu/2018/tavasz/kab-mufajok-a-magyar-filmtortenetben/.
4 See Balázs Varga, "Paradoxes of popularity," *Ekrany* 56, no. 4 (2020).
5 Supported by a grant from the Hungarian National Research, Development and Innovation Office (grant no. 116708). While working on this essay, I relied greatly on the criticism and comments from research team members.

Downward mobility has hit former Eastern Bloc countries hard in the wake of the regime changes of 1989–1990. The collapse of the plan-governed economy, and the forced end of hidden unemployment were among the more crucial factors that contributed to large masses of people suddenly experiencing social instability. However, it has to be noted that these social phenomena were not entirely new for Hungarian society in 1989. The downfall of the Hungarian economy was only temporarily delayed by the Western loans during the early 1980s, and in the mid-80s there were already a number of signs that projected a deep crisis of the Kádár-era socialist welfare state.[6] Overall, during the early 1990s large segments of the Hungarian population experienced changes in their social status: upward or downward movement, or stagnation. Tibor Valuch points out that one main trend in these complex social shifts is the decreasing significance of the middle classes,[7] while Erzsébet Bukodi and Péter Róbert underline the growing presence of the petty bourgeoisie.[8] Hungarian sociologists have developed various approaches to the analysis of social mobility and stratification, from various perspectives.[9] Valuch summarizes these trends by focusing on three differing approaches.[10] Tamás Kolosi and Péter Róbert, analyzing occupational and income data, consumption, and life standards combined with mobility information, arrived at the conclusion that the consequences of the regime change need to be understood as structural changes to work and earning relations.[11] Describing the new class structure of Hungarian society, the two researchers still see the middle classes as the most significant social strata. On the other hand, László Laki focused on the disintegrating consequences of the economic regime

---

6 Ignác Romsics, *Magyarország története a XX. században* (Budapest: Osiris, 2010), 456.
7 Tibor Valuch, *A jelenkori magyar társadalom* (Budapest: Osiris Kiadó, 2015), 92.
8 Péter Róbert and Erzsébet Bukodi, "Changes in intergenerational class mobility in Hungary, 1973–2000," *Social mobility in Europe*, ed. Richard Breen (Oxford: Oxford University Press, 2004), 292.
9 Social mobility as a phenomenon has been studied in detail since the regime change in Hungary. While being aware of the rich findings of these studies, I have simplified the conceptual frame of my study on several fronts in order to make the scope of my essay manageable. Nonetheless, it is probably worth acknowledging here that, on top of the individual's class position, mobility can be studied as changes in various categories relating to family situation, lifestyle, prestige- and value preferences, education, spatial location, etc. Additionally, mobility can be interpreted as an intergenerational or intragenerational phenomenon.
10 Valuch, *A jelenkori magyar társadalom*, 117–122.
11 Tamás Kolosi and Péter Róbert, "A magyar társadalom szerkezeti átalakulásának és mobilitásának főbb folyamatai a rendszerváltás óta," in *Társadalmi riport 2004*, ed. Kolosi Tamás, Tóth István György, and Vukovich György (Budapest: Tárki, 2004).

change, and underlines the increasing polarization of society.¹² Using a more complex methodology, Bukodi has argued that aspects of everyday life (mentalities, value systems, consumption and cultural preferences, status inheritance, etc.) also have to be included in analyses of mobility and stratification.¹³ Furthermore, she argues that occupation relations in Hungary have shifted towards intellectual forms of employment (commercial and service industries, office employment), and groups not in possession of these skills or cultural capital are increasingly being pushed towards lower social strata. These general trends are also underlined by the empirical study Osztálylétszám 2014,¹⁴ which Valuch summarizes in the following way: Since the regime change, middle classes have lost their significance and the predominance of lower classes moved into the foreground, and the social distance between urban and rural areas has risen dramatically.

The consequences of the mentioned directions in mobility research are important for the purposes of my query, as they identify the fundamental social polarization of Hungarian society and propose that economic *and* cultural-symbolic capital should be conceptually differentiated in interpretations of social mobility. While it needs to be acknowledged that the conceptual tools of the briefly outlined stratification and mobility studies are much more complex than that of the feature film database compiled by researchers at ELTE, the differentiation between economic and cultural-symbolic capital and the roles these play in the changes of the film characters' fates are points of departure for my essay as well. Pierre Bourdieu has analyzed the difference between types of capital: In a text authored in 1983, he argued that "capital can present itself in three fundamental guises: economic [. . .], cultural [. . .] and social capital."¹⁵ The database of Hungarian feature films deploys two different variables for the negative changes in the characters' fates in the narratives: downward economic mobility and the loss of social status. These were separated in order to make manageable the categorizations of events where characters simply lose money or properties as opposed to others where their downward mobility is marked by a degrading social network (family, colleagues, friends), occupational situation, life world, mental state, etc. The two changes often occur simultaneously, or stand in a causal relation,

---

12 László Laki, "Rendszerváltások Magyarországon," in *Társadalmi metszetek*, ed. Imre Kovács (Budapest: Napvilág Kiadó, 2006).
13 Erzsébet Bukodi, "Társadalmunk szerkezete különböző nézőpontokból," in *Társadalmi metszetek*, ed. Imre Kovách (Budapest: Napvilág Kiadó, 2006).
14 The results of the study have been published online: https://politikatudomany.tk.mta.hu/osztalyletszam-a-magyar-tarsadalom-szerkezete.
15 Pierre Bourdieu, "The Forms of Capital," *Handbook of Theory and Research for the Sociology of Education* [1983], ed. John Richardson (Westport, CT: Greenwood, 1986), 16.

and therefore their theoretical separation is beyond the scope of this study. Nonetheless, their intuitive or practical differentiation allows for various insights about the forms of the filmic representation of precarity.

Numbers

In the period between 1985 and 2018, 599 films were produced in Hungary. Among these films, 398 have a contemporary setting. Searching the database for films that feature characters losing either economic or social status results in 77 hits with an almost equal distribution between auteur and genre films.[16] Some critics have argued that contemporary Hungarian cinema does not pay much attention to social change or poverty,[17] but the numbers show that about one-fifth of all films that take place in the post-1989 world feature characters who are well acquainted with precarity. The database reveals that these 77 motion pictures include 100 protagonists who experience at least one of the two types of downward mobility.[18] The chart below (Fig. 1) displays the different ways in which arthouse and genre films address downward mobility through its two distinct formations.

Representations of the loss of social status are by far more common than depictions of economic downturns in auteur films.[19] In genre movies, the proportion is much more balanced, but still leans towards social crisis.[20] Protagonists in the films can undergo both a social and an economic crisis, and the query for a chosen type of downward mobility confirms the findings of the previous inquiry.[21]

---

16 From the 77 films of the corpus on downward mobility, 38 are auteur films and 39 genre pieces (dramas, melodramas, crime films, and comedies).
17 Gusztáv Schubert, "Rejtőzködő évtized. A magyar rendszerváltás filmjei," *Metropolis* 6, no. (2002): 2–3; Zsófia Mihancsik, "Kiürült agóra. A rendszerváltás filmjei – Beszélgetés György Péterrel, Hirsch Tiborral és Révész Sándorral," *Filmvilág*, no. 1 (2002): 16–21.
18 Women and men do feature proportionately here, if we factor in the unequal occurrence of female and male protagonists (statistically, each film in the period includes 0,6 female- and 1,5 male protagonist) in contemporary Hungarian cinema: out of 100 leading characters experiencing downward mobility 29 are women and 71 are men.
19 Compared to 39 protagonists in this group who undergo social crisis there are only 14 protagonists whose economic decline is depicted.
20 The 36 protagonists sliding down socially are trailed by 26 protagonists who experience economic crisis.
21 In the arthouse films there are 35 protagonists who experience social decline but no economic crisis, while there are only 10 protagonists in the same group who lose economically without losing social status. And the same holds for genre film protagonists and the type of crisis they endure: the database lists 24 characters who suffer a social downfall without losing their possessions and 15 protagonists who endure an economic crisis without a social downfall.

Additionally, I ran an inquiry on the database about the social standing and the possessions of the films' protagonists: Who experiences the social or economic crises in question? The data shows an overwhelming dominance of middle-class protagonists losing social and economic status, closely followed by lower class protagonists sliding even further down. Upper middle-class characters are found fairly rarely in this query, while upper-class protagonists barely register.[22] Overall, there is no significant difference between arthouse and genre films with regard to social class.[23] When considering wealth, a similar distribution appears among protagonists.[24] It seems that these numbers among film protagonists confirm the findings of the sociological studies on post-1989 social change in Hungary. Overall, genre films display more average characters moving down, while auteur films feature more poor protagonists declining.[25] According to the statistical investigation, contemporary Hungarian cinema is much more preoccupied with the cultural-symbolic aspects of downward mobility than with its economic aspects. Both auteur and genre film protagonists who endure downward mobility overwhelmingly come from the middle classes with an average financial situation. Second most common are films featuring lower-class characters and poor people as protagonists.[26] The numbers reveal how contemporary Hungarian cinema tackled downward mobility overall, but only give us a static impression of the period between 1985 and 2018. In order to be able to examine the modalities of the filmic representations and consider *how* they depict, for example, the loss of social status of a middle-class protagonist, I turn to the temporal distribution of the numbers, and attempt to define periods based on the tendencies that can be discerned.

---

[22] Middle-class protagonists: 49, lower-class protagonists: 41, upper middle-class protagonists: 9, upper-class protagonists: one.

[23] Auteur films do not feature upper-class characters slipping down, while we find five upper middle-class, 23 middle-class and 21 lower-class protagonists displaying the same dynamic. Genre films include only one upper-class character moving down, while we find four upper middle-class, 25 middle-class and 20 lower-class protagonists displaying the same dynamic.

[24] Downward mobility (social and economic combined) affects one rich, 11 wealthy, 52 average, 34 poor and one extremely poor protagonist in the corpus of films.

[25] Auteur films show no rich character moving down, while we find seven wealthy, 21 average, 20 poor and one extremely poor protagonist who move downwards. Genre films show one rich character declining, while we find four wealthy, 31 average, 14 poor and 0 extremely poor protagonist suffering a downturn.

[26] Auteur films tend somewhat more to feature poor protagonists and genre films slightly more financially average protagonists with downward mobility.

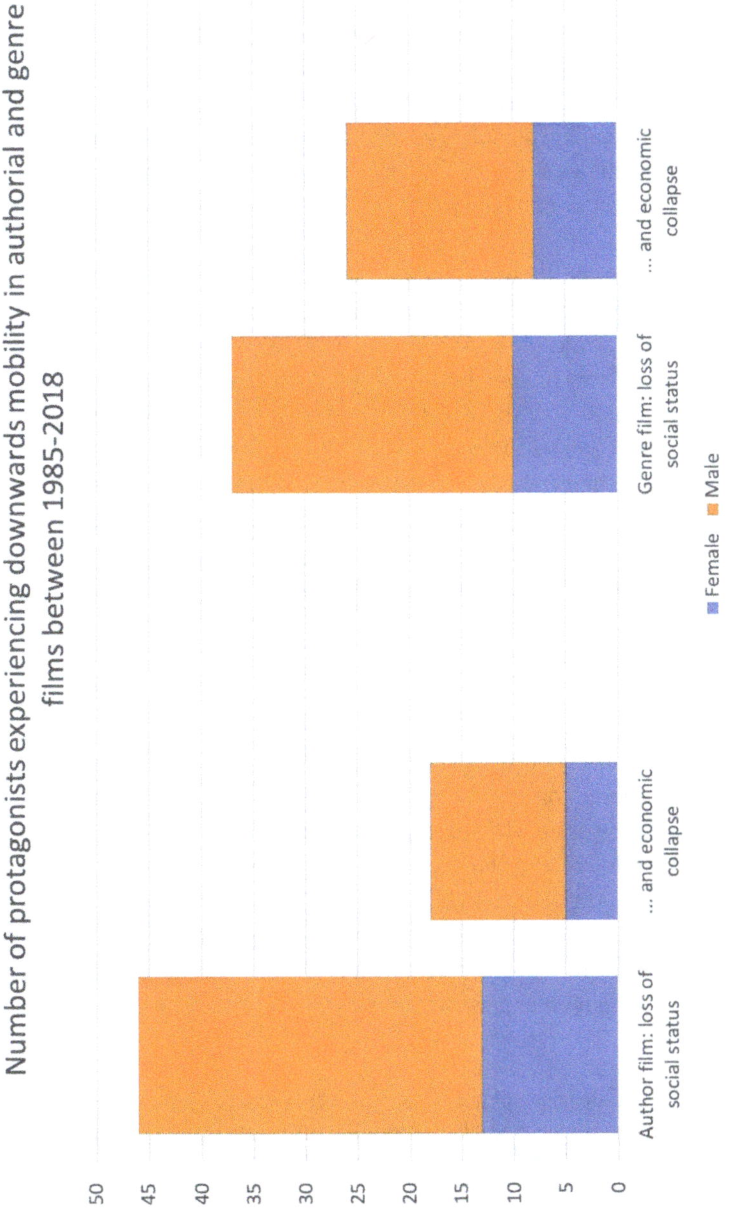

Fig. 1: Downward Mobility Chart.

Periods

Three more or less distinct phases appear in the period where representations of downward mobility take different forms. The first phase features stories about middle or lower-class characters who lose their social or economic standing due to the social situation, which lies outside their personal disposition (situational precarity).[27] This phase corresponds with the years before and after the regime change. Signs of situational instability already started to appear in the narratives of feature films during the mid-1980s. Both genre and auteur cinema represent characters' fates that spiral downward, and the films typically revolve around the disintegration of the protagonists' social world. The second phase starts around 1994 and is characterized by a sharp turn towards the personal: middle- or lower-class protagonists' lives deteriorate due to their own decisions, and much less as a result of their precarious social world (dispositional precarity), and films still focus on social decline, but here with crime and criminality as main root causes. Again, both auteur and genre films follow the trend in roughly equal numbers. During the third phase from about 2003/2004 onwards until 2018, genre movies slightly outnumber auteur films in depicting downward mobility, and in this phase social factors that cause the decline surface again, but only in auteur films and dramas. However, the dividing line between phases two and three is rather soft as one can see a gradual shift during the mid-2000s instead of a clear-cut boundary.

Decline as Inevitability

In the first phase that lasts approximately from 1985 to 1995, the protagonists are struggling to make it in a rapidly changing social setting. Irrespectively of the arthouse or generic framework of the stories, the characters come up against larger forces they cannot control and that threaten to squash their efforts to prevail and/or prosper. While the Kádár-regime was still in place and there was little sign of the political shifts of 1989, precarity already became an important theme in the films of the mid- to late 1980s. This general story pattern extends a few years beyond the immediate experience of the regime change. We find exactly

---

27 In her analysis on social mobility of female protagonists in contemporary Hungarian film, Margitházi ("Up the Slope. Women's Mobility Stories in Post-Transition Hungarian Cinema," *Acta Univ. Sapientiae, Film and Media Studies*, no. 18 (2020): 225) deploys Weiner's theory of social attribution (Bernard Weiner, *Achievement motivation and attribution theory* (New York: General Learning Press, 1974)) and differentiates between dispositional (personal, internal) and situational (external) factors that guide social actors' actions.

the same number of genre and auteur films where protagonists slip downwards: out of 34 characters, 17 are in auteur and 17 in genre films. Among these protagonists, social disintegration (24) features in larger numbers than those with economic hardship (15), and the social reasons for the decline (28) by far outnumber the private reasons (6).

Three films that are useful for the characterization of various depictions on precarity in the period are *Visszaszámlálás* (*Countdown*, Pál Erdőss, 1986, *Sweet Emma, dear Böbe*, and *Hoppá* (*Oops*, Gyula Maár, 1993). They also show a broad range and various types of representations of instability through protagonists who find themselves in dissimilar phases in their lives. In *Countdown*, the local cooperative auctions off an IFA truck and Sanyi purchases the vehicle by investing a large amount of money. It is a very good investment, however, since he is able to take on private jobs to deliver various kinds of goods. Hinting at the somewhat more permissive stance of late state socialist Hungary towards small entrepreneurship, the film lines up a number of characters who actually use the state's resources to run small side-businesses. As long as he has jobs, Sanyi and his family thrive, and they start to build their own family home from the earnings realized with the truck. He is constantly on the road, and there is no way for him to put in enough hours. An employer tells him: when I was your age, I worked 26 hours a day. The limitation of the protagonist's options already becomes visible in those scenes of the film in which Sanyi takes on more and more assignments, often forcing him to work far into the night. The image of the truck's weak headlights cutting into the darkness of a desolate country highway is a compelling visualization of the forced trajectory of self-exploitation that leads to the protagonist's injury. Sitting at the window of the family house he built, looking out the barren winter landscape shot in black and white, the film effectively depicts the lack of perspective of the disabled Sanyi, who cannot drive the truck anymore. Ultimately, the truck, the symbol of Sanyi's ventures, has to be sold. *Countdown* features a character who loses both social position and money due to health reasons. The film, however, effectively depicts that the injury is caused in turn by the contradictions of late-state socialism: the entrepreneur's only capital is labor. Therefore, s/he exploits it to the maximum. This point is powerfully enforced by the film's coda, where his wife Jutka has to jump in as the breadwinner of the family. It is now she who works frantically around the clock . . . just like Sanyi did before. There are several other films that depict the failure of the small entrepreneur in that period, such as *Hülyeség nem akadály* (*Silliness is no Problem*, János Xantus, 1986), *A nagy generáció* (*The Great Generation*, Ferenc András, 1986), or the small-time criminal ventures *Képvadászok* (*Image Hunters*, Miklós Szurdi, 1986) and *A nagy postarablás* (*The Great Post Robbery*, Sándor Söth, 1992).

Fig. 2: Édes Emma, drága Böbe (Sweet Emma, Dear Böbe, István Szabó, 1992).

The protagonists of *Sweet Emma, dear Böbe* (Fig. 2) are emblematic characters of post-regime change Hungary, and the precarity of their identity is foregrounded in the film in multiple ways. As former teachers of Russian, they became suddenly obsolete with the changing curricula in schools and are considered pariahs at work as instructors of a language that represents a hated era. Their social fall is complimented by their economic hardships: the two women from the country who hardly make any money live in a workers' shelter, sharing a small room. The rapidly shifting power dynamics of society are repeatedly expressed through gender conflicts. Thus the female protagonists are involved in conflicts with various men, such as the headmaster of the school with whom Emma is having an affair, with the wealthy German tourists that Böbe suggests they should meet, and with the sexist police officers who accuse Böbe of various crimes. The theme of sexuality as an arena in which social insecurities are played out returns in several films of this first period: good examples are the asymmetrical affair between János and the elusive French woman Odette in *A rejtőzködő* (*The Hidden*, Zsolt Kézdi-Kovács, 1986), the power games between Mari and Réb over their daughter in *The Great Generation*, and the love affair verging on insanity in *A skorpió megeszi az ikreket reggelire* (*The Scorpion Eats Up the Geminis for Breakfast*, Péter Gárdos, 1992).

The inability to adapt to a new, threatening, and unknowable world is another topic that many of the films in this first period pick up in order to express precarity and social turmoil. The regime change brings nothing but (primarily social) problems for the elderly couple Kati and Ede in *Oops*. They fail to understand the rules of the new, post-socialist game and both escape into their own secrets, thereby drifting further and further away from each other. Kati writes a dream-diary, in which she takes exotic journeys and leads conversations with her long-deceased patriarchal father in order to compensate for their dull life and for Ede's failure to step up as an authority figure. At the same time Ede accidentally bumps into a former lover, who tells him they have a now-20-year-old son together. Through the figure of the son, the film is able to stage the re-emergence of the (socialist) past as unknown territory. The episodes powerfully reiterate not only their weary relation to current precarious social circumstances but also the constructedness of their version of an idealized past, an era they thought they knew and were comfortable with. Initially it seems that they also suffer from monetary problems (their savings evaporate quickly when the car dealership they made prepayments to goes bankrupt), but the film resolves this issue as Ede is able to buy a house in the country after all. This shows that money problems never were their main issue. In the final scene, Kati rejects Ede's offer to live peacefully in their new house, says goodbye to her husband, and walks away. In a quasi-point-of-view shot from the helpless Ede's perspective, we watch her stepping onto a balloon and drifting off. Apparently, she goes on to embrace the imaginary world she constructed for herself, while Ede wallows in denial. The escape into a fantasy world as a tool of rejection keeps coming up in several other films of this period: in *Silliness is no Problem* the protagonist literally turns into a childish fool in order to escape reality, while *The Great Generation*, *The Scorpion Eats Up the Geminis for Breakfast,* and *Laura* (Géza Böszörményi, 1987) deploy the deceptive myths of ever-lasting friendship, love, and youthful rebelliousness, respectively, as useful devices of escapism.

Agency and Decline

During the second period, films still focus on social decline and depict economic crisis only sporadically: among the 28 protagonists between 1995 and 2003 there are 26 whose social downfall, and only six whose economic downfall we witness. However, the inevitability of the forces that bring about the social decline of the characters (five protagonists) shifts towards stories where precarity is caused by the protagonists' own decisions (23 protagonists). Most importantly, these choices relate to criminality and its consequences, such as getting arrested and going to jail: we can see this in the case of 14 protagonists. However, during this period we also find characters whose downfall is brought about by fateful love affairs.

A good example for the aforementioned transformation is *Gengszterfilm* (*Gangster Film*, György Szomjas, 1999), a farcical tale of two criminals, Gábor and Sanyi, whose actions turn more and more violent and spiral out of their control (Fig. 3). Continuing with an emblematic visual style of handheld, tight close-ups already visible in Szomjas's prequel *Roncsfilm* (*Junk Film*, György Szomjas, 1992), cinematographer Ferenc Grunwalsky gets uncomfortably close to the characters, who discuss their violent, antisocial actions in a detached, matter of fact, but at the same time ludicrous way, just like they talk about lunch items and repairing cars.

Fig. 3: Gengszterfilm (Gangster Film, György Szomjas, 1999).

The exaggerated, caricature-like acting style of Zoltán Mucsi and Péter Scherer[28] confuses audiences through the seeming incompatibility of the dialogues' tonality and their subject. *Gangster Film* is propelled forward by this uncomfortable lack of moral consideration, thereby catching an important sentiment of the post-1989 wild capitalism of Hungary. The transformation between the two films is worth mentioning here, as it effectively highlights the structural differences between the first phase of the corpus, where the characters' decline is caused by situational factors, and the second where it results from their own dispositions. In *Junk Film*, the social decline is due to poverty and alcoholism that gets worse as the film progresses. Overall, however, it has little to do with the actions of the protagonists and much rather seems to be a permanent social condition. The deranged-drunk petty criminals and their penniless neighbors do not act with conscious intentionality, but rather play in an arena demarcated by the social-material circumstances of their life world. In this regard, the contrast between Zoltán Mucsi and Péter Scherer's characters across the two films could not be stronger. In *Gangster Film*, the two talk about, meticulously plan, and conduct robberies, some of which end up in murder. Gábor's girlfriend attempts to run a video store, a bar, a floral shop, but fails in each venture. Therefore, they have to rely financially on Gábor's job, again and again. Szomjas's two films, and the

---

28 Grunwalsky and the two actors went on to make a number of films with Miklós Jancsó, which are based on the absurd adventures of the two characters they established in Szomjas's films. For more on this, see László Strausz, "The Politics of Style in Miklós Jancsó's *The Red and The White* and *The Lord's Lantern in Budapest*," *Film Quarterly* 62, no. 3 (2009).

characters' transformation between them, highlight this shift in agency that marks contemporary Hungarian films on precarity.

In this second period within the corpus, there is a significant number of crime films in which crime and its consequences play a central role in the protagonists' downfall. This cause dominates overall among the reasons that lead to social/economic decline. The gritty television style of *Pattogatott kukorica* (*Popcorn*, Gábor Péter, 1999) on a group of violent criminals in Budapest's infamous 8th district redraws the silly innocence of *Junk Film*, which played in and around the same blocks. *Balekok és banditák* (*Losers and Bandits*, Péter Bacsó, 1997) introduces a character who starts a shady "scapegoat" business: for good money he takes the blame for other people's mistakes. After initial success, the plan fails, and the man loses everything. In *A rózsa vére* (*The Rose's Blood*, Dezső Zsigmond, 1998) characters participate in an oil smuggling scheme at the country's eastern borders that ultimately falls short. *Anarchisták* (*Anarchists*, Tamás Tóth, 2001) depicts two idealistic youngsters who criminally rebel against the selfish, materialistic life around them, triggered by an incident where co-workers of a charity organization steal donations only to sell them abroad. The young protagonists of *Kísértések* (*Temptations*, Zoltán Kamondi, 2002) and *Vagabond* (György Szomjas, 2003) are arrested after being caught committing financial fraud and robbery, respectively. In each of these examples, the social downfall of the protagonists, generally depicted as more crucial than the material aspects, is a deliberate reaction to the precarious social circumstances.

Additionally, there are three films in this group in which the protagonists' downfall is brought about by romantic feelings. *Érzékek iskolája* (*School of Senses*, András Sólyom, 1996) depicts an intense love affair crossing various social boundaries with the man ultimately returning to his upper-class family, leaving a young woman to social fall. In *Sztracsatella* (*Stracciatella*, András Kern, 1996) the protagonist, a middle-class artist, experiences a midlife crisis in the form of a love affair leaving his life in ruins, and in *Közel a szerelemhez* (*Close to Love*, András Salamon, 1999) a policeman falls for a Chinese woman and has to overcome the systemic prejudices of state institutions. From the perspective of the question of agency, these pieces also stage decline as a consequence of personal choices.

Variations of Decline

In the third and last phase, we see a gradual shift back towards a more equal distribution of social and economic decline, and social and private reasons for these changes in the characters' fates. Overall, there are 38 protagonists whose fates decline: 18 in auteur films and 20 in genre films. Economic crisis features more strongly than in the previous period there are 19 protagonists who suffer economic loss against 25 who decline socially. More importantly, the reasons for the changes in the characters' lives also become somewhat more balanced, with 12 cases where social forces cause the precarious situations and 26 where crisis is the result of their own decisions. Dispositional factors still appear twice as often as situational ones, but this ratio is much less extreme compared to the almost complete disappearance of social causes during the late 1990s. For this reason, this third phase is less distinct and can be conceptualized as the gradual fading of the almost complete dominance of dispositional reasons for slipping into precarity.

Auteur films and dramas produced during the period show a variety of factors that lead to downfall. In *Fekete kefe* (*Black Brush*, Roland Vranik, 2005), four youngsters hang around in Budapest, taking odd jobs to make some money and pass the time. They start working for a gangster entrepreneur, only to lose most of his money at a cockfight, steal a car from an oriental sect, get stoned, etc. In the end they find themselves even more broke than they were in the beginning but take this turn of events with stoic resignation. Vranik's film depicts the hopelessness and lack of perspective in the lives of his four drifter protagonists, whose only ambition is to make it to the end of the day. Other auteur films such as *Dallas Pashamende* (Róber Pejó, 2005) revolve around the structural racism against Roma: the protagonist, a teacher who once escaped the quasi-feudal circumstances of the village where he was born, gets helplessly sucked back into this world. Made towards the end of the period, *Genezis* (*Genesis*, Árpád Bogdán, 2018) tackles the tragic murders of Roma people in Hungary: its young protagonist loses everything as a group of far-right killers mow down his entire family.[29] *Az állampolgár* (*The Citizen*, Roland Vranik, 2016) depicts the disillusioning troubles of two Black refugees in Hungary. Portraying underage prostitution, two films made in the same year stage the tragic events from different perspectives: situational and dispositional. Young Iszka is forced into prostitution in the gritty *Iszka utazása* (*Iszka's Journey*, Csaba Bollók, 2007), while the protagonists of *Lányok* (*Girls*, Anna Faur, 2007) prostitute themselves to earn some money and pass the time. *Out* (György Kristóf, 2017) introduces a protagonist who is tricked into accepting a non-existent job abroad, and after milling about he ends up working on a fishing boot. As the examples reveal, auteur films and dramas

---

[29] Bence Fliegauf's 2012 film *Csak a szél* (*Just the Wind*) also depicts the aforementioned racist murder series. The reason this film is not part of the corpus is technical: Protagonists who pass away (and thus do not experience social or economic decline) are not included in my search in the database. Whether this exclusion is justifiable or not is debatable, but I used this criterion to limit the number of films in the corpus.

depict both economic and social downfall and offer a variety of explanations for the events that befall their protagonists.

Genre films (with the exception of dramas noted above) explain crisis exclusively through dispositional attributes, of which, just like in the previous phase, crime and its consequences feature most importantly. In this phase, we find films about runaway robbers such as *A miskolci boniésklájd* (*Who the Hell's Bonnie & Clyde*, Krisztina Deák, 2004) and *A viszkis* (*The Whiskey Robber*, Nimród Antal, 2017), gang rivalries and crime stories in *Zuhanórepülés* (*Nosedive*, Erik Novák, 2007) and *Cop mortem* (József Kovalik, 2016). There are other factors here however. *Gondolj rám* (*Think of Me*, András Kern, 2016) revolves around the late-midlife crisis of a doctor who is diagnosed with a terminal illness, which mysteriously disappears from his body after he has wrecked his entire social life. An outstandingly popular Hungarian genre film, *Üvegtigris 2* (*Glass Tiger 2*, Péter Rudolf, 2006) goes on from its prequel through the comic story of its lovable losers who stumble around in this burlesque-like film. Protagonist Lali owns a roadside trailer selling refreshments for drivers passing by (Fig. 4).

Fig. 4: Üvegtigris 2 (Glass Tiger 2, Péter Rudolf, 2006).

Similar to the first installment and in line with comedy storylines, the film follows the abrupt changes of fortune in the protagonists' lives. While it seems to offer the simple-minded protagonist and his friends a chance to break out (they sell the piece of land under the trailer for a large sum), in the end the film finds them in the exact same situation as in the beginning, or even lower. The directions of these changes, however, follows a distinct pattern: when their fates change for better, it is always the results of a coincidence, and when for the worse, it is due to their own mishaps. From the perspective of precarity, *Glass Tiger 2* fits well with the pattern of other 2000s genre films that depict downward mobility as a dispositional change. Falling behind, however, is depicted not so much as a threat looming over the characters' fates, but rather as change that does not break their will. This might explain the immense therapeutic popularity of each part of the *Glass Tiger* trilogy: they all turn precarity into a manageable affect, into something that audiences can laugh about. Nonetheless, even in these genre films, decline is the immediate result of the protagonists' decisions.

Overall, Hungarian film on social and economic decline from the mid-2000s onwards swings back from the extreme polarization of the two previous phases. While social forces dominated the films around the regime change for about ten years, the pieces produced from the mid-1990s place the responsibility on their protagonists when representing precarity. Around 2003–2004, this trend slows down and swings around, and protagonists with situational attributes for decline reappear, although still in lower numbers.

By Way of Conclusion: Some Hypotheses on Social Factors

The relationship between the shifts in the cinematic representations of precarity described here and the changes in the fabric of Hungarian society are very complex, and I cannot attempt to offer a comprehensive portrayal of this correlation here. What follows are a few hypothetical ideas on the turning points that frame the three phases of situational, dispositional, and mixed representation of decline into precarity.

A crucial question for the periodization of Hungarian cinema's social history is the films' deemphasizing of 1989: why do films not react to this historical juncture? Potential answers suggest that Hungarian films do not so much (or at least not just) reflect the changes in the structure of society, but much rather mirror the disposition of the filmmakers, or more broadly speaking that of middle-class intellectuals. While 1989 undoubtedly introduces social changes that affect the entire society, intellectuals already started to experience precarity in terms of social status during the mid-1980s. According to Erzsébet Szalai, this is partially due to late Kádárism's weakening reliance on intellectuals and increasing reliance on technocrats for self-legitimization.[30] Additionally, intellectuals also felt economically precarious due to the rising financial possibilities of

---

30 Erzsébet Szalai, "Feljegyzések a cethal gyomrából. A kulturális elit válsága és az értelmiség dilemmái," *Az elitek átváltozása* (Budapest: Cserépfalvi Kiadó, 1998).

small entrepreneurship. On the other hand, the dominance of situational factors in the articulations of precarity lasting until the mid-1990s is also related to intellectuals' general disposition of powerlessness since the late 1960s: "their positions [or the lack thereof] were primarily not the results of their knowledge, but their displayed loyalty towards an external power."[31] In 1981 critics already noted that Hungarian cinema had a strong inclination towards depicting "whining" intellectuals. Several commentators lamented on the possible social causes of the phenomenon,[32] but a simple answer is that this feeling of dismissal (or whining) does not just belong to the diegetic characters but even more importantly to the creators of the films themselves. This dominant disposition of social displacement does not change with the regime change, but rather further destabilizes the status of intellectuals.

By the mid-1990s, however, it becomes increasingly clear that formations of Hungarian society, and with them questions of social mobility, can no longer be explained with reference to an oppressive regime. Thus, individual agency moves into the center of the filmmakers' themes, a trend that is clearly reflected in the cinematic output of the era until the mid-2000s. Another factor is probably the further spreading of genre film conventions in filmmaking. Genre films were made in larger numbers from the mid-1990s onwards, and these kinds of stories are generally driven by the individual motivation of the characters and less by social factors. As I have demonstrated, the period between around 1994 and 2004 is characterized by an almost complete reversal of the situational attributes in cinema, and dispositional factors dominate the protagonists' fates. Around the mid-2000s, the dominance of individual agency as the main motivator of precarity or downward mobility starts to fade. This slow, less marked, and progressive shift is arguably related to the exhaustion of the hopes that neoliberal capitalism in Hungary will translate into broadly available, improved living standards and social security. As Gábor Scheiring and Kristóf Szombati put it, "[t]he hope that liberalisation [implemented during the early 2000s] would help the emergence of efficient enterprises and mobilise inactivated segments of the labor force failed to materialise."[33] This frustration of the expectations is also expressed in the frequent social withdrawal of protagonists, and

---

31 Erzsébet Szalai, "Az értelmiség útja a semmibe?," *Lépték és irónia*, ed. András Bozóki and Katalin Füzér (Budapest: L'Harmattan, 2018), 141.
32 On pages of the monthly journal Filmvilág in 1981, four articles discuss the thematic of the "whining intellectual." See for example Elemér Hankiss, "Nyafogás vagy társadalomkritika?," *Filmvilág* 1981, no. 9 (1981): 33.
33 Gábor Scheiring and Kristóf Szombati, "From neoliberal disembedding to authoritarian reembedding: The making of illiberal hegemony in Hungary," *International Sociology* no. 35 (2020): 726.

the sentiment is reflected in the filmmakers' dispositions on social change, and thereby in the re-appearance of situational attribution of cinematic precarity. Arguably, the analyzed phases in Hungarian cinema are not simply reflections of social transformations, but also mirror the dispositions of the filmmakers themselves about social mobility, and intellectuals' fears about precarity and the loss of social status in general.

Bibliography

Bourdieu, Pierre. "The Forms of Capital" [1983]. In *Handbook of Theory and Research for the Sociology of Education*, ed. John Richardson. Westport, CT: Greenwood, 1986, 241–158.
Bukodi, Erzsébet. "Társadalmunk Szerkezete Különböző Nézőpontokból." In *Társadalmi Metszetek*, ed. Imre Kovách. Budapest: Napvilág Kiadó, 2006, 109–160.
Hankiss, Elemér. "Nyafogás Vagy Társadalomkritika?" *Filmvilág*, no. 9 (1981): 33.
Kolosi, Tamás and Péter Róbert. "A Magyar Társadalom Szerkezeti Átalakulásának És Mobilitásának Főbb Folyamatai a Rendszerváltás Óta." In *Társadalmi Riport 2004*, ed. Kolosi Tamás, Tóth István György, and Vukovich György. Budapest: Tárki, 2004, 48–74.
Kovács, András Bálint. "Műfajok a Magyar Filmtörténetben." *Apertúra*, 3 April, 2018. https://uj.apertura.hu/2018/tavasz/kab-mufajok-a-magyar-filmtortenetben/.
Laki, László. "Rendszerváltások Magyarországon." In *Társadalmi Metszetek*, ed. Imre Kovács. Budapest: Napvilág Kiadó, 2006, 39–78.
Margitházi, Beja. "Up the Slope. Women's Mobility Stories in Post-Transition Hungarian Cinema." *Acta Univ. Sapientiae, Film and Media Studies*, no. 18 (2020): 223–250.
Mihancsik, Zsófia. "Kiürült Agóra. A Rendszerváltás Filmjei – Beszélgetés György Péterrel, Hirsch Tiborral És Révész Sándorral." *Filmvilág*, no. 1 (2002): 16–21.
Róbert, Péter, and Erzsébet Bukodi. "Changes in Intergenerational Class Mobility in Hungary, 1973–2000." In *Social Mobility in Europe*, ed. Richard Breen. Oxford: Oxford University Press, 2004, 287–314.
Romsics, Ignác. *Magyarország Története a XX. Században*. Budapest: Osiris, 2010.
Scheiring, Gábor, and Kristóf Szombati. "From Neoliberal Disembedding to Authoritarian Reembedding: The Making of Illiberal Hegemony in Hungary." *International Sociology* no. 35 (2020): 721–738.
Schubert, Gusztáv. "Rejtőzködő Évtized. A Magyar Rendszerváltás Filmjei." *Metropolis* 6, no. 2–3 (2002): 10–24.
Strausz, László. "The Politics of Style in Miklós Jancsó's *The Red and the White* and *The Lord's Lantern in Budapest*." *Film Quarterly* 62, no. 3 (2009): 41–47.
Szalai, Erzsébet. "Feljegyzések a Cethal Gyomrából. A Kulturális Elit Válsága És Az Értelmiség Dilemmái." In *Az Elitek Átváltozása*. ed. Szalai, Erzsébet. Budapest: Cserépfalvi Kiadó, 1998, 107–138.
———. "Az Értelmiség Útja a Semmibe?" In *Lépték És Irónia*, ed. András Bozóki and Katalin Füzér. Budapest: L'Harmattan, 2018, 139–60.
Szelenyi, Ivan. "Pathways from and Crises after Communism: The Case of Central Eastern Europe." *Belvedere Meridionale* 26, no. 4 (2014): 7–23.

Valuch, Tibor. *A Jelenkori Magyar Társadalom*. Budapest: Osiris Kiadó, 2015.
Varga, Balázs. "Paradoxes of Popularity." *Ekrany* 56, no. 4 (2020): 11–17.
Weiner, Bernard. *Achievement Motivation and Attribution Theory*. New York: General Learning Press, 1974.

Filmography

A miskolci boniésklájd (*Who the Hell's Bonnie & Clyde*). Dir. Krisztina Deák. Hungary, 2004.
A nagy generáció (*The Great Generation*). Dir. Ferenc András. Hungary, 1986.
A nagy postarablás (*The Great Post Robbery*). Dir. Sándor Söth. Hungary, 1992.
A rejtőzködő (*The Hidden*). Dir. Zsolt Kézdi-Kovács. Hungary, 1986.
A rózsa vére (*The Rose's Blood*). Dir. Dezső Zsigmond. Hungary, 1998.
A skorpió megeszi az ikreket reggelire (*The Scorpion Eats Up the Geminis for Breakfast*). Dir. Péter Gárdos. Hungary, 1992.
A viszkis (*The Whiskey Robber*). Dir. Nimród Antal. Hungary, 2017.
Anarchisták (*Anarchists*). Dir. Tamás Tóth. Hungary, 2001.
Az állampolgár (*The Citizen*). Dir. Roland Vranik. Hungary, 2016.
Balekok és banditák (*Losers and Bandits*). Dir. Péter Bacsó. Hungary, 1997.
Cop mortem. Dir. József Kovalik. Hungary, 2016.
Csak a szél (*Just the Wind*). Dir. Bence Fliegauf. Hungary/Germany/France, 2012.
Dallas Pashamende. Dir. Róber Pejó. Hungary, Germany/Hungary/Romania, 2005.
Édes Emma, drága Böbe (*Sweet Emma, Dear Böbe*). Dir. István Szabó. Hungary/Germany, 1992.
Érzékek iskolája (*School of Senses*). Dir. András Sólyom. Hungary, 1996.
Fekete kefe (*Black Brush*). Dir. Roland Vranik. Hungary, 2005.
Genezis (*Genesis*). Dir. Árpád Bogdán. Hungary, 2018.
Gengszterfilm (*Gangster Film*). Dir. György Szomjas. Hungary, 1998.
Gondolj rám (*Think of Me*). Dir. András Kern. Hungary, 2016.
Hoppá (*Oops*). Dir. Gyula Maár. Hungary, 1993.
Hülyeség nem akadály (*Silliness is no Problem*). Dir. János Xantus. Hungary, 1996.
Iszka utazása (*Iszka's Journey*). Dir. Csaba Bollók. Hungary, 2007.
Képvadászok (*Image Hunters*). Dir. Miklós Szurdi. Hungary, 1986.
Kísértések (*Temptations*). Dir. Zoltán Kamondi. Hungary, 2002.
Közel a szerelemhez (*Close to Love*). Dir. András Salamon. Hungary, 1999.
Lányok (*Girls*). Dir. Anna Faur. Hungary, 2007.
Laura. Dir. Géza Böszörményi. Hungary, 1987.
Out. Dir. György Kristóf. Slovakia/France/Hungary/Czech Republic, 2017.
Pattogatott kukorica (*Popcorn*). Dir. Gábor Péter. Hungary, 1999.
Roncsfilm (*Junk Film*). Dir. György Szomjas. Hungary, 1992.
Sztracsatella (*Stracciatella*). Dir. András Kern. Hungary, 1996.
Üvegtigris 2 (*Glass Tiger 2*). Dir. Péter Rudolf. Hungary, 2006.
Vagabond. Dir. György Szomjas. Hungary, 2003.
Visszaszámlálás (*Countdown*). Dir. Pál Erdőss. Hungary, 1986.
Zuhanórepülés (*Nosedive*). Dir. Erik Novák. Hungary, 2007.

Katarína Mišíková
Social Martyrs in Slovak Social Film Drama and Documentary

Since the end of the first decade of the new millennium, the artistic reputation of Slovak fiction film has been boosted by the trend toward social film dramas. After a period of economic and creative stagnation in the industry in the 1990s and early 2000s, marked by a lack of reflection on current reality, this new trend brought long-awaited issues of post-socialist transformation to Slovak cinema, as well as new aesthetic forms, merging elements of fiction and nonfiction.[1] This trend is closely related to the previous movement of social documentary filmmaking by the so-called Generation 90, which introduced current issues, such as economic transformation, multiculturalism, globalization, politics, disadvantaged social groups, precarity, problems of the Roma minority, etc. into Slovak cinema.[2] After the foundation of the Slovak Audiovisual Fund in 2010 and the beginning of systematic public financial support for cinema, many of the Generation 90 documentary filmmakers and their younger colleagues shifted from low-budget nonfiction production to fiction. Although not all social film dramas and documentaries deal with the subject of precarity, they offer a valuable insight into how poverty and precarity are represented in the highbrow arthouse cinema trends of a post-socialist country.

Both social film drama and social documentary have been quite successful on the international festival circuit and have received predominantly positive critical response domestically.[3] However, while social documentaries of the

---

1 For a closer explication of the social drama trend see Katarína Mišíková, "Hľadanie žánru v slovenskom hranom filme," in *Nový slovenský film: Produkčné, estetické, distribučné a kritické východiská*, ed. Katarína Mišíková and Mária Ferenčuhová (Bratislava: Vysoká škola múzických umení 2015), and Katarína Mišíková, "The Real Story: Indexing Strategies of Slovak Social Film Dramas," in *Transformation Processes in Post-Socialist Screen Media*, ed. Jana Dudková and Katarína Mišíková (Bratislava: Academy of Performing Arts in Bratislava, 2016).
2 The term Generation 90 was first coined by the influential film critic Pavel Branko to describe common characteristics of nonfiction works by Jaroslav Vojtek, Peter Kerekes, Marko Škop, Robert Kirchhoff, Juraj Lehotský, Zuzana Piussi, and Marek Kuboš. Most of them are graduates of documentary filmmaking at the Film and Television Faculty of the Academy of Performing Arts in Bratislava. See Pavel Branko, "Slovenský dokumentárny film – Generácia 90," *Film.sk* 5, no. 2 (2004).
3 The most significant success of this trend is represented by several films premiered at A-list film festivals, e.g. *Môj pes Killer* (*My Dog Killer*, Mira Fornay, 2013), one of the three Hivos Tiger Awards at the IFF Rotterdam in 2013; *Eva Nová* (Marko Škop, 2015), FIPRESCI at the

Open Access. © 2022 Katarína Mišíková, published by De Gruyter. This work is licensed under the Creative Commons Attribution-NonCommercial-NoDerivatives 4.0 International License.
https://doi.org/10.1515/9783110707816-011

Generation 90 have been almost unanimously praised by domestic critics, the social drama films have been criticized by Slovak filmmakers and film critics who object to the arthouse exclusivity and alleged elitism of these films, as well as to certain stereotypical narrative patterns and character types. These objections stem partly from the fact that these works, often seen as a film festival commodity, are not able to compete with popular genre films on the local film market. Film critic Miloš Krekovič summed up reservations regarding social film drama in his article "Why is Social Drama a Pejorative in Slovakia?"[4] in which he compared Slovak social realism with the Dardenne brothers' films. He blamed Slovak filmmakers for focusing on extreme situations when portraying social problems, showing only the very lowest parts of society, and for emotionally manipulating the viewers by emphasizing the suffering of victims instead of analyzing the causes of social problems. In light of this critique, we can perceive the paradox of Slovak social film drama. Firstly, filmmakers who moved from documentary to fiction changed the dominant aesthetic paradigm of Slovak cinema through a realist style and through interest in social issues, but their gloomy stories from the social periphery give a somewhat deformed view of Slovak reality, which is much more nuanced than what we see in these films. Secondly, although these films have an ambition to reflect the reality of common people, they isolate themselves in the ivory tower of arthouse cinema, hence not reaching the audiences to whose lives they refer. Looking back at the history of cinema, these paradoxes may remind us of controversies about Italian neorealism in the 1950s as well as of the current debate about the ethics of so-called "poverty porn."[5]

Toronto IFF in 2015; *Koza* (Ivan Ostrochovský, 2015), premiered in the Panorama section at the Berlinale in 2015; *Out* (György Kristóf, 2017), premiered in the Un Certain Regard section at the Cannes IFF in 2017; *Piata loď* (*Little Harbor*, Iveta Grófová, 2017), winner of the Generation KPLUS section at the Berlinale; *Slepé lásky* (*Blind Loves*, Juraj Lehotský, 2008), premiered in the Directors' Fortnight at the Cannes IFF in 2008; and *Hotel Úsvit* (*Hotel Sunrise*, Mária Rumanová, 2016), premiered at the International Documentary Filmfestival Amsterdam in 2016).

4 Miloš Krekovič, "Prečo je sociálna dráma na Slovensku nadávkou?," *Denník N*, March 19, 2015, https://dennikn.sk/75337/socialne-dramy/.

5 Although the term is used by film critics mainly to refer to cinematic depictions of the Global South—such as *Slumdog Millionaire* (Dir. Danny Boyle and Loveleen Tandan, 2008) or *Cidade de Deus* (*City of God*, Dir. Fernando Meirelles and Kátia Lund, 2002)—,which feature exploited and impoverished protagonists in order to excite disgust and pity in Western white and middle-class cinema audiences, some of the objections against the false sense of compassion and against exoticization of poverty can also be applied to the cinemas of post-socialist countries, especially to films about the Roma community. In the context of Slovak cinema, this is a subject that has not been sufficiently analyzed, although some of these issues can be identified in Mária Ferenčuhová, "Obrazy 'iných' a 'druhých' v súčasnom slovenskom dokumentárnom

Both Slovak social documentary and social film drama are rather heterogeneous in regard to style and genre, with individual film directors employing different, often contradictory formal elements. However, what these films share is a general tendency towards hybridization of fiction and nonfiction (from staging techniques in documentary film through employing fiction film techniques in documentaries to featuring real-life protagonists and settings in a fictional plot) and considerable similarities in the themes they depict. Circulation and repetition of thematic motifs is due partly to the input of scriptwriter Marek Leščák, who co-wrote almost half of these films, and partly to the generational bond and creative coherence of the filmmakers, who have been cooperating since their university studies. An almost universal trait of these social dramas and documentaries is a character who is placed in a socially unfavorable situation, often resulting in his or her social and emotional isolation. I argue that the model for most of the characters of social dramas as victims who accept or resist their fates is the archetype of the social martyr, rooted in Slovak cultural tradition. But not all characters of social dramas conform to the passive victim model, as we will see; some social martyrs find strength, hope, or a certain awakening through their struggles.

In this article, I will examine prevalent themes and motifs tied to representations of precarity in contemporary Slovak fiction and nonfiction cinema. A brief overview of social themes in Slovak literature, fine art, and cinema will define the archetype of the social martyr that is characteristic of contemporary depictions of poverty and precarity. After a concise comparison with the Czech cinema, I will then examine various reincarnations of this archetype and analyze thematic motifs and poetic tropes that they are tied to as well as dominant narrative and stylistic traits of social film dramas and documentaries. This should help us pin down the complexity and variability of representations of social martyrs.

Tracing the Tradition of Social Martyrs

The archetype of the martyr, a socially excluded individual going through trials and tribulations of poverty and suffering, can be found in several literary works of the Slovak realist tradition.[6] Social motifs and imagery are also present in

---

filme," in *Nový slovenský film. Prudukčné, estetické, distribučné a kritické východiská*, ed. Katarína Mišíková and Mária Ferenčuhová (Bratislava: Vysoká škola múzických umení, 2015).

6 For example the short story "Neprebudený" (translated as "An unawakened boy, or the village idiot") by Martin Kukučín (1886), the socialist novel *Čenkovej deti* (*Čenková's Children*) by Fraňo Kráľ (1932), and most notably *Jozef Mak* (1933) by Jozef Cíger-Hronský, who named his

Slovak fine art of the interwar avant-garde:[7] we can find figures collapsing under heavy burdens, images of poor people suffering from hunger, motifs of emigrants and refugees forced to leave their homes because of hardships or war. Most social motifs are tied to village life, but we can also find several images of social martyrs in the cities, for example portraits of prostitutes or fallen women.

The advent of socialist realism after 1948 brought about a change in the paradigm of social motifs in Slovak art: instead of suffering and poverty, victory and industrial progress were accentuated. The dominant character of socialist cinema was an active hero, representing a collective group, who overcomes obstacles of reactionary forces and brings about social change. Although the short period of political liberalization in the creative heyday of the 1960s brought much more differentiated narratives and character types, the normalization period following the occupation of Czechoslovakia in 1968 was marked by the return to thematic and ideological schematism.

An exceptional phenomenon from this period pertaining to the representation of socially disadvantaged people is the documentary *Obrazy starého sveta* (*Pictures of the Old World*, 1972) by Dušan Hanák. The film features portraits of several old village people, who lived a life of hardship and suffering in a turbulent historical era and who reply to the director's questions about the real meaning of life. Communist officials disapproved of the aesthetics of ugliness of the film, and therefore it could not be screened publicly for 15 years. After 1989, Dušan Hanák became a film professor and a key influence on the Generation 90 documentary filmmakers. It might be precisely that this nonfiction background shared by many directors of social film dramas is the cause of a significant presence of social subject matter in both Slovak fiction and nonfiction film.

The situation is quite different from that of Czech cinema. Despite its being considerably more productive than Slovak cinema, with more stratified genres and higher domestic attendance, Czech cinema presents only two fiction directors who continually deal with the subject of poverty and precarity in a realist

---

hero symbolically as Mak—Poppy Seed and called him "man-million"—an Everyman. Hronský created a new type of social novel by shifting the accent from the portrayal of specific social circumstances of his characters to suffering as a constant determinant of the lives of common people—his hero is a representative of the whole social group, who seems to accept tragic strokes of fate passively, but at the same time is endowed with an inner strength and invincibility that helps him to endure everything.

7 E.g. František Reichentál, Imrich Weiner-Kráľ, Ladislav Čemický, František Studený, Koloman Sokol, Cyprián Majerník, Mikuláš Galanda, Konštantín Bauer.

style: Petr Václav and Bohdan Sláma. In his debut feature film *Marian* (1996), Petr Václav presented a psychological portrait of a Roma boy from a foster home. Although the state took care of his basic material needs, it has not provided him with any authentic interpersonal skills and relationships. Václav returned to the Roma community in his film *Cesta ven* (*Zaneta*, 2014), a story of a young mother, who despite racial and economic challenges fights for a better future for her daughter and herself. In *Nikdy nejsme sami* (*We Are Never Alone*, 2016), he analyzed the impact of the economic situation on his characters' relationships and life choices. As a loose follow-up to the fate of one of the protagonists of *Zaneta*, he later dealt with the subject of criminal recidivism in the Roma community in the comedy *Skokan* (*The Jumper*, 2017). Like many Slovak social film dramas, Václav often works with amateur actors in actual settings and some of his films are even connected to the real lives of his non-professional protagonists, who portray themselves.

In contrast, Bohdan Sláma most often works with professional actors in somewhat melancholic comedies set in the Czech countryside. In his debut *Divoké včely* (*Wild Bees*, 2001) he combined an authentic depiction of Moravian village life with a coming-of-age story. In *Štěstí* (*Something Like Happiness*, 2005), he contrasted the rough village lifestyle of working-class protagonists with the need for authentic emotional ties and values. In his comedy *Čtyři slunce* (*Four Suns*, 2012), he portrayed four anti-heroes working in precarious jobs and surviving from day to day in a dreary everyday life, who are trying to find various ways to change their fates. Other works with social subject matter worth mentioning are *Poupata* (*Flower Buds*, Zdeněk Jiránský, 2011) and *Kobry a užovky* (*The Snake Brothers*, Jan Prušinovský, 2015), both of which deal with the impact of the economic downfall on the disintegration of families. Representation of social subject matter is considerably more systematic in Czech non-fiction cinema. For several decades, Helena Třeštíková has been continuously dealing with socially marginalized heroes, as in *René* (2008), *Katka* (2010) and *Mallory* (2015) as well as with various challenges to the middle class—mostly in her cycle *Manželské etudy* (*Marriage Stories*, 1987, 2006, 2018) and *Strnadovi* (*A Marriage Story*, 2017) in long-term observational films. Other filmmakers with an interest in social documentary are Vít Janeček with his *Závod ke dnu* (Race to the Bottom, 2011), a film about unemployment, and Vít Klusák with *Vše pro dobro světa a Nošovic* (*All for the Good of the World and Nosovice*, 2010) about the desperate fight of countrymen against the construction of a car factory, or his portrait of a neo-nazi *Svět podle Daliborka* (*The White World According to Daliborek*, 2017). Together with Filip Remunda, Klusák made several films dealing with the impact of neoliberalism on post-socialist society—e.g. *Český sen* (*Czech Dream*, 2004 or *Český mír* (*Czech Peace*, 2010). Together they also created a television cycle for Czech public TV *Český žurnál* (*Czech Journal*), which among other subjects tackles also social issues such as in *Exekuce* (*Don't Take My Life*, Andrea Culková, 2016) or *Hranice práce* (*The Limits of Work*, Apolena Rychlíková, 2017). Czech public television also deals with problems of poverty and precarity in other nonfiction series, e.g. in the film *Chudoba cti netratí* (*Poverty is no Sin*, Dana Gébová, 2013) from the series *Why Poverty?*[8]

Motifs and Figures of Contemporary Social Martyrs

With regards to Slovak cinema, I would claim that the social film drama and documentary trend follows the tradition of social realism that has been present in Slovak art long before the advent of socialist realism. Of course, we can hardly trace specific aesthetic inspirations or reiterations of the same thematic motifs, because current reality poses different challenges for the films' protagonists: they do not have to face wars and have moved away from isolated villages in the mountains. However, the archetype of the social martyr is still present in them.

If the figures of social martyrs can be identified in contemporary social film dramas and documentaries, what common themes and tropes do they represent? The dominant subject matter of social film dramas is unemployment, economic migration, problems of the Roma community, racism, issues of socially excluded individuals, alcoholism, drugs, prostitution, sexual violence, and most of all the subject of disintegrated, incomplete, or dysfunctional families, in which materially and emotionally neglected children cannot find a reliable orientation to form their own system of values. This subject matter determines the character typology of social film dramas: their protagonists are unemployed who become economic migrants; madonna types of suffering mothers or on the contrary heartless mothers who refuse their maternal role; unloved or insufficiently loved children, waiting in vain for support from their parents; fallen women hoping for redemption; ordinary people struggling to elevate their standard of living; or victims of their social situation, enduring oppression.

Although social documentaries of the Generation 90 deal with various subjects ranging from politics, the rise of nationalism, and reflection of the socialist past to portrayals of physically or mentally challenged protagonists, those

---

[8] I would like to thank Martin Šrajer for valuable tips and advice on Czech cinema.

dealing with representations of precarity are mostly concerned with the Roma community. Besides depictions of hardships of living in excluded settlements mainly in Eastern Slovakia, these films about an ethnic minority challenged by generational poverty, unemployment, and educational underdevelopment often focus on the relationship of Sinti and Roma to music as a unique form of communication within and outside of this community.

Let us examine various character types deriving from the archetype of the social martyr in order to identify key themes, motifs, tropes, and figures of precarity of Slovak fiction and non-fiction cinema.

The Unemployed

Economic transformation after the downfall of communism drastically changed the social structure. In areas where state-owned industry was located, former proletarian heroes turned into beggars, now forced to find work in other professions and away from their homes. A pioneering reflection on these transformation processes and the resulting precarization is the documentary *Hej, Slováci!* (*Hey, Slovaks!*, 2002) by Robert Kirchhoff. In the form of a documentary mosaic, the film features heterogenous portraits of protagonists from different parts of Slovakia, whose lives have been impacted by the changing social landscape: former heroes of socialist work, who became unemployed after the privatization of state-owned industry; a winner of the TV show "Who Wants to Be a Millionaire?," who plans to buy a house but fears that he will be robbed of his small fortune; a single mother struggling to support her children with odd jobs; young unemployed men who are dreaming of moving abroad for work; or expats who came to visit the native country of their fathers and grandfathers and reflect on the contrast between their own standards of living and those of their ancestors. Kirchhoff is interested in the subject of poverty as a social phenomenon with considerable political consequences in the forms of nationalistic or communist sentiment, but concentrates mainly on the essence of precarity as a deficit of motivation, the inability to change one's social situation. His protagonists are not martyrs, but casualties of transformation processes in the first post-socialist decade: they were thrown into a world where the rules they had learned to follow were not valid anymore, where the tools they were taught to use became useless. Economic crisis, in Kirchhoff's interpretation, thus turns into a crisis of identity.

Slnečný štát (*The City of the Sun*, 2005) by Martin Šulík deals with a similar subject, but in a completely different genre. This fiction film is about four friends who lost their jobs in metal works in the Moravian city of Ostrava and try to adapt to the new economic situation by starting their own business. It combines inspiration from the popular genre of comedy—the most notable inspiration is the British comedy *The Full Monty* (Peter Cattaneo, 1997)—with the depiction of the social situation of a specific region and its precarized inhabitants. Several social film dramas like *Punk je hned!* (*Punk Never Ends*, 2019) by Juraj Šlauka, *Stanko* (Rasťo Boroš, 2016) or *Pirko* (*Little Feather*, 2016) by Lucia and Petr Klein Svoboda also mix a realist style (non-professional actors, authentic settings and language in the dialogue) with traits of popular genres, such as crime plots, character identification, humor, and more traditional music scores.

While the above-mentioned films focus on transformation, Mária Rumanová's documentary *Hotel Úsvit* (*Hotel Sunrise*, 2016) is dominated by the atmosphere of post-apocalyptic decay. It is set in a town near the borders with Hungary and Ukraine—one of the poorest regions in Slovakia. Its multiethnic population is leaving the town because of a high unemployment rate and those staying behind are doomed to ultimate downfall amidst the ruins of this dying town. The decrepit building of the hotel Úsvit (Sunrise), where gatherings of the local communist activists take place, can be perceived as its symbolic representative. The film offers fragmentary glimpses of the lives of three protagonists living in the town. The true tragedy of their lives is not their social situation itself, but rather their ultimate stagnation, the twilight of hope, the lack of any outlook for a positive change. The director seems almost reluctant to take a sociological approach to the protagonists and their environment. Instead, she concentrates on abstract visual structures, eliminates all informative titles, commentary, or interviews, and weakens referential relations to social reality. Thus, the film presents the viewer only with fragments of a decaying world accompanied by sound footage characteristic more of fiction than nonfiction film: indexical sounds become a part of the music score, telephone dialogue between two protagonists is shot from outside of a car, but the viewer gets access to both parties talking, like in a traditional fiction film. The director does not manipulate or initiate events in the profilmic reality, she observes them from afar, but by using two cameras simultaneously she is able to transform everyday situations into dramatic ones in postproduction. For example, the film adds a motif of platonic love between one protagonist and a train attendant only through the editing. However, the dramatic situations are only implied and have no resolution. The combination of abstraction and fragmentation creates impressions of the town that lack precise social coordinates, narrative development, subjectivation, or interaction with protagonists, but the form of the film renders the feeling of decay and disillusion.

Emigrants

Several social film dramas deal directly or indirectly with the phenomenon of economic migration caused by the lack of employment opportunities in the post-socialist economy. In *Líštičky* (*Little Foxes*, Mira Fornay, 2009), Eastern-European girls go to Ireland as au-pairs and are treated as second-rate citizens. The heroine of the film, impulsive Betka, is struggling to make a living in a foreign country. She sees her only opportunity for survival in casual relationships with men. While her situation apparently contrasts with that of her sister, who is employed and engaged to an Irishman, their male counterparts perceive both female immigrants as stray foxes, wandering around the city: there are too many girls like them, somehow wild and uncivilized, spreading diseases and looking for food everywhere.

Prostitution is the next step downward from Eastern-European girls' economic dependance on men from more economically stable countries. The figure of a fallen women—a naive and young girl, forced to leave home because of her economic situation, who later becomes a prostitute—is a reoccurring motif in several social film dramas. In her film *Až do mesta Aš* (*Made in Ash*, 2012), Iveta Grófová depicts girls from poor backgrounds from various post-socialist countries who come to the Czech town of Aš on the border to Germany, the symbolic end of the post-socialist world, to work as precarized seamstresses in a textile factory. After losing their jobs and not having enough money to go back to their families, they are left with no other option than to fall prey to German sex tourists. *Made in Ash* is one of the formally most daring art-house social film dramas, consistently employing para-documentary style. Grófová originally developed her debut film as a documentary but encountered limits in the representation of intimate situations and decided instead to use non-professional actresses in a scripted story inspired by real life and set in a real environment. She combined documentary observation with footage from security cameras and mobile phones in order to strengthen the film's relation to actual reality. But she also rendered the narration subjective by using blurred visual compositions and animations as representations of the main protagonist's perceptions. In this way she created a suggestive portrayal of the milieu and at the same time accentuated the viewer's identification with the main character.

One of the most tragic aspects of characters precarized by the social and economic transformation is their social and psychological isolation. Economic migration and unstable work take their toll on family relationships. In *Eva Nová*, the main character, a former actress recovering from alcoholism and as an aging woman struggling to find a job, had once left her son in the countryside to be taken care of by her sister so that she could pursue the career of a prominent socialist actress. In post-socialist times, her daughter-in-law leaves for Austria in order to support her family and work as a caretaker (similarly to many Slovak nurses), leaving her unemployed husband and children at home.

In *Out* by György Kristóf, a slightly absurd social road movie, a middle-aged man from the Hungarian minority in Eastern Slovakia leaves his family and tries to find a job in the faraway Baltics. His odyssey to find employment in a foreign world becomes a solitary journey on which he meets several bizarre characters, but also a quest for self-liberation of this passionate amateur fisherman. Contrary to the majority of social film dramas, the absurd edge of the story gives the film an almost optimistic twist despite the rather gloomy subject matter.

The depicted emigrants usually wish to leave post-socialist Slovakia and move west in search of an economically brighter future. However, once abroad, they have to face challenges and the disappointment of their hopes. In a single film, the documentary *My zdes* (*Here We Are*, 2005) by Jaro Vojtek, Slovakia becomes the deceitful promised land for a family, which after World War II had moved to Kazakhstan, leaving the eastern region of Czechoslovakia that became part of the USSR. In 2000, the new generation of the family decides to move back to the country of its origin, only to struggle with financial distress and fear of immigrants.

Middle and Working Class Men

The unemployed and emigrants live at the edges of social dignity, but the situation of the working and middle class, struggling to keep their standard of living and achieve financial security for their children, is not much better. Constant economic pressure and a lack of financial stability act as catalysts in the erosion of family ties.

In *Dom* (*The House*, Zuzana Liová, 2011), the authoritative and hardworking father is willing to sacrifice his health and his family time in order to build a house for his daughter. He is reluctant to admit that he is forcing his own values and ideals on the girl, who instead is dreaming of leaving for Britain. The house acts as a complex trope in the film. It is the metonymy of a family home, but also a metaphor of a stable way of living, a straightforward life trajectory in pre-1989 society. This mode of living did not leave much room for freedom, but it provided security. Hence, the house under never-ending construction symbolically also refers to the post-socialist society as a whole. In the end, the daughter escapes from the safe, but restrictive family nest and abandons the unfinished house to break away from the tradition, to find both a new place to live and a new way of living.

Relationships among family members in *Ďakujem, dobre* (*Thanks, Fine*, Mátyás Prikler, 2013) are brought to boil by the economic crisis and financial conflicts. The film analyzes the current situation of *homo economicus* in three interconnected stories: an elderly couple with a tiny retirement income struggles to cope; their children, with unstable jobs and living unsatisfying family lives in a suburb, try to earn some money by selling the parental apartment after their mother's death and to put their mentally declining father into a rest home; a successful businessman fires his employees with no regrets, while his own family life suffers from his emotional shutdown after the trauma of his son's death.

In *Nech je svetlo* (*Let there be Light*, Marko Škop, 2019), the loving but always absent father is away from his family in northern Slovakia to do construction work in Germany. Up until the Christmas break, he is completely unaware that his eldest son has been ideologically brainwashed by a paramilitary extremist group, which victimizes its younger members and indoctrinates them with racial hatred, with tacit approval by the local priest and the church-going community. He has to find out that the main challenge is not only to provide for his family, but to become a husband for his estranged wife and a father for his son again, who is in desperate need of true paternal authority.

Suffering and Heartless Mothers, Despotic and Helpless Fathers, and Their Children

Relations between parents and children, disrupted by the decay of traditional social ties, are manifested in specific types of maternal and paternal figures. The main protagonist of *O Soni a jej rodine* (*Sona and Her Family*, 2006), a short documentary by Daniela Rusnoková, epitomizes this and is in a way a precursor of suffering and all-enduring mothers in other films. Soňa is a devoted and loving wife and a mother of 15 children, living in a settlement in eastern Slovakia. The director depicts her everyday struggles with her family and material circumstances and interlays them with Soňa's intimate confessions. Thus, the film offers not only an insight into problems of the Roma community, but also a uniquely empathetic opportunity for intercultural dialogue between the social minority and the majority.

The antithesis of mothers as martyrs are heartless mothers, who are reluctant to take on their maternal role. Underaged Ela from *Zázrak* (*Miracle*, Juraj Lehotský, 2013) was physically forced by her mother to live in a detention center. Only after she escapes to her drug addict boyfriend and agrees to be sold as a prostitute to human traffickers in order to pay off his debts, does she realize that neither her mother nor her boyfriend cares for her. When she finds herself pregnant, the only parental advice from her mother is to get rid of the unwanted child in order not to ruin her life as she once did. Ten-year-old Jarka from *Little Harbour* longs for the attention and affection of her mother, who is too young to take care of her and who herself was rejected by her mother because of unwanted pregnancy. Jarka abducts baby twins from an alcoholic stranger and tries to create a new family together with a boy from the neighborhood in a remote garden above the city. The nameless Roma girl from *Stanko* was abandoned by her mother who left for Italy, and when she finally finds her, her mother only tries to get rid of her.

The protagonists of *Miracle* and *Eva Nová* go through a complicated process of accepting their motherhood. Ela, betrayed by both her mother and her boyfriend, decides to give birth to the unwanted child and give it up for adoption. The tenderness in her face shown in the film's finale is a miracle of authentic human emotion, the only one she experiences during the whole story. After years spent in alcoholic rehab, the former star Eva Nová tries to reestablish her relationship with her son. The film closes with a scene of both a symbolic fight and embrace of the mother with her son in an inflatable swimming pool. The water inside metaphorically refers to oblivion, which both mother and son sought in alcoholism. Its circular shape refers to their disintegrated family that has to reconnect again and also evokes the mother's womb with amniotic fluid, in which the bond between the mother and the son is reborn—at least temporarily.

The figure of a despotic father, who wants the best for his children, but cannot accept their own needs, is a recurring character type, which can be found in films like *The House*, *Thanks, fine* or *Nina* (Juraj Lehotský, 2017).

On the other hand, characters of helpless fathers are featured in films like *Hotel Sunrise*, *Thanks, Fine,* and *Deti* (*Children*, 2014) by Jaro Vojtek. A variation of this figure is the protagonist of the film *Punk Never Ends*. A junkie, torn between his addiction and love and duty towards his small son, tries to provide for his partner and their child, but is only able to secure a temporary shelter and in the midst of his own temptations steals the last remaining money from the family budget. After his partner leaves him and he finds himself unable to take care of his son, he seeks the easiest escape in suicide. However, since he is to a large degree a figure of a precarious Sisyphus, he survives the fall from a cliff, and after getting out of the demolished car, he can only laugh at the tragic absurdity of his own situation.

There are only a few loving paternal figures in Slovak social drama. The film *Let There be Light*, which can also be interpreted as a commentary on the overarching crisis of paternal authority, presents the viewer with the central character of the loving father, who wants to do everything for his family, because his own father was despotic, cold, and cruel. However, he must escape the trap of his own toxic masculinity to become a reliable moral compass for his own children.

Martyrs

Several socially excluded and suffering protagonists literally become martyrs, whose sacrifice, however, gives little hope for redemption. In *Koza*, the last boxing tour of a former Olympic champion now living in a Roma ghetto turns into a calvary. When he has to secure money for his partner's abortion, he sets out on a journey through unidentified Western-European countries where he lets himself be beaten in a series of fixed matches. In a similar vein to *Made in Ash*, this film combines inspiration by the real-life protagonist Peter Baláž, called Koza, who played himself in the film, with a fictional plot. Other former real-life boxers are featured in minor roles and the role of Koza's manager is played by a non-professional actor. TV footage, which shows Koza's Olympic match in Atlanta, serves an authentication function. The para-documentary style of the emotionally detached and elliptical narrative is based on observational realism and consists of long, mostly static shots. Emotional attachment with the protagonist is cued only by images of physical suffering, by poetic tropes, and by metaphysical landscapes. The representation of the hero draws heavily on mythological and biblical imagery of martyrdom: he carries heavy burdens to a junk yard as Sisyphus, he experiences hunger and thirst as Tantalus when he tries to drink from a bottle of frozen coke or gets a taste of lollipop stolen from his manager during his sleep. He also runs with a heavy tire tied to his body by a rope (Fig. 1), similar to Jesus Christ carrying his cross. He carries his wounds or metaphorically "walks" on water like Christ when crossing a river on a ferry. Koza, which means goat, is a true scapegoat, ironically carrying the title Slovakia on his jacket. He is accompanied by his Judas, his manager Zvonko. Together they represent two radically different life principles as well as two post-socialist social survival strategies: the devoted exploited and his unscrupulous exploiter.

The protagonists of *Made in Ash* and *Miracle* are portrayed as crucified by the ruthlessness of the world: in *Made in Ash* a stripper is visually "crucified" on the pole, while in a scene in a swimming pool in *Miracle*, Ela, who has no one to teach her how to swim (literally and metaphorically), is at the risk of drowning, which can be seen as a visual metaphor of her life situation.

My Dog Killer by Mira Fornay follows one day in the life of a young neo-Nazi who is ashamed of his estranged mother because she left her father for a Roma man. The protagonist's younger Roma half-brother is killed by a dog. It is not clear whether this was a tragic accident or an intentional murder, and the

Fig. 1: Koza (Ivan Ostrochovský, 2015).

film's ambiguous ending does not indicate whether the event might prospectively change the neo-Nazi teenage protagonist or if the boy is going to be just another tragic victim of racial intolerance.

In the documentary *Comeback* (Miro Remo, 2014), a portrayal of two recidivists, the protagonists are not depicted as innocent victims. Remo shows the destructive patterns that are the cause of their desperate life situations. However, he also points out that the cycle of crime and punishment they entered as teenagers is a vicious circle that is impossible to break because they are no longer capable of living outside the walls of prison and do not know how to cope with freedom. An expressive close-up of one of the zonked-out protagonists screaming directly into the camera, in its visual and affective saliency reminiscent both of Edvard Munch's famous painting *The Scream,* and the close-up of Sergei Eisenstein's cinema of attractions in the image of the lady with eyeglasses from *Bronenosets Potemkin* (*Battleship Potemkin,* 1925*)*, is a picture of despair and at the same time a cry for help (Fig. 2).

Fig. 2: Comeback (Miro Remo, 2014).

It seems that these martyrs of social film dramas and documentaries were born to suffer or—at least some of them—to find the strength to endure suffering.

Documentary Depictions of the Roma Community

The subject of the Roma minority, racial discrimination, and extremism is present in several social film dramas, but the main domain of Roma protagonists as specific types endangered by precarity and poverty are social documentaries. While Ladislav Kaboš' film *Všetky moje deti* (*All My Children*, 2013) deals with issues of the ethnic minority, it can instead also be seen as a portrayal of a modern-day messianic figure of a priest who dedicated his life to charity work. A similar figure can be found in the character of the manager in *Kapela* (*The Band*, 2018) by the same director. In this film, several men try to break free from the ghetto through music. They form a band and try to play gigs at music festivals, but have to deal with racial prejudices, tensions in their own community, as well as perpetual problems with music instruments being pawned in order to pay off loan sharks. Both films follow the mainstream nonfiction cinema pattern of a portrait and success story.

While music is often the dominant paradigm through which Slovak cinema depicts the Roma community, there are several variations on musical themes among social documentaries, which are more experimental in way they deal with the documented subject through staging, interaction, and reenactment. In *Zvonky šťastia* (*Bells of Happiness*, Jana Bučka and Marek Šulík, 2012), we observe two peculiar protagonists, Mariena and her cousin Roman, who are fans of the popular music stars Karel Gott and Dara Rollins. The film presents their everyday life and their admiration of celebrities, as well as the game of switching both identities and gender roles, during which female Mariena impersonates male Karel and male Roman becomes female Dara. The protagonists shift their own position from documented objects to self-staged subjects, becoming their own metteurs-en-scène by taking on the roles of their musical idols. Through this playful self-staging, the film emphasizes the contrast between the stark reality of the Roma ghetto and the unreal world of celebrities and, at the same time, offers its protagonists at least the temporary freedom to choose their fate and an escape from reality.

This therapeutic function of music is also prominent in *Ťažká duša* (*Heavy Hearth*, 2017), a documentary by Marek Šulík, which by comparing the three teenage protagonists and their parents offers an insight into the realm of Roma sad songs and examines their meaning for the community. For generations, these songs have been helping the Roma to struggle with hardship. They are able both to evoke sadness and to ease it through a sort of catharsis.

In contrast, Pavol Pekarčík approaches the depiction of life in a Roma ghetto without any musical romanticism in his film *Hluché dni* (*Silent Days*, 2019). His four child protagonists are excluded from society not only by their ethnic origin, but also by a hearing handicap. The film follows everyday micro stories without a salient narrative arc, reenacted in authentic settings, that do not offer these children a lot of chances for self-realization, but still cannot prevent them from sticking to their own dreams.

Conclusion

The significant presence of social subject matter dealing with poverty and precarity in Slovak cinema is directly connected to the nonfiction output of the Generation 90 filmmakers who awakened an interest in current reality in Slovak cinema. They were soon followed by younger filmmakers, but also by already well-known directors of the middle generation like Martin Šulík. There is a clearly visible trend toward socially engaged cinema in Slovakia. It draws not only on the traditions of international arthouse social film dramas, but also on the archetype of the social martyr, which has been present in Slovak art at least since the interwar period. By connecting current subject matter of post-socialist society with this archetype, these filmmakers are able to go beyond sheer observation of reality towards visual tropes. Instead of merely reporting, they offer more abstract and universal stories about the human condition, suffering, and endurance, while employing various narrative and stylistic techniques to engage the viewers emotionally and make them empathize with characters from a social universe often completely different from their own.

This work was supported by the Slovak Audiovisual Fund.

Bibliography

Branko, Pavel. "Slovenský dokumentárny film – Generácia 90." *Film.sk* 5, no. 2 (2004): 22–24.

Cíger-Hronský, Jozef. *Jozef Mak* [1933], trans. Andrew Cincura. Columbus, OH: Slavica Publishers, 1985.

Ferenčuhová, Mária. "Obrazy 'iných' a 'druhých' v súčasnom slovenskom dokumentárnom filme." *Nový slovenský film. Produkčné, estetické, distribučné a kritické východiská*, ed.

Katarína Mišíková and Mária Ferenčuhová. Bratislava: Vysoká škola múzických umení, 2015, 37–61.
Kollár, Martin. *Slovensko 001*. Bratislava: Inštitút pre verejné otázky, 2001.
Krekovič, Miloš. "Prečo je sociálna dráma na Slovensku nadávkou?" *Denník N*, March 19, 2015. https://dennikn.sk/75337/socialne-dramy/.
Kráľ, Fraňo. *Čenkovej deti* [*Čenková's Children*, 1932]. Bratislava: Mladé letá, 1980.
Kukučín, Martin. "An unawakened boy, or the village idiot" [1886]. In *Seven Slovak Stories*, trans. Norma Leigh Rudinsky. Cleveland, OH: Slovak Institute, 1980.
Mišíková, Katarína. "Hľadanie žánru v slovenskom hranom filme." In *Nový slovenský film. Produkčné, estetické, distribučné a kritické východiská*, ed. Katarína Mišíková and Mária Ferenčuhová. Bratislava: Vysoká škola múzických umení, 2015, 9–36.
——. "The Real Story: Indexing Strategies of Slovak Social Film Dramas." In *Transformation Processes in Post-Socialist Screen Media*, ed. Jana Dudková and Katarína Mišíková. Bratislava: Academy of Performing Arts in Bratislava, 2016, 60–76.

Filmography

Až do mesta Aš (*Made in Ash*). Dir. Iveta Grófová. Slovakia/Czech Republic, 2012.
Bronenosets Potemkin (*Battleship Potemkin*). Dir. Sergei M. Eisenstein. Soviet Union, 1925.
Cesta ven (*Zaneta*). Dir. Petr Václav. Czech Republic/ France,2014.
Chudoba cti netratí (*Poverty is no Sin*). Dir. Dana Gébová. Czech Republic, 2013.
Cidade de Deus (*City of God*). Dir. Fernando Meirelles and Kátia Lund. Brazil/France/Germany, 2002.
Cigán (*Gypsy*) Dir. Martin Šulík. Czech Republic/ Slovakia,2011.
Comeback. Dir. Miro Remo. Slovakia, 2014.
Český mír (*Czech Peace*). Dir. Vít Klusák and Filip Remunda. Czech Republic, 2010.
Český sen (*Czech Dream*). Dir. Vít Klusák and Filip Remunda. Czech Republic, 2004.
Čtyři slunce (*Four Suns*). Dir. Bohdan Sláma. Czech Republic, 2012.
Deti (*Children*) Dir. Jaro Vojtek. Slovakia/Czech Republic, 2014.
Divoké včely (*Wild Bees*). Dir. Bohdan Sláma. Czech Republic, 2001.
Dom (*The House*). Dir. Zuzana Liová. Czech Republic/ Slovakia,2011.
Ďakujem, dobre (*Thanks, Fine*). Dir. Mátyás Prikler. Slovakia, 2013.
Eva Nová. Dir. Marko Škop. Slovakia/Czech Republic, 2015.
Exekuce (*Don't Take My Life*). Dir. Andrea Culková. Czech Republic, 2016.
Hej, Slováci! (*Hey, Slovaks!*). Dir. Robert Kirchhoff. Slovakia, 2002.
Hluché dni (*Silent Days*). Dir. Pavol Pekarrčík. Slovakia/Czech Republic, 2019.
Hotel Úsvit (*Hotel Sunrise*). Dir. Mária Rumanová. Slovakia, 2016.
Hranice práce (*The Limits of Work*). Dir. Apolena Rychlíková. Czech Republic, 2017.
Kapela (*The Band*). Dir. Ladislav Kaboš. Slovakia/Czech Republic, 2018.
Katka. Dir. Helena Třeštíková. Czech Republic, 2010.
Kobry a užovky (*The Snake Brothers*). Dir. Jan Prušinovský. Czech Republic, 2015.
Koza. Dir. Ivan Ostrochovský. Slovakia/Czech Republic, 2015.
Líštičky (*Little Foxes*). Dir. Mira Fornay. Ireland/Czech Republic/ Slovakia,2009.
Mallory. Dir. Helena Třeštíková. Czech Republic, 2015.

Manželské etudy (*Marriage Stories*). Dir. Helena Třeštíková. Czechoslovakia, 1987.
Manželské etudy po dvaceti letech (*Marriage Stories 20 Years Later*). Dir. Helena Třeštíková. Czech Republic, 2006.
Manželské etudy po 35 letech (*Marriage Stories 35 Years Later*). Dir. Helena Třeštíková. Czech Republic, 2018.
Marian. Dir. Petr Václav. Czech Republic/France, 1996.
Môj pes Killer (*My Dog Killer*). Dir. Mira Fornay. Slovakia/Czech Republic, 2013.
My zdes (*Here We Are*). Dir. Jaro Vojtek. Slovakia, 2005.
Nech je svetlo (*Let There be Light*). Dir. Marko Škop. Slovakia/Czech Republic, 2019.
Nikdy nejsme sami (*We Are Never Alone*). Dir. Petr Václav. Czech Republic, 2016.
Nina. Dir. Juraj Lehotský. Slovakia/Czech Republic, 2017.
Obrazy starého sveta (*Pictures of the Old World*). Dušan Hanák. Czechoslovakia, 1972.
O Soni a jej rodine (*Sona and Her Family*). Dir. Daniela Rusnoková. Slovakia, 2006.
Out. Dir. György Kristóf. Slovakia/France/Hungary/Czech Republic, 2017.
Piata loď (*Little Harbor*). Dir. Iveta Grófová. Slovakia/Czech Republic, 2017.
Pirko (*Little Feather*). Dir. Lucia and Petr Klein Svoboda. Czech Republic/ Slovakia,2016.
Poupata (*Flower Buds*). Dir. Zdeněk Jiránský. Czech Republic, 2011.
Punk je hned! (*Punk Never Ends*). Dir. Juraj Šlauka. Slovakia, 2019.
René. Dir. Helena Třeštíková. Czech Republic, 2008.
Skokan (*The Jumper*). Dir. Petr Václav. Czech Republic, 2017.
Slepé lásky (*Blind Loves*). Dir. Juraj Lehotský. Slovakia, 2008.
Slnečný štát (*The City of the Sun*). Dir. Martin Šulík. Slovakia/Czech Republic, 2005.
Stanko. Dir. Rasťo Boroš. Slovakia, 2016.
Slumdog Millionaire. Dir. Danny Boyle and Loveleen Tandan. United Kingdom/United States, 2008.
Strnadovi (*A Marriage Story*). Dir. Helena Třeštíková. Czech Republic, 2017.
Svět podle Daliborka (*The White World According to Daliborek*). Dir. Vít Klusák. Czech Republic/Slovakia/UK, 2017.
Štěstí (*Something Like Happiness*). Dir. Bohdan Sláma. Czech Republic, 2005.
The Full Monty. Dir. Peter Cattaneo. United Kingdom/United States, 1997.
Ťažká duša (*Heavy Hearth*). Dir. Marek Šulík. Slovakia, 2017.
Vše pro dobro světa a Nošovic (*All for the Good of the World and Nosovice*). Dir. Vít Klusák. Czech Republic, 2010.
Všetky moje deti (*All my Children*). Dir. Ladislav Kaboš. Slovakia/Czech Republic, 2013.
Závod ke dnu (*Race to the Bottom*). Dir. Vít Janeček. Czech Republic, 2011.
Zázrak (*Miracle*). Dir. Juraj Lehotský. Slovakia/Czech Republic, 2013.
Zvonky šťastia (*Bells of Happiness*). Dir. Jana Bučka and Marek Šulík. Slovakia, 2012.

Melanie Letschnig
Pandemic (Dis)Proportions
On the Depiction of Precarized Work and Living Conditions in Austrian Film

During the period when Austria experienced its first lockdown due to the coronavirus in March 2020, people began applauding. For a few weeks, every day at 6 p.m. people in cities all over the country stepped out on their balconies, terraces, or onto the streets to celebrate so-called "key or essential workers" (*systemrelevante Arbeitskräfte*): supermarket and medical staff, cleaners, care workers, teachers, and public transportation drivers.

This performance was somewhat paradoxical, because the recipients who were meant to be addressed by this gesture were generally not able to perceive the cheering. They were working when it happened: filling shelves with groceries, taking care of sick people, cleaning and disinfecting public and semi-public spaces, guiding children and young adults, driving buses, trams, and undergrounds. Suddenly the cleaning ladies, our supermarket cashier, and the women taking care of my grandmother in the nursing home became the so-called "heroes of everyday life." They were holding things together and most of them did not have time to step out for one or two minutes to receive any applause. What is far more significant for this extreme situation: they did not receive permanent pay raises from their employers, just a one-time bonus in some cases.

The pandemic and its consequences made the imbalance visible that exists between interpersonal appreciation, on the one hand, and the complete lack of economic fairness and attention by the state and society as a whole for the representatives of the above-mentioned groups, on the other hand. Their occupations all share one crucial feature: precarious working conditions that are continuously becoming worse under the influence of an amalgamation of neoliberalism, increasing nationalism, sexism, and classism in Austria. Sociologist Susanne Völker mentions "the politically based multiplication of social instabilities" as one of the results of the insidious shift from welfare to workfare states that took and is still taking place in Europe.[1] The coronavirus has brought these interrelations even more closely into focus in public discourse.

---

[1] Susanne Völker, "Phänomene der Prekarisierung: Entsicherung und erschöpfte Arbeits- und Lebensarrangements," in *Feministische Kapitalismuskritik. Einstiege in bedeutende Forschungsfelder*, ed. Brigitte Aulenbacher, Birgit Riegraf and Susanne Völker (Münster: Westfälisches Dampfboot, 2015), 131. All translations, if not otherwise stated in the bibliography, are by me, M.L.

Open Access. © 2022 Melanie Letschnig, published by De Gruyter. This work is licensed under the Creative Commons Attribution-NonCommercial-NoDerivatives 4.0 International License.
https://doi.org/10.1515/9783110707816-012

Precarity and Othering: The Advantages of a Feminist Approach

I would like to take this recent exposure of social imbalances through a worldwide pandemic as a starting point for an examination of the depiction of precarious living and working conditions in Austrian cinema since 2000. My aim is to examine if and how films have the power to analyze the politically motivated slant between social relevance and appropriate compensation in the form of money and recognition of so-called "essential workers."

It is important to note that precarization not only relates to working conditions. It also has a fundamental impact on concepts of gender/sexuality, race, and class. Referring to the theoretical debate about the terms precarization/precarity initiated by leading sociologists like Robert Castel and Pierre Bourdieu, a critical feminist approach to their derivation of these terms is very important and suitable to draw parallels to feminist film studies. Völker states that the definition of precarious work and living conditions starts from a concept of "standard employment" ("fordistisches Normalarbeitsverhältnis"[2]) meaning a permanent full-time contract, which was and mostly still is the privilege of men. When this work concept started to erode, precarization perpetuated a broad sociological and social discourse leaving out the fact that there were always precarious fields of work, for example in sex work, care, the cultural sector, and creative industries—of course with different degrees of severity depending on the field.[3] Therefore setting Fordistic standard employment as the metric for defining the parameters of precarious work conditions determines men as the measure of all things, against whom women, trans and inter persons, migrants, Black persons and People of Color are "the Other." This is a discriminating concept that has also been criticized in feminist film studies, for example in the analytic works of Laura Mulvey, Teresa de Lauretis and bell hooks, who use psychoanalysis and postcolonial theories to disassemble the construction of the Other as non-white and non-male. Also important to mention is the prefabricated position of the Other as subject/object of cinematographic inspection in which "a massive imbalance of power" is already created as a premise, as Anette Baldauf, cultural

---

2 Völker, "Phänomene der Prekarisierung," 12.
3 Volker Woltersdorff, "Neue Bündnispotenziale und neue Unschärfen. Zum Begriff der Prekarisierung von Geschlecht, Arbeit und Leben," *Zeitschrift für interdisziplinäre Frauen- und Geschlechterforschung* 29, no. 2 (November 2011), https://doi.org/10.1515/fs-2011-0205.

scientist and filmmaker, states in a talk with the director Katharina Weingartner about the political in documentary cinema.[4] Cinematic modes and forms that question this imbalance are crucial to the films discussed in this article.

Precarious jobs in the low wage segment concern mostly marginalized groups of people who are affected by economic, identity-forming, and sociopolitical uncertainties in overlapping ways. Therefore, I would like to determine the following professions and their work and living environments as subjects of my examination: seasonal workers in agriculture and gastronomy, cleaners, sex workers, and caregivers.

Movies by renowned filmmakers like Barbara Albert, Anja Salomonowitz, and Ulrich Seidl address aspects of precarized work and living conditions: Albert's *Nordrand* (*Northern Skirts*, 1999) centers the two female protagonists Tamara and Jasmin within the environment of the Viennese suburbs. Tamara, daughter of Yugoslavian parents, working as a nurse in the hospital, leads a more stable life than her elementary school friend Jasmin, who earns her money as a vendor in a traditional cake shop and is still living with her parents, the mother an alcoholic, the father abusive. The everyday life of both women is marked by crises involving involuntary pregnancy, by relationships of dependence in both their private and working lives, and by dreams and wishes that are impossible to fulfill in the social and emotional environment they are living in. *Nordrand* interrogates these unrealizable life concepts politically by intertwining the stories of Tamara and Jasmin with topics like xenophobia and body politics, which are also present in Anja Salomonowitz's *Kurz davor ist es passiert* (*It Happened Just Before*, 2006) and Ulrich Seidl's *Import/ Export* (2007). The exploitative and violent dimension of sex work is a central issue in both films, but the aesthetic approach of the filmmakers is significantly different: While Seidl uses his characteristic central perspective gaze to show sex work as a degrading spectacle, Salomonowitz chooses abstraction and alienation effects to analyze mechanisms of power and abuse. The five protagonists—all of them non-professional actors—in *Kurz davor ist es passiert* recite monologues based on the real-life experiences of sex workers. In a highly stylized manner, the performers are placed in allegedly authentic locations while speaking, with the intended effect being to call up a sense of possibility in the

---

4 Anette Baldauf and Katharina Weingartner, "Selbstreflexion und politische Verantwortung im neueren österreichischen Dokumentarfilm. Anette Baldauf im Gespräch mit Katharina Weingartner," in *Zooming in and out. Produktionen des Politischen im neueren deutschsprachigen Dokumentarfilm*, ed. Aylin Basaran, Julia B. Köhne, and Klaudija Sabo (Vienna: Mandelbaum, 2013), 30.

spectators, to "evoke images" that result in "consciousness-raising"[5] (*Bewusstseinsarbeit*) about the social tabooing of sex work, as Anja Salomonowitz puts it.

There are numerous Austrian film productions that illuminate the complex of precarious working and living conditions in countries all over the world, examples are *In den Straßen von Dehli* (*In the Streets of Dehli*, Sabine Derflinger, 2006), *Mind the Gap* (Robert Schabus, 2020), and *Talleres Clandestinos* (*Clandestine Workshop*, Catalina Molina, 2010).[6] However, the focus of this article is on Austrian movies that set their stories in Austria, with an emphasis on women as the main protagonists, depicted as working in sectors in which the work is mainly carried out by women. The discrepancy of hard physical work versus lousy payment and social insecurity is show as characteristic, for example in *Gute Arbeit* (*Good Work*, 2004) by Karin Macher, in *Hörmanns* (2018) by Siegmund Skalar, and in Sudabeh Mortezai's *Joy* (2018), which highlights the explicit criminalization of workers. The movies I chose for this article were made with small budgets—a fact referring to the precarious situations of many (female) filmmakers in Austria. Concerning the genres, *Gute Arbeit (Good Work)* is a documentary, *Hörmanns* a short fictional film, and *Joy* a "documentarily researched, fictionalized story."[7] Aesthetic strategies of distance and non-voyeuristic intimacy provoke the spectator's understanding for the overdetermined disadvantages in the lives of the main characters and their everyday struggles.

The following observations were strongly influenced by social developments in Austria in 2020/2021 related to the Covid-19 pandemic. However one insight I won from studying the reflection of precarious work and living conditions in Austrian cinema is that if one views cinematic representations as a mirror of society, very little has changed for essential workers in Austria during the last twenty years and during the pandemic the situation has even worsened for many. It is disenchanting.

---

[5] Anja Salomonowitz, interviewed by Karin Schiefer, "Anja Salomonowitz über KURZ DAVOR IST ES PASSIERT," *Austrian Film Commission*, 2007, https://www.austrianfilms.com/news/bodyanja_salomonowitz_kurz_davor_ist_es_passiert__interviewbody.

[6] For further references on Austrian films that deal with the subject matter of poverty and precarity, see Eva Flicker and Irene Zehenthofer, "Repräsentationen von Armut und sozialer Ausgrenzung im Österreichischen Film," in *Armut in Österreich. Bestandsaufnahme, Trends, Risikogruppen*, ed. Roland Verwiebe, Vienna: Braumüller (2011).

[7] Sudabeh Mortezai, interviewed by Karin Schiefer, "Joy | Sudabeh Mortezai," *Verband Filmregie Österreich*, August 2018, https://www.austrian-directors.com/filme/joy-sudabeh-mortezai/.

Narrations of Struggle

When Martina has to get up for work with the help of three alarm clocks, it is 2:35 in the morning. The bus reaches Senica in Slovakia at 3 a.m. to pick up the workers, leaving for Marchfeld, a landscape in Lower Austria called "the Granary of Austria" for its wealth of corn and vegetable fields. When the bus arrives at its destination it is 6 a.m., which means six hours commuting time in total every day. Martina works as an asparagus picker; the hourly wage is 3.27 euros and the employees have to pay for the bus themselves. The structure of her working life is representative for thousands of seasonal workers in agriculture from Eastern European countries working in Austria during spring, summer, and autumn.

Martina is one of three main protagonists in Karin Macher's documentary film *Good Work*, which portrays three women working in precarious jobs in Austria. Besides Martina, we get to know Julietha from Namibia, a seasonal worker at a mountain inn in Bad Goisern, and Gordana, an Austrian based cleaner from Bosnia. The director accompanies the women through their daily lives. In voice-overs commenting on images of themselves and in interviews staged in front of the camera, the women provide us with insights into their realities, wishes, and dreams. They speak frankly about the difficulties in their jobs, which are representative of the exploitative structures of highly precarious "essential" work environments: terminable contracts, backbreaking work in all weather, lousy remuneration, no social network, little social appreciation.

The sociologist Brigitte Aulenbacher mentions different factors that exacerbate precarious working conditions, like being a migrant and a woman.[8] These factors apply to Martina, Julietha, and Gordana, but with different degrees of severity, not only concerning work but also their personal lives. One example is the mobility that is demanded. While Gordana settled in Vienna years ago and is surrounded by a group of peers at work and Martina is not willing to pay for an unacceptable accommodation provided by the employer, Julietha barely has any opportunity to leave her seasonal working and living space on a mountain in Upper Austria, thus making it nearly impossible to create an ongoing personal environment. In one of the interviews, Julietha mentions a friend who is based in Bad Ischl, one and a half hours walk away, practically unreachable when you

---

8 Brigitte Aulenbacher and Fabienne Décieux, "Prekaritäten: internationale Forschung zu globalen Ungleichheiten, Ungleichzeitigkeiten und Geschlecht," in *Handbuch Interdisziplinäre Geschlechterforschung*, ed. Beate Kortendiek, Birgit Riegraf, and Katja Sabisch (Wiesbaden: Springer, 2019), 817; see also Mona Motakef, *Prekarisierung* (Bielefeld: Transcript, 2015), 6–11; 70–117.

have to work until late at night and get up early in the morning. Julietha is caught in a microcosm that is defined by a 17-hour workday, watching TV, and sleeping. One gets a feeling for her loneliness when Julietha takes a walk in the snow or is confronted with a group of male guests who treat her passive-aggressively as if she was invisible.

The camera (operated by Clemens Lechner) acts as a silent observer of this humiliation in order for the spectator to develop a sense of the appalling behavior of the group of drinking buddies. The innkeeper's words full of praise for Julietha do not help either, they seem patronizing. Even when bosses like the innkeeper are indignant about the ill treatment seasonal workers from poorer countries experience in Austria, they are ultimately beneficiaries of the system.

One of the main motivations for Martina and Julietha to earn money in Austria despite precarious working conditions is that they earn much more than in their countries of origin. Martina reports that she used to be a tailor in Slovakia, but the wages were so bad that cutting asparagus is lucrative in comparison. Julietha can sustain her whole family of nine—including herself—with the earnings from one season. Like Martina, Julietha does not want to live permanently in Austria, partly because she is aware of the blatant disparity between the work done and the pay for seasonal workers.

In comparison, Gordana has been living in Austria for quite a while. After leaving Sarajevo, where she had studied law, Gordana and her husband left Bosnia at the beginning of the 1990s. This new start in Austria is representative for a 'normal' curriculum vitae for migrants:[9] Her first boss, the owner of a café, promised a work permit that she never received. At her next place of employment, she was finally granted a residence permit, so that her family could immigrate.

Gordana works as a cleaner. With three colleagues she is responsible for the cleanliness of Wohnpark Donaucity, a gigantic housing estate with 1001 flats in the 22nd district of Vienna. The four of them need one week to clean the whole complex. Gordana seems to have settled in Austria, nevertheless she still experiences inequalities in comparison to people that were born here. In one of the last scenes of the film, Gordana and her daughter stroll through the Christmas market, talking about their feelings and thoughts regarding the mother's profession. Both hint at struggling with the mother's work, especially the daughter, because her classmates' mothers are lawyers or office administrators. But Gordana remains calm, noting that it is good the way it is. In the following shot,

---

9 The base of this statement is my personal observations resulting from work teaching German language for migrants.

mother and daughter make their way home arm in arm, and this shot reinforces the impression of solidarity between the two generations.

In addition to the voice-over of the protagonists and their intimate interviews on set, Karin Macher uses inserts after each of the three episodes that provide information about the legal situation of workers like Martina, Julietha and Gordana. Using this technique, the personal stories are put into a larger context that identifies them as representative not only of a few but of many. If *Gute Arbeit* had been shot in the year 2020 instead of 2004, maybe the media coverage about a seasonal worker, Mrs. A., who informed the public about the absolutely inacceptable accommodation and working conditions on an asparagus farm[10] in Marchfeld would have found its way into Macher's film. In the meantime, little to nothing had changed between Martina's everyday work life and that of Mrs. A.

Another film that deals with the complex of systematized exploitation of seasonal workers is Ruth Mader's *Struggle* (2003), which Barbara Pichler—former festival director of *Diagonale – Festival of Austrian Film*—describes as "a film about affluent societies, the losers within the system, and the loss of human dignity."[11] *Struggle* is a fictional film with documentary elements, a "factual narration."[12] Ewa, the female protagonist, is a single mother from Poland working as a seasonal worker, picking strawberries. One day, during a comfort stop on the bus ride, Ewa takes advantage of it as a chance to stay in Austria instead of returning to Poland. She hopes to settle there with her daughter and start a new life. Shots of Ewa looking out of the bus window, similar to ones that had been shown earlier in the film, are repeated here and dissolve into images of rows and rows of plain, tasteless detached houses in Lower Austria that show what she is longing for.

After leaving the strawberry picking behind, Ewa earns her money in different branches: the meat industry (Fig. 1), polishing bric-a-brac for a professional dealer, cleaning the pool of a wealthy family. Presumably, Ewa works illegally in all of these jobs. She is hired straight from the line of people waiting for jobs. One time, Ewa has to run to flee from the labor inspectors. Mader documents the details of manual labor in all of Ewa's work environments by filming in part on original locations with non-professional actors, i.e. real workers. The severity of the monotonous and hyper-efficient workflows is shown from a certain

---

10 Colette M. Schmidt, "Eine Erntearbeiterin will Gerechtigkeit," *Der Standard*, June 16, 2020, https://www.derstandard.at/story/2000118110455/eine-erntearbeiterin-will-gerechtigkeit.
11 Barbara Pichler, "The Construction of Reality: Aspects of Austrian Cinema between Fiction and Documentary," in *Cinema and Social Change in Germany and Austria*, ed. Gabriele Mueller und James M. Skidmore (Waterloo: Wilfried Laurier University Press, 2011), 269.
12 Ibid.

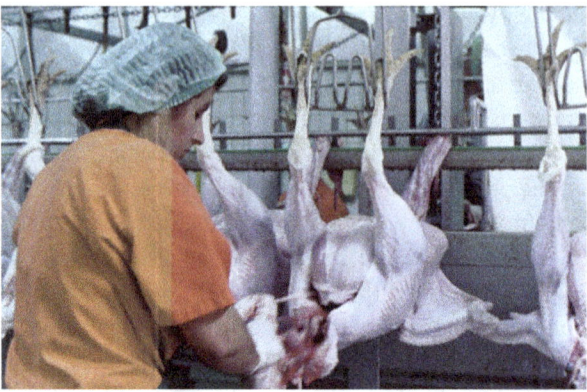

Fig. 1: Struggle (Ruth Mader, 2003).

distance, providing "no room for subjectivity."[13] We do not share Ewa's exertions and are relegated to looking on as bystanders, having no feeling for how exhausting it must be to work these jobs because everything seems so effortless and efficient.

Sex Work and (Im)possible Solidarity

As a result of the first lockdown regulations in March 2020, the practice of sex work in Austria was forbidden until July, when the easing of the restrictions also applied to sex workers. In November of the same year the next shutdown ensued. Currently (March 2021) escort services (i.e. sex work at the home of the customer) are permitted, if the worker can exhibit a negative Covid-test and wears a FFP2 face mask. The already often precarious situation of sex workers in Austria worsened with the pandemic: A lot of the professionals lost not only their income but also their working spaces, which are often where they live. Many sex workers commute between Austria and their home country, which is nearly impossible if quarantine is compulsory after crossing the border. During the first lockdown sex workers could not get the official medical examinations that are mandatory to carry on the profession officially. Therefore, a lot of them were forced to work illegally, according to Christian Knappik, senior administrator of the *Sexworker-*

---

13 Pichler, "The Construction of Reality," 270.

Forum.[14] Brothels are not listed as business enterprises in the Austrian classification of economic activities (ÖNACE), so sex workers who practiced their profession in a brothel are excluded from compensation payment because listing in ÖNACE is a prerequisite for the payments.[15] These factors worsen the situation of legal sex workers, but have always been the status quo of persons in Austria illegally who earn their money with sex work. In "Criminalisation kills," an article written by clumsycolours from RED EDITION – MIGRANT SEX WORKERS GROUP VIENNA, the author points out that sex work will not just disappear, even if it is made illegal.[16]

A fictional film from 2018 that puts the precarized professional and living conditions of sex workers into the center of attention is Sudabeh Mortezai's second feature film, *Joy*. The film will be analyzed by highlighting the following aspects: What is the motivation for the protagonists to work in their profession? Which situations are adduced by Mortezai to give an insight into the lives of the women? What social and emotional dynamics shape the existence of the protagonists? Of course, all three aspects are intertwined, so the following analysis is meant to shed light on the interrelations between the severity of enforcement, (impossible) solidarity, group dynamics, and solitariness.

Joy is the name of the heroine of the film. The spectators do not learn much about how and when Joy came to Vienna to do sex work for a living. Only in comparison to Precious, the second protagonist of the film, do we get an insight of the overall situation of women forced to leave Nigeria, getting objectified by a perfectly organized system of women trafficking, landing in Europe where they have to pay off their debts for being brought here, earning money with sex work to pay their own debts and provide for their families in Nigeria.[17] The opening of *Joy* shows Precious in a one-on-one ritual with a juju priest as preparatory measure for her future life in Europe. She has to swear not to cooperate with the police. The priest inculcates her with the idea that the Iroko tree always knows when a child is killed, and he tells her that she can always invoke him, but if

---

14 Sophie Wochenalt, "Verschlechterung der Situation von Sexarbeiter/-innen während der Corona-Pandemie," *A&W blog*, November 27, 2020, https://awblog.at/sexarbeiterinnen-waehrend-corona-pandemie/.
15 Ibid.
16 "Criminalisation kills," *Red Edition – Migrant Sex Worker's Group Vienna*, October 30, 2020, https://rededition.wordpress.com/2020/10/30/criminalisation-kills/. I cordially would like to thank Marty Huber for bringing my attention to RED EDITION.
17 For an overview on the mechanisms of women trafficking in Austria see Mortezai, "Joy | Sudabeh Mortezai."

she does not pay the money in time, the priest will haunt her. The conversation reveals that Precious is being sent off to settle her family's debts.

How Precious arrives in Europe is not shown. The plot jumps directly to an illegal streetwalkers spot in Vienna at night: the street lighting is sparse, no sanitation facilities to be seen. Joy is popular amongst the customers, but it is obvious that Precious feels deeply uncomfortable, not being able to attract clients. The relationship between Joy and Precious emerges as a kind of training situation, decreed by the "madam." Her role as mentor causes Joy additional distress as she has almost paid back her debts but is now put in the position of having to pay for Precious if she does not earn enough money. So, Joy is caught between maintaining her own existence and the imposed responsibility for Precious, an "infinite loop of dependency and desolidarization."[18] The power of Mortezai's directional work is to portray this disjointedness with a sensitivity that always sets the protagonists at eye level with the spectator. One the one hand, this is accomplished by the participatory involvement of the actors in the development of the film: Mortezai found them via casting within the Nigerian community in Vienna, some of them can relate their biographies to the women in the movie, others do not share that background but were empathically interested in the project. Due to their horizon of experience, they are by all means "co-authors" of the film but were not able to read the script in advance, as improvising was a key method in the film.[19] On the other hand, the camera work (Klemens Hufnagl) produces an intimate relationship between the spectator and the women, sometimes closely involved, sometimes distanced, sometimes doomed to be petrified as in the scene when Precious gets raped by the madam's handymen. Mortezai does not show the violence directly, but we see the reactions of the women in the room next to the scene of crime, and we hear Precious. We see how Joy is affected, but neither she nor one of the other women interfere.

To emphasize the level of brutality, a harsh cut introduces the next sequence, which takes place in a beauty salon where Joy's "mentee" is equipped with the stereotyped outward appearance of a sex worker: long hair, short dress, high heels (Fig. 2).

The visual transformation is accompanied by a lecture from Joy who states that all the women are lone warriors, a typical truism, but one that the film repeatedly puts into question by means of identification. One example is the scene shortly after the exposition in which Joy and Precious visit a shop to

---

18 Ibid.
19 Ibid.

Fig. 2: Joy (Sudabeh Mortezai, 2018).

transfer money to their families and to call them. In one shot, Joy is reflected in the glass door of the phone booth from which Precious tells her family that the boat to Europe almost keeled over during the crossing and she cannot swim. The countenances of two women are dissolved in the glass, Joy's facial expression hard to read for the spectator, but it is noticeable that they share experiences.

Another device to produce a feeling of solidarity is the over-shoulder shot, for example when Joy has an appointment with the NGO for Human Rights to discuss if there is a possibility to get out of prostitution by cooperating with the Austrian authorities, which is extremely risky for illegal persons because they have no guarantee of not being deported after testifying. In this scene, Joy is accompanied by her admirer, a customer, a man with family, who—as it turns out in the course of the film—is not at all interested in helping her to live an autonomous life, but rather has a distinct paternalistic complex. While he is filmed in profile, the camera relocates us in a position behind Joy, a setup that was already used in an earlier scene in the film when Precious has to endure a speech by the madam who states that there are countless other girls who would love to replace her. In this moment, Joy is accompanying Precious in a way that is similar to how we are positioned in relation to Joy in the situation with the man at the NGO. Here the spatial relationship shows the women closing ranks to fend off their attackers.

A third way of breaking with the lone wolf stereotype is for example a situation after the madam instructed Joy to take Precious to Lienz where she will be handed over to Italian traffickers. The women miss their train connection, it is evening and winter, in a phone call they are told to stay where they are, so Joy and Precious stop by at an inn. Shortly after their arrival, costumed figures of St. Nicholas and several Krampusse (horned, devilish-looking characters in Alpine folklore who accompany St. Nick and punish bad children in the advent period) enter the guest room to entertain and frighten the audience. Precious and Joy seem to be unimpressed and to share a certain kind of disconcertment at the same time. This scene, depicting a traditional Austrian ritual linked to religion and with pagan roots, is crucial because it refers to juju—not only as one part of the introduction of *Joy*, but as a motif that is repeatedly addressed throughout the film—especially when Austrians are disparaging it as nonsense, as if St. Nicholas and Krampus were any less fictitious.

After Precious is handed over to the traffickers, the story continues in Vienna, where Joy is finally free from her debts—but not in a situation where she can start a new life apart from sex work. This represents a downward spiral that is typical for the lives of Nigerian sex workers in Austria. First they have to pay back ten thousand euros to the madam, which they can only do through sex work, since they cannot find other jobs without a work permit, which they can only get if they are granted asylum in Austria. As a result, Joy begins to refer the girls to the clients, competing with the other madams who eventually reveal her illegality, leading to her deportation. In the end, we see the heroine negotiating about documents with a man on the street in Lagos and entering into a new dependency. The downward spiral is recycling.

Joy is the story of a complex structure of inexorable relationships determined by self-protection, motherliness, temporary sisterhood, and future prospects that will never lead to social and financial freedom for the women portrayed. Altruistic attachment is impossible. The way Mortezai stages these dynamics of the lack of alternatives and the continually reproduced violence does not criticize the sex workers, but dissects the mechanisms of brutal exploitation that constitute the trafficking of women in Austria.

Innuendos and Emotional Workloads

When the first lockdown in Austria in the spring of 2020 made it apparent that there would be a massive bottleneck in regard to 24-hour-caregivers from abroad due to entry regulations in European countries, the Austrian government organized means of travel to bring back the caregivers—mostly from Slovakia and Rumania.[20] They came with corridor trains and were flown in because it was clear that the care system in Austria would melt down completely if those workers

---

20 In 2017, 88.000 self-employed caregivers in Austria were on the business registers, 71.000 of them were from Slovakia and Rumania. ORF, "Pflege kommt nicht ohne Osteuropa aus," *ORF-News*, October 22, 2018, https://orf.at/stories/3073921/.

broke away. When the caregivers arrived, they had to undergo testing for Covid; if they were tested negative, they were able to resume work. A lot of them were hesitating between the decision to visit their families and possibly risking loss of pay (in case of a mandatory quarantine after traveling back to Austria), or not to see their relatives and friends for weeks or even months. In October 2018 the national council in the first Austrian government under Chancellor Kurz passed a law on indexation of child support for people from other EU-countries working in Austria.[21] The indexation was based on the average living expenses in the countries concerned and resulted in less money for workers from Eastern European countries while they still had to pay their full taxes in Austria.[22]

Caregivers from Eastern European countries are vital to the Austrian health system while constantly being underpaid for their physically and mentally hard work. In the beginning of times of crisis, the red carpet is rolled out for them, but soon everything is back to (not) normal.

Elena is one of them. She is the protagonist of Siegmund Skalar's *Hörmanns*,[23] titled after the village with a population of 200 in Lower Austria where Elena is taking care of Stefanie, an older woman. Like Martina in *Good Work* and Ewa in *Struggle,* she arrives by bus, a common introductory motif in films telling the stories of precarious migrant workers in order to point out that working under difficult conditions is further complicated by the personal loss of time due to traveling.

Hörmanns is a short fiction film which relies on the method of allusion. When Elena arrives there, she takes over the house key from a colleague from the previous shift. Elena is a young woman, probably new at the job as is suggested by one scene in which we see Elena asking an experienced friend, also working as caregiver, how to give injections. There are absolutely no attractions for Elena as a young woman in Hörmanns. Stefanie is the only person with whom she has a relationship. It is tense in the beginning but starts to open up the longer Elena stays. However, she is confronted with resentment from Stefanie's family. In one scene they come for visit and Stefanie's son asks his mother whether Elena cooks well ("Mocht's da wo Gscheits zum Essen?" ["Does she

---

[21] Victoria Reinberg and Thomas Soxberger, "Nationalrat stimmt Indexierung der Familienbeihilfe zu," *Parlamentskorrespondenz*, no. 1160, August 24, 2018, https://www.parlament.gv.at/PAKT/PR/JAHR_2018/PK1160/.
[22] The European Commission filed charges against this legislation with the European Court of Justice in May 2020. ORF, "EU-Kommission klagt Österreich," *ORF-News*, May 14, 2020, https://orf.at/stories/3165666/.
[23] I would like to thank Isabella Reicher so much for helping me finding this movie again after I lost my notes.

cook decent food for you?"]) while bringing an unappetizing looking pie as a present. The family members constantly undervalue and humiliate her. An example is a scene in which Stefanie's daughter delivers the groceries and checks how many slices of cheese are still in the package already there by flipping through the cheese with her fingers as if it was index cards. Also, the daughter stresses that the beer she brought is exclusively for Stefanie: Elena is treated more like a potential criminal than as a professional worker.

This incident is similar to a scene from Mader's *Struggle* in which Ewa is served a snack brought by the teenage son at the house where she cleans the pool. After the boy puts down the tray he goes back to the house, closing the iron grille door through which Ewa is filmed like a zoo animal, trapped in the relationships of dependency that still make it impossible for her to live a safe life in Austria. Only after Ewa meets Harold, a divorced, unsuccessful real estate agent, does a realistic possibility of a steady life for her and her daughter seem within reach. Harold uses his new girlfriend, whom he introduces to his teenage daughter as an "open minded partner," as a prosthetic for his emotional and sexual impotence. Mader touches an important point that emphasizes that precarization not only means unstable working and living conditions but also emotional and sexual dependencies that would never allow for equal relationships, a precarization Volker Woltersdorff—following Robert Castel and Judith Butler—calls "social vulnerability," "fragility," or "de-securing."[24]

The cinema offers strategies to counteract these vulnerable positions. When in the final scene of *Struggle*, Ewa visits a puppet theater performance with her daughter and Harold in a shopping center, her enraptured look in close-up refers to an inversion of roles that is hers alone, since it remains opaque, illegible for the spectator. Or when Gordana serves coffee and cake to her co-workers, pointing out in front of the film team that this is a one-time occasion because a movie is being shot, and everybody understands the joke. Or when Elena in *Hörmanns* puts on one of Stefanie's evening dresses and dances to pop music in front of the mirror while drinking one of the bottles of beer she was not supposed to touch. Cinema also offers possibilities of depicting the brutality of sexualized exploitation without serving voyeurism by exhibiting vulnerable persons, but rather by creating a distressing sense of dilemma.

All these cinematic strategies are methods of self-empowerment and awareness to be acted out on screen.

---

24 Woltersdorff, "Neue Bündnispotenziale und Unschärfen," 206.

Conclusion

It is the cinema's task to disclose violent forms of subjugation and exploitation and to suggest possibilities of overcoming them. Whether it chooses fictional, documentary, hybrid, or essayistic forms is not the first concern. Most important is that it does not portray people with precarious work and living conditions as victims of their social relations, but rather exposes the social and political circumstances that are causing these conditions. In any case, it is important to avoid a voyeuristic view and projection or inappropriate identification that only elicits a superficial experience of being affected and allows one to feel good because one's life is so much better.

A visual regime of allusions like in *Hörmanns*, a deeper interest in one's protagonists expressed by portraying the mechanical mode of work and the loneliness in leisure time like in *Gute Arbeit*, or a realistic artificiality as in *Struggle* seem to be appropriate cinematic techniques. They point out the existential distance between the exploited and the profiteers without diminishing the former.

Now that Austria has experienced several lockdowns due to the coronavirus and the national film industry has been in a kind of artificial coma, it will become apparent how much sensibility it has truly developed for the numerous essential workers who often toil under unacceptable conditions to maintain our daily lives. Otherwise, there will be nothing to applaud here.

Bibliography

Aulenbacher, Brigitte, and Fabienne Décieux. "Prekaritäten: internationale Forschung zu globalen Ungleichheiten, Ungleichzeitigkeiten und Geschlecht." In *Handbuch Interdisziplinäre Geschlechterforschung*, ed. Beate Kortendiek, Birgit Riegraf, and Katja Sabisch. Wiesbaden: Springer VS, 2019, 813–822.

Baldauf, Anette, and Katharina Weingartner. "Selbstreflexion und politische Verantwortung im neueren österreichischen Dokumentarfilm. Anette Baldauf im Gespräch mit Katharina Weingartner." In *Zooming in and out. Produktionen des Politischen im neueren deutschsprachigen Dokumentarfilm*, ed. Aylin Basaran, Julia B. Köhne, and Klaudija Sabo. Vienna: Mandelbaum, 2013, 23–38.

Flicker, Eva, and Irene Zehenthofer. "Repräsentationen von Armut und sozialer Ausgrenzung im Österreichischen Film." In *Armut in Österreich. Bestandsaufnahme*, Trends, *Risikogruppen*, ed. Roland Verwiebe. Vienna: Braumüller, 2011, 328–347.

Mortezai, Sudabeh, interviewed by Karin Schiefer. "Joy | Sudabeh Mortezai." *Verband Filmregie Österreich*, August 2018. https://www.austrian-directors.com/filme/joy-sudabeh-mortezai/.

Motakef, Mona. *Prekarisierung*. Bielefeld: Transcript, 2015.
ORF. "EU-Kommission klagt Österreich." *ORF-News*, May 14, 2020. https://orf.at/stories/3165666/.
——. "Pflege kommt nicht ohne Osteuropa aus." *ORF-News*, October 22, 2018. https://orf.at/stories/3073921/.
Pichler, Barbara. "The Construction of Reality: Aspects of Austrian Cinema between Fiction and Documentary." In *Cinema and Social Change in Germany and Austria*, ed. Gabriele Mueller and James M. Skidmore. Waterloo: Wilfried Laurier University Press, 2011, 267–281.
Red Edition – Migrant Sex Worker's Group Vienna. "Criminalisation kills." October 30, 2020. https://rededition.wordpress.com/2020/10/30/criminalisation-kills.
Reinberg, Victoria, and Thomas Soxberger. "Nationalrat stimmt Indexierung der Familienbeihilfe zu." *Parlamentskorrespondenz*, no. 1160, August 24, 2018. https://www.parlament.gv.at/PAKT/PR/JAHR_2018/PK1160/.
Salomonowitz, Anja, interviewed by Karin Schiefer. "Anja Salomonowitz über KURZ DAVOR IST ES PASSIERT." *Austrian Film Commission*, 2007. https://www.austrianfilms.com/news/bodyanja_salomonowitz_kurz_davor_ist_es_passiert__interviewbody.
Schmidt, Colette M. "Eine Erntearbeiterin will Gerechtigkeit." *Der Standard*, June 16, 2020. https://www.derstandard.at/story/2000118110455/eine-erntearbeiterin-will-gerechtigkeit.
Völker, Susanne. "Phänomene der Prekarisierung: Entsicherung und erschöpfte Arbeits- und Lebensarrangements." In *Feministische* Kapitalismuskritik. *Einstiege in bedeutende Forschungsfelder*, ed. Brigitte Aulenbacher, Birgit Riegraf, and Susanne Völker. Münster: Westfälisches Dampfboot, 2015, 126–138.
Wochenalt, Sophie. "Verschlechterung der Situation von Sexarbeiter/-innen während der Corona-Pandemie." *A&W blog*, November 27, 2020. https://awblog.at/sexarbeiterinnen-waehrend-corona-pandemie/.
Woltersdorff, Volker. "Neue Bündnispotenziale und neue Unschärfen. Zum Begriff der Prekarisierung von Geschlecht, Arbeit und Leben." *Zeitschrift für interdisziplinäre Frauen- und Geschlechterforschung* 29, no. 2 (November 2011): 206–216. https://doi.org/10.1515/fs-2011-0205.

Filmography

Gute Arbeit (*Good Work*). Dir. Karin Macher. Austria, 2004.
Hörmanns. Dir. Siegmund Skalar. Austria, 2018.
Import/Export. Dir Ulrich Seidl. Austria/France/Germany, 2007.
In den Straßen von Dehli (*In the Streets of Dehli*). Dir. Sabine Derflinger. Austria, 2006.
Joy. Dir. Sudabeh Mortezai. Austria, 2018.
Kurz davor ist es passiert (*It Happened Just Before*). Dir. Anja Salomonowitz. Austria, 2006.
Mind the Gap. Dir. Robert Schabus. Austria, 2020.
Nordrand (*Northern Skirts*). Dir. Barbara Albert. Austria, 1999.
Struggle. Dir. Ruth Mader. Austria, 2003.
Talleres Clandestinos (*Clandestine Workshop*). Dir. Catalina Molina. Austria/Argentina, 2010.

Marcy Goldberg
Precarity and Paradox in Swiss Cinema

As far as national stereotypes go, Switzerland is not likely to be associated at first glance with precarity—either in general terms or as a central theme for its artistic output. Its branding is dominated by luxury goods such as high-end watches, fine chocolate, and expensive Alpine ski holidays. And with an economy based to a large extent on the banking and finance sector (with its infamous secrecy laws), Big Pharma, the arms industry, and commodities trading, Switzerland is more likely to be viewed as a culprit in perpetuating poverty, precarity, and inequality abroad, as the flip side of the affluence and security enjoyed within its borders.

Indeed, the question of the country's complicity in some of the most painful chapters of world history, from the colonial slave trade to collaboration with the Nazis and Cold War espionage, has been a dominant theme in Swiss literature and scholarly research for the past several decades. But it has not been a frequent theme in fiction film production—with a few notable exceptions. Two of the most significant domestic film productions since the 1970s dramatized Switzerland's often fatally strict immigration policies: *Das Boot ist voll* (*The Boat Is Full*, Markus Imhoof, 1981) highlighted "neutral" Switzerland's rejection of Jewish refugees during the Second World War, while *Reise der Hoffnung* (*Journey of Hope*, Xavier Koller, 1990) looked at a tragic case, based on a true story from the 1980s, of a Turkish Alevi family attempting to cross the border illegally in hopes of a better life.

It may seem surprising that Swiss cinema has only produced a handful of such gripping dramas drawn from real-life tragedies or scandals, especially since these have tended to be exceptionally successful at home and sometimes even abroad. *The Boat Is Full*, for instance, won a Silver Bear at the 1981 Berlin Film Festival and was one of the rare Swiss films to be nominated for an Academy Award for Best Foreign Language Film, while *Journey of Hope* won the 1991 Oscar in that category. One of the biggest domestic box-office successes of all time—and a perennial favorite of German-language television programming—is Rolf Lyssy's *Die Schweizermacher* (*The Swissmakers*, 1978), a comedic portrayal of a pair of bumbling bureaucrats charged with spying on immigrants who have applied for Swiss citizenship.

And yet, there have been few other major feature films critically targeting the country's establishment or focusing on the shadow side of its wealth and its complacent self-image as a haven for neutral diplomacy. One rare exception from the contemporary era is—tellingly—a mix of fiction feature and documentary: *Grounding – Die letzten Tage der Swissair* (*Grounding – The Last Days of Swissair*, Michael Steiner, 2006) used both dramatized scenes and interviews with real-life protagonists to chronicle the 2001 bankruptcy of the airline once dubbed the "flying bank." The demise of this icon of Swiss financial stability and international prestige coincided with, and helped intensify, a period of national self-questioning, as Switzerland was forced to confront the failure of its neoliberal policy elite and rethink its role in a globalized world shaped by new international alliances.

Where fiction films skewering the moneyed classes do exist, they tend to focus on the existential angst or the hollowness of their affluent protagonists' lives, rather than explicitly contrasting these lifestyles with actual poverty. This tone seems to have been set by the Swiss New Wave of the 1960s and 1970s, usually termed the New Swiss Cinema (*nouveau cinéma suisse* in French and *der neue Schweizer Film* in German). Among its foundational films are most notably Alain Tanner's *Charles mort ou vif* (*Charles, Dead or Alive*, 1969) and Claude Goretta's *L'Invitation* (*The Invitation*, 1973), both compelling debut fiction features by directors who would go on to achieve sustained international prominence. Tanner's film is an eccentrically told tale of a businessman in the throes of a mid-life crisis, while Goretta's satirizes a group of *petit-bourgeois* office workers attempting to emulate an upper-class garden party, with both comical and disastrous consequences.

Two more recent and noteworthy films focusing on this type of affluent anomie both happen to have been produced by the Zurich-based Dschoint Ventschr Filmproduktion. In *Snow White* (Samir, 2005), the spoiled but unfulfilled daughter of an upper-class family begins to question the emptiness of her life as a party girl after meeting an ambitious young rapper from an immigrant family. Although the film alludes to his working-class background, it is set primarily in the glittering but ultimately sterile world of the *jeunesse dorée* and its cocaine-fueled escapades. *Nachbeben* (*Going Private*, Stina Werenfels, 2006) is similarly set in a milieu of lakeside villas and high-class substance abuse, but achieves more psychological depth and complexity in probing the imminent collapse of an investment banker's career and family life following a major financial reversal.

These two films follow in the tradition of the New Swiss Cinema classics mentioned above, in that they take up an ironic distance toward their well-to-do protagonists, but do not set up a dramatic conflict between social classes. That type of tension—as exemplified by a film like *Gisaengchung* (*Parasite*, Bong Joon-ho, 2019), the South Korean black-comedy thriller in which the members of a destitute family take revenge on the wealthy household where they are all employed as servants—is virtually nonexistent in Swiss fiction filmmaking. Nor do Swiss fiction features tend to make use of the "upstairs, downstairs" dynamic typical of the costume film genre of British cinema and television. And yet, the list of films made in and about Switzerland on topics related to precarity is quite long, ranging from economic instability to social discrimination and other forms of marginality. The vast majority of these films, however, are documentaries.

The (Cultural) Politics of Swissness

Before moving on to look at noteworthy recent examples of films that engage with precarity, poverty, and social exclusion, it is important to examine some of the reasons why these topics remain relatively underrepresented within Swiss fiction filmmaking, while they have been highly formative to the development of documentary film movements since the 1960s. To do that, it will be necessary to provide some brief background information on both the Swiss socio-political context and the Swiss film industry, such as it is.

Within the framework of this publication, it is worth mentioning several particularities of Swiss political structures that also affect cultural policy and, in turn, the film sector, with implications, ultimately, for the theme of this study. Although Switzerland is located geographically in the center of Europe, and functions as a global financial hub, it has remained largely politically isolated due to its traditional policy of neutrality: a paradoxical status characterized by historian André Holenstein as "Verflechtung und Abgrenzung" (entanglement and isolation).[1] Switzerland is not a member of NATO or the European Union; although it maintains areas of bilateral cooperation with both organizations, this state of affairs has also had implications for the cultural sector. In the aftermath of a 2014 referendum aiming to unilaterally limit immigration, thus violating the bilateral accord with the EU, Switzerland was excluded from participating in Creative Europe initiatives, including the MEDIA program, to which it had belonged on and off over the years.[2] As a result, Swiss film production has been cut off from both important funding resources and opportunities to collaborate internationally.

But even before these more recent developments, Swiss cinema had maintained something of an outsider status, for both financial and political reasons. On the one hand, this has been due in part to what sociologist Olivier Moeschler has diplomatically called the "discreet" role of the state in shaping—and in funding—cultural policy on a national scale.[3] Because Switzerland is a federal republic, the role of supporting culture falls primarily to the 26 cantons, bolstered further by smaller regional funds. The existence of a national law for funding film production represents a significant exception to this state of affairs—and a recognition that there would be no national cinema without federal support. But the contributions

---

[1] André Holenstein, *Mitten in Europa. Verflechtung und Abgrenzung in der Schweizer Geschichte* (Baden: Hier und Jetzt, 2014).
[2] See for instance Media Desk Suisse, "Die Schweiz und Media," *Media Desk Suisse*, accessed January 31, 2022, https://www.mediadesk.ch/a-propos-die-schweiz-und-media/.
[3] Olivier Moeschler, *Cinéma Suisse. Une politique culturelle en action: l'Etat, les professionels, les publics* (Lausanne: Presses polytechniques et universitaires, 2011), 16.

made by the federal film fund to individual film productions, while almost always necessary, are rarely sufficient to finance a project fully, and so budgets must be cobbled together from a variety of other sources on cantonal and municipal levels, as well as from foundations, television pre-sales, and so on. Due to the dearth of public funding as well as the modest size of potential audiences—currently about 8 million inhabitants, further subdivided into multiple linguistic groups—Swiss film productions face the paradoxical reality of being chronically underfunded in spite of the country's overall wealth, and of having to appeal to a wide variety of potential funders, all of whom expect to exercise some degree of creative input into a given project. That Switzerland tends to produce considerably more documentaries than fiction features is partly due to these financial constraints. But there is also an ideological aspect to the pre-eminence of documentary, which I will outline below.

In terms of economics, output, and scope, Switzerland remains a "cinema of small nations" with the resulting implications for the kinds of topics and narratives that tend to be handled. Like many small cinematic nations, it is typically preoccupied with questions of local culture and national identity—what Mette Hjort and Duncan Petrie have called "thematic aboutness"—as well as "the role that film might play as a form of public criticism or critical intervention."[4] In addition, it is a heterogeneous film nation, somewhat analogous to the "cinemas"—in the plural—of countries like Canada and Belgium, where different linguistic groups and geographical regions produce distinctively different kinds of work that nevertheless share certain common characteristics. The linguistic diversity of Swiss cinema includes standard ("high") German, Swiss-German regional dialects, standard French with some dialect elements, to a lesser extent Italian, including regional inflections, and occasionally the country's fourth official language Romansh, which is spoken only in the mountain canton of Grisons. As Jerry White has suggested,[5] such forms of "sub-national cinema" often function as an alternative to, or a reckoning with, centralist nationalist impulses: a notion that meshes perfectly with the foundational concept of the Swiss Confederation as a "*Willensnation*" or "nation of intent." As political scientist Michael Hermann explains, this "nation of intent" is not bound by an essentialist unifying ethnic, linguistic, or religious identity, but rather by the political will of the citizens, as well as by a constant process

---

[4] Mette Hjort and Duncan Petrie, eds., *The Cinema of Small Nations* (Edinburgh: Edinburgh University Press, 2007), 7.
[5] Jerry White, "Introduction: Four Kinds of Minor Cinema (and Some Thoughts on a Fifth)," *Canadian Review of Comparative Literature/Revue Canadienne de Littérature Comparée* 45, no. 3 (September 2018): 360–361.

of renegotiating power relations and polarities.[6] Consequently, both Swiss political discourse and Swiss arts and culture tend to be dominated by explorations, meditations, and debates on what it means to be "Swiss" and how national or cultural identity might be defined at a given point in history: a practice of self-interrogation that, Hermann warns, can verge on the narcissistic.

The Citizen as Cinéaste

Similarly, several critical observers of Swiss film since the New Wave of the 1960s and 1970s have pointed out that a chief characteristic of the New Swiss Cinema beginning in that era was an emphasis on "Suissitude" or "Swissness," which granted local filmmaking an autonomy that distinguished it from the international mainstream. To the critic and filmmaker Alexander Seiler, this very "provincialism" was what made the Swiss films of the time potentially interesting to both domestic and foreign audiences.[7] It is important to note that this renewed preoccupation with the territory amid the rebellious movements of the period represented a rupture with, and not a continuation of, the tradition of the bucolic and patriotic *Heimatfilme* that had dominated the previous era, from the 1930s to the 1950s: leaving behind nationalist myth-making in order to focus critically on the home territory, with all its faults and inequities.[8]

However, in an influential book-length essay published as a special issue of the journal *CINEMA*, looking back at the first two decades of New Swiss Film from the vantage point of the mid-1980s, the author and critic Martin Schaub[9] pointed out an important difference between the documentaries and the fiction films of this movement. While documentary filmmaking actively and self-assuredly assumed a critical stance, which he called "the nation's conscience" ("das Gewissen der Nation"),[10] the fiction films tended to provide a much more oblique and

---

6 Michael Hermann, *Was die Schweiz zusammenhält* (Bern: Zytglogge, 2016).
7 Alexander Seiler, "David und Goliath. Zur aktuellen Lage des Filmschaffens hier und anderswo. Eine Preisrede," [1984] in *Daneben geschrieben* (Zurich: Hier und Jetzt, 2008), 138–146.
8 For a detailed discussion of both the nationalist mythmaking and the self-critical possibilities attached to the Heimatfilm genre, albeit in the German context, see Johannes von Moltke, *No Place Like Home Locations of Heimat in German Cinema* (Berkeley, CA: University of California Press, 2005) and Alexandra Ludewig, *Screening Nostalgia: 100 Years of German Heimat Film* (Bielefeld: Transcript, 2011).
9 Martin Schaub, *Die eigenen Angelegenheiten: Themen, Motive, Obsessionen und Träume des neuen Schweizer Films 1963–1983* (Basel: Stroemfeld/Roter Stern, 1983).
10 Martin Schaub, *Die eigenen Angelegenheiten*, 92–110.

"discreet" critique of social wrongs and injustices—although in many cases the same filmmakers worked in both areas. In Schaub's view, both approaches represent versions of "committed" filmmaking. The documentaries' critical standpoint was made plain through their chosen subjects: migration, housing, industrialization, pollution, the marginalization of both the youth and the elderly, and so on. Schaub saw the minimalism and lack of bombast of the fiction films as a critical act on formal and ideological levels: a refusal of grand narratives and blockbuster storytelling; understatement as an antidote to "kitsch"; and the outsider or marginalized figure as a metaphor for precariousness beyond the (merely) economic.

In the decades since Schaub's 1983 assessment, this basic dichotomy has persisted, although it is arguable whether it can still be attributed to the political attitudes of the 1968 generation. But Schaub's analysis also touched on a further explanation for the fundamentally self-critical tendency of Swiss cinema: the identification of many of its practitioners with the concept of the *citoyen*, the engaged citizen on whom the system of direct democracy rests. In this connection, Schaub borrowed from the renowned Swiss literary figure Max Frisch the notion of the "layperson" as someone who "meddles in his [sic] own affairs":[11] the filmmakers had assigned themselves the task of meddling in society's affairs, as part of their civic duty. In a country based as strongly on a consensus model of governing as the Swiss Confederation, it followed that the citizen filmmaker would choose to engage in the role of chronicler and critic rather than through a discourse of class struggle and conflict. In the interest of historical accuracy, it is important to note here that the concept of "citoyen" was originally narrowly defined, in an era in which voting was restricted to Swiss males. With the introduction of women's suffrage in 1971 (a relatively late date in Europe) and the ongoing process of migration and assimilation of so-called foreigners into the country, the question of what it means to be a Swiss citizen continues to be expanded and redefined.

Precarity and Swissness

It should be clear by this point that the case of Switzerland involves several layers of paradox: a wealthy nation with a film sector that is itself precariously

---

[11] The title of Schaub's volume cited above is drawn from a 1966 quote from Frisch: "Der Laie ist ein Mann, der sich in seine eigenen Angelegenheiten einmischt," which translates as "the layman is someone who meddles in his own affairs" (Schaub, *Die eigenen Angelegenheiten*, 7). It reflects the Swiss political system's emphasis on widespread lay participation in civic affairs, rather than technocratic rule by experts.

funded; a country focused in on itself even as it exerts geopolitical and international financial influence; and a preoccupation with questions of national and regional identity that might be deemed provincial or narcissistic but is actually self-critical on a number of levels. All of these elements are worth touching on here, because they continue to shape the ways in which Swiss cinema engages with precarity, poverty, and social exclusion.

As I have already mentioned, one main result is that the number of documentaries on these subjects far outweighs the number of fiction films. A further important aspect is the way in which films about precarity often also engage with questions of "Swissness" and the extent to which the protagonists' plight may, or may not, be considered typical or representative of the country or its people. It is important to mention that Swiss film history also includes a tradition of globe-trotting documentaries that necessarily connect with themes of poverty, deprivation, and injustice around the world. But because the focus on Swissness is so central to Swiss cinema, I have chosen to concentrate in the following sections on contemporary examples of films dealing with precarity that, in one way or another, also participate in the discourse around questions of national identity. Finally, for the purposes of this study I have chosen to focus on films in which the themes related to precarity intersect with formal choices, because—following Martin Schaub's insight—certain narrative strategies and structures may also be understood as self-critical, analytical approaches that engage with precarity on a more abstract or metaphorical level.

A Constellation of Themes

One of the most masterful contemporary examples of a film that reflects all these elements also happens to be the most recent of the films I have selected for this study: the documentary essay *Nemesis* by Thomas Imbach (2020). For seven years, Imbach filmed the view from his studio window near the railway lines in Zurich, as the nineteenth-century freight depot facing his building was demolished and replaced by a high-security prison and police complex. The film weaves together several thematic strands: the disappearance of the historic freight yards connected to Zurich's industrial past as a manufacturing and shipping hub; closely observed scenes of the goings-on at the construction site; and interviews with incarcerated immigrants and asylum-seekers awaiting deportation at a different jail, whose testimonies foreshadow the fate of the future inmates of the new, repressive building. Particularly striking visually is Imbach's use of fast-motion cinematography through much of the film, which lends a jerky, sometimes playful, and often disturbing quality to the demolition and construction scenes (Fig. 1). In between the different phases of wreckage and reconstruction, the site is used casually by city dwellers who relax or hold impromptu parties amid the ruins, even as the terrain is also briefly reclaimed by stray animals.

Fig. 1: Nemesis (Thomas Imbach, 2020).

Nemesis offers a complex look at multiple forms of precariousness including, but not restricted to, classic economic precarity: from the perilous aspects of the construction work (there are several references to on-site accidents), the migrant backgrounds of many of the laborers, and the suffering of the prisoners' awaiting deportation, to the erosion of viable urban living spaces and the seeming rootlessness, randomness, and loneliness of contemporary urban life. Imbach uses voiceover commentary, spoken in the first person by an actor, to introduce personal elements, such as his family's own experience during Switzerland's evolution from a rural to an industrial and a post-industrial economy, or his grief at the deaths of relatives and friends. In tracing the history of the new police and prison complex, the film also emphasizes the political struggles and power imbalances surrounding the project, which had been contested by various groups including historical preservation societies and residents' associations. In an interview on Swiss-German public radio,[12] Imbach explained that his use of fast-motion cinematography, which requires filming fewer frames per second, was not only an aesthetic choice but also an economical one, because it allowed him to save film stock during the years-long filming process: in other words, a kind of material precarity is built into the very image.

---

12 Michael Sennhauser, "Der Blick aus dem Fenster: *Nemesis* von Thomas Imbach," *SRF Kontext*, April 26, 2020, https://www.srf.ch/audio/kontext/der-blick-aus-dem-fenster-nemesis-von-thomas-imbach?partId=11752881.

Nemesis also stands out among recent Swiss film productions because it weaves together nearly all the thematic elements most typical of the treatment of precarity in Swiss cinema: outsider status, both inadvertent and self-imposed; shifting political and economic power and inequality; abuses of justice; the marginalization of immigrants and refugees; work-related alienation and anomie. One further set of themes would complete this constellation: addiction and mental illness, which are not really touched on by Imbach in this film, but which often intersect with these other elements, as we shall see in the examples that follow.

Views from the Margins

Platzspitzbaby (*Needle Park Baby*, Pierre Monnard, 2020), a feature film released around the same time as *Nemesis*, is a case in point. Based on Michelle Halbheer's 2013 memoir of the same title, a bestselling account of growing up in the mid-1990s with a single mother addicted to heroin, the film revisits Switzerland's evolving policies of the time around drug addiction treatments and child welfare cases. Told from the point of view of the preteen Mia—a fictionalized version of Halbheer, created with her input—and set in the same historical period as Halbheer's childhood, *Needle Park Baby* dramatizes both the material precarity of the young girl's life with her mother and the complex emotional challenges she faces as she struggles to play the role of her unstable mother's caretaker.

While Mia's mother Sandrine belongs to the hard-drug subculture that developed as a self-destructive spinoff of the countercultural youth movements of the 1970s and 1980s, and is often shown socializing with fellow addicts from her peer group, Mia is relegated to the position of a complete outsider and outcast. She suffers emotional and to some extent physical abuse at the hands of her mentally unstable mother, and is ostracized at school. There is also an element of racism invoked in the bullying, as Mia—like Halbheer—is the biracial child of a white Swiss mother and a father who is a person of color, although details of his ethnic background are never revealed. One of the film's main plot twists revolves around Mia's attempt to form a friendship with a couple of other young teens from equally troubled families: an attempt that is tragically thwarted by their abusive and unstable addict parents' behaviors. But the main source of dramatic tension in the film is the constant threat of separation from her mother, which takes on several forms: from incompetent administrative decisions by social services, to periodic abandonment by her unfit mother, and her mother's risk of fatally overdosing. Mia also witnesses Sandrine's forays into prostitution and drug-dealing as attempts to finance her drug habit; in these scenes, the spectacle of Sandrine's victimization becomes an additional burden borne by Mia.

As befits a coming-of-age narrative, this tension is only resolved when Mia is finally able to make her own choices and break the cycle of co-dependency. But in keeping with Swiss self-critical cinema's tendency to reject bombastic, overly dramatic plot twists and unrealistic happy endings, the film's resolution remains discreetly open-ended. Still, *Needle Park Baby* represents an indictment of a social system that failed both addicts and their families, within the context of the repressive drug policies that had only begun to be phased out around the time in which the film's plot is set. Although most of the film takes place in the small town in which the welfare authorities have placed mother and daughter, its title, as well as its opening sequence, evoke the infamous "Needle Park" once located behind the main train station in Zurich, which came to symbolize those failed policies that have since been replaced by more liberal, and more effective, therapy programs.

The 2013 fiction feature *Traumland (Dreamland)* coincidentally also features a young protagonist named Mia: in this case, a teenage single mother from Bulgaria who has been trafficked into Switzerland by a vicious pimp to work the streets during the lucrative pre-Christmas season. *Dreamland* brutally juxtaposes the misery, abjection, and violence that Mia experiences as an illegal migrant prostitute on the streets of Zurich with the affluent but sterile lives of her clients and other figures she encounters. The entire story is set within one twenty-four-hour period, starting in the wee hours on the day before Christmas and ending with a tragic denouement on Christmas morning. Much of the film takes place after dark, with the glittering seasonal decorations providing an ironic contrast to the physical and emotional chill that dominates the characters' lives. Amid the festive trappings, the impending holiday is shown to be an emotional trial for all the characters, for different reasons, underscoring the brittleness or lack of family ties and friendships.

Director and scriptwriter Petra Volpe based the film, her first fiction feature, on extensive research conducted over several years, including interviews with sex workers, social workers, and police officers, as well as on her own experiences living in Zurich's red-light district and working as a phone sex operator. The narrative is crafted as a multi-protagonist structure in which all the main characters are connected through their interactions with Mia. They include: a middle-aged man estranged from his family; a pregnant wife who has discovered her husband's infidelity; a lonely, bitter older woman who herself is an immigrant from Spain; a frustrated social worker helpless against the dilemmas faced by the migrant sex workers she is supposed to protect. As Volpe herself has confirmed, in a statement from the film's press kit, the ultimate goal was to represent Swiss society critically by portraying it through the eyes of a marginalized outsider, thus demonstrating how the most vulnerable within it are treated. Volpe's statement echoes a line from the preamble to the Federal Constitution of the Swiss Confederation: "the strength of a people is measured by the well-being of its weakest members."[13] The stories told in her "dreamland," however, belie the ideal of solidarity promised by the constitution's ringing words.

Hunger, cold, the attendant dangers of working the streets, the indifference or hostility of neighbors: all the story strands are gradually woven together, leading to a tragic ending for Mia that the narrative structure has rendered inevitable, as one character after another fails to help or (unwittingly) betrays her. Beginning with its ironic title and ending with its inexorably bleak resolution, *Dreamland* is a hard-hitting indictment of the indifference and coldness of a society in which the bodies of young foreign women are subject to the brutal logic of commodity consumption, and where even those living materially secure lives suffer from a sense of alienation and emotional poverty, and an inability to communicate with those closest to them or to help others in need that borders on the pathological.

The portrayal of destitute outsiders living on the margins of an affluent, yet repressive society is a relatively common trope in the work of New Swiss Cinema pioneers like Alain Tanner or Markus Imhoof. It is a significant mark of continuity between generations and regions that this same trope is found in fiction films by younger (female) filmmakers like the Swiss-German Volpe—or the francophone Swiss Ursula Meier. Meier's 2012 crime drama *L'Enfant d'en haut* (*Sister*) is a particularly apt example of an outsider figure whose very existence serves to highlight the gap between the haves and have-nots. In this case, the "boy from the heights" of the original French title is the prepubescent waif Simon, who in fact lives on the edge of a semi-industrial plain near a well-frequented ski slope in the Canton of Valais. During the ski season he regularly rides the cable car up to the summit, where he pilfers gear casually left lying around by well-to-do skiers to sell it for cash down in the valley. It is not clear whether he goes to school at all. It seems clear that he lives with his moody and volatile older sister, who works dead-end jobs, possibly on the verge of prostitution, and struggles with substance abuse—though their circumstances and their emotional bond are gradually revealed to be abject in different ways than they appear at first. From the highway that runs past their tiny, squalid apartment, there is a clear view of the majestic and not-so-distant snowy peaks where tourists and vacationers cavort.

---

13 In the official German version: " . . . dass die Stärke des Volkes sich misst am Wohl der Schwachen." Full text available here: *Bundesverfassung der Schweizerischen Eidgenossenschaft*, March 7, 2021, https://www.fedlex.admin.ch/eli/cc/1999/404/de.

Sister contains almost no explicit references to Switzerland, but the film's visual design engages constantly with the iconography of Swissness as it has been constructed through the history of self-critical Swiss filmmaking. In particular, the constant contrast between the fantasy world of the snowy slopes and the tedium of the concrete sprawl of highways and high-rises evokes a long tradition of filmic negotiations with the landscape as a symbolic representation of national characteristics, both positive and negative (Fig. 2).[14]

Fig. 2: L'Enfant d'en haut (Sister, Ursula Meier, 2012).

Meier's choice to link the material and spatial dimensions by emphasizing the contrast between the valley and the mountain lends simplicity, rigor, and elegance to her narrative. As an interloper in the world of luxury and leisure, Simon serves as a link between the dreary and hopeless grind of the industrial valley and the dreamlike brightness and ease of the ski resort. Because, as the film gradually reveals to us by following Simon behind the scenes, precarity also lurks in the fancy restaurants, rental bungalows, and equipment counters: in the form of the temporary workers who run the machinery, cook the food, do the cleaning, and dispose of the garbage, until the season ends and they leave to chase other jobs. Simon's own boyish dreams of pilfering his way to wealth and a "better" family are dashed soon enough, and at the narrative's close he is

---

14 See for instance Maria Tortajada, "Cinéma suisse: comment échapper au paysage narcissique?", in *Derrière les images*, ed. Marc-Olivier Gonseth, Jacques Hainard, and Roland Kaehr (Neuchâtel: Publications du Musée d'ethnographie, 2000), 279–306.

shown riding a cable car back down to the valley all alone. Even the landscape has lost its splendor, as the formerly gleaming snow-covered slopes have transitioned into muddy thaw. With an ending less bleak than *Dreamland*, but more open-ended and ambivalent than *Needle Park Baby*, *Sister* leaves its main character stuck between freedom and desolation.

Forms of Engagement: From Documentary to Collaborative Filmmaking

As previously mentioned, committed filmmaking in Switzerland long tended to emphasize documentary forms over fiction features. Even today, the list of documentary films dealing with aspects of precarity, poverty, insecurity, and injustice would be very long. It would be even longer if the definition of *precarity* were expanded to include films about the decline of family farming and the erosion of rural communities, on the one hand, and films about people with mental and physical disabilities or illnesses, on the other hand. Although these avenues of inquiry would undoubtedly be fruitful as well, including them here would go beyond the scope of what this essay can cover.

One body of work that must be mentioned in this connection, however, is that of the francophone-Swiss filmmaker Fernand Melgar, and most particularly his direct-cinema documentaries on asylum seekers and so-called *"sans-papiers"* (illegal immigrants). As the son of Spanish "guest workers" who came to Switzerland in the 1960s, Melgar had begun his career in the 1990s by focusing on themes of immigration, assimilation, and exile. With *La Forteresse* (*The Fortress*, 2008) he began what is arguably his most important work to date: a trilogy looking at how asylum seekers are processed, and all too often ultimately deported, within the Swiss system. *The Fortress* was shot inside a factory-like transit facility for asylum applicants; the second film, *Vol spécial* (*Special Flight*, 2011) was filmed inside a detention center near Geneva airport where rejected applicants await their mandatory flights out of the country. In a follow-up film, *Le monde est comme ça* (*The World Is Like That*, 2013), Melgar sought out five of the deportees in their countries of origin, to chronicle the brutal after-effects of having been separated from their families and sent back to the countries from which they had sought to escape. Taken together, the three films offer a devastating look at the hypocrisy, callousness, and brutality of Swiss immigration and asylum policy. Although the employees portrayed in *The Fortress* and *Special Flight* are largely well-meaning and kind to the prisoners they are detaining, they are powerless against a judicial system and a political climate where the priority is deterring asylum-seekers rather than upholding and protecting human rights.

After completing the trilogy, Melgar pursued his method of observational filmmaking within an institution to make *L'Abri* (*The Shelter*, 2014), filmed throughout the winter season in an emergency homeless shelter in his own city, Lausanne. As in the asylum trilogy, *The Shelter* combines scenes with recurring protagonists and fleeting glimpses into the lives of people in transit, while also documenting the daily routines and regulations practiced by the facility's staff. Each night, the staff are compelled to turn away more people than they can accommodate at the shelter; those who are rejected must spend the night out in the cold. Melgar's observational filming style, unobtrusive but precise, contributes to the sense of mounting rage and despair one feels while watching these chronicles of inequality and powerlessness. In the spirit of documentary activism, Melgar has made all four films available for free online streaming, so that their impact can be strewn as widely as possible.

The figure of the Swiss social worker powerless to effect any meaningful change is a recurring element in both documentary and fiction films about precarity, including several mentioned here. A more light-hearted and optimistic version of this character can be found in *Tapis Rouge* (*Red Carpet*, Frédéric Baillif and Kantarama Gahigiri, 2014). A Dogme-style scripted film made in collaboration with non-professional youth actors, and shot in loose vérité-style camera work, *Red Carpet* tells the story of a group of disaffected teenagers from a housing project on the outskirts of Lausanne, who are encouraged by their local caseworker for sociocultural animation to collaborate on writing a screenplay. The youths take this advice so seriously that they come up with an entire production dossier for a film, which they then decide they should pitch to producers at the upcoming Cannes Film Festival. The hapless caseworker, unwilling to quash their enthusiasm, agrees to take them on a camping trip to the Côte d'Azur. Along the way, these so-called "troubled" kids, most of them from African or North African backgrounds, share details of their personal and familial struggles, squabbling but also bonding more deeply with each other. The film ends with "guerilla filming" scenes on the Croisette at Cannes, where the youths, dolled up in tuxedos and evening gowns as per the Cannes Festival dress code, mingle with what seem to be actual tourist crowds, collecting business cards and handing out flyers for their project.

Red Carpet is not only a rare example of a playful and hopeful depiction of housing project culture, it is also an actual product of that culture: the film was developed as part of a socio-cultural education program, and the youths who collaborated on it essentially play themselves. In addition, with help from the film production, they were ultimately able to make the short film they had scripted as part of the program. It remains a promising example of a new phase of self-critical Swiss cinema: one which expands the portrayal of Swiss identities to include more visible diversity, with the children of immigrants taking their place within the national cinema landscape, both in front of and behind the camera. And one which places ostensible outsiders at the center of the story, not only as the film's subjects, but also as its makers and agents of change.

Paradox Revisited

If Melgar's documentaries, and most of the other films discussed here, present a critical and generally pessimistic view of Swiss society as marked by marginalization, alienation, injustice, and hypocrisy, *Red Carpet* presents a refreshingly optimistic alternative, while remaining within the tradition of "discreet" narrative arcs that eschew full-blown happy endings in favor of more contemplative conclusions. Each of these films, in its own way, illustrates the paradoxical nature of Swiss cinema's preoccupation with themes of precarity and social inequality: a generally affluent society with a poorly funded film sector engaging in self-critical representations of marginalization as part of a larger ongoing discourse around national identity, while insisting on open-ended narratives that often call into question the possibility of positive change.

To conclude this essay, I would like to briefly mention one more film that embodies this paradox on several levels. The fiction feature *Dene wos guet geit* (*Those Who Are Fine*, Cyril Schäublin, 2017) corresponds remarkably well to Schaub's formulation of a "discreet" mode of storytelling that is all the more devastating for its narrative restraint. Ostensibly a thriller about a young telemarketing employee who tricks vulnerable elderly people out of large sums of money by posing as their granddaughter, Schäublin's film depicts contemporary urban Swiss life as depressive, repressed, morally out-of-kilter, materialistic, and yet curiously anhedonic. The potentially gripping thriller plot fades into the background amid the close attention paid to details of sterile city life—with its grid-like streets and building structures, monotonous minimum-wage jobs, and electronic surveillance apparatus—and gradually unravels as it becomes clear that the thief's goal is merely to deposit the stolen funds with an exclusive private investment bank. *Those Who Are Fine* fascinates precisely through its ironic obsession with laconic speech, repetitive sales patter, and poetically filmed tedium. Most telling of all is the film's title, which is a reference to a classic 1970s Swiss-German dialect ballad by singer-songwriter Mani Matter, about the paradoxical nature of social justice.

> Dene wos guet geit, giengs besser
> Giengs dene besser wos weniger guet geit
> Was aber nid geit, ohni dass's dene
> Weniger guet geit wos guet geit[15].

Leaving out the untranslatable wordplay of the original, the lyrics say: Those who are well-off would feel better if those who are worse off could also do better—but that would require those who are well-off to be a little worse off. In Schäublin's telling, the promise of prosperity turns out to be a trap, which is perhaps another way of expressing what Lauren Berlant has called "cruel optimism's double bind": in spite of the obvious failures of the current state of affairs, "it is awkward and it is threatening to detach from what is already not working."[16] And yet, navigating this paradox is the prerequisite for change.

Bibliography

Bundesverfassung der Schweizerischen Eidgenossenschaft. March 7, 2021. https://www.fedlex.admin.ch/eli/cc/1999/404/de.
Berlant, Lauren. *Cruel Optimism*. Durham, NC: Duke University Press, 2011.
Hermann, Michael. *Was die Schweiz zusammenhält*. Bern: Zytglogge, 2016.
Hjort, Mette, and Duncan Petrie, eds. *The Cinema of Small Nations*. Edinburgh: Edinburgh University Press, 2007.
Holenstein, André. *Mitten in Europa. Verflechtung und Abgrenzung in der Schweizer Geschichte*. Baden: Hier und Jetzt, 2014.
Ludewig, Alexandra. *Screening Nostalgia: 100 Years of German Heimat Film*. Bielefeld: Transcript, 2011.
Media Desk Suisse. "Die Schweiz und Media." *Media Desk Suisse*. Accessed January 31, 2022. https://www.mediadesk.ch/a-propos-die-schweiz-und-media/.
Moeschler, Olivier. *Cinéma Suisse. Une politique culturelle en action: l'Etat, les professionels, les publics*. Lausanne: Presses polytechniques et universitaires, 2011.
Schaub, Martin. *Die eigenen Angelegenheiten: Themen, Motive, Obsessionen und Träume des neuen Schweizer Films 1963–1983*. Basel: Stroemfeld/Roter Stern, 1983.
Seiler, Alexander. "David und Goliath. Zur aktuellen Lage des Filmschaffens hier und anderswo. Eine Preisrede" [1984]. In *Daneben geschrieben*. Zurich: Hier und Jetzt, 2008, 138–146.
Sennhauser, Michael. "Der Blick aus dem Fenster: *Nemesis* von Thomas Imbach." SRF Kontext, April 26, 2020. https://www.srf.ch/audio/kontext/der-blick-aus-dem-fenster-nemesis-von-thomas-imbach?partId=11752881.

---

15 Mani Matter, "Dene wo's gut geit," from his 1970 EP *Hemmige*.
16 Lauren Berlant, *Cruel Optimism* (Durham, NC: Duke University Press, 2011), 263.

Tortajada, Maria. "Cinéma suisse: comment échapper au paysage narcissique?" In *Derrière les images*, ed. Marc-Olivier Gonseth, Jacques Hainard, and Roland Kaehr. Neuchâtel: Publications du Musée d'ethnographie, 2000, 279–306.
Von Moltke, Johannes. *No Place Like Home: Locations of Heimat in German Cinema.* Berkeley, CA: University of California Press, 2005.
White, Jerry. "Introduction: Four Kinds of Minor Cinema (and Some Thoughts on a Fifth)." *Canadian Review of Comparative Literature/Revue Canadienne de Littérature Comparée* 45, no. 3 (September 2018): 357–380.

Filmography

Charles mort ou vif (*Charles, Dead or Alive*). Dir. Alain Tanner. Switzerland, 1969.
Das Boot ist voll (*The Boat Is Full*). Dir. Markus Imhoof. Switzerland, 1981.
Dene wos guet geit (*Those Who Are Fine*). Dir. Cyril Schäublin. Switzerland, 2017.
Die Schweizermacher (*The Swissmakers*). Dir. Rolf Lyssy. Switzerland, 1978.
Gisaengchung (*Parasite*). Dir. Bong Joon-ho. South Korea, 2019.
Grounding – Die letzten Tage der Swissair (*Grounding – The Last Days of Swissair*). Dir. Michael Steiner. Switzerland, 2006.
L'Abri (*The Shelter*). Dir. Fernand Melgar. Switzerland, 2014.
L'Enfant d'en haut (*Sister*). Dir. Ursula Meier. Switzerland/France, 2012.
L'Invitation (*The Invitation*). Dir. Claude Goretta. Switzerland, 1973.
La Forteresse (*The Fortress*). Dir. Fernand Melgar. Switzerland/France, 2008.
Le monde est comme ça (*The World Is Like That*). Dir. Fernand Melgar. Switzerland, 2013.
Nachbeben (*Going Private*). Dir. Stina Werenfels. Switzerland, 2006.
Nemesis. Dir. Thomas Imbach. Switzerland, 2020.
Platzspitzbaby (*Needle Park Baby*). Dir. Pierre Monnard. Switzerland, 2020.
Reise der Hoffnung (*Journey of Hope*). Dir. Xavier Koller. Switzerland/Italy/Germany, 1990.
Snow White. Dir. Samir. Switzerland/Austria, 2005.
Tapis Rouge (*Red Carpet*). Dir. Frédéric Baillif and Kantarama Gahigiri. Switzerland/France, 2014.
Traumland (*Dreamland*). Dir. Petra Volpe. Switzerland/Germany, 2013.
Vol spécial (*Special Flight*). Dir. Fernand Melgar. Switzerland, 2011.

Hanna Prenzel
Individualization as a Shared Experience?
Precarious Conditions Negotiated in German Film:
Individual Refusal and Collective Agency

A harvested cornfield under the blue morning sky. The camera is static and shows the sunny landscape in a long shot. It films a barefooted woman with wild curly hair dressed in a fancy black jumpsuit who stares into the void, holding her high heels in her hands. After remaining motionless for a while, she staggers drunkenly across the dry ground, trying to keep her balance as she approaches the camera.

This is how the opening scene of *Eine flexible Frau* (*The Drifter*, 2010) by Tatjana Turanskyj introduces the film's main character Greta, a middle-class, unemployed architect and single mother who is trapped in a downward spiral of precarization. The film reveals how the all-encompassing uncertainty, dependance, and vulnerability affect the precarized subject and demonstrates the (unfulfilled) mobility demanded by neoliberal capitalism.[1]

Turanskyj's film has often been discussed as an exemplary film dealing with the precarization of gendered subjects in a post-Fordist society.[2] Hence it can be regarded as a paradigmatic case of the German "cinema of precarity."[3] Before focusing on two exemplary cinematic works, I will give a cursory overview of films that deal with the precarization of the working sphere in Germany on the basis of a brief socio-political and historical framing.

The echo of the German *reunification* and the transformation of the working sphere, especially in the former GDR, are addressed in innumerous films. *Kehraus*

---
[1] Hester Baer, "Future Feminism: Political Filmmaking and the Resonance of West German Feminist Film Movement," in *German Cinema in the Age of Neoliberalism*, ed. Hester Baer (Amsterdam: Amsterdam University Press, 2021), 157.
[2] See Barbara Mennel, "From Utopian Collectivity to Solitary Precarity: Thirty Years of Feminist Theory and the Cinema of Women's Work," *Women in German Yearbook* 30, (2014); Carolyn Veldstra, "Bad feeling at work: emotional labour, precarity, and the affective economy," *Cultural Studies* 34, no. 1 (December 2020), https://doi.org/10.1080/09502386.2018.1555269.
[3] Whereas Lauren Berlant and Alice Bardan use the specific term "cinema of precarity," Francesco Sticchi maps films connected to affective states in precarious conditions. Lauren Berlant, *Cruel Optimism* (Durham, NC: Duke University Press, 2011), 201; Alice Bardan, "The New European Cinema of Precarity: A Transnational Perspective," in *Work in Cinema: Labor and The Human Condition*, ed. Ewa Mazierska (New York: Palgrave Macmillan, 2013); Francesco Sticchi, *Mapping Precarity in Contemporary Cinema and Television: Chronotopes of Anxiety, Depression, Expulsion/Extinction* (Cham, Switzerland: Springer & Palgrave Macmillan, 2021).

(*Sweeping*, 1990) by Gerd Kroske, *HALLE 101* (2010) by Andreas Dresen or Thomas Stuber's *In den Gängen* (*In the Aisles*, 2018)—to name only very few examples—deal with the impact of the changes in wage labor and the working class, as well as the spread of West Germany's capitalist logic, tangible till today. The resulting unemployment culminated in the restructuring of the entire German social system through the so-called *Agenda 2010* at the beginning of the twenty-first century, which had an enormous impact on the self-esteem of the unemployed. This is portrayed in films like *Halbe Treppe* (*Grill Point*, 2002) and *Sommer vorm Balkon* (*Summer in Berlin*, 2005) by Dresen or Robert Thalheim's *Netto* (2005) that oscillate between tragedy and comedy. While these films address the effects of unemployment mostly on German citizens within the (social) system, films such Hans-Christian Schmid's *Lichter* (*Distant Lights*, 2003) and *Wundersame Welt der Waschkraft* (*Wondrous World of Laundry*, 2009)—both set at the Polish-German border—or the documentary film *Regeln am Band, bei hoher Geschwindigkeit* (*Rules of Assembly Line, by High Speed*, 2020) by Yulia Lokshina deal with structurally precarious and exploitative working conditions for migrants in Germany. Some documentary films such as *Family Business* (Christiane Büchner, 2015) and *Marina* (Werkgruppe 2, 2018) depict transnational care work by mostly young migrants while Judith Keil and Antje Kruska underline the precarious working conditions of older female cleaners in *Glanz von Berlin* (*Queens of Dust*, 2002).[4]

Numerous scholars have theorized the complex and wide-ranging effects of precarity as a structural phenomenon that encompasses not only the working but also the living sphere.[5] Some scholars have diagnosed the emergence of a new "precarious class"[6] or—as Guy Standing puts it—"a class-in-the-making," which understands itself as a heterogenous multitude. Others use a feminist perspective on becoming precarious[7] or focus on the potential for a shared

---

[4] The effects of precarity and its intergenerational trauma are especially virulent for a younger generation; cf. Aleksandra Miljković's contribution to this volume. These topics are also discussed in Maria Speth's documentary *9 Leben* (*9 Lives*, 2011) about young homeless people or in films by Henner Winckler such as *Klassenfahrt* (*School Trip*, 2002) and *Lucy* (2006).
[5] Pierre Bourdieu, "Job Insecurity is Everywhere Now," in *Acts of Resistance: Against the New Myths of our Time*, trans. Richard Nice (Cambridge: Polity Press, 1998).
[6] Andreas Reckwitz, *Das Ende der Illusionen. Politik, Ökonomie und Kultur in der Spätmoderne* (Frankfurt/Main: Suhrkamp, 2019), 63–135.
[7] Silvana Schmidt, *Prekär sein. Feministische Einführung in die Prekaritätsdebatte* (Münster: Edition Assemblage, 2020).

experience and thus for novel forms of connection, ranging from political organization to activist protest.[8]

Inspired by the latter approaches, I will explore how resistant forms of refusal and dissent in precarious conditions are represented and negotiated in the German cinema of precarity. I will consider narration as well as formal and aesthetic choices. Given the myriad range of possible forms of articulating dissent in film, the scope of this chapter is deliberately limited to two case studies: one film that portrays *individual refusal* and one that portrays *collective resistance* as responses to an all-encompassing precarization.

Turanskyj's *The Drifter* will be my main reference in analyzing the filmic negotiation of individual strategies of refusal in a precarized and isolated working sphere. My analysis is centered on the formal devices that are used to represent individual refusal, boycott, and the disruption of the status quo in fragmented and solitary working and living conditions. *The Drifter*'s subject matter is closely related to the reform of the welfare system in the early 2000s—the aforementioned *Agenda 2010* and its consequences such as impoverishment, pressure on the unemployed, ideologies of self-responsibility, and the propagation of techniques of self-management. Therefore, I will contextualize my film analysis by referring to other films dealing with the "work on the self."[9]

The following part is devoted to collective intersectional struggles in precarious living conditions with reference to *Miete essen Seele auf* (*Rent Eats Your Soul*, Angelika Levi, 2015). This film about a tenants' movement in Berlin-Kreuzberg shows how collective agency may be possible even when precarized subjects are affected differently by structural inequality.[10] In this context, I will explore the political and cinematic landscape by providing an overview of

---

8 See Oliver Marchart, *Die Prekarisierungsgesellschaft. Prekäre Proteste. Politik und Ökonomie im Zeichen der Prekarisierung* (Bielefeld: Transcript, 2013); Brett Neilson and Ned Rossiter, "Precarity as a Political Concept, or, Fordism as Exception," *Theory,Culture & Society* 25, no. 7–8 (December 2008), https://doi.org/10.1177/0263276408097796; Maribel Casas-Cortés, "A Genealogy of Precarity: A Toolbox for Rearticulating Fragmented Social Realities in and out of the Workplace," *Rethinking Marxism* 26, no. 2 (2014), https://doi.org/10.1080/08935696.2014.888849; Judith Butler, *Frames of War: When is Life Grievable?* (London/New York: Verso, 2009), and Isabell Lorey, *State of Insecurity: Government of the Precarious*, trans. Aileen Derieg (London: Verso, 2015).
9 Maurizio Lazzarato, "Immaterial Labor," in *Radical Thought in Italy: A Potential Politics*, ed. Michael Hardt and Paolo Virno (Minneapolis, MN: University of Minnesota Press, 1996).
10 Kimberle Crenshaw, "Demarginalizing the Intersection of Race and Sex: A Black Feminist Critique of Antidiscrimination Doctrine, Feminist Theory and Antiracist Politics," *University of Chicago Legal Forum*, no. 1 (1989); Magdalena Freudenschuss, *Prekär ist wer? Der Prekarisierungsdiskurs als Arena sozialer Kämpfe* (Münster: Westfälisches Dampfboot, 2013), 228–241.

documentary films dealing with Berlin's housing crisis and resulting processes of gentrification and urban displacements, specifically centering on social housing.

"Encourage and Challenge": The Reformation of the German Welfare System

Between 2003 and 2005, the coalition of Social-Democrats and Greens introduced a welfare system reform in Germany, known as *Agenda 2010*. This series of changes included the *Hartz* reforms,[11] which were aimed at reducing unemployment by significantly tightening the rules for claiming welfare or unemployment benefits. Based on post-Fordist ideas of self-responsibility and flexibility, the reforms are anchored in a logic of *Fördern and Fordern* (to support/encourage and to challenge/demand something). This stipulates that recipients of the Hartz IV benefits are obliged to attend regular meetings with a job center adviser to prove that they are actively looking for work or are enrolled in sanctioned skills-training programs. From its implementation the Hartz reform has been much criticized. The benefits are insufficient to live a dignified life and the sanctions for missing job center meetings or programs are disproportionally harsh.[12]

When the Hartz reforms were being introduced, the media and politicians made excessive use of the stereotype of long-term, lazy unemployed, who have only themselves to blame. This stereotyped image focused on physical appearance (such as obesity), the housing situation, and vices (such as lazing about on the sofa watching TV, drinking, and smoking). The cliché of the "lazy unemployed" was reproduced by comedians (such as *Cindy from Marzahn*, 2000–2016), late night shows, scripted reality shows, and the press. Social stereotypes were thus propagated in the public sphere and fulfilled a specific political function.[13] Chancellor Gerhard Schröder's famous quotation from 2001 illustrates these dynamics vividly: "Those who can work but don't want to, cannot count on solidarity. There is no right to laziness in our society!" The societal condemnation of unemployed persons and the so-called "detached precariat" (*abgehängtes Prekariat*) formed an antipode to the ideal image of meritocracy: getting up early, eating well,

---

11 The Hartz reforms were named after the head of the commission (Peter Hartz) that presented recommendations for reforms in the German labor market in 2002.
12 Even though in 2019, the Federal Constitutional Court declared the government cuts to welfare benefits are partially unconstitutional, the reform exists until today.
13 Sebastian Friedrich, "Fett, faul, fernsehsüchtig: Das Arbeitslosenstereotyp in den Medien und seine Funktion," *Journal der Rosa Luxemburg Stiftung*, no. 2 (2015).

exercising, and working from nine to five. Through the Agenda 2010 and systematic stigmatization, the discourse on responsibility for unemployment shifted from the state to the individual. This historically rooted focus on the individuals as solely responsible for their own fates went hand in hand with a continuous work on the self, the flexibilization of working hours, and the establishment of an "entrepreneurial self."[14]

Individual Strategies of Dissent under Precarious Working Conditions: *The Drifter*

At first glance, the main character in *The Drifter* embodies the social counterpart of the stereotypical unemployed described above. Greta is a good-looking, smart, 40-year-old single parent and job-seeking architect living in post-Wall neoliberal Berlin shortly after the financial crisis. Her search for employment is one of the film's main motifs, revealing the absurdity of self-management and self-responsibility. As she is hoping to get a job offer through acquaintances, old friends, or former business partners, we watch her attending quirky parties, calling ex-colleagues, consulting a pushy job coach specialized in optimizing performances. The absurdity of the reality of job-seeking is consistently parodied in the film, for instance in a scene in which a drunk job center employee wants to draw conclusions about Greta's work biography by reading her hands.

We witness how Greta's life becomes a downward spiral: While drinking heavily, she drifts through the gentrified city, from industrial wastelands to areas with newly built townhouses. The changing city of Berlin becomes the stage for performative, absurd moments in which the protagonist playfully comments on the urban space. Trying to gain a foothold in the precarious service society and earn at least a small income, she accepts a call-center-job to sell prefabricated houses for a telemarketing firm. Greta is trying to take part and to adhere to the logic of work as providing identity through status and money.[15] But at the same time, she refuses the role she is required to play in a globalized, flexible capitalist system. This simultaneous process of adaptation and dissent is reflected by

---

14 Ulrich Bröckling, *The Entrepreneurial Self. Fabricating a New Type of Subject* (London: California Sage, 2016).
15 Birgit Kohler and Sabine Nessel, "A Woman Under the Influence – in Berlin zu Beginn des 21. Jahrhundert. Zu Tatjana Turankskyjs Spielfilm-Debüt EINE FLEXIBLE FRAU (D 2010)," *Frauen und Film*, no. 66 (July 2011).

Greta's self-isolation, unwillingness, stubbornness, and anger when dealing with her place in the precarious work regime.

The process of becoming precarious is accompanied by different dimensions of societal expectations: On the one hand, gender-specific expectations that Greta, as a woman with a—albeit precarious—middle class background, is expected to fulfill; on the other hand, the requirements of the labor market to which she is exposed. Gender-specific demands are reflected by displaying different contemporary *female* lifestyles in precarious conditions: helicopter-mothers, additional income earners, workers in leadership positions supervising workers in the low-wage sector, career coaches, and faithfully serving teachers. They all have different strategies to deal with societal expectations, but nevertheless share a constant discontent with their professional and/or personal situation, finding unsatisfying ways to deal with having to try to meet the simultaneous and contradictory demands of capitalist society. Greta distances herself clearly—and in a harsh, ashamed, lonely, and sarcastic way—from the other female characters. Her strategy to escape the situation of multi-layered expectations on her—be it regarding the upbringing of the adolescent son, correct behavior as an ex-wife, or being appropriately sexy—is to drink excessively:[16] numb, staggering, she lets herself go and only on rare occasions (mostly for her son) takes on the sacrificial task of the care work demanded of her.

Even though the film depicts a shared experience of individualization and fragmentation, the female characters in the film do not seem to perceive it as a common basis for political action but remain solitary. In *The Drifter* we witness a multitude of "all-round reduced personalities," quite similar to those in 1978 Helke Sander's classic feminist film *Die allseitig reduzierte Persönlichkeit – Redupers (The All-Around Reduced Personality – Redupers)*. *The Drifter* can be interpreted as a continuation of the story of *Redupers's* main character Edda, a single parent, freelance photographer, and member of a women's-only creative collective in West-Berlin struggling along with different interwoven forms of labor.[17] Sander's film encompasses spheres of paid labor as a freelance photographer, collective and self-organized work in the cultural sector, and care work for her child. To quote Marion von Osten, the film

> represents a possible historical starting point for the current debate over forces of production, precarity, and critical potential by illustrating that, even in the upheaval of changes in the capitalist as well as gender order that took place in the transition from Fordism to

---

16 Baer, "Future Feminism," 163.
17 Mennel, "From Utopian Collectivity to Solitary Precarity," 129.

post-Fordism, many networked and self-organizing production conditions [. . .] were already present—and were being analyzed by feminists.[18]

Whereas *Redupers* was produced during the second wave feminist movement integrating moments of collective work or shared care work, in Turanskyj's film, a utopian, collective perspective including solidarity and resistant strategies remains entirely absent.

In addition to being confronted with various gendered societal expectations, Greta is exposed to a labor market that requires her to constantly perform labor on the self, to which she often responds in a cynical manner by offering different versions of not wanting to meet expectations. These examples are clearly formulated in the telemarketing firm: while the other young employees effortlessly accomplish the task of "always being friendly" (as Ann, the supervisor, phrases it), Greta remains uninvolved, unwilling to use the instructed vocabulary. When her supervisor teaches her how to persuade clients, almost rejoicingly, and knowing she's going to be fired, she does just the opposite of what she was told to do, saying: "Ah, if you are not interested, I do fully understand. No problem. Have a good day then!" This scene is only one of many in which Greta unmasks work as a performative activity through exaggeration, taking the sales strategies ad absurdum. Scholar Carolyn Veldstra argues that the demand for enthusiasm or passion belongs to the large field of affective labor required in the service economy.[19] Thus, Greta's workplace illustrates and ridicules these expectations when she is not willing to fulfill them. Be it in a training session at the telemarketing company or in other situations, we witness Greta's unconventional and unenthusiastic behavior, as well as indifferent reactions incompatible with entrepreneurialism demanding a certain form of emotional labor. By focusing on the lack, inability, and refusal of meeting the required demands, Turanskyj represents these claims through their negation—and thus undermines and highlights them.

In one of the performative scenes in the urban space, Greta acts out the process of precarization, the downward spiral of becoming fragile and vulnerable: Like a stand-up figure, she staggers, loses her balance, and falls—over and over again—on the dusty sandy ground in the bright midday sun. After a few minutes, she remains motionless on the ground while two eccentric performers, who taught her "how to fall down properly," enjoy this endless process of collapsing

---

18 Marion von Osten, "Irene ist Viele! Or what we call 'Productive' Forces," *e-flux journal* 8, (September 2009), https://www.e-flux.com/journal/08/61381/irene-ist-viele-or-what-we-call-productive-forces/.
19 Veldstra, "Bad feeling at work," 11.

and regaining stability. The experimental dance is staged on Teufelsberg, a small mountain on the outskirts of Berlin, and is one among several performative elements in the gentrified and changing urban environment, giving the film a commenting and anti-realistic momentum. The creative and powerful moment in this scene is Greta's transformation of her situation of precarity into a performative dance, an abstract and absurd gesture of interruption to escape the constant pressure of exploitation.

Are Greta's small acts of refusal—as a lonely drinker, a recalcitrant employee in a call center, and an experimental dancer of embodied precariousness—strategies of denial, or even resistance?

Although Greta is fired from the call center and as a dancer stays motionless on the dusty ground, I would indeed argue that the situations described above are ways and strategies of fleeing when trapped in an impasse of uncertainty, experienced loss of status, unemployment, and precarization.[20] They are fragmented moments exemplifying the destruction of the precarized subject caused by the circumstances. In systematic, organizing, and material terms, they are only short-term exit strategies, unraveling and illustrating the mechanisms of the system instead of changing them. Nevertheless, these moments of a "politics of withdrawal"[21] are necessary to unmask structural mechanisms of neoliberal subjugation and to open up forms of dissent as ways of dealing with it.

"Work-for-Labor"- Job Application Trainings in Film

An important motif of Turanskyj's film is the depiction of a job training, in which Greta is taught self-management techniques to optimize her performance. The mise-en-scène of the self-confident career coach, who has a "97% guarantee of success," emphasizes the notion of self-scrutiny: Greta has to observe herself on an over-sized screen having an emotional break down and sobbing incessantly (Fig. 1). The recording is running fast-forward. As the coach stops and replays the tape, we hear Greta crying out in tears, "I'm all alone! I don't have anyone who..."

---

20 Berlant, *Cruel Optimism*, 200.
21 Pepita Hesselberth and Joost de Bloois, *Politics of Withdrawal: Media, Arts, Theory* (Lanham: Rowman & Littlefield, 2020).

Fig. 1: *Eine flexible Frau* (*The Drifter*, Tatjana Turanskyj, 2010).

When the projection stops, the coach nods and turns to Greta: "You have to work on your performance. Define goals. Learn to come across the right way." This scene exemplifies the absurdity of entrepreneurialism at the intersection of emotional labor and the personalization of precarity.[22]

The staging of the neoliberal demand to perform labor on one's self in job application trainings is a recurrent topic used in many contemporary fiction and documentary films from this period in Germany.[23] For example, imagery connected to training, consulting, and further education permeate Harun Farocki's oeuvre: *Die Bewerbung* (*The Interview*, 1996) analyzes powerful hierarchies between coach and applicants and *Die Umschulung* (*Retraining*, 1994) shows how ex-GDR-workers are being trained and trimmed to fit the selling strategies and the behavioral habitus of a FRG company.

There are several film examples directly connected to the job centers' logic of integration into the job market. Both *Summer in Berlin* and *Netto* are dramacomedies from 2005 Berlin in which the main characters are single parents with severe alcohol problems. Katrin Rothe's documentary film *Dunkler Lippenstift macht seriöser* (2003) presents the experience of unemployed university graduates as a Sisyphean task of finding a first job. The film is structured by what Guy Standing calls "work-for-labor":[24] finding job offers, writing applications,

---

22 Veldstra, "Bad feeling at work," 12.
23 Christoph Büttner, "'In dir muss brennen!' Self/Change-Management in Arbeitswelt und Dokumentarfilm," in *Opus und Labor: Arbeit in autobiographischen und biographischen Erzählungen*, ed. Luditha Balint, Katharina Lammers, Kerstin Wilhelms, and Thomas Wortmann (Essen: Klartext 2018).
24 Guy Standing, *The Precariat: The New Dangerous Class* (London/New York: Bloomsbury, 2011), 120.

pimping the CV, traveling to interviews, preparing for interviews, performing at the interviews, while being exposed to constant competition, getting rejections, and then looking for new job offers, and so on. Being unemployed is revealed to be a full-time job itself.

Interestingly, job center benefits are not mentioned as an alternative source of income in *Dunkler Lippenstift macht seriöser*. In contrast, the 2-channel-video *40 Stunden, max. 2 Monate* (*40 hours, max. 2 months*, Stefanie Schröder, 2017) takes the situation at the job center as a starting point for creating a new piece of art. The video is based on the filmmaker's experiences from a series of self-management workshops—funded by the job center—aimed at training artists' entrepreneurial skills. Notes from conversations in the workshop and a dream diary of the artist are mixed up with the formal language of the job center documents and scripted into an installation piece about artistic self-optimization. Not only on a narrative level, but also aesthetically and formally, the installation is emblematic for what Brigitta Kuster and Isabell Lorey call "voluntary precarization"[25] or "self-precarization":[26] The prospect of self-realization conflates with subordination to the marketized logic of artistic labor, including the logic of and demands for self-realization and entrepreneurial self-marketing.

Although the film examples share the subject of application trainings for integration into the labor market, the way the precarized subjects are able to react to, or even use and adopt the *work on the self* situations for their genuine aspirations, depend on their particular intersection of gender, nationality, ethnicity, and access to economic resources.[27] What they have in common is the depiction of individualized subjects in a system in which they are obliged to take part in measures that are supposed to integrate them into the job market. We witness situations in which precarized individuals are being trained or coached for successful job interviews, either on a voluntary basis or through *measures* like job application sessions through the job center—the institution that grants basic security benefits for job seekers and is commissioned to discipline the recipients of these benefits to integrate them as soon as possible into the job market. These scenes of job application trainings function as a magnifying glass for structural

---

[25] Brigitta Kuster, "Die eigenwillige Freiwilligkeit der Prekarisierung," *Grundrisse. Zeitschrift für linke Theorie & Debatte*, no. 18 (2006), http://www.grundrisse.net/grundrisse18/brigitta_kuster.htm.

[26] Isabell Lorey, "Gouvernementalität und Selbst-Prekarisierung. Zur Normalisierung von KulturproduzentInnen," *Transversal Journal* (November 2006), https://transversal.at/transversal/1106/lorey/de.

[27] Freudenschuss, *Prekär ist wer?*, 228–241.

mechanisms of *work-for-labor* situations, their absurdity, as well as the (emotional) dependencies for those precarized subjects affected.

Berlin's Social Housing Politics: Some Fragments

Having emphasized individual strategies of resistance in *The Drifter* and the tropes of *work-for-labor* situations in this and many other films, I will now shift my focus to situations in which individualized precarization is taken not as a hindrance but as a starting point for collective political agency,[28] despite the division along intersectional lines.[29] In recent years, such situations are often connected to the housing crisis as it indiscriminately affects people with quite different social backgrounds.

Exploding rents, insecure and precarious housing conditions, and gentrification have increased globally since the financial crisis in 2008 and finding affordable housing has become difficult for many. According to a 2021 study by the Hans Böckler Foundation, 49.2 percent of approximately 8,4 million households in German major cities spend almost a third of their household income for rent.[30]

In Germany, the welfare benefits no longer cover high rent costs when they exceed a certain fixed amount of a *reasonable rent*. This means that people with low incomes are pushed to the outskirts or into social housing. However, the number of social housing units has declined drastically over the last thirty years. While there were 339,687 social housing units in Berlin in 1990, only 116,597 such units were registered in 2016. This decline is related to the legal and political framework under which social housing was built. After the first

---

28 "Our situations are so diverse, so singular, that it is difficult for us to find common denominators from which to depart or clear differences with which to mutually enrich ourselves. It is complicated for us to express ourselves, to define ourselves from the common ground of precariousness: a precariousness which can do without a clear collective identity in which to simplify and defend itself, but in which some kind of coming together is urgent." Precarias a la deriva, "Adrift through the circuits of feminized precarious work," *Transversal Journal* (2004), http://translate.eipcp.net/transversal/0704/precarias1/en.html.
29 Crenshaw, "Demarginalizing the Intersection of Race and Sex," 139–167.
30 A quarter of households pay at least 40 percent of their income for rent and utilities. Almost twelve percent of city households need even more than half of their income for rent, i.e. warm rent and extra costs. Cf. Andrej Holm, Valentin Regnault, Maximilian Sprengholz, and Meret Stephan, "Die Verfestigung sozialer Wohnversorgungsprobleme," *Hans Böckler Foundation*, Working Paper 217 (June 2021), https://www.boeckler.de/de/faust-detail.htm?sync_id=HBS-008039.

laws for social housing were introduced in the 1950s, private investors, municipal companies, or cooperatives agreed to build social housing in the early 1960s. In return, the investors were subsidized by the state, for example through favorable loans tied to conditions such as occupancy and rent control. After 30 years, the contracts on these conditions expired and profitable market prices could be applied. This development marked a neoliberal turn in rental policy, not only for social housing but in general. The scenarios of displacement and unaffordable rents affect not only the residents of social housing, but a large part of Berlin's population, because half of them live in rental apartments that are at risk of being sold by investors.[31]

These developments led to a rise of social movements and initiatives for collective tenant struggles. The political fight for affordable housing has now become a widespread phenomenon in Berlin, and Germany more generally.

Tenant Collective Struggles in Film

Tenant movements and protest against homeowners, investors, and antisocial rental policies have a long history in Germany. Since the mid-eighteenth century, precarious housing conditions and rent struggles have been documented and portrayed visually in socially critical drawings and photography.[32] Later, in the Weimar Republic, films such as *Wie wohnen wir gesund und wirtschaftlich?* (*How do we Live in a Healthy and Economical Way?*, Richard Paulick, 1926–1928) or Slatan Dudow's *Zeitprobleme: wie der Arbeiter wohnt* (*Time Problems. The Way the Worker Lives*, 1930) addressed issues like modern urban planning, the social consequence of housing politics, and evictions.[33] In the 1970s, antisocial rent politics

---

[31] Nevertheless, in Germany 58 percent of the population lives in rented apartments and pays on the average about a quarter of their net income for rental payments. Compared to the rest of Europe, where the majority of people live in their own apartments, the rental situation is a specifically German one.

[32] Philipp Mattern, Mieterkämpfe. *Vom Kaiserreich bis heute: das Beispiel Berlin* (Berlin: Bertz + Fischer, 2018).

[33] Thomas Elsaesser, "Die Stadt von morgen: Filme zum Bauen und Wohnen," in *Geschichte des dokumentarischen Films in Deutschland. Vol. 2: Weimarer Republik: 1918–1933*, ed. Klaus Kreimeier, Antje Ehmann, and Jeanpaul Goergen (Stuttgart: Reclam 2005), and Guido Kirsten, "Armut und Alltag: Zur Darstellung von proletarischer und subproletarischer Lebensrealität im Kino der Weimarer Republik," in *Sichtbar machen. Politiken des Dokumentarfilms*, ed. Elisabeth Büttner, Vrääth Öhner, and Lena Stölzl (Berlin: Vorwerk, 2018).

in social housing areas have been tackled in films in Märkisches Viertel in Berlin and other parts of the city.[34]

The contemporary political struggles from 2010 onwards form the backdrop of quite a number of documentary films. Most of these independent productions have an activist background. Filmmaker Katrin Rothe takes her struggle against modernization measures and rent increases as a starting point to depict psychological demoralization as a strategy of investors, while giving concrete advice for organizing tenants in *Betongold – wie die Finanzkrise in mein Wohnzimmer flatterte* (*Concrete Gold – How the Financial Crisis Fluttered into My Living Room*, 2012). In *Verdrängung hat viele Gesichter* (*Displacement has Many Faces*, Samira Fansa, 2014) perspectives of precarious residents are juxtaposed with the viewpoints of future investors from residential joint building ventures. The struggle for housing thus becomes visible as class struggle. Whereas *Mietrebellen – Widerstand gegen den Ausverkauf der Stadt* (*Rent Rebels – Resistance against the Sellout of the City*, Matthias Coers and Gertrud Schulte Westenberg, 2014) focuses on tenants' movements and successful moments in collective struggles for empowering other tenants, the documentary film *Halbes Hähnchen vom Himmel* (*Half a Chicken from the Heavens*, Mireia Sanjaume Guzmán, 2018) portrays the 74-year-old protagonist Mevla and her inexhaustible strength and sense of humor while she faces homelessness after an eviction from her apartment. The neighborhood of Berlin-Kreuzberg, where she had lived for thirty years, is one of many urban spaces undergoing massive transformations and increasing rents. It is also at the center of Angelika Levi's 3-channel installation *Miete essen Seele auf*, which I will now discuss in more detail.[35]

Collective Agency in Precarious Housing Conditions: *Rent Eats Your Soul*

Rent Eats Your Soul brings together different facets of the community at the south side of Kottbusser Tor. It draws a complex portrait of neighborhood organizing and protest by the tenant movement *Kotti&Co*, which in 2012 occupied

---

[34] Fabian Tietke, "A Laboratory for Political Film: The Formative Years of the German Film and Television Academy and Participatory Filmmaking from Workerism to Feminism," in *Celluloid Revolt: German Screen Cultures and the Long 1968*, ed. Christina Gerhardt and Marco Abel (Rochester: Camden House 2019).
[35] Besides the 64 min. long 3-channel-installation there is also an alternate version of 54 minutes which was produced for the television-channel ARTE by Angelika Levi and Christoph Dreher.

public space for constructing a *Gececondu* (Turkish: *informal house set up by night*). By addressing political struggles of today's neighborhood in Kreuzberg, the context of the discriminatory logic of the housing question is broadened. Levi's work explicitly deals with intersectional discrimination and reveals how different individuals are affected by precarity. Levi's interweaving of historical and current perspectives creates a kaleidoscopic multi-perspectivity, a choir of different voices, and connects the housing problem to the history of migration. *Rent Eats Your Soul*—the title alludes to Rainer Werner Fassbinder's 1974 film *Angst essen Seele auf (Fear Eats the Soul)*, in which the relationship between a German widow and a Moroccan guest worker results in housing and societal problems—demonstrates racist continuities connected to urban displacement and participatory urban politics.[36]

Fig. 2: *Miete essen Seele auf (Rent Eats Your Soul*, Angelika Levi, 2015).

> You have reached the repair service line of 'Deutsche Wohnen.' If your name is Ahmed or Hatice, or for some other reason you have a low income push '1'! [. . .] Please don't hang up. As soon as possible, we'll take care of the termination of your rental contract. Please be patient.[37]

A small experimental choir, which recurs at several points in the installation, sings these lyrics that imitate a telephone waiting loop of the housing association Deutsche Wohnen. Parallel to that, the tenants of a social housing complex receive invitations for a general house assembly from two Kotti&Co organizers (Fig. 2).[38] Ironically commenting on inequity and the interconnectedness of structural racism and urban displacement, the choir's declaration can be linked to a "differential distribution" of protection and precarity.[39]

---

36 Earlier debates about participatory decision-making with residents and tenants to change housing policy toward municipal ownership are represented as frighteningly similar to today's discussions—as archival footage of a 1985 interview with former city building council Werner Orlowski demonstrates.
37 Min. 20:12–20:54.
38 I thank Angelika Levi for her kind permission to use the still of *Rent Eats Your Soul* in this text.
39 "From this perspective, domination means the attempt to safeguard some people from existential precariousness, while at the same time this privilege of protection is based on a

Rent Eats Your Soul uses various situations in the neighborhood of Kottbusser Tor to show how multi-layered this unequal distribution can be. Discussing and juxtaposing current struggles—against the eviction of refugees who found shelter in a school building—and current racist attacks with archival footage of Kreuzberg's housing situation in earlier decades, the film contextualizes today's urban displacement with the history of (mostly Turkish and Kurdish) migration to Berlin-Kreuzberg since the 1960s. On two screens of the installation, black and white archival footage shows Kreuzberg's everyday street activity in the 1960s and 1970s—vendors, children playing, people strolling along, family picnics—while an interview partner recounts that Turkish families were often not allowed to move into the front house facing the street.

Towards a Political Collective Agency in Differences?

While Angelika Levi's work depicts the history and motivation of some individual tenant movement activists, its focus remains on the heterogeneity and complexity of the movement and the processes of getting to know one another in order to unite in the fight for affordable social housing. Processes of negotiation and creating space for each other are crucial factors for the political practice and self-conception of Kotti&Co[40] and are reflected in many observational scenes.

---

differential distribution of the precarity of all those who are perceived as other and considered less worthy of protection." Lorey, *State of Insecurity*, 22.

40 Kotti&Co, "'Alles muss man selber machen': Multi-Layer-Organizing für eine soziale Wohnraumversorgung in Berlin," *sub \ urban. zeitschrift für kritische stadtforschung* 4, no. 2–3 (2016).

Kotti&Co, "The form of our protest: Merhaba, Salam, and welcome!" (May 14, 2021), https://kottiundco.net/english/?iframe=true&preview=true.

"We are Kreuzberg–and not just since yesterday. We! There really is no one term that can grasp us, no category. In fact, the following colloquial expressions reflect how helpless the German language is at the moment since it cannot even adequately describe us: 'Germans,' 'foreigners,' 'guest workers,' 'people with a migration history,' 'Turkish-Germans,' etc., etc. We are a community that the world of Sarrazin & Co has no space for. We are trainees, doctor's assistants, nurses, engineers on unemployment; we are insurance sales people who studied sociology, we are metal workers who are writing their dissertation, marketers, designers who work in the cultural industry; we are the children of people who have worked hard all their lives after coming here through the recruitment agreements Germany upheld with Turkey and other nation-states form the 1950 to the 1970s. [. . .] We've had to fight racism and social exclusion all our lives, as well as Hartz VI and poverty among the elderly in this society. We are old, and we are young. We believe in Allah, God, or simply in a just society."

United through their common political goal, a "headscarf-woman can sit next to an atheist woman," as they themselves comment in the film. Throughout, the protesters emphasize both their differences and their common struggle for a less discriminatory housing policy. Working together, and attempting a shared agency, implies as a fundamental element the precarious endeavor of communication, as one of the protesters underpins in an interview:

> Everyone always understands the things we share, whether it's through language or with other expressions, on the basis of their own biography. Communication is always something of a precarious matter and it's always growing out of positive mis- or half-understandings. When I create a picture in a conversation, then the other person fills out this image out of their own experience. If I say *tree*, I might mean *palm*, and someone else thinks *oak*, for example.[41]

How is it possible to articulate alliance without falling back on identity, without ignoring the differences of specific precarious situations? If the housing situation is a common denominator for heterogenous individuals who form a collective agency despite intersectional differences, one can ask if precarity can be used as a shared condition for other situations as well. Isabell Lorey refers to social movements from 2000 to 2010 such as the *EuroMayDay* movement or the Spanish social movement *Precarias a la Deriva*, which address precarization and aim to turn the multitude of isolated workers into political agents.[42] Precarity as a starting point for common action is not something to which one may resort, but something that must first emerge in the process of political negotiation.[43] In Angelika Levi's work, these processes of negotiation are reflected on the one hand in the fragmented and simultaneous storytelling decisions, but also on an aesthetic and formal level. Multi-perspectivity and the temporal simultaneity of present and past political situations are stressed through the use of a 3-channel installation. As an instance of expanded cinema, it engages the audience in a specific way.

Conclusions

The attempts and cinematic strategies that negotiate forms of resistance and refusal in precarious conditions on a narrative and formal level are as diverse as the formal choices and thematic fields of the cinema of precarity in general. Using a fragmented and raw style of storytelling, Tatjana Turanskyj's film ends

---

41 Min. 34:53–35:19.
42 Precarias a la deriva, *Was ist dein Streik? Militante Streifzüge durch die Kreisläufe der Prekarität* (Vienna: Transversal, 2014).
43 Lorey, *State of Insecurity*, 8.

with its beginning, with Greta's loneliness as she loiters drunkenly in the dusty cornfield before finally stumbling towards the horizon. If anything, the editing intensifies the spiral of precarization into an endless circle of precarization since there is no defined enemy anymore but only the incorporated logic of having to work on one's own self. I have discussed Greta's obstinate unwillingness to take her place in capitalist society as individual acts of refusal and dissent. I have argued that these fragmented moments of denial can be interpreted as moments of self-empowerment by exposing and unmasking mechanisms of subjugation and the absurdity of the neoliberal condition. According to Lorey, this "governmental precarization [is] not only destabilization through employment, but also destabilization of the conduct of life and thus bodies and modes of subjectivation":

> Understanding precarization as governmental makes it possible to problematize the complex interactions between an instrument of governing and the conditions of economic exploitation and modes of subjectivation, in their ambivalence between subjugation and self-empowerment.[44]

Turanskyj presents this ambivalence by proposing a sharp social analysis. Her film exhibits and thereby undermines the logic of simultaneous processes of adaptation and dissent within the working field and as a *flexible woman.*

Whereas shared experiences remain individualized and devoid of moments of hopeful relief, togetherness, or collective solidarity in *The Drifter*, Levi's 3-channel installation *Rent Eats Your Soul* takes the structural effects of intersectional differences as a starting point to approach neighborhood collective agency in difference. Through the simultaneous use of three screens and the inclusion of historical footage, Levi creates a multi-perspective kaleidoscope that addresses the intersection of racism and displacement as well as parallel political struggles related to the crisis of social housing.

The protest against rent politics proves that precarious subjects can unite to form a cross-class protest. This protest follows the logic of acknowledging differences and intersectional discrimination. While processes of precarization do not necessarily create a common identity, what they do appear to create is a common experience. And if this experience—that of a threat to one's living space—is linked to a concrete material unifying factor, then a multitude of precarized subjects, in this case the Berlin-Kreuzberg tenants with their manifold biographies and political backgrounds, are able to organize and fight together. Then, I would argue—and this is what we can learn from *Rent Eats Your Soul*—intersectional differences and individualization (as the shared experience of precarity) are taken not as a hindrance but as a starting point for a collective form of resistance.

---

44 Ibid., 13.

Bibliography

Baer, Hester. "Future Feminism: Political Filmmaking and the Resonance of West German Feminist Film Movement." In *German Cinema in the Age of Neoliberalism*, ed. Hester Baer. Amsterdam: Amsterdam University Press, 2021, 157–192.

Bardan, Alice. "The New European Cinema of Precarity: A Transnational Perspective." In *Work in Cinema: Labor and The Human Condition*, ed. Ewa Mazierska. New York: Palgrave Macmillan, 2013, 69–90.

Berlant, Lauren. *Cruel Optimism*. Durham, NC: Duke University Press, 2011.

Bourdieu, Pierre. "Job Insecurity is Everywhere Now." In *Acts of Resistance: Against the New Myths of our Time*, trans. Richard Nice. Cambridge: Polity Press, 1998, 81–87.

Bröckling, Ulrich. *The Entrepreneurial Self. Fabricating a New Type of Subject*. London: California Sage, 2016.

Butler, Judith. *Frames of War: When is Life Grievable?* London/New York: Verso, 2009.

Büttner, Christoph. "'In dir muss brennen!' Self/Change-Management in Arbeitswelt und Dokumentarfilm." In *Opus und Labor: Arbeit in autobiographischen und biographischen Erzählungen*, ed. Luditha Balint, Katharina Lammers, Kerstin Wilhelms, and Thomas Wortmann. Essen: Klartext, 2018, 191–212.

Casas-Cortés, Maribel. "A Genealogy of Precarity: A Toolbox for Rearticulating Fragmented Social Realities in and out of the Workplace." *Rethinking Marxism* 26, no. 2 (2014): 206–226. https://doi.org/10.1080/08935696.2014.888849.

Crenshaw, Kimberle. "Demarginalizing the Intersection of Race and Sex: A Black Feminist Critique of Antidiscrimination Doctrine, Feminist Theory and Antiracist Politics." *University of Chicago Legal Forum*, no. 1 (1989): 139–167.

Elsaesser, Thomas. "Die Stadt von morgen: Filme zum Bauen und Wohnen." In *Geschichte des dokumentarischen Films in Deutschland*, ed. Klaus Kreimeier, Antje Ehmann, and Jeanpaul Goergen. Vol. 2: *Weimarer Republik: 1918–1933*. Stuttgart: Reclam, 2005, 381–410.

Freudenschuss, Magdalena. *Prekär ist wer? Der Prekarisierungsdiskurs als Arena sozialer Kämpfe*. Münster: Westfälisches Dampfboot, 2013.

Friedrich, Sebastian. "Fett, faul, fernsehsüchtig: Das Arbeitslosenstereotyp in den Medien und seine Funktion." *Journal der Rosa Luxemburg Stiftung*, no. 2 (2015): 15–16.

Hesselberth, Pepita, and Joost de Bloois. *Politics of Withdrawal: Media, Arts, Theory*. Lanham: Rowman & Littlefield, 2020.

Holm, Andrej, Regnault, Valentin, Sprengholz, Maximilian, and Meret Stephan. "Die Verfestigung sozialer Wohnversorgungsprobleme." *Hans Böckler Foundation*, Working Paper 217 (June 2021). https://www.boeckler.de/de/faust-detail.htm?sync_id=HBS-008039.

Kirsten, Guido. "Armut und Alltag: Zur Darstellung von proletarischer und subproletarischer Lebensrealität im Kino der Weimarer Republik." In *Sichtbar machen. Politiken des Dokumentarfilms*, ed. Elisabeth Büttner, Vrääth Öhner, and Lena Stölzl. Berlin: Vorwerk, 2018, 208–222.

Kohler, Birgit, and Sabine Nessel. "A Woman Under the Influence – in Berlin zu Beginn des 21. Jahrhundert. Zu Tatjana Turanskyjs Spielfilm-Debüt EINE FLEXIBLE FRAU (D 2010)." *Frauen und Film*, no. 66 (July 2011): 171–180.

Kotti&Co. "'Alles muss man selber machen': Multi-Layer-Organizing für eine soziale Wohnraumversorgung in Berlin." *sub \ urban. zeitschrift für kritische stadtforschung* 4, no. 2–3 (2016): 121–126.

——. "The form of our protest: Merhaba, Salam, and welcome!" (May 14, 2021). https://kottiundco.net/english/?iframe=true&preview=true.

Kuster, Brigitta. "Die eigenwillige Freiwilligkeit der Prekarisierung." *Grundrisse. Zeitschrift für linke Theorie & Debatte*, no. 18 (2006). http://www.grundrisse.net/grundrisse18/brigitta_kuster.htm.

Lazzarato, Maurizio. "Immaterial Labor." In *Radical Thought in Italy: A Potential Politics*, ed. Michael Hardt and Paolo Virno. Minneapolis: University of Minnesota Press, 1996, 133–147.

Lorey, Isabell. "Gouvernementalität und Selbst-Prekarisierung. Zur Normalisierung von KulturproduzentInnen." *Transversal Journal* (November 2006). https://transversal.at/transversal/1106/lorey/de.

——. *State of Insecurity: Government of the Precarious*. Trans. Aileen Derieg. London: Verso, 2015.

Marchart, Oliver. *Die Prekarisierungsgesellschaft. Prekäre Proteste. Politik und Ökonomie im Zeichen der Prekarisierung*. Bielefeld: Transcript, 2013.

Mattern, Philipp. *Mieterkämpfe. Vom Kaiserreich bis heute: Das Beispiel Berlin*. Berlin: Bertz + Fischer, 2018.

Mennel, Barbara. "From Utopian Collectivity to Solitary Precarity: Thirty Years of Feminist Theory and the Cinema of Women's Work." *Women in German Yearbook* 30, (2014): 125–137.

Neilson, Brett, and Ned Rossiter. "Precarity as a Political Concept, or, Fordism as Exception." *Theory, Culture & Society* 25, no. 7–8 (December 2008): 51–72. https://doi.org/10.1177/0263276408097796.

Precarias a la deriva. "Adrift through the circuits of feminized precarious work." *Transversal Journal* (2004). http://translate.eipcp.net/transversal/0704/precarias1/en.html.

——. *Was ist dein Streik? Militante Streifzüge durch die Kreisläufe der Prekarität*. Vienna: transversal, 2014.

Reckwitz, Andreas. *Das Ende der Illusionen. Politik, Ökonomie und Kultur in der Spätmoderne*. Frankfurt/Main: Suhrkamp, 2019.

Schmidt, Silvana. *Prekär sein. Feministische Einführung in die Prekaritätsdebatte*. Münster: Edition Assemblage, 2020.

Standing, Guy. *The Precariat: The New Dangerous Class*. London: Bloomsbury Academic, 2011.

Sticchi, Francesco. *Mapping Precarity in Contemporary Cinema and Television: Chronotopes of Anxiety, Depression, Expulsion/Extinction*. Cham, Switzerland: Springer & Palgrave Macmillan, 2021.

Tietke, Fabian. "A Laboratory for Political Film: The Formative Years of the German Film and Television Academy and Participatory Filmmaking from Workerism to Feminism." In *Celluloid Revolt: German Screen Cultures and the Long 1968*, ed. Christina Gerhardt and Marco Abel. Rochester: Camden House 2019, 105–121.

Veldstra, Carolyn. "Bad feeling at work: emotional labour, precarity, and the affective economy." *Cultural Studies* 34, no. 1 (December 2020): 1–24. https://doi.org/10.1080/09502386.2018.1555269.

Von Osten, Marion. "Irene ist Viele! Or what we call 'Productive' Forces." *e-flux journal* 8 (September 2009). https://www.e-flux.com/journal/08/61381/irene-ist-viele-or-what-we-call-productive-forces/.

Filmography

9 Leben (*9 Lives*). Dir. Maria Speth. Germany, 2011.
40 Stunden, max. 2 Monate (*40 hours, max. 2 months*), 2-Channel-Installation. Dir. Stefanie Schröder. Germany, 2017.
Angst essen Seele auf (*Fear Eats the Soul*). Dir. Rainer Werner Fassbinder. FRG, 1974.
Betongold – wie die Finanzkrise in mein Wohnzimmer flatterte (*Concrete Gold – How the Financial Crisis Fluttered into My Living Room*). Dir. Katrin Rothe. Germany, 2012.
Die Bewerbung (*The Interview*). Dir. Harun Farocki. Germany, 1996.
Die Umschulung (*Retraining*). Dir. Harun Farocki. Germany, 1994.
Dunkler Lippenstift macht seriöser (*Dark Lipstick Makes More Serious*). Dir. Katrin Rothe. Germany, 2003.
Eine flexible Frau (*The Drifter*). Dir. Tatjana Turanskyj. Germany, 2010.
Family Business. Dir. Christiane Büchner. Germany, 2015.
Glanz von Berlin (*Queens of Dust*). Dir. Judith Keil and Antje Kruska. Germany, 2002.
Halbe Treppe (*Grill Point*). Dir. Andreas Dresen. Germany, 2002.
Halbes Hähnchen vom Himmel (*Half a Chicken from the Heavens*). Dir. Mireia Sanjaume Guzmán. Germany, 2018.
HALLE 101. Dir. Andreas Dresen Germany, 2010.
In den Gängen (*In the Aisles*). Dir. Thomas Stuber. Germany, 2018.
Sommer vorm Balkon (*Summer in Berlin*). Dir. Andreas Dresen. Germany, 2005.
Kehraus (*Sweeping*). Dir. Gerd Kroske. Germany, 1990.
Klassenfahrt (*School Trip*). Dir. Henner Winckler. Germany, 2002.
Lichter (*Distant Lights*). Dir. Hans-Christian Schmid. Germany, 2003.
Lucy. Dir. Henner Winckler. Germany, 2006.
Marina. Dir. Werkgruppe 2. Germany, 2018.
Miete essen Seele auf (*Rent Eats Your Soul*), 3-Channel-Installation. Dir. Angelika Levi. Germany, 2015.
Mietrebellen – Widerstand gegen den Ausverkauf der Stadt (*Rent Rebels – Resistance against the Sell-Out of the City*). Dir. Matthias Coers and Gertrud Schulte Westenberg. Germany, 2014.
Netto. Dir. Robert Thalheim. Germany, 2005.
redupers – die allseits reduzierte Persönlichkeit (*The All-Round Reduced Personality – Redupers*). Dir. Helke Sander. FRG, 1978.
Regeln am Band, bei hoher Geschwindigkeit (*Rules of Assembly Line, by High Speed*). Dir. Yulia Lokshina. Germany, 2020.
Verdrängung hat viele Gesichter (*Displacement has Many Faces*). Dir. Samira Fansa. Germany, 2014.
Wie wohnen wir gesund und wirtschaftlich? (*How do we Live in a Healthy and Economical Way?*). Dir. Richard Paulick. Germany, 1926–1928.
Wundersame Welt der Waschkraft (*Wondrous World of Laundry*). Dir. Hans-Christian Schmid. Germany, 2009.
Zeitprobleme. Wie der Arbeiter wohnt (*Time Problems. The Way the Worker Lives*). Dir. Slatan Dudow. Germany, 1930.

Ewa Mazierska
Representation of Poverty and Precarity in Post-Communist Polish Cinema

In this chapter I discuss the representation of poverty and precarity in Polish cinema after the end of state socialism in 1989. What especially interests me is the relationship between the type of poverty shown on screen and the political and economic situation in Poland during the time when the given film was made. In order to explain the specificity of this situation, I draw on the concepts of poverty and precarity and the political and economic history of Poland from the time it regained independence in 1918 to the present day. My assumption is that cinema engages with social and political reality, but not through simple mirroring of this reality, but through hiding or emphasizing certain of its features. Poverty tends to be hidden, beautified, or dramatized, because by itself it is rather mundane and its existence reflects badly on the government as well as the country's elites and its citizens. This is also the case with Polish cinema, which adopted different approaches to this topic in different periods.

Poverty and Precarity

What constitutes a poor person in one culture might not apply to someone in a different culture. For this reason, authors differentiate between absolute and relative poverty. Absolute poverty is defined in terms of survival; more commonly it refers to subsistence, linked to a basic standard of physical capacity necessary for production (paid work) and reproduction (unpaid work in the household). Nutrition is central to such a definition.[1] The first recognition of poverty understood in such terms was probably the English Poor Laws of the sixteenth to nineteenth centuries, which defined the *pauper* as a condition of deprivation in the basic sense of food, shelter, occupation, and wellbeing.[2]

With the passage of time, when absolute poverty was gradually eradicated in various parts of Europe, the concepts of *percentiles* and *relative poverty* were introduced.

---

[1] Ruth Lister, *Poverty* (Cambridge: Polity Press, 2004), 21.
[2] Jane I. Guyer, "Pauper, Percentile, Precarity: Analytics for Poverty Studies in Africa," *The Journal of African History* 59, no. 3 (November 2018): 438.

ᵭ Open Access. © 2022 Ewa Mazierska, published by De Gruyter. This work is licensed under the Creative Commons Attribution-NonCommercial-NoDerivatives 4.0 International License.
https://doi.org/10.1515/9783110707816-015

> Percentiles entered the British administrative system with the expansion of statistical records on income and wealth distribution, most clearly in the twentieth century, building from the growth of a participatory class politics. Those in the bottom percentiles, whatever process placed them there, would qualify as poor according to their monetary income. Considered in class terms, this would be seen as an enduring structural condition of whole categories of the population in the industrial economy.[3]

Relative poverty is defined as occurring when individuals, families, and groups in the population

> lack the resources to obtain the types of diet, participate in the activities, and have the living conditions and amenities, which are customary, or are at least widely encouraged or approved of, in the societies to which they belong. Their resources are so seriously below those commanded by the average individual or family that they are, in effect, excluded from ordinary living patterns and activities.[4]

Relative poverty thus affects those who are significantly *below average* in a given society, even if their standard of living is high in comparison with other countries.

Precarity brings another concept into the equation: that of security or its lack, uncertainty and unhappiness. As Jane Guyer observes, American Catholic activist Dorothy Day was one of the first to link modern poverty to precarity in 1952. However, her argument was a religious one. The secular referent of precarity comes later in the neoliberal era of shifting markets, exchange rates, and insurgent capitalization of assets.[5] The economist Guy Standing devoted a book to the emergence of a class of western populations, whose jobs, hours of work, and incomes are all unpredictable, while many of the components of the cost of living are inflexible. He referred to them as "the precariat."[6] Members of the precariat might not be particularly poor, but they are vulnerable to changes in the global and local economy and have little control over their lives, which likens them to poor people. At the same time, it is worth mentioning that precarity is always an aspect of poverty, as poor people have greater exposure to the negative changes in the national and global markets than rich people.

---

[3] Ibid.
[4] Peter Townsend, *Poverty in the United Kingdom* (London: Allen Lane and Penguin Books, 1979), 31.
[5] Guyer, "Analytics for Poverty Studies in Africa," 438.
[6] Guy Standing, *The Precariat: The New Dangerous Class* (London: Bloomsbury, 2011).

Poverty in Polish History and Cinema

In 1918, the First World War ended and Russia, Prussia, and the Habsburg Empire, which had ruled Poland since the end of the eighteenth century, ceased to exist. In this way the Polish dream of living again in one independent country could be fulfilled. It was officially achieved in June 1919, when Poland's right to sovereignty was confirmed by the victorious powers through the Treaty of Versailles. Regaining statehood was a great cause for celebration for Poles. Other aspects of their situation, however, provided grounds for concern. The borders of Poland were fragile, due to conflicts with its neighbors about regions with mixed populations and Soviet Russia's initial ambition to export communism to the whole of Europe. Following the Great War, industry was paralyzed and in 1918 over four-fifths of the industrial workers were unemployed. Agricultural production had fallen dramatically, and poverty and malnutrition stalked the land. According to the 1921 census, the geographic distribution of the population put 25 percent in towns and 75 percent in the countryside; the occupational structure was made up of manual workers (27 percent, of which almost half were agricultural laborers), peasants (65 percent), intelligentsia and professionals (5 percent), entrepreneurs (2 percent), and landowners (under 1 percent).[7] Polish industry was mostly on a small scale and a large proportion of the firms were in foreign hands, mostly German. According to the main standards of modernity, namely urbanization and industrialization, Poland was one of the most backward countries in Europe in this period, somewhat suspended between feudalism and capitalism, not unlike Russia before the Bolshevik revolution.

From the mid-1920s the economic situation started to get better and kept improving up to the end of the 1920s, thanks to the financial stability brought by the non-party government of Władysław Grabski and the state taking an active role in reinvigorating the economy. Subsequently Poland was hit by various crises, but the overall situation kept improving, particularly in the second half of the 1930s. Unfortunately, this development was halted by the outbreak of the Second World War.

Although Poland was a poor country in absolute terms, Polish cinema did not show absolute poverty, because cinema was mainly for entertainment and a tool used to boost national morale. Films showing people getting sick and dying of hunger would be seen as having little entertainment value. This rule applies to practically the entire commercial cinema, but especially to Polish

---

7 Norman Davies, *God's Playground: A History of Poland, Volume II: 1975 to the Present* [1979] (Oxford: Oxford University Press, 2005), 304.

cinema between the wars, because it had virtually no state protection and had to be self-sustaining. Another reason why it avoided showing poverty was that it was produced mostly by and for urban dwellers, where the level of poverty was lower than in the countryside, where the majority of the population lived. Precarity featured more often than simple poverty. Many films drew attention to the uncertainty of life for all social classes. Middle-class types or even aristocrats were often at risk of bankruptcy or were bankrupt and worked hard to conceal their predicament or tried to overcome it, often by marrying above their means. Another sign of precarity is the abundance of prostitutes in this cinema, typically girls from the province who move to the city and fell victim of unscrupulous men, as in *Skłamałam* (*I Lied*, 1937), directed by Mieczysław Krawicz.

After the Second World War, Poland was again suffering poverty, due to the extensive war destruction. It lost almost 40 percent of its wealth and the bulk of its intelligentsia. To exist, it had to rebuild its infrastructure, the factories, the housing stock, the roads and railway lines, and its cultural capital. Poland entered this period from a position of economic backwardness, with the vast majority of its citizens living in the countryside, lacking basic amenities. Around the same time the country underwent a profound political and economic change: from capitalism to state socialism. This was not a consequence of the political choice of a majority of Polish citizens, but of a new political order, imposed by the victorious powers of Britain, the United States and the Soviet Union, which agreed to incorporate parts of Poland directly into the Soviet Union and the rest into the Soviet sphere of influence.

Eradicating poverty was one of the main goals of the new government. One means to achieve this was a successful land reform. From being a country that could not feed itself, Poland even became an exporter of food. Land reform was followed by the nationalization of industry and banks. This reform was driven as much by sheer pragmatism as by ideological principles, because many factories lost their owners during the war or were so devastated that they could not be rebuilt without state support.[8] A negative assessment of Polish industry under state socialism prevails after 1989, but in many ways it was a success story. For example, industrial production of the post-war period increased by a factor of 38, and in some periods grew faster than in the West. The geography of industry also changed in the sense that at the end of the state socialist period industrialization was more balanced than in the interwar period thanks to building many industrial centers in regions that were previously underdeveloped. During the period

---

[8] Zbigniew Landau and Jerzy Tomaszewski, *The Polish Economy in the Twentieth Century*, trans. Wojciech Roszkowski (London: Croom Helm, 1985), 196.

of state socialism absolute poverty was practically eradicated and the level of relative poverty was low, due to socialist policies of full employment, universal education, healthcare, and subsidized childcare. This does not mean that Poland was free from social problems. Some persisted, most importantly housing shortages and alcohol abuse.

Films about poverty were relatively rare during this period. This reflected the objective reality that the authorities were eradicating the most obvious causes of poverty and that cinema was meant to present socialism in a positive light. This was a given in that the state financed these films and was in a position to censor them. Spikes in the number of films about poverty and other negative features of the country typically appeared after a change in government and the easing of censorship. One such moment followed the end of Stalinism and resulted in a series of documentaries, known as the "dark series" (*czarna seria*), which tackled such problems as prostitution and the demise of small towns, caused by a government policy which was hostile to small traders and craftsmen. One of these films is *Ludzie z pustego obszaru* (*People from an Empty Zone*, 1957), directed by Kazimierz Karabasz and Władysław Ślesicki. Ostensibly, it is about the boredom and anomie of young people, but we can conjecture that more important factors in their dissatisfaction were low wages and a lack of career prospects. Finally, we learn that the "people from an empty zone" usually live in poor accommodations, often with parents and siblings in one-bedroom apartments with minimal facilities.

Another surge in films about poverty came in the second half of the 1970s and the early 1980s. Its occurrence can be attributed to two factors. One was a drastic worsening of the economic situation in Poland, leading to long lines and empty shelves in shops; another was, again, the easing of censorship, especially during the successes of the solidarity movement, allowing filmmakers to tackle problems that the government tried to hide. A seminal example is *Kobieta samotna* (*A Woman Alone*, Agnieszka Holland, 1981), which is one of the last examples of the Cinema of Moral Concern, a wave of films focused on social problems afflicting Poland under late state socialism. It centers on a single mother who works as a postwoman and lives on the outskirts of town, in a room without running water or heating. Not only are her housing conditions inadequate, but another poor family hopes that she will move out, so they can take over her room. Marred by lack of money and prospects, she steals money from her work and tries to escape abroad with her lover, which ends with her being killed by him. Although it was made almost a decade before state socialism would finally fall, when watching this film one gets the impression that this system already offered no prospects for the working class.

Exotic Poverty in the Countryside in Polish Cinema in the 1990s

The end of state socialism and the introduction of market capitalism changed the lives of Poles immensely. Most importantly, the rule that the state must ensure full employment of its citizens was abolished. Another change was the privatization of state assets, which brought the impression that everybody became wealthier overnight, due to the sense that these assets previously belonged to everybody. Finally, Poles got easier access to credit. These changes, initially seen positively, as injecting dynamism into the moribund economy of the late-socialist period, in due course proved to be a crude instrument of social stratification. Many privatized factories went bankrupt, resulting in a surge of unemployment, which in the 1990s was between 10 percent and 20 percent. The hardest hit were regions like Lodz and the North West (Mazury), where individual factories were the single major employer and had a mostly female workforce, as in the textile industry or cooperative farms. This dire situation was exacerbated by rolling back the welfare state. As a result, absolute poverty returned to some parts of Poland. Documentary cinema was first to capture this, in part because of its immediacy, contrasting with the longer time needed to produce full-length fiction films, and in part because during this decade of crisis the authorities prioritized historical films. Several of them, such as *Mgła* (*Fog*, 1993), directed by Irena Kamieńska, *Trzynastka* (*Thirteen*, 1997) and *Arizona* (1998), directed by Ewa Borzęcka, focus on the countryside, especially places where there used to be cooperative farms (State Agricultural Farm, Polish: *Państwowe Gospodarstwo Rolne*, PGR).

Fog is set in an unnamed place where there was previously a PGR. Shots of what had been a functioning microcosm and now looks like a ghost town are juxtaposed with the statements of the inhabitants, who compare the present, which for them is a time of misery, resulting from unemployment, with the communist past. A man states: "When I had work, I had everything. Now, with no work, I'm a common beggar." Some try to pinpoint the reasons why they cannot get work. Firstly, they were deprived of their means of production by being excluded from the privatization of the common land. One man says that if he got ten hectares, a horse, and a cow, he would be fine now. Others express the view that a cooperative farm should be created on the ruins of the old PGR and the old workers should be its new owners and managers. This raises the question of why this did not happen, suggesting that privatization of state land in Poland was conducted according to the neoliberal rule of accumulation through dispossession.[9] As ex-farm workers, whose professional capital became obsolete, they have no chance of finding employment in agriculture elsewhere. Nor do they get a chance to increase their capital by attending courses to learn new professional skills. On top of that, they are not eligible to get credit to set up their own businesses. The only help they get from the state is unemployment benefits, which are so low that they fall behind with rent and owe money to the local grocery shops. One woman declares that she has no money to call a doctor or buy medicine for her sick child. Kamieńska's interlocutors admit that under state socialism there was always enough work, which ensured both income and self-respect. The post-communist regime took all of this away, bringing nothing of value in its place.

In their discussion of *Fog*, Mikołaj Jazdon and Mirosław Przylipiak argue that the title refers to the state of mind of the inhabitants of the post-PGR village. Their minds are "clouded" by their sense of helplessness, which prevents them from improving their lot.[10] Such an explanation is plausible, but the titular *fog* might also refer also to an invisible calamity coming from outside, as suggested by shots showing the village enveloped in this immaterial substance. I read the *fog* as the means through which the village and its inhabitants are cut from the center and condemned to civil and eventually material downfall.

Kamieńska presents her characters in an objective manner, although she does not allow us to come too close to them. In contrast, in her films Ewa Borzęcka appears to come as close as possible to her characters, but she does not share in their anguish, rather attempting to exoticize them. *Arizona* is set in the post-PGR village of Zagórki in the Słupsk region of northern Poland. Its title is taken from the main entertainment of its inhabitants, which is drinking a cheap wine of this name. The film paints a picture of the world going through a slow apocalypse. This is manifested in the end of profitable production and the return of the inhabitants of Zagórki to a sort of state of nature. We learn that they poach animals living in the nearby forest and that it is easier for them to survive in summer than in winter because in summer they collect berries and mushrooms which they sell in the city of Słupsk. One of Borzęcka's interviewees admits with pride that he has enough wood for five years; this is wood that he *gleaned* rather than bought. Deprived of paid employment and money, they

---

[9] David Harvey, *A Brief History of Neoliberalism* (Oxford: Oxford University Press, 2005), 160–162.
[10] Mikołaj Jazdon, "Irena Kamieńska" (booklet added to a DVD box of the films of Polish female documentary filmmakers) (Warsaw: Polskie Wydawnictwa Audiowizualne, 2008); Mirosław Przylipiak, "Dokument polski lat 90tych," in *Historia polskiego filmu dokumentalnego*, ed. Małgorzata Hendrykowska (Poznań: Wydawnictwo Naukowe UM, 2015), 522–523.

amuse themselves by spying on each other and drinking Arizona. Alcohol allows them to forget their miserable existence and reach a kind of utopia, but on the other hand it reduces their chance to leave the vicious cycle of unemployment, poverty, and social exclusion.

The majority of people presented in the film looked after animals when they worked in the PGRs, with many milking cows. Their attachment to the animals crops up throughout the narrative. Some look after the few animals that survived the privatization of the PGR, such as a pig and a horse. The horse is now over thirty years old, and the owner takes it for walks as if it were a beloved pet. An old woman, who introduces herself as an ex-prisoner of the Nazi concentration camp Ravensbrück, lives with numerous cats and dogs, which is her way of redeeming her shameful deed of eating a dog after she left the camp (probably out of hunger). This draws attention to the danger that the unemployed farmhands may also be reduced to eating their pets. (Fig. 1) Borzęcka also points to the fact that they are treated like animals rather than human beings by the authorities and by each other.

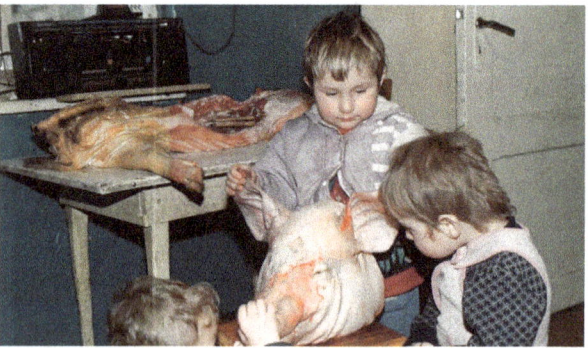

Fig. 1: Arizona (Ewa Borzęcka, 1998).

The title of the film can be interpreted as referring to the post-PGR village as a new *Wild West* that needs to be re-captured and re-civilized the neoliberal way. However, on repeated viewing, one picks up signals that it is the neoliberal system that produces those whom one critic describes as *degenerates*. For example, one of the characters, a wealthy incomer who apparently wanted to rejuvenate the bankrupt PGR, mentions that under state socialism the PGR had 300 cattle and 300 hectares of land that went wild post-1989. One wonders who is responsible for this decline—surely not the workers who lament the disappearance of their livelihood.

Arizona received some important awards, such as the Grand Prix at the 1998 Kraków Film Festival, and is widely regarded as one of the most important Polish films of the 1990s. But it also brought accusations that the filmmaker behaved in an immoral way by picking characters who best illustrated her point and buying them Arizona so that they would play the role of degenerated lumpenproletariat better. One critic compared the reality presented by Borzęcka to that created by Pieter Bruegel.[11] Without diminishing this comparison, I will evoke here the concept of *ruin porn*,[12] which refers to the phenomenon of the special interest granted to sites of poverty and misery and the attempts to make money out of them. No doubt Borzęcka uses the aesthetics of ruin porn by exaggerating the negative aspects of life in Zagórki.

The strategy of exoticization was intensified in Borzęcka's subsequent film, *Thirteen*. The film shows the life of a single mother with thirteen children, presented without any authorial commentary. All that we hear are the dialogues of the characters, mainly the mother and children, and some people with whom she interacts as well as the off-screen comments of children and their mother. There is no doubt that the family in Borzęcka's film is poor in absolute terms. The best indicator of that is the food they eat and their comments on food. Food is the most important thing in life for them and they distinguish people according to the amount and type of food they eat. One of the children says that rich people eat good food, such as meat and butter, and they have plenty of it, while they eat mostly bread. At one point we see the mother buying over twenty loaves of bread, all on credit and bringing it back in large sacks. Other food we see the children eating is home-made sauerkraut, made in the way it was done traditionally with the children trampling cabbage with their bare feet so that the juice comes out. The rest of their diet is supplemented by what they catch in the woods: rabbits and fish. There is no cutlery in their home—they eat all their food with their hands. This would be enough to portray the family as reduced to an animal-like existence, but Borzęcka goes on to play up this aspect by focusing on animals and human interaction with animals. Even before we see the characters, when film titles are shown on screen, we hear cats meowing wildly as if they were being tortured or were in a fight. Later we see three cats the children hold by their backs and bring close to other cats so that they attack each other with their paws and meow to scare the other cat off. Obviously, the

---

11 Maciej Nowak, "*Arizona* Ewy Borzęckiej, czyli notatki z buszu," in *Polskie kino dokumentalne 1989–2009. Historia polityczna*, ed. Agnieszka Wiśniewska (Warsaw: Wydawnictwo Krytyki Politycznej, 2011), 47.
12 Nate Millington, "Post-Industrial Imaginaries: Nature, Representation and Ruin in Detroit," *International Journal of Urban and Regional Research* 37, no. 1 (January 2013).

children (all boys) find it very funny and there is nobody in the room to stop this cruel entertainment. The scene of fighting cats is repeated several times throughout the film, suggesting that this is the kids' main entertainment. We also see them fascinated by images of cats hunting for mice, a cat fighting with a dog, and animals showing signs of life after seemingly being killed. Apart from showing limited opportunities of entertainment, such images encourage an allegorical reading—the family is like a pack of animals fighting for limited resources. There is no information about where the family lives, although it looks like a village somewhere in the mountains, but more likely on the outskirts of the village than at its center. The house is made of wood and has minimal facilities. There is no bathroom and no gas or electrical heating; the house is heated by an old-fashioned stove using wood or coal.

Although it would be possible to present the children as individuals, by showing how different they are from each other, this is not the case in the film. Their names remain unknown and any personal characteristics are curtailed, as encapsulated by the very title of the film. There is no reference to them going to school, although the majority are of school age and school would be their main source of learning about the wider environment and an opportunity for social advancement. This adds to the sense that they are excluded from the wider world. There seems to be only two daughters of this single mother and they are excluded from play and have (literally) no voice. We see them only once for a short time. Such exclusion of women might seem surprising in a film made by a woman, but might be explained by in that foregrounding the girls would undermine the Darwinian vision of the family that Borzęcka offers.

Despite Borzęcka's attempts to render the family as both animal-like and condemned to social exclusion and possibly criminality, there are moments when this family's life seems almost idyllic. This is because the children are able to enjoy small things and capture the moment. For example, when there is snow, they use any equipment available, such as a large bowl, to slide down the hill. Moreover, having so many siblings makes them immune to arguably the greatest malaise of contemporary times: solitude. Such observations confirm the point made by Oscar Lewis that "living immersed in the present [characteristic for poor people] may develop a capacity for spontaneity, for enjoyment of the sensual, the indulgence of impulse, which is too often blunted in our middle-class future-oriented man."[13]

---

[13] Oscar Lewis, "Culture of Poverty," in *Poor Americans: How the White Poor Live*, ed. Marc Pilisuk and Phyllis Pilisuk (New Brunswick: Trans-Action Books, 1971).

Given the consistency in Borzęcka's interest and her approach, it is natural to regard *Thirteen* as the work of a documentary *auteur*. However, it is also worth adding that the film was produced by *Telewizja Polska – I Program*—the First Program of Polish State Television, hence one can expect that it would reflect the dominant ideology, in this case the government view of poverty. The film scores well on this account, divorcing the issue of poverty in post-communist Poland from that of the collapse of the socialist welfare state and neglect of rural communities. Instead, it suggests that poverty is a personal problem—in this case having too many children. Moreover, it does so in a subtle way, avoiding any commentary from the author and seemingly only showing how things are.

The Violence of Precarious Life

The end of state socialism not only caused widespread poverty, but also brought insecurity to the lives of people of all classes. The new situation not only resulted in a worsening of the circumstances of thousands of people who lost their livelihood—as mentioned in the previous section—but also brought the promise of becoming wealthy in a short period of time through setting up one's own business or speculating on the stock market. Consequently, Polish cinema of the 1990s and early 2000s is full of images of businessmen and traders. Many of such films focus on the opportunities of capitalism, but the best-known of them *Dług* (*Debt*, 1999), directed by Krzysztof Krauze, points to the risks of engaging in the *capitalist games*. The title refers to what was a new phenomenon in Poland and Eastern Europe at large: personal debt. The socialist economy was based on the principle of postponing gratification, of sacrificing the present for the future through saving. By contrast, debt is at the heart of the capitalist economy, because to develop their businesses, entrepreneurs have to take out credit and as Maurizio Lazzarato observes, the neoliberal economy has a particularly intimate and dangerous relation to debt, because the majority of citizens living under this system begin and finish their lives having debt and debt affects their behavior and identity to a greater extent than labor affected earlier generations.[14]

Because debt is so common under neoliberalism, it is presented as something normal or even positive. *Borrow now and do not worry about tomorrow* is the approach propagated by the media. Yet, by borrowing we sentence ourselves to precarious life. Debt forecloses our future: it not only fails to multiply

---

[14] Maurizio Lazzarato, *The Making of the Indebted Man: An Essay on the Neoliberal Condition*, trans. Joshua David Jordan (Amsterdam: Semiotexte, 2012), 29.

our income but extracts what we possessed. Krauze's film presents such an extreme case of dispossession, based on the true story of two budding businessmen who in the 1990s set up a wholesale firm selling cosmetics, but who lacked capital to import the first consignment. As a result, they contacted an acquaintance who promised to lend them the cash they lacked. He did not fulfil his promise, but demanded compensation for his effort and when they were unable to pay, increased their debt and began a campaign of intimidation with his bodyguard. Brought to the end of their tether, the friends killed their oppressors, and cut off their heads so that the murder looked as if committed by the Russian mafia. They were caught and in 1997 received a severe sentence of twenty-five years in prison. Their story attracted the attention of some journalists, who argued that the punishment was too severe in proportion to the crime. Krauze shared this view and wanted his film to become a "socially engaged film."[15] *Debt* was successful as a social intervention—President Kwaśniewski pardoned one of the men in 2005 and his successor, President Kaczyński, pardoned the other man in 2006, largely as a result of the film's outcry.

The main characters in the film are Adam and Stefan, two friends in their late twenties, whose main ambition is to set up a successful business. In their dealings, Adam and Stefan come across as amateurs, lured by the mirage of fast and easy *post-communist money*. However, they are not into consumption for consumption's sake. For them money is chiefly a means of achieving an ideal of bourgeois life. They want to have families and ensure their prosperity. Their ambitions render them easy prey for all sorts of unscrupulous people and institutions: they are ideal debtors. We meet them when a bank refuses them credit. Anxious that their plan may never materialize, they accept the offer of an acquaintance, Gerard, that they contact somebody who can guarantee their credit in exchange for paying him a bribe. The transaction is not finalized, but Gerard asks the friends to pay his expenses of several thousand dollars. The story of Adam and Stefan finishes like the real story I described.

What Krauze shows is the immense precarity of Adam and Stefan's lives. Eventually it feels as if every day might be the last day of their lives—if they do not pay their oppressors, they will be killed—until the tables are turned when they kill the loan sharks. Although the downfall of the young businessmen takes place under the conditions of neoliberalism, it is not neoliberalism per se, but its criminal fringe that is responsible for it. We are to believe that if they

---

15 Tadeusz Lubelski, "Krzysztof Krauze – młodszy brat kina moralnego niepokoju," in *Autorzy Kina Polskiego*, ed. Grażyna Stachówna and Bogusław Zmudziński (Kraków: Wydawnictwo Uniwersytetu Jagiellońskiego, 2007), 206–214.

had received credit from the bank that refused their request or if they asked for help from their parents, all would have gone well. However, as Jakub Majmurek argues, their story would not have been much different if the characters had been given credit, given that interest rates in the 1990s were expensive, leading to many bankruptcies and suicides.[16] In this sense *Debt* is not very different from *Thirteen*, in which capitalism is not the main culprit, but their personalities and the specific situation in which the characters found themselves.

Subsequently, however, we find more films in which precarity is presented not as an aberration, but a systemic feature of capitalism.[17]

A seminal example is *Dzień kobiet* (*Women's Day*, 2012), directed by Maria Sadowska. Its title alludes to International Women's Day, which celebrated women's fight for their rights as workers. Under state socialism, this holiday was used to celebrate the achievements of women under this system. Therefore many Eastern European feminists boycotted it, seeing it as a smokescreen obscuring the real gender inequality which was not properly addressed by the authorities. However, while state socialism fell short of its promise to emancipate women, it offered them certain benefits, such as heavily subsidized childcare. After its fall, these privileges were withdrawn. Instead of allowing women to work at a time convenient to them, flexible employment—a cornerstone of neoliberal working practices—forces them to work when it suits their employers, which usually means longer hours on lower wages at more inconvenient times. The retail sector, where more women than men find employment, is particularly disadvantageous, because shops under neoliberalism tend to be open much longer than under state socialism and cost cutting means that fewer employees are required to do more work. Stories about exploitation of workers by supermarket managers started to fill the pages of national newspapers in Poland in the 2000s. One of them concerned Bożena Łopacka, a shop assistant in the Biedronka supermarket chain, who took her employer to court on the grounds of particularly harsh and unfair working conditions, including having to do extra hours without pay and not being able to leave the cash register for many hours, even to go to the toilet. Łopacka's story was the main source of inspiration for Sadowska's movie.

Women's Day begins when Halina (Fig. 2), an ordinary employee in the Motylek supermarket (*Motylek* means *butterfly*, a nod to the infamous *Biedronka*, which means *ladybird*), is promoted to a managerial position. For Halina it

---

16 Jakub Majmurek, "Wychodzenie ze ślepoty: Przemoc ekonomiczna i klasowa w kinie polskim," *Ekrany*, no. 01 (2020): 42.
17 Ibid., 42–43.

Fig. 2: Dzień kobiet (Women's Day, Maria Sadowska, 2012).

means more money that she badly needs, being a single mother with a teenage daughter. She also believes that her promotion will lead to improvement for her work mates. However, she soon learns that it means more duties than privileges. Halina is asked to work extra hours for free and to force others to work the same way, including a pregnant colleague who miscarries while on duty. She also has to fire another woman to ensure more savings for her company. All the work the women have to do is back-breaking physical labor, such as unloading large quantities of goods, because the firm, to create more profit, refuses to use trolleys. As a reward for her loyalty to the firm, Halina is sent to a training camp for Motylek's managers, where she learns that the highest value for her firm is productivity. Another *perk* that Halina receives at work is sex with her boss. Initially she believes that he is seriously interested in her, only to learn later that he also has sex with other female employees. In Motylek private and public spheres intermingle; sex is used by men in positions of power to extract pleasure for themselves and extra commitment from the gullible women, as demonstrated by the fact that the type of sex prevailing in this environment is fellatio. Ultimately Halina's promotion in Motylek not only fails to bring her any real improvement, but actually worsens her material situation and drives a wedge between her and her female co-workers, making her life more precarious. Brought to the brink of despair, she decides to fight back, and wins in court, receiving compensation, moral satisfaction, and a victory for other mistreated employees. The director herself compared her film to a western,[18] but it has more in common with melodrama, a genre that uses exaggeration to illuminate the plight of (often naive) women. To strengthen its emotional effect, the film is filled with

---

[18] Maria Sadowska, "Dzień kobiet to western," Trójka: Polskie Radio, March 12, 2013, http://www.polskieradio.pl/9/396/Artykul/799193,Maria-Sadowska-Dzien-kobiet-to-western.

(melo)dramatic events, such as the death of Halina's mother. There is also an obligatory episode with a bailiff trying to evict Halina from her apartment. This accumulation of misfortune does not render the film particularly subtle, yet registers the precarious position of Polish manual workers in the neoliberal reality, as well as, perhaps, pointing to the Polish audience's desensitization to ordinary misfortunes. Although *Women's Day* criticizes neoliberalism, its political program is modest, merely requiring that employers respect some minimal standards. A return to any form of socialism is nowhere on the agenda.

Conclusions

Polish post-communist cinema has engaged with the issues of poverty and precarity, presenting in detail the deprivations and uncertainties suffered by those on the receiving end of neoliberalism. However, it has avoided researching deeper causes of poverty and precarity, namely neoliberal policies, instead emphasizing the specific circumstances of characters. It should be added that films about poverty and precarity have become rarer since 2015. This was largely because of the greatly reduced poverty in Poland that resulted from policies, such as generous child benefit, which the then elected government introduced. The topic of precarious lives of the middle classes also largely disappeared from Polish cinema, in part because capitalism has become more settled and better regulated. That said, precarity has remained an important aspect of Polish workers' lives, especially of young people. In 2018, 46.3 percent of the workers between 15 and 29 years old did not have stable employment, which was one of the highest proportions in the European Union.[19] In this group, working itself often does not save one from poverty. It remains to be seen whether this fact will inspire filmmakers, especially younger ones, who often share the condition of precarity with their characters.

---

19 Juliusz Gardawski, Adam Mrozowicki, Vera Trappmann et al., *Young Precarious Workers in Poland and Germany. Insights into Life Strategies, Political Consciousness and Activism*, (January 2020), DOI:10.34616/26.20.002.

Bibliography

Davies, Norman. *God's Playground: A History of Poland, Volume II: 1975 to the Present* [1979]. Oxford: Oxford University Press, 2005.
Gardawski, Juliusz, Adam Mrozowicki, Vera Trappmann et al. *Young Precarious Workers in Poland and Germany. Insights into Life Strategies, Political Consciousness and Activism.* (January 2020), DOI:10.34616/26.20.001.
Guyer, Jane I. "Pauper, Percentile, Precarity: Analytics for Poverty Studies in Africa." *The Journal of African History* 59, no. 3 (November 2018): 437–448.
Harvey, David. *A Brief History of Neoliberalism.* Oxford: Oxford University Press, 2005.
Jazdon, Mikołaj. "Irena Kamieńska." Booklet added to a DVD box of the films of Polish female documentary filmmakers. Warsaw: Polskie Wydawnictwa Audiowizualne, 2008.
Landau, Zbigniew, and Jerzy Tomaszewski. *The Polish Economy in the Twentieth Century*, trans. Wojciech Roszkowski. London: Croom Helm, 1985.
Lazzarato, Maurizio. *The Making of the Indebted Man: An Essay on the Neoliberal Condition*, trans. Joshua David Jordan. Amsterdam: Semiotexte, 2012.
Lewis, Oscar. "Culture of Poverty." In *Poor Americans: How the White Poor Live*, ed. Marc Pilisuk and Phyllis Pilisuk. New Brunswick: Trans-Action Books, 1971, 20–26.
Lister, Ruth. *Poverty.* Cambridge: Polity Press, 2004.
Lubelski, Tadeusz. "Krzysztof Krauze – młodszy brat kina moralnego niepokoju." In *Autorzy Kina Polskiego*, ed. Grażyna Stachówna and Bogusław Zmudziński. Kraków: Wydawnictwo Uniwersytetu Jagiellońskiego, 2007, 195–219.
Majmurek, Jakub. "Wychodzenie ze ślepoty: Przemoc ekonomiczna i klasowa w kinie polskim." *Ekrany*, no. 53 (1/2020): 39–44.
Millington, Nate. "Post-Industrial Imaginaries: Nature, Representation and Ruin in Detroit." *International Journal of Urban and Regional Research* 37, no. 1 (January 2013): 279–296.
Nowak, Maciej. "*Arizona* Ewy Borzęckiej, czyli notatki z buszu." In *Polskie kino dokumentalne 1989–2009. Historia polityczna*, ed. Agnieszka Wiśniewska. Warsaw: Wydawnictwo Krytyki Politycznej, 2011, 45–50.
Przylipiak, Mirosław. "Dokument polski lat 90tych." In *Historia polskiego filmu dokumentalnego*, ed. Małgorzata Hendrykowska. Poznań: Wydawnictwo Naukowe UM, 2015, 471–572.
Sadowska, Maria. "Dzień kobiet to western." *Trójka: Polskie Radio*, March 12, 2013. http://www.polskieradio.pl/9/396/Artykul/799193,Maria-Sadowska-Dzien-kobiet-to-western.
Standing, Guy. *The Precariat: The New Dangerous Class.* London: Bloomsbury, 2011.
Townsend, Peter. *Poverty in the United Kingdom.* London: Allen Lane and Penguin Books, 1979.

Filmography

Arizona. Dir. Ewa Borzęcka. Poland, 1998.
Dług (*Debt*). Dir. Krzysztof Krauze. Poland, 1999.
Dzień kobiet (*Women's Day*). Dir. Maria Sadowska. Poland, 2012.

Kobieta samotna (*A Woman Alone*). Dir Agnieszka Holland. Poland, 1981.
Ludzie z pustego obszaru (*People from an Empty Zone*). Dir. Kazimierz Karabasz and Władysław Ślesicki. Poland, 1957.
Mgła (*Fog*). Dir. Irena Kamieńska. Poland, 1993.
Skłamałam (*I Lied*). Dir. Mieczysław Krawicz. Poland, 1937.
Trzynastka (*Thirteen*). Dir. Ewa Borzęcka. Poland, 1997.

Eva Näripea, Renata Šukaitytė, Zane Balčus
Economic and Social Precarity in Baltic Cinema

This article explores some of the ways in which economic and social precarity is depicted and narrated in films produced in the Baltics after the introduction of neoliberal capitalism in the early 1990s. Laura Lapinskė writes that the dramatic collapse of the Soviet Union was followed by "immediate restructuring of major industries, the initiation of land reforms and privatization of state property."[1] The period of 1991–1995/1996 is often referred to as a "post-Communist transformation" or a time of "extraordinary politics" and "radical reforms."[2] The decline of the industrial sector, high inflation, weak national currencies, and the unstable banking system generated social and economic insecurity, as the rates of unemployment and poverty soared. Thus, the drastic transition from state-controlled to free-market economy "caused a shock-therapy with regular people bearing the cost of these transformations."[3] The prioritization of economic issues led to steadily increasing social and economic polarization and precarity of vulnerable groups, such as the low-educated, unskilled, low-waged, women, elderly, disabled, ethnic minorities, and migrant workers.

Although the EU accession in 2004 promoted economic stabilization and growth, the Baltic trio remained truly "neoliberal economies and even neoliberal welfare states" due to "their low public spending on social protection, high income inequality, and low social dialog."[4] The global financial crisis of 2007–2008 hit the Baltics hard, largely due to extensive financial vulnerability of the population and weak social systems. Moreover, the Baltic governments introduced the most aggressive austerity measures in the EU between 2008 and 2011, including cuts in social expenditures, pensions, and family and unemployment benefits.[5] While the

---
1 Laura Lapinske, "Living in Precarity: Ethnography of Everyday Struggles of Single Mothers in Lithuania," *Sociologija* 60, no. 1 (January 2018): 67.
2 Marju Lauristin, Zenonas Norkus, and Peeter Vihalemm, "On the Sociology's Contribution to Knowledge of the Baltic Way," *Sociologija. Mintis ir veiksmas* 29, no. 2 (2011): 129.
3 Lapinske, "Living in Precarity," 67.
4 Jolanta Aidukaitė and Sven E. O. Hort, "Editorial Introduction: Baltic States after the Crisis? The Transformation of the Welfare System and Social Problems," *Journal of Baltic Studies* 50, no. 1 (2019): 1, https://doi.org/10.1080/01629778.2019.1571754.
5 Karsten Staehr, "Austerity in the Baltic States during the Global Financial Crisis," *Intereconomics* 48, no. 5 (September 2013): 293.

∂ Open Access. © 2022 Eva Näripea, et al., published by De Gruyter. [CC BY-NC-ND] This work is licensed under the Creative Commons Attribution-NonCommercial-NoDerivatives 4.0 International License.
https://doi.org/10.1515/9783110707816-016

economies recovered relatively quickly, this "Baltic miracle" did not produce "social security and well-being for all," largely excluding the most vulnerable groups, such as low-wage workers or recipients of public benefits.[6] The post-crisis period was marked by the introduction of more flexible terms of employment in all sectors, both private and public, as well as precarious contracts issued by foreign agencies for temporary work in Western countries, which fundamentally weakened workers' financial security as well as the stability of families. Despite the steady though modest growth of the GDP, the number of people living in poverty or at risk of poverty has remained above 20 percent in all three countries. Furthermore, the majority of the Balts fit into the category of working poor, as illustrated by low minimum and average monthly wages, compared to the Western countries[7]—a factor that stimulates economic emigration to the West.

Despite the fact that precarity of working people has remained the most stable element for at least half of the Baltic population in the last 30 years, no codified or universal representations and narratives of this human condition can be observed in Baltic visual media and film, the mainstream of which prefers to concentrate on past traumas, identity politics, and images of accomplishment. This tepid interest can partly be explained by noting that the Baltic cinemas have no established tradition of the social problem film, a genre that typically focuses on workers and other precarious subjects. However, a growing body of cinematic work on precarity has emerged as (in particular the younger generation of) filmmakers confront the consequences of the neoliberal transformation, the global financial crisis, and the situation of economic migrants, ethnic minorities, and other at-risk groups. This article seeks to identify cinematic responses to the various manifestations of social vulnerability and provide an overview of some of the ways in which Baltic films represent and narrate the experiences of precarity. However, we do not aim to construct a universal precarious subject in the Baltic cinemas. Our intention is rather to make the Baltic

---

6 Aidukaitė and Hort, "Editorial Introduction," 4.

7 In 2021, the minimum monthly wages in the EU Member States ranged from €332 to €2,202 per month. In Lithuania the monthly minimum wage was €642, in Estonia €584 and in Latvia €500. Since 2010, the minimum wages in the Baltic states have increased more than 50 percent. ("Statutory Minimum Wages," *Eurofound*, February 3, 2021, https://www.eurofound.europa.eu/data/statutory-minimum-wages.) In 2020, the average monthly salary in the Baltic countries was the highest in Estonia (€1,472), followed by Lithuania (€1,381) and Latvia (€1,152). ("Average Monthly Salary in European Union 2020," Reinis Fischer, last modified June 26, 2020, https://www.reinisfischer.com/average-monthly-salary-european-union-2020.)

precariat visible because, as Tom Zaniello suggests, the precariat tends to remain invisible despite being seen every day.[8]

The films discussed in this article represent some of the key motifs of precarity in Baltic cinema: systemic deprivation of the working class; domestic migration prompted by regional inequality; emigration, in particular for seeking employment abroad; and the underprivileged status of the Russophone minority that remains a thorny issue for the Baltics.

Invisible Precariat

In the Baltic countries, the end of the twentieth and the beginning of the twenty-first century witnessed an abrupt decline of the working class as a collective social and political actor due to the collapse of traditional industries and the socialist system. As in most neoliberal capitalist countries, the traditional working class was brutally replaced by a new social entity—the precariat. However, only a relatively small number of authors have chosen to zoom in on the social and economic dilemmas of the working poor in films that mainly target the festival circuit. Wholesale, retail, and food industry workers, cleaners, paramedics, police patrols, hotel workers, migrant laborers from the provinces, young temporary workers, and single underpaid parents are the most frequently represented fields of labor and subclasses of the precariat. Although "the precariat finds itself more and more concentrated in urban configurations"[9] and while many Baltic films indeed represent the city as a terrain for the underpaid, underemployed, and exploited, the impoverished countryside is also a frequent trope, indicating that peripheralization and rural exodus are pervasive social issues.

2007 witnessed two feature-length fiction debuts that are central to the representation of precarity in Baltic cinema. *Sügisball* (*Autumn Ball*, 2007) by the Estonian director Veiko Õunpuu provides gripping insights into the consequences of the neoliberal transformation for ordinary Estonian people and the deterioration of social cohesion as a cost of economic growth. Employing a social realist style, *Autumn Ball* portrays a broad gallery of Estonian precarious workers whose low income and low social status cause their lack of satisfaction with

---

[8] Tom Zaniello, *The Cinema of the Precariat: The Exploited, Underemployed, and Temp Workers of the World*, (London: Bloomsbury Academic, 2020), x.
[9] Ibid, 1.

their lives.[10] The multi-protagonist format of the film, in combination with its setting in a Soviet prefab residential district of Tallinn, suggests that social exclusion is an omnipresent condition brought about by the desire of the neoliberal political elite to shed everything reminiscent of the Soviet period, including the safety nets that the socialist state provided. *Monotonija* (*Monotony*, 2007), directed by Juris Poškus, an established Latvian filmmaker, draws on Dogme 95 conventions by casting a mixed ensemble of young and experienced actors and non-professionals and relying on improvisation in rehearsals in order to encourage the actors to adapt real-life experiences in conceiving their roles.[11] This approach serves to create convincing portrayals of precarious subjects and a credible social milieu. The film focuses on Laura, a girl working on a fish farm who moves to Riga in search of alternatives to her precarious village life. However, in the city her social status does not change. The Estonian Liina Paakspuu with *Soovide puu* (*The Wish Tree*, 2008) and the Lithuanian Saulius Drunga with *Anarchija Žirmūnuose* (*Anarchy in Žirmūnai*, 2010) tell similar stories of young girls' internal migration and their precarious work experiences in the capital cities, expressing explicit criticism of the capitalist system and its exploitation of young, inexperienced workers.

Lošėjas (*The Gambler*, 2013), a Lithuanian-Latvian co-production directed by Lithuanian Ignas Jonynas and shot in the port city of Klaipėda, portrays paramedics whose meager income and financial problems draw them into the dangerous territory of gambling and dramatic life situations. Meanwhile, *Šventasis* (*The Saint*, 2016), a social problem film by Andrius Blaževičius, looks into the repercussions of the global financial crisis on workers in the Lithuanian provinces, leaving a significant part of the population, notably young people, unemployed, causing their emigration to the Western countries, and tearing families apart.

Tracing the consequences of the neoliberal transformation for the working class, the Latvian documentary *Tārps* (*The Worm*, Andis Mizišs, 2005) was one of the first films to engage both with precarious work and the politics of precarity by displaying the miserable existence of Kārlis and Inese who, after losing their jobs, moved to an illegally built shack in a garden located somewhere on the outskirts of Riga. The couple suddenly finds themselves on the margins of

---

10 Õunpuu has continued to detail the plight of the working class in his subsequent films. See, e.g., Eva Näripea, "Representing and Escaping the Crisis of Neoliberalism: Veiko Õunpuu's Films and Methods," in *Cinema of Crisis: Film and Contemporary Europe*, ed. Thomas Austin and Angelos Koutsourakis (Edinburgh: Edinburgh University Press, 2020), 119–135.
11 Poškus borrowed this method from Alvis Hermanis, a stage director at the New Riga Theater where a number of the film's actors worked.

society, forced to survive on meager social benefits, the vegetables they grow, and the delicacies the forest offers. The birth of a child makes their life even more complicated. *Bekons, sviests un mana mamma* (*My Mother's Farm*, 2008), a personal documentary by the Latvian-Norwegian director Ilze Burkovska Jacobsen also tells a story of the losers of the new economic and political system by observing her mother who, as a small farmer, led a precarious life till the end of her days. Meanwhile the filmmaker and her younger siblings emigrated to the West. Ivars Zviedris, another Latvian director, has portrayed people forced to live in destitute conditions in several documentary films. *Ērik, atnāc!* (*Get Lost*, 2005), for instance, focuses on an elderly man finding shelter near the Latvian-Estonian border in a container with no electricity. In *Dokumentālists* (*Documentarian*, 2012), Inta scrapes by on hardly any income in a similar living arrangement near a national park.

Transient Workers

After the fall of the Iron Curtain, and even more so after the 2004 accession to the EU, previously non-existent opportunities for travel and work abroad emerged for the Baltic people. While a deliberate quest for self-realization can prompt cross-border mobility, in the Baltic countries it has often resulted from unfavorable socioeconomic circumstances such as unemployment, low-wage poverty, or social exclusion. Furthermore, in many cases moving abroad undermines the emigrants' social condition, impairing their communal, familial, and intimate connections, and suppressing their political agency or even violating their basic human rights, especially when they are forced to work illegally.

The first wave of emigration from the Baltics took place in 1992 and 1993, when a large proportion of the Russian-speaking population returned to their home countries.[12] Although the native Balts move abroad chiefly for economic

---

12 Jakub Bijak and Marek Kupiszewski, "International Migration Trends in Europe Prior to 2002," in *International Migration and the Future of Populations and Labour Force Resources in Europe*, ed. Marek Kupiszewski (Heidelberg/New York/London: Springer Dordrecht, 2013). It is estimated that around 50 percent of the Russophones left Lithuania for their original homelands after the collapse of the USSR, while in Latvia the percentage was 25 and in Estonia only 15. See: Monika Frejūtė-Rakauskienė, Andrius Marcinkevičius, and Kristina Šliavaitė, "Etninių mažumų grupės Lietuvoje: demografinė kaita ir socialinės padėties aspektai," in *Lietuvos gyventojų grupių socialinė kaita*, ed. Meilutė Taljūnaitė (Vilnius: Lietuvos socialinių tyrimų centras, 2016), 86; Pārsla Eglīte and Zaiga Krišjāne, "Dimensions and Effects of Labour Migration to EU countries: The Case of Latvia," in *EU Labour Migration since Enlargement: Trends, Impacts and Policies*, ed.

reasons,[13] a notable difference exists in the spatial patterns of the exodus. In Estonia, the main destination of emigration (including transnational commuting) since the early 1990s has been Finland, due to the linguistic and geographical proximity of the two countries.[14] Latvians and Lithuanians, however, have preferred to relocate to the United Kingdom and Ireland, which can be partly explained by the fact that these two English-speaking countries decided not to instate a transition period for opening their labor markets to the newcomers after the 2004 enlargement of the EU.[15] A substantial tide of emigration followed the global financial crisis and the subsequent upsurge of unemployment. Becoming part of the labor market of another country was the only way to survive for many families. Thus, the situation of a divided family became a trait of the time, which can also be observed in cinematic representations.

In terms of cinematic geography, the Baltic films that portray the post-Soviet emigration obviously reflect these trends. Interestingly, though, the extent to which resettlement or transnational commuting has attracted the attention of filmmakers varies in each Baltic country rather significantly. For instance, migration—including job-related commuting—of Estonians to Finland, which has had a considerable impact on Estonian society, has rarely been tackled in cinematic form, and typically by early-career, or even student, filmmakers. Lithuanian cinema has also taken relatively little notice of emigration, despite the consistent increase in cross-border resettlement.

In Latvia, by contrast, the predominant trends of post-Soviet emigration have been addressed in several documentaries that focus on Latvians seeking work, higher income, better life, and opportunities in the USA and Ireland. As in other Baltic countries, these films were often made by early-career authors. Usually based on interviews with multiple characters, these works explore the

---

Béla Galgóczi, Janine Leschke, and Andre Watt (Farnham, Burlington: Ashgate, 2009), 271; Kristi Anniste, *East-West Migration in Europe: The Case of Estonia after Regaining Independence*. Dissertationes geographicae Universitatis Tartuensis 57 (Tartu: University of Tartu Press, 2014), 18.
13 Mihails Hazans, "Emigration from Latvia: A Brief History and Driving Forces in the Twenty-First Century," in *The Emigrant Communities of Latvia*, ed. Rita Kaša and Inta Mieriņa (Cham: SpringerOpen, 2019), 43.
14 Kaja Kumer-Haukanõmm and Keiu Telve, "Estonians in the World," in *Estonian Human Development Report 2016/2017: Estonia at the Age of Migration*, ed. Tiit Tammaru (Tallinn: Foundation Estonian Cooperation Assembly, 2017), https://www.2017.inimareng.ee/en/open-to-the-world/estonians-in-the-world/.
15 Jakub Bijak, Anna Kincinger, and Marek Kupiszewski, "International Migration Scenarios for 27 European Countries, 2002–2052," in *International Migration and the Future of Populations and Labour Force Resources in Europe*, ed. Marek Kupiszewski (Heidelberg/New York/London: Springer Dordrecht, 2013), 77.

reasons for leaving Latvia and the current conditions or prospects of their subjects. *Sprīdītis Amerikā* (*Does It Look Like Happiness?*, Ieva Salmane) and *Atrasts Amerikā* (*Found in America*, Sandris Jūra), both made in 2003, concentrate on Latvians in the USA and feature a wide spectrum of experiences, while *Un tad es atgriezīšos pa īstam* (*And Then I Will Return for Real*, Una Celma, 2003) and *Bēgums* (*Tide*, Ivars Zviedris, 2009) portray economic migrants in Ireland. In *Found in America*, a woman in her 40s working several odd jobs expresses her satisfaction with life in the US and conveys a belief shared by characters in all of the films—hard work abroad results in a better income than at home and secures a more carefree life. In addition to the recurring topic of earning money, which is often sent back home to support families or in some cases invested in new ventures, the films also bear witness to the emotional hardships of leaving children behind in Latvia. In *Tide*, the focus is on people gathering sea clams. They work in the wee hours during the tide; the image of the changing coastline serves as a metaphor for migration. It is reflected also in the narrative—some people come to Ireland, some leave, corresponding to the fluctuating migration statistics. In general, the films set in Ireland appear to underline pragmatic reasons for emigration, in contrast to those about Latvian expatriates in the USA, who seem to be fueled by their adventurous spirit. Ireland also features in the Lithuanian-Latvian co-production *Nereikalingi žmonės*/*Nevajadzīgie ļaudis* (*Loss*, Māris Martinsons, 2008), a fiction film where the paths of several characters cross, relating to the topics discussed in the documentaries.

A fair number of narrative films that tell stories of emigration revolve around children left in the care of their grandparents or other adults while the parents look for work abroad—typically in London, as in *Ūdensbumba resnajam runcim*/*Veepomm paksule kõutsile* (*Waterbomb for the Fat Tomcat*, Varis Brasla, 2004), a family film co-produced by Latvia and Estonia, and *Es esmu šeit* (*Mellow Mud*, Renārs Vimba, 2016), a Latvian coming-of-age drama. *Laikinai* (*Temporary*, 2011), a Lithuanian short by Jūratė Samulionytė, even goes a step further, as a 14-year-old girl is forced to mind her 5-year-old sister Liucija without any adult supervision. *Mazie laupītāji* (*Little Robbers*, Armands Zvirbulis, 2009) introduces yet another strategy of solving the family's financial difficulties. After the father loses his job and fails to pay the mortgage, the bank confiscates the family apartment, and the children decide to rob the bank in an effort to get their former life back. All of these films present children or adolescents forced to take action and responsibilities normally in the hands of grown-ups. The Lithuanian-Irish co-production *Pilis* (*The Castle*, Lina Lužytė, 2020) also features a determined teenage protagonist, but this coming-of-age story takes place in Dublin and reflects on what migration means for different generations of Lithuanians (and Eastern Europeans in general)—for the 13-year-old

Monika who dreams of becoming a singer; for her mother Jolanta, a professional pianist working in a fish factory; and for Monika's highly demented grandmother. *Emigrantai* (*Emigrants*, Justinas Krisiūnas, 2013), a Lithuanian low-budget drama, presents a broader picture of Lithuanian emigrants from the point of view of social class and age, analyzing the effects of emigration on both those who leave and those who stay behind. The harshest look on the downside of labor migration in contemporary Latvian cinema is *Oļegs* (*Oleg*, Juris Kursietis, 2019). Based on real events, the film follows a young Russian-speaking resident of Riga who, seeking work in Belgium, falls victim to a modern-day slavery circuit run by Polish emigrants. He finds himself in a desperate situation without knowing the language, stripped of his passport, with no protection from authorities, and no money to return home. Although somewhat lighter in tone, the immensely popular 12-part Estonian TV series *Kalevipojad* (*The Sons of Kalev*, Ergo Kuld, 2011) powerfully summarizes the collective experiences of thousands of Estonian men forced to seek low-skilled employment in Finland, often in humiliating conditions, and the dire consequences of this on their personal lives and families.

"Miserable" Minority

As a legacy of the Soviet industrialization program, the Russophone community forms the largest ethno-linguistic minority in Estonia and Latvia.[16] In 2009, Russian-speaking people made up 29 percent of the Estonian and 34 percent of the Latvian population.[17] The majority of them are migrants (and their descendants)

---

[16] Enforced industrialization and the accompanying influx of migrants affected Lithuania to a smaller extent as the country remained more agricultural than its northern neighbors and was able to fulfill the required economic targets largely without recruiting labor force from other republics, while the increasingly national orientation of the Lithuanian communist party also provided certain protection against migration, cf. Kjetil Duvold, Sten Berglund, and Joakim Ekman, *Political Culture in the Baltic States: Between National and European Integration* (Cham: Palgrave Macmillan, 2020), 7. As a result, the Russophones only accounted for 12.3 percent of Lithuania's population in 1989, cf. Mare Ainsaar and Vlada Stankūnienė, "Demographic Costs of Transition and the Future of the Baltic States," in *Estonian Human Development Report 2010/2011. Baltic Way(s) of Human Development: Twenty Years On*, ed. Marju Lauristin (Tallinn: Eesti Koostöö Kogu, 2011), 45 (table 2.2.1).

[17] In addition to ethnic Russians, these figures include Ukrainians and Belarusians, Ainsaar and Stankuniene, "Demographic Costs," 45. In 1939, the titular ethnic group constituted 88.2 percent of the population in Estonia and 75.5 percent in Latvia, cf. Duvold, Berglund, and Ekman, *Political Culture*, 7.

who were brought to the two annexed Soviet republics to man the newly established large factories and the military industrial complex. Compared to the native population they enjoyed "a higher than average status, income and better access to services," regardless of their rank or skills.[18] After the USSR ceased to exist and the nation states were reinstated, these people were stripped of their former privileges and social status, as well as their de facto homeland. The Russophones in Estonia probably fared the worst. Unlike in Estonia, the share of Russian-speaking immigrants in Latvia constituted the majority not only of blue-collar workers but also of the higher ranks of professionals, many of whom switched to business, forming up to 80 percent of the new entrepreneurial class in Latvia by the mid-1990s.[19] In Estonia, however, the access of the typically unilingual settlers, even those with higher education, to white collar positions was significantly inhibited for many years after the collapse of the Soviet Union.[20] In addition to the neoliberal "shock therapy" conceived by the right-wing political elite that undermined the social security of the best part of the population, the social exclusion of the Russophones was aggravated by major structural reforms that disproportionately burdened the Russian-speaking manufacturing labor force. Finally, both Estonia and Latvia, unlike Lithuania, opted for restitutionist citizenship laws. As opposed to the descendants of the citizens of the inter-war republics who were automatically offered citizenship in 1991, Soviet immigrants had to undergo a cumbersome naturalization process, including successfully taking compulsory tests on language proficiency and citizenship law. As a result of this divisive policy, the non-citizens in both countries still constitute around 15 percent of the population in 2020.[21] Hence, perhaps in Estonia in particular, under the rule of the right-wing parties that combine extreme neoliberal market ideology with populist nationalist sensibility, the Russophone community has been deeply marginalized—politically, economically, as well as socially and culturally.

It is then perhaps surprising to find that the plight of this community has earned plenty of screen time in Estonian cinema of the past three decades, principally in documentary form. The discourse of these titles is generally sympathetic toward the Russophones, especially the most disenfranchised among them—the elderly, the unemployed, the addicted—, as opposed to the mainstream Estonian

---

18 Avo Trumm, "The Socio-Economic Situation of Non-Estonians," in *Estonian Human Development Report 2007*, ed. Mati Heidmets (Tallinn: Eesti Koostöö Kogu, 2008), 47.
19 Zenonas Norkus, "Estonian, Latvian and Lithuanian Post-Communist Development in the Comparative Perspective," in *Estonian Human Development Report 2010/2011. Baltic Way(s) of Human Development: Twenty Years On*, ed. Marju Lauristin (Tallinn: Eesti Koostöö Kogu, 2011), 30.
20 Trumm, "The Socio-Economic Situation," 49–50.
21 Duvold, Berglund, and Ekman, *Political Culture*, 8–9.

press, which reproduced the toxic revanchist paradigm for many years.[22] The darker side of this mode of representation, of course, lies in normalizing the Russian-speaking minority as the miserable, pitiful Other. While films like *Jõulud Leninita* (Christmas without Lenin, Andres Sööt, 1994) and *Äraneetud linn* (Accursed Town, Andres Sööt, 1996), and especially *Pronksiöö: Vene mäss Tallinnas* (Bronze Night: The Russian Riot in Tallinn, Urmas Eero Liiv, 2007) lean towards group-based portrayals that are particularly prone to sweeping generalizations, most documentary-makers increasingly focus on individual subjects and protagonists. This is perhaps most evident in the films of the younger-generation, Russian-speaking documentarists, such as Alyona Surzhikova with her *Generatsioon 0* (Generation Zero, 2008), *Laulev Nadežda* (Singing Nadezhda, 2011), and *Poissmees ja Volga* (The Bachelor and Volga, 2014). While Surzhikova tracks the rather ordinary, although sometimes financially strapped, everyday life of the "little people" among the minority community, thus bridging the cognitive gap between the different ethnic groups, the most poignant cinematic representations of the Russophone people come from two Estonian auteurs, Meelis Muhu and Sulev Keedus. Muhu's *Aljoša* (Alyosha, 2008) observes the escalation of the single most serious inter-ethnic crisis in post-Soviet Estonia, related to a Soviet war monument in central Tallinn, an anchor for Russian identity and a sore spot for Estonian nationalists, that was removed by the authorities in 2007 just weeks before the annual celebration of the end of World War II (or the Great Patriotic War, as it is known among the Russians). Street riots broke out as a result, fueled by far-right factions of both communities. Muhu's film brilliantly highlights the embarrassing fact that "during the 15 years of independence [the Estonian majority's] desire for revenge, indifference and 'forceful integration' has created a social stratum in Estonia whose attitude towards their country of birth is estranged and hostile."[23] Meanwhile, Keedus's much-polemicized *Varesesaare venelased* (The Russians on Crow Island, 2012) presents a series of heart-breaking testimonies by the "wretched of Narva," drug addicts from a predominantly Russian-speaking industrial town on the Estonian-Russian border that acutely suffered from the post-Soviet structural changes. Although in an extreme manner, the film summarizes with great empathy the existential condition of many post-Soviet Russophones:

---

22 See, e.g., Piia Tammpuu, "Construction of the Russian-Speaking Minority in the Estonian Press," in *Estonian Press about Integration: Media Monitoring of Integration of Russian-Speaking Population 1999–2001*, ed. Ragne Kõuts (Tartu: Mitte-eestlaste Integratsiooni Sihtasutus, 2002).
23 Jaak Allik, "Annaks jumal, et järge ei tuleks," *Teater. Muusika. Kino*, no. 7 (July 2008): 88.

They are not needed in Russia and Estonians do not want to embrace them. The country they once came from no longer exists on the world map, and the country they are in would like to deport them to non-existence. They are a homeless mass of people that was supposed to vanish together with the Soviet empire; children stillborn in the shadow of capitalist society, no longer needed by anyone.[24]

In contrast to Estonia, filmmakers in Latvia have largely overlooked the Russophone minority. Russian-speaking characters are rare and they usually do not take a central place in the narrative. In addition to the above-mentioned *Oleg*, the title character of which is a Russian-speaking non-citizen, Aik Karapetian's drama *Cilvēki tur* (*People Out There*, 2012) is one of the very few Latvian films to take an immediate interest in this minority community.[25] It is the first state-funded film in post-Soviet Latvia that features Russian as its main language of dialogue. The protagonist Jan, trying to find his place in life, drifts between his neighborhood—a drab multi-story residential district from the Soviet era—and a new high-rise estate that promises a getaway from his lack of steady income and prospects for the future and his environment of crime, bullying, alcohol, drugs, and pornography.[26]

All ethnic minorities are underrepresented in Lithuanian cinema, primarily because Lithuanians make up 84.2 percent of the country's population. However, multiethnic subjects are treated in many documentaries that focus on social-risk families, poverty, and unemployment, such as *Romano vaikystė* (*Roman's Childhood*, 2020) and *Pietūs Lipovkėje* (*Dinner*, 2013) by Linas Mikuta and *Stebuklų laukas* (*The Field of Magic*, 2011) by Mindaugas Survila. The precarious Russophones and their problems are made visible by Oksana Buraja and Olga Černovaitė, documentarists of Russian origin. For instance, Černovaitė's *Drugelio miestas* (*Butterfly City*, 2017) investigates the situation of Visaginas, a predominantly Russian-speaking city, after the Ignalina nuclear power plant was closed down in 2009. Visaginas was built in the 1970s for the immigrant workers recruited from other republics of the USSR to serve the plant. It used to be a wealthy city, but became impoverished after 2009. The majority of its inhabitants do not feel at home in Lithuania and are nostalgic about the Soviet past, although the young try to build their lives in a new reality.

---

24 Marianne Kõrver, "Kaotatud paradiis," *La Strada: Kinoleht*, no. 2 (2012): 2.
25 Karapetian was born in Armenia (1983), raised in Latvia, and studied filmmaking in Latvia and France. *People Out There* was his feature debut.
26 Even though the film's producer Roberts Vinovskis has stated that their goal was to avoid any political statements, it has proved difficult not to read one into it, cf. Kristīne Matīsa, "Intuīcija bez vīzijām," *Kino Raksti*, no. 35 (Spring 2012): 7.

Conclusion

Our study on precarity and social exclusion in Baltic cinema suggests that only a small number of filmmakers deal with the new precariat as a social class. Narratives explicitly focusing on precarious experiences remain rather peripheral, especially considering the high relevance of the problem in the region, while the mainstream of Baltic cinema is largely made up of films that examine the historic traumas of the three nations, engaging in identity politics, or that celebrate the entrepreneurial spirit of the new era of restored statehood. Moreover, stories of precarity tend to be found in documentaries rather than narrative films, and the plight of the marginalized groups principally attracts a younger generation of auteurs who are inclined to value social consciousness over popular success. Precarious workers with a low level of education dominate as subjects of both fiction and documentary films in all three countries, while other at-risk social groups seldom take the central stage. While precarity is often represented by Russophone characters in Estonian cinema, this is rarely the case in Latvia and Lithuania. At the same time, Latvians and Lithuanians appear to be more attentive to the predicament of migrant workers and the concomitant issue of dysfunctional families, while the dilemma of cross-border flows of labor earns far less screen time in Estonian cinema.

Bibliography

Aidukaitė, Jolanta, and Sven E. O. Hort. "Editorial Introduction: Baltic States after the Crisis? The Transformation of the Welfare System and Social Problems." *Journal of Baltic Studies* 50, no. 1 (2019): 1–6. https://doi.org/10.1080/01629778.2019.1571754.

Ainsaar, Mare, and Vlada Stankuniene. "Demographic Costs of Transition and the Future of the Baltic States." In *Estonian Human Development Report 2010/2011. Baltic Way(s) of Human Development: Twenty Years On*, ed. Marju Lauristin. Tallinn: Eesti Koostöö Kogu, 2011, 44–51.

Allik, Jaak. "Annaks jumal, et järge ei tuleks." *Teater. Muusika. Kino*, no. 7 (July 2008): 84–90.

Anniste, Kristi. *East-West Migration in Europe: The Case of Estonia after Regaining Independence*. PhD diss. University of Tartu, 2014.

Bijak, Jakub, Anna Kincinger, and Marek Kupiszewski. "International Migration Scenarios for 27 European Countries, 2002–2052." In *International Migration and the Future of Populations and Labour Force Resources in Europe*, ed. Marek Kupiszewski. Heidelberg, New York, London: Springer Dordrecht, 2013, 75–92.

Bijak, Jakub, and Marek Kupiszewski. "International Migration Trends in Europe Prior to 2002." In *International Migration and the Future of Populations and Labour Force Resources in Europe*, ed. Marek Kupiszewski. Heidelberg/New York/London: Springer Dordrecht, 2013, 57–74.

Duvold, Kjetil, Sten Berglund, and Joakim Ekman. *Political Culture in the Baltic States: Between National and European Integration*. Cham, Switzerland: Palgrave Macmillan, 2020.
Eglīte, Pārsla, and Zaiga Krišjāne. "Dimensions and Effects of Labour Migration to EU countries: The Case of Latvia." In *EU Labour Migration since Enlargement: Trends, Impacts and Policies*, ed. Béla Galgóczi, Janine Leschke, and Andre Watt. Farnham and Burlington: Ashgate, 2009, 269–290.
Eurofound. "Statutory Minimum Wages." February 3, 2021. https://www.eurofound.europa.eu/data/statutory-minimum-wages.
Frejūtė-Rakauskienė, Monika, Andrius Marcinkevičius, and Kristina Šliavaitė. "Etninių mažumų grupės Lietuvoje: demografinė kaita ir socialinės padėties aspektai." In *Lietuvos gyventojų grupių socialinė kaita*, ed. Meilutė Taljūnaitė. Vilnius: Lietuvos socialinių tyrimų centras, 2016, 85–108.
Fischer, Reinis. "Average Monthly Salary in European Union 2020." Last modified June 26, 2020. https://www.reinisfischer.com/average-monthly-salary-european-union-2020.
Hazans, Mihails. "Emigration from Latvia: A Brief History and Driving Forces in the Twenty-First Century." In *The Emigrant Communities of Latvia*, ed. Rita Kaša and Inta Mieriņa. Cham, Switzerland: SpringerOpen, 2019, 35–68.
Kõrver, Marianne. "Kaotatud paradiis." *La Strada: Kinoleht*, no. 2 (2012): 2.
Kumer-Haukanõmm, Kaja, and Keiu Telve. "Estonians in the World." In *Estonian Human Development Report 2016/2017: Estonia at the Age of Migration*, ed. Tiit Tammaru. Tallinn: Foundation Estonian Cooperation Assembly, 2017. Last modified March 13 2022. https://www.2017.inimareng.ee/en/open-to-the-world/estonians-in-the-world/
Lapinske, Laura. "Living in Precarity: Ethnography of Everyday Struggles of Single Mothers in Lithuania." *Sociologija* 60, no. 1 (January 2018): 64–83.
Lauristin, Marju, Zenonas Norkus, and Peeter Vihalemm. "On the Sociology's Contribution to Knowledge of the Baltic Way." *Sociologija. Mintis ir veiksmas* 29, no. 2 (2011): 128–155.
Matīsa, Kristīne. "Intuīcija bez vīzijām." *Kino Raksti*, no. 35 (Spring 2012): 7–15.
Näripea, Eva. "Representing and Escaping the Crisis of Neoliberalism: Veiko Õunpuu's Films and Methods." In *Cinema of Crisis: Film and Contemporary Europe*, ed. Thomas Austin and Angelos Koutsourakis. Edinburgh: Edinburgh University Press, 2020, 119–135.
Norkus, Zenonas. "Estonian, Latvian and Lithuanian Post-Communist Development in the Comparative Perspective." In *Estonian Human Development Report 2010/2011. Baltic Way(s) of Human Development: Twenty Years On*, ed. Marju Lauristin. Tallinn: Eesti Koostöö Kogu, 2011, 22–30.
Staehr, Karsten. "Austerity in the Baltic States during the Global Financial Crisis." *Intereconomics* 48, no. 5 (September 2013): 293–302.
Tammpuu, Piia. "Construction of the Russian-Speaking Minority in the Estonian Press." In *Estonian Press about Integration: Media Monitoring of Integration of Russian-Speaking Population 1999–2001*, ed. Ragne Kõuts. Tartu: Mitte-eestlaste Integratsiooni Sihtasutus, 2002, 31–39.
Trumm, Avo. "The Socio-Economic Situation of Non-Estonians." In *Estonian Human Development Report 2007*, ed. Mati Heidmets. Tallinn: Eesti Koostöö Kogu, 2008, 47–54.
Zaniello, Tom. *The Cinema of the Precariat: The Exploited, Underemployed, and Temp Workers of the World*. London: Bloomsbury Academic, 2020.

Filmography

Aljoša (Alyosha). Dir. Meelis Muhu. Estonia, 2008.
Anarchija Žirmūnuose (Anarchy in Žirmūnai). Dir. Saulius Drunga. Lithuania, 2010.
Äraneetud linn (Accursed Town). Dir. Andres Sööt. Estonia, 1996.
Atrasts Amerikā (Found in America). Dir. Sandris Jūra. Latvia, 2003.
Bēgums (Tide). Dir. Ivars Zviedris. Latvia/Ireland, 2009.
Bekons, sviests un mana mamma (My Mother's Farm). Dir. Ilze Burkovska Jacobsen. Latvia/Norway, 2008.
Cilvēki tur/Lyudi tam (People Out There). Dir. Aik Karapetian. Latvia, 2012.
Dokumentālists (Documentarian). Dir. Ivars Zviedris, Inese Kļava. Latvia, 2012.
Drugelio miestas (Butterfly City). Dir. Olga Černovaitė. Ireland/Belgium/Denmark, 2017.
Emigrantai (Emigrants). Dir. Justinas Krisiūnas. Lithuania, 2013.
Ērik, atnāc! (Get Lost). Dir. Ivars Zviedris. Latvia, 2005.
Es esmu šeit (Mellow Mud). Dir. Renārs Vimba. Latvia, 2016.
Generatsioon 0 (Generation Zero). Dir. Alyona Surzhikova. Estonia, 2008.
Jõulud Leninita (Christmas without Lenin). Dir. Andres Sööt. Estonia, 1994.
Kalevipojad (The Sons of Kalev). Dir. Ergo Kuld/Kanal 2. Estonia, 2011.
Laikinai (Temporary). Dir. Jūratė Samulionytė. Lithuania, 2011.
Laulev Nadežda (Singing Nadezhda). Dir. Alyona Surzhikova. Estonia, 2011.
Lošėjas (The Gambler). Dir. Ignas Jonynas. Lithuania/Latvia, 2013.
Mazie laupītāji (Little Robbers). Dir. Armands Zvirbulis. Latvia/Austria, 2009.
Monotonija (Monotony). Dir. Juris Poškus. Latvia, 2007.
Nereikalingi žmonės/Nevajadzīgie ļaudis Loss. Dir. Māris Martinsons. Lithuania/Latvia, 2008.
Oļegs (Oleg). Dir. Juris Kursietis. Latvia/Lithuania/Belgium/France, 2019.
Pietūs Lipovkėje (Dinner). Dir. Linas Mikuta. Lithuania, 2013.
Pilis (The Castle). Dir. Lina Lužytė. Lithuania/Ireland, 2020.
Poissmees ja Volga (The Bachelor and Volga). Dir. Alyona Surzhikova. Estonia, 2014.
Pronksiöö: Vene mäss Tallinnas (Bronze Night: The Russian Riot in Tallinn). Dir. Urmas Eero Liiv. Estonia, 2007.
Romano vaikystė (Roman's Childhood). Dir. Linas Mikuta. Lithuania, 2020.
Soovide puu (The Wish Tree). Dir. Liina Paakspuu. Estonia, 2008.
Sprīdītis Amerikā (Does It Look Like Happiness?). Dir. Ieva Salmane. Latvia, 2003.
Sügisball (Autumn Ball). Dir. Veiko Õunpuu. Estonia, 2007.
Šventasis (The Saint). Dir. Andrius Blaževičius. Lithuania/Poland, 2016.
Stebuklų laukas (The Field of Magic). Dir. Mindaugas Survila. Lithuania, 2011.
Tārps (The Worm). Dir. Andis Mizišs. Latvia, 2005.
Ūdensbumba resnajam runcim/Veepomm paksule kõutsile (Waterbomb for the Fat Tomcat). Dir. Varis Brasla. Latvia/Estonia, 2004.
Un tad es atgriezīšos pa īstam (And Then I Will Return for Real). Dir. Una Celma. Latvia, 2003.
Varesesaare venelased (The Russians on Crow Island). Dir. Sulev Keedus. Estonia, 2012.

Anders Marklund
Screening Precarity Scenes
Precariousness and the Welfare State in Scandinavian Film

"Wait!" A key scene in Pernilla August's debut feature *Svinalängorna* (*Beyond*, 2010), ends with the young girl Leena hurrying towards the door to halt the two persons who just left. They are social workers. Leena asks them, whispering so her parents cannot hear, to take her brother Sakari with them: "You have to take him, you have to . . ."

I will call this a precarity scene, drawing on the Latin word *prex*, "entreaty, prayer," and the later English *precarious* in the meaning of "depending on favour, pertaining to entreaty, obtained by asking or praying."[1] I will explore similar situations where someone depends on others and asks them for help to get by. Precarity scenes often capture the essence of a serious and vulnerable situation, how it affects the individual, how it articulates responsibility, and how foregrounded it is within the film as a whole. A key question that will be explored regards how this is constructed differently in different kinds of films.

In *Beyond* the requested help is denied. We will soon see the consequences: Leena's young brother will never recover from the neglect he suffered because of their parents' drinking. He will die a few years later, fourteen years old, from an overdose. Later Leena will bluntly state that "Sakari perished, he broke down in our family, because of us, and those disgusting orphanages." What Leena sees clearly, and what this chapter will foreground, is how the individual (Sakari) is abandoned by both the family (drinking parents) and the welfare state (the social workers, orphanages). The discussion of precarity scenes thus needs to be framed in a wider context, including the key relationships between the individual, the welfare state, and the family (as part of the community and civil society).

The negotiations among these three aspects plays a particular role in recent Scandinavian history. Henrik Berggren and Lars Trägårdh underscore how Scandinavian welfare societies[2] strive for a direct relationship between the state and the

---

[1] "Precarious," Online Etymology Dictionary, *Etymonline*, accessed January 31, 2022, https://www.etymonline.com/search?q=precarious.
[2] For an outline of this see, for example, Henrik Berggren and Lars Trägårdh, "Pippi Longstocking: The autonomous child and the moral logic of the Swedish welfare state," in *Swedish Modernism: Architecture, Consumption and the Welfare State*, ed. Helena Mattsson and Sven-Olov Wallenstein (London: Black Dog, 2010), or Mary Hilson, "The Nordic Welfare Model," in *Introduction to Nordic Cultures*, ed. Annika Lindskog and Jakob Stougaard-Nielsen (London: UCL Press, 2020).

∂ Open Access. © 2022 Anders Marklund, published by De Gruyter. [CC BY-NC-ND] This work is licensed under the Creative Commons Attribution-NonCommercial-NoDerivatives 4.0 International License.
https://doi.org/10.1515/9783110707816-017

individual, thus reducing the traditional significance of family and civil society. Their concept "state individualism" clarifies how the ideal goal appears to be to

> liberate the individual citizen from all forms of subordination and dependency in civil society: the poor from charity, the workers from their employers, wives from their husbands, children from parents (and vice versa when the parents have become elderly). [. . .] The aim, it appears, is to avoid subjecting individuals to the charity of others and to make even relationships within the family as equal and voluntary as possible.[3]

This clearly fails in *Beyond*. Leena and her brother are too young to have this direct relationship with the state. They are subordinated and dependent on a failing family. The welfare state also fails them, not responding to Leena's prayer for help, instead accepting the parents' lies and evasions. In this manner, precarity scenes can point to how roles and responsibilities are distributed.

The precarity scene described above occurs within one of the film's many flashbacks. The first flashback is particularly interesting, not only for its staging, but also for how it moves audiences into Leena's grave situation—and out of it again. The young Leena stands next to an older version of herself at an indoor swimming pool, both ready to dive into the water. The older Leena is married, has two children, and has just learned that her mother is in hospital and will not live much longer. The two Leenas look at each other, briefly noticing each other's presence, dive in, and swim alongside one another. The older Leena forges through the water but cannot leave her younger self behind. When she raises her head above the surface, she is the young Leena, back in her childhood. She tries to wake her drunken, barely conscious mother. Realizing it cannot be done, she herself helps Sakari get ready for his first day in school.

What the older Leena dives into is a world where her life goes very wrong. When, in this case and after other flashbacks, she returns from it she is back in the world where she has a supportive and loving husband, two sweet daughters, a big car, and a modern house. Alternating between these two worlds, these double times, is related to the double meaning of the word "to screen" that Linda Williams has used to analyze representations and their conventions. Screening means both revelation and concealment: "To screen is to reveal on a screen. But a second, equally important meaning [. . .] is 'to shelter or protect with or as a screen.' Movies both reveal and conceal [. . .]. Every revelation is also a concealment that leaves something to the imagination."[4] With this in mind, I will explore how films not only reveal precarity but also how they, in different ways and to different degrees, conceal it, making viewers less concerned about the

---

[3] Berggren and Trägårdh, "Pippi Longstocking," 52–53.
[4] Linda Williams, *Screening Sex* (Durham, NC/London: Duke University Press, 2008), 2.

precarity shown. *Beyond's* original novel, written by Susanna Alakoski (based in part on her own childhood experiences), is entirely set in the past, with Leena as a young girl. August explains why she and co-screenwriter Lolita Ray created the film adaptation's contemporary frame story: "We wanted Leena to meet a healthy man as an adult [. . .] there must be hope. Leena has put on a tight lid on things: she has a job, a family, she creates a life jacket for herself."[5] The decision allows the film to capture how the consequences of Leena's childhood trauma linger into her adult life, and how she reluctantly deals with them at this later point in her life, but the frame story's key function is to add hope, a safety net, and "to put a tight lid" on the earlier problems. Young Leena's precarity is revealed, but it is also concealed by contemporary Leena's success.

In the following discussion I will use a model of different film practices as a framework to distinguish how filmmakers elaborate similar themes in different kinds of films. The model has been suggested by Birger Langkjær to position realism as a third textual practice, in between the traditional opposition of Hollywood mainstream and European art films. There is much to be said about each of these three practices—classic narration, realism, and art film—but since their characteristics should be familiar, I will only briefly introduce some of the relevant concepts in relation to *Beyond*. Langkjær foregrounds that realist films "deal with their themes in narrative forms that do not apply to basic genre rules, but, nevertheless, they tell their stories in accessible and often engaging ways that differentiate them from art films."[6] Regarding realism, I will use a distinction which is central to Langkjær's discussion: the distinction between social realism and psychological realism.

Langkjær underlines social realism's "emphasis on social aspects of the fictional world depicted and how it influences characters," and he also notes how structural conditions are of key importance in creating a dramatic conflict and exploring challenges to the protagonist.[7] Importantly, he suggests that rather than showing people who are entirely confined by social structures, these films are about the "ways individuals deal with those structures."[8] As we will see, this emphasis will play out differently as we look at precarity scenes in films of different kinds. *Beyond*, for example, offers a varied and nuanced view of social structures and how Leena's parents are formed by them, including the experience of

---

5 Sanna Thorén Björling, "Pernilla August," *Dagens Nyheter*, March 2, 2011, https://www.dn.se/arkiv/kultur/pernilla-august/.
6 Birger Langkjær, "Realism as a third film practice," *MedieKultur: Journal of Media and Communication Research*, no. 51 (2011): 52.
7 Ibid., 48.
8 Ibid., 49.

migrating from Finland to Sweden, precarious work, class, and social hierarchies. The precarious situation is, in this case, caused by alcoholism, but it should be seen against the background of structural challenges of settling into a new society. The welfare state and institutions of civil society (i.e. Leena's swimming club) are there, but they do not make any difference.

If Leena's past is characterized by social realism, her present is rendered in terms of psychological realism, nuancing how she responds to the memories resurfacing from her traumatic childhood. Langkjær describes psychological realism as a practice focusing on "micro-sociological relations and intimate psychological development," rather than larger social structures. And it often includes "love, friendship and liberation from parents" as central themes.[9] Contrasting psychological realism with genre films and art films he suggests that it

> is more about coming to terms with oneself than about actions in the outer world [as in genre films], and the narrative structure mirrors this inner development, which is more comprehensible than the fleeting existential conflicts in art films, but without the outer story arc and the melodramatic moralism central to the Hollywood version of serious, psychological dramas.[10]

What does it mean that *Beyond* presents its story using typical elements from social realism for the diegetic past and the devices of psychological realism for the present? It appears to restrict viewers from seeing structural problems in contemporary society—such problems are in the past. In the present, there are "only" individual psychological conflicts dealing with a traumatic childhood and the scars it has left unremedied. Furthermore, the look back is from the point of view of someone who has managed to escape misery. Audiences know that things will turn out quite well for Leena (without forgetting about the scars the past has left on her), allowing them to look forward to a reassuring conclusion. The past is where social structures are relevant, today is where lingering psychological traumas are dealt with. When Leena dives into the social realism of the past, revealing the struggles of the migrant, working-class family, the film simultaneously conceals comparable social issues in contemporary society.

Beyond has served to give a first example of precarity scenes, of how the relations between family, welfare state, and individual are articulated in them, and how precarity can also be seen in a larger framework, where different filmmaking practices may reveal or conceal precarities viewers should be aware of. In the following I will look at precarity scenes in a small selection of contemporary Scandinavian films. The aim is to see how different film practices articulate

---

9 Ibid., 51.
10 Ibid.

situations where someone is in a position of needing help. I will look at the interactions between the individual (in need), the family, and the welfare state (and its institutions). What particularly interests me is how these films, to varying degrees and through different means, reveal persons, problems, and precarious situations, but also conceal them.

Screening a Dark Past Through Different Film Practices

Looking at different film practices, I will begin with four quite unalike films. I discuss the first one, Christoffer Boe's crime thriller *Journal 64* (2018), more extensively than the others. The other three, introduced briefly as contrasting examples, are Felix Herngren's comedy *Hundraåringen som klev ut genom fönstret och försvann* (*The Hundred-Year-Old Man Who Climbed Out the Window and Disappeared*, 2013), Amanda Kernell's biographic realist drama *Sameblod* (*Sami Blood*, 2016), and Ali Abbasi's *Gräns* (*Border*, 2018), a difficult film to characterize, sharing features of all three of Langkjær's practices, but probably mostly those of the art film.[11]

The topic these films approach, through different practices, is eugenics.[12] Regarding this topic, we should remember both the involvement of state institutions and that key ideas were aligned with the development of the welfare state. Here too, we will see differently articulated relations between individuals, the welfare state, and the family (civil society).

Journal 64 begins in 1961 with the story of Nette and how an actual Danish state institution incarcerated young women on the small island Sprogø. Many of them were forced into abortion and sterilization. The institution's founder, Christian Keller, wrote that these women were "a certain class of young, slightly mentally retarded girls who, by their unbounded sexual encounters, become a serious danger to society and to themselves."[13] The film's concluding titles will later reveal

---

[11] Ali Abbasi, "Sommar: Ali Abbasi," *Sveriges radio*, August 5, 2019, https://sverigesradio.se/avsnitt/1319480.
[12] For an outline on how eugenics emerged and was practiced within Scandinavia, see: Gunnar Broberg and Nils Roll-Hansen, eds., *Eugenics and the Welfare State: Sterilization Policy in Denmark, Sweden, Norway, and Finland* (East Lansing, MI: Michigan State University Press, 1996).
[13] Quoted from news statement written by Keller in 1920 and reproduced in: Katrine Becker, *Sprogø: Lidt om kvindeanstalten på Sprogø* (Slagelse: Dansk Forsorgshistorisk Museum, no year), np.

the consequences: "Between 1934 and 1967, more than 11,000 Danish women were forcibly sterilized."

In the precarity scene that takes place just after she has failed to escape the island, Nette lies tied to a bed in a small cell. A doctor enters, cold and powerful. Nette repeatedly asks him not to touch her—including not to rape her or to take away the child she is expecting. He does not answer. Nette stops him from raping her by biting off a piece of his ear but cannot stop the abortion and sterilization. Before the intervention, the doctor nods to a framed portrait of the man who created the Danish social reform in 1933 and states—simultaneously degrading Nette and justifying his own actions: "Now we send our regards to K.K. Steincke. We cannot have too many underperformers [. . .] for the welfare society to work." The scene not only gives a frightfully clear motive for the crime thriller's revenge story and its discourse on justice, but also presents the ideology behind the doctor's actions and its association with the welfare state.

Apart from the extended flashbacks to 1961, the film is set in the present, revealing the persistence of ideologies regarding reproduction and on superiority and inferiority. We meet Nour, a young woman from an immigrant family, in a precarity scene early in the film. She enters a private clinic with her friend. Nour is insecure: "Perhaps I should wait. I don't feel safe here." She is about to have an abortion, feeling it is her only option, fearing that her father will kill her if he finds out. She lets the doctor go ahead. Placed at this point, the scene gives the viewer a cold feeling of vulnerability, of desperation and compulsion, increased by the combination of shots of her being given sedatives, of the bare room with the medical apparatus that she is surrendering to, plus the eerie formality of the dialogue and the music.

Later, the viewer will know that there is more, that Nour will be unknowingly sterilized. The procedure is done by the doctor who half a century earlier did the same to Nette. He follows the same line of reasoning as earlier, but now targeting immigrants and for a private foundation instead of the welfare state.

In this film it becomes clear, although perhaps not clear enough, that the welfare state has its share of responsibility and guilt. Nette asks to be free, to keep her child, and later to get justice for what was done to her. Her doctors and the welfare state deny her that. Nour is not directly harmed by the welfare state, as Nette is, but the film suggests that she becomes dependent on the charity of a private clinic because the welfare state is not there to help her.[14] It is clear that

---

14 Lars Trägårdh, Per Selle, Lars Skov Henriksen, and Hanna Hallin, "Inledning: Civilsamhället klämt mellan stat och kapital: välfärd, mångfald, framtid," in *Civilsamhället klämt mellan stat och kapital: välfärd, mångfald, framtid*, ed. Lars Trägårdh, Per Selle, Lars Skov Henriksen, and Hanna Hallin (Stockholm: SNS förlag, 2013), 25.

the seemingly altruistic clinic is not governed by welfare state ethics—equality and caring for its citizens—but by an ideology hostile towards immigrants. Leaving room for this is a failure of the welfare state.

Although these crimes and supremacist ideologies are revealed, the film and its crime thriller approach allow the seriousness of it to be somewhat softened (but not entirely concealed). Boe explains the dynamic between genre-driven pleasure and exploration of dark themes:

> [B]ecause of the genre's conventions you are allowed to explore the most macabre, the most evil, the most morbid that humanity can offer, and everyone sits there enjoying it with their big popcorn [. . .]. Had it been within another genre, people would have run away, screaming, and no one would have seen it, but because it is a crime film which has some conventions [. . .] we are able to tell some really, really coarse things about ourselves as humans, our existence and our society.[15]

These conventions, also discussed by Langkjær, involve the focus on police officers where their goal-oriented uncovering of crimes shifts the focus, to some degree, away from the young female victims and how they suffer traumas. The strong emotions in and following the precarity scenes motivate action, but the emotional consequences are not equally foregrounded. Instead, in terms of closure, the film formulates a rather optimistic ending. It is satisfying to see Nette sitting comfortably in a house in Spain and watching the news, with a faint smile, seeing how the crimes are uncovered and the doctor and his associates put to justice. It is equally satisfying to see Nour, and others like her, take courage and talk in public media about their experiences, denouncing the doctors and their helpers in the bureaucracy.

There is a great difference between *Journal 64* and the picaresque comedy *The Hundred-Year-Old Man* and its brief sequence relating to eugenics. In a flashback to the 1930s, the young Allan has been placed in a mental institution because he accidentally killed a man. Lundborg, a doctor—apparently named after Herman Lundborg, who instituted and lead the state Institute for Race Biology, founded in 1922[16]—seeks to determine what may have caused Allan's violent behavior. He compares Allan's facial traits with two portrait photographs, of a Sami and a "negro" (sic!). Unable to see any clear similarities, he is puzzled, but

---

15 Christoffer Boe, interviewed by Daniel Bentien, "Krimien er en dejlig fribillet til livets grumhed," *Kino.dk*, Youtube, October 18, 2018, https://www.youtube.com/watch?v=QO5TIR8p2BQ.
16 Gunnar Broberg and Mattias Tydén, "Eugenics in Sweden: Efficient Care," in *Eugenics and the Welfare State: Sterilization Policy in Denmark, Sweden, Norway, and Finland*, ed. Gunnar Broberg and Nils Roll-Hansen (East Lansing, MI: Michigan State University Press, 1996), 87.

nevertheless decides to "play it safely," and consequently and casually performs a vasectomy on Allan. Afterwards, Allan leaves the institution while his voice-over (as an old man) ponders that perhaps the professor's hands were a bit unsteady, but the operation was still a success, and he never regretted it.

This is not a precarity scene. Allan never asks for help. Not because he cannot, or because asking will be pointless, but because it does not occur to him that this will cause him harm. The whole matter is made light of, not only through the humorous and trivializing dialogue but also through the mise-en-scène, with absurd facial comparisons, casually performing surgery in an elegant office while simultaneously having a coffee break, etc. (It should be noted, however, that not only the negative consequences of eugenics are trivialized, but also the credibility of Lundborg and racial biology is undermined.) Taking the precarity out of a scene like this makes for an entirely different experience than what we saw in *Journal 64*, comedy instead of passion and suffering. Also, the scene is void of social or psychological realism, its function being to characterize Allan and contribute to the film's overall comic mood. Still, in its own way, a scene such as this can also be effective in drawing attention to a not much talked about part of national history.

Like *The 100-Year-Old Man*, *Sami Blood* is also partly set in the 1930s. It follows the young Sami girl Elle-Marja as she breaks away from her Sami culture and challenges race hierarchies in order to pursue education and become a teacher. As in *The 100-Year-Old Man*, representatives from the Institute for Race Biology in Uppsala also play a role in *Sami Blood*. They have traveled far to visit Elle-Marja's Sami school. Not out of care or interest, as she believes, but to make observations and measurements of her presumably inferior race and culture. In *Sami Blood* the comic mood of *The 100-Year-Old Man* is replaced by psychological realism and an embodied experience of being subjected to a demeaning and discriminatory treatment by authorities she thought would show her respect and interest. Stylistically, a series of bright flashes from the institute photographer's camera and the strongly foregrounded sound of the flashes, are combined with images of Elle-Marja's exposed body and of close-ups of her sad, angry, defiant, deluded face. The resulting subjective and embodied experience of humiliation is effectively communicated to the viewer (Figs. 1 and 2).

In *Border* there are no flashbacks or a protagonist who has experienced (and remembered) a eugenic institution. Still, together with *Sami Blood* it might be the film that most strongly shares an enduring embodied experience of eugenics. There is no looking back at the past with forgiving eyes, as in *The 100-Year-Old Man*, or through the knowledge that past and present crimes will be uncovered and prosecuted, as in *Journal 64*. Instead, there is, as in *Sami Blood*, a strong feeling that past injustices are inscribed in the body and identity of those who are still alive. Everything essential about the main character Tina, who is a troll (a

Fig. 1: Observing Others and determining difference in Hundraåringen som klev ut genom fönstret och försvann (The Hundred-Year-Old Man Who Climbed Out the Window and Disappeared, Felix Herngren, 2013).

Fig. 2: Hundraåringen som klev ut genom fönstret och försvann (The Hundred-Year-Old Man Who Climbed Out the Window and Disappeared, Felix Herngren, 2013) and in Sameblod (Sami Blood, Amanda Kernell, 2016).

human-like being in Nordic folklore, often big, mean, and ugly, and also not particularly clever) but adopted by humans and raised as a human, was kept away from her: her troll identity, body, culture. Learning about this only when she is a grown-up woman is beyond understanding or forgiving.

There is no precarity scene. The agony of her real parents at St Jacob's mental institution is not shown. Her adoptive father succinctly informs that Tina's parents, and trolls like them, had their children taken away, that they usually did not live long, that they were buried behind the church. Without visualization, but guided by seeing Tina's restrained but apparent pain, the viewer simulates their suffering and the ungraspable ideology behind it.

Apart from the different practices, these four films differ in how they arrange their oscillation between the past and the present. The most light-hearted approach is in *The Hundred-Year-Old Man*, where the troubling episode is securely situated as something that happened at one point in the past and anyway had no significance. Both *Journal 64* and *Sami Blood* show their protagonists (also) as ageing women, as survivors, able to look back to their past. *Journal 64* makes a mystery of Nette being still alive, and when she is eventually found and tells her story it is one of grief but also including good years later. In contrast, *Sami Blood* shows how leaving her family and traditions, and remembering all injustices, has left Elle-Marja with wounds that never healed. Similarly, comparable emotions are formed not only in *Beyond* but also in *Border* as Tina vicariously senses how her parents and her race were treated and regarded. It is done differently, but in their own way these contemporary framings of the past contribute to our memories of it.

Identity and Individuality

If the previous four films related to traumatic historical events, the two following, Joachim Trier's *Thelma* (2017) and Iram Haq's *Hva vil folk si?* (*What Will People Say?*, 2017), are contemporary stories focusing on identity and individuality. The precarious situations concern two young women, their emotions and close relations—both family and romance/sexuality. In *What Will People Say?*, Pakistani-Norwegian Nisha is seeing a Norwegian boy, which upsets her father to the extent that he beats up the boyfriend, and later kidnaps his daughter and takes her to Pakistan to make her get to know his (and her) culture. In *Thelma*, Thelma has just left her parents in rural Vestlandet and moved to Oslo to study where she falls in love with Anja. This is complicated by her father's conservative religiousness and by Thelma's feature of having supernatural powers that can make people disappear, including her girlfriend Anja. Both films—and both precarity scenes—focus on a destructive daughter-father relationship, but they present it quite differently; one more aligned with social realism, the other with art film.

In *What Will People Say?* Nisha is trapped in a car and pleads to her brother: "Asif, help me! I don't want to!" Just a few minutes earlier she was happy and hopeful. After a call from her mother, she was looking forward to leaving the emergency social shelter where she stayed since her father had beaten her boyfriend. She is looking forward to being reunited with her family and to settling everything. Expecting to replace the welfare state's care with that of her family, she rushes into the car and drives away with her father and brother. However, when her father sternly lectures her about how she has brought shame on him, herself, and their family, when her father throws away her mobile phone, and when she realizes they are not heading home, she becomes afraid and wants to get out of the car and escape from whatever plans they have for her. But she cannot. And her brother cannot help her.

What Will People Say? is an example of social realism. Haq, who used her own traumatic experiences when she wrote the story about Nisha, could very well have emphasized the individual experience in the manner of psychological realism but instead strived to understand the social structures and everyone's perspective. This includes the film's father. Instead of making him an ominous power, impossible to understand, the film shows that he too is constrained by pressures from community and tradition. Haq regards everyone within a (Pakistani) community as being confined and unable to break free:

> For me, it was very important to understand their point of view. And I understood that in these types of oppressive family structures, everyone—both the parents and the children—is in this kind of jail because they are all more focused on what other people may think instead of on doing what's good for them.[17]

The result is a narration where in each scene it is possible to understand each character's choices. In the precarity scene the controlling patriarchal power is obvious, but it is also clear how insecure the father is, caught between his care for his daughter and the pressure from their community.

The precarity scene in *Thelma* is quite different. Thelma sits on her knees praying to God, her father standing behind her. She asks the dear Lord and heavenly Father to have mercy on her, to purify her heart, and to redeem her by the holy ghost. Continuing, she declares her anger, with God and with her father, and goes on to say that her father "has to stop. I can't bear it any longer." Instead of God it is her father who answers. He makes Thelma become confused about her feelings for Anja and Anja's feelings for her, exposing them as selfishness and coercion. Thelma remains passive, endures a bit longer, because of the drugs her father gives her and her insecurity about who she is and how to handle the powers she has.

If *What Will People Say?* could be characterized as a nuanced social realist film, *Thelma* mixes film practices in a complex exploration of subjectivity. It does not quite belong within social realism or classical narration but has more elements in common with art film and psychological realism. *Thelma* explores the psychology of Thelma's desires, but the addition of supernatural elements (and framing these within a tradition of regarding independent and knowledgeable women as witches) distracts from a social and psychological view on Thelma, her parents, and Anja, and it devalues the social contexts surrounding them. Instead of departing from or mimicking real experiences, as *What Will People Say?* does, Thelma's existential conflicts are explored using devices from both genre filmmaking and art film.

---

17 Iram Haq, interviewed by Arnau Salvadó, "Rebellious, wise and free," *Metal* (no date), https://metalmagazine.eu/en/post/interview/iram-haq-rebellious-wise-and-free.

Trier has described the process of creating *Thelma* (together with co-screenwriter Eskil Vogt) as moving from the kind of experience they strived for, to finding the means to achieve it:

> We decided early on about a certain vibe, mood, [. . .] a genre [. . .] to open up for more nightmarish scenes, concepts, spaces, moods that were darker, more sinister, more occult, to try to liberate ourselves in terms of form for what kind of story we could tell. And after a while of talking about all these kinds of set pieces, or ideas of under water, and snakes and all these images it came to us we also realized that at the core of it there was still that human character-driven story of a young woman who needs to be herself, to liberate herself from her father, so I think it is a classical human tale.[18]

It is, of course, an anecdotal example and although Trier mentions the young woman and her struggles only after first mentioning genre, effects, moods etc., this does not necessarily mean that she is less important. Still, what Trier says captures a particular approach to telling stories about a person in a precarious situation. *Thelma* can be seen as a genre film, but with several features—such as the existential conflict, the narrative ambiguities, and the protagonist's search for meaning—common in art film traditions.

Both Thelma and Nisha are dependent on and subordinated to their families in a very harmful way. As mentioned earlier, Scandinavian welfare states aim for a direct relationship with individuals, partly to secure independence from families in situations like these. Nisha's contacts with the welfare state are realistically motivated, part of the film's social realism, but also part of how the film articulates the differences between two value systems between which Nisha has to navigate. The social welfare workers Nisha meets on a few occasions not only offer her shelter, physical independence from family, but also assert her right, as a Norwegian, to act differently than her family wants. She is not to blame and should feel no guilt. The film, in its nuanced social realism and its precarity scene, makes clear how well everyone is aware of this, but how difficult it still is to embrace a new culture and lifestyle, and to let go of another.

In *Thelma*, the most important welfare state institution is the hospital where Thelma goes to find out what causes her epileptic seizures. In contrast to *What Will People Say?*, Thelma's hospital visit does not clarify anything in terms of social situation or regarding her bodily weakness. Instead, it is a setting for a *tour de force* montage sequence and a consultation with the doctor that introduces clues to the plot construction and to a psychoanalytic reading of Thelma.

---

[18] Joachim Trier, interviewed by Scout Tafoya, "Video Interview: Joachim Trier on 'Thelma'," *RogerEbert.com*, November 11, 2017, https://www.rogerebert.com/interviews/video-interview-joachim-trier-on-thelma.

The fundamental difference between the films' views on identity and individualism is concisely contrasted through the questions in the title *What Will People Say?* and in *Thelma's* poster tag line, "Do you dare being the one you are?" The former regards a community's restricting norms whereas the later turns existentialist concerns into a question of personal choice and courage.

Help Without Precarity Scenes

In Aki Kaurismäki's film *Toivon tuolla puolen* (*The Other Side of Hope*, 2017), the key precarity scene is positioned in relation to the protocols of international agreements on human rights. Although the scene is of fundamental importance, driving the narration through the first part of the film, it is nevertheless the absence of precarity scenes on several later occasions that allows the film's humanistic sensibility to permeate the story, written in the wake of the refugee crisis of 2015.

The Other Side of Hope opens with a sequence relating how the Syrian refugee Khaled arrives in Finland in a boatload of coal, and how he, in a typical matter-of-fact Kaurismäkian scene, finds a police station, enters, hands over his passport, and asks for asylum. This is the prescribed way for refugees to ask for help, and Kaurismäki goes on to detail procedures: Khaled being brought to a cell, moved to a refugee center, investigations of his story about how he escaped from Syria, and, after due deliberation, being summoned to the migration agency only to learn that he is denied asylum and will be deported the following day. Kaurismäki contrasts the migration agency's view that Syria is now safe enough for Khaled to return to, with contradicting television news covering air strikes against hospitals and civilians. The film argues that official procedures for asking and administering help are just that—procedures—and that these will not help a person in need.

The remaining part of the film gradually affirms an alternative to relying on the welfare state or international bureaucracy for help. The ensuing absence of precarity scenes is aligned with Kaurismäki's laconic and linguistically sparse style—gently moving viewers a step or two away from mainstream storytelling and into his own auteurist brand, where only the essentials of a situation are shown. But eliding precarity scenes goes beyond sustaining a brand of filmmaking. It is a strategy that invites viewers first to experience surprise, then to realize that someone has recognized Khaled's need and offered help, and finally and importantly, to conclude that this is just how all of us should act towards one another. Two examples: First, in the refugee center on the morning he will be deported, Khaled makes his bed, packs his things, and appears to walk towards the arriving officers. Now, however, a woman working at the asylum center unlocks a door so Khaled can get away. This surprise, accompanied by lovely Finnish rock music, grants the viewer a moment of relief. Second, soon afterwards, Khaled awakes exhausted outside of a restaurant, has a brief argument and exchange of nose-punches with the restaurant owner before the next scene shows him at a table being served a meal by the restaurant crew. The owner asks him: "Wanna work, Khaled?" Khaled gratefully accepts. With additional situations like this in the film, Khaled will get what he, and indeed any human, would need: First, freedom (in a country without war), food, and a job. Later, identity and family. In Kaurismäki's film, Khaled never explicitly asks for any of this—at least not after he asked for asylum. Instead, viewers are invited to see and feel what Khaled needs, what anyone else in his situation would need, and to re-learn that what the refugee center worker, the restaurant owner, and others do is both right and natural.

The contrast is clear. The welfare state and official international agreements respond to precarity with detached procedures that involve waiting, bureaucracy, limited freedom, and ultimately a return to despair. Ordinary citizens respond by granting what is needed. Omitting precarity scenes is significant. It lets audiences construct characters who can see the pain and need of others, who respond to it with empathy, and who extend an offer of help. As if it were human to do so. In Kaurismäki's world it is, and viewers may wonder if our world could not also be like that.

A similar approach to helping others is found in Mika Kaurismäki's most recent film, *Mestari Cheng* (*Master Cheng*, 2019). Here too, it is striking how generous people can be without being required to help, without compensation, or without even being asked. In the film, the Chinese cook Cheng happens to visit an uninspiring diner along a Lapland countryside road, when a busload of hungry Chinese tourists unexpectedly appears. Cheng sees that Sirkka, the diner's owner, is not able to provide them with food, at least not food they would enjoy. Cheng simply steps up, says "I can help," and then proceeds to do just that. Afterward, Sirkka offers to pay him, but he declines, saying that there is no need, and motivating it with "I cook, you happy, the Chinese people happy, everybody happy." The logic is simple. And, as in *The Other Side of Hope*, viewers vicariously experience the pleasure of altruistically having done something good.

In *On the Other Side of Hope* Khaled is integrated into the workings of the restaurant and, it appears, within Finnish society. Ordinary citizens have granted him asylum—a place of refuge. *Master Cheng* goes further. Beyond confirming that a foreigner, quite naturally, can be accommodated in Finnish society, it foregrounds how foreign culture—Cheng's skills, traditions and personality—breaks stagnation and enriches Finnish society. Cheng's cooking secures the diner's economy, it enlivens the citizens, and it brings personal happiness to himself, his son, and Sirkka.

None of these films can be comfortably characterized as arthouse, realist, or mainstream cinema. At least partly, it seems, this lies in the characters and their agency. They are not arthouse characters dealing with internal struggles that are difficult to understand, they are not goal-oriented in the way mainstream cinema characters usually are, and the situations, and how characters respond to them, are not quite what you would expect in realist filmmaking. Instead, the characters are designed to show, clearly and simply, people who need help and people who still know how to offer it.

Approaching Realism from Reality

Although I have already discussed films with a realist aesthetics, I would like to conclude with *Engelen* (*Angel*, Margreth Olin, 2009) and *Lof mér að falla* (*Let Me Fall*, Baldvin Zophoníasson, 2018), two films even more firmly positioned within realism.

Apart from both films' tragic drug addiction stories, they have in common Olin's and Z's urge to engage with reality—with little explored and very dark sides of reality. Baldvin Z saw "a whole world in Iceland that I didn't know about, and I decided to delve deeper into it. I met the girls living on the streets and doing drugs. They allowed us to enter their lives and follow them for one year."[19] Somewhat differently, the already well-established documentary filmmaker Olin followed a mother and daughter over a period of two years, before concluding that it would be too sensitive to make a documentary about them. Instead, Olin invented a new family and explored its damaging relations in what would be her fiction film debut. Still, the film is grounded in the same observations of reality and the strong conviction that this is an urgent story to tell.

In the precarity scene in *Angel*, Lea, a young mother, visits a doctor and asks him to take her one-year-old daughter: "I am not fit to be a mother. I am addicted to heroin. I want someone else to take care of her." The social services arrange for a foster family to take in the girl. A social and psychological realist film, it allows us to understand this scene, and Lea's painful plea, as formed by Lea having experienced not only how families (in this case particularly mothers, including Lea herself) can fail to care for their children (or indeed for themselves) but also how

---

[19] Baldvin Zophoníasson, interviewed by Vassilis Economou, "Baldvin Z • Director," *Cineuropa*, September 21, 2018, https://cineuropa.org/en/interview/360691.

the welfare state can provide help, but will not impose it on you unless you ask and are ready to receive it. Lea asks for help. Her daughter needs to receive it.

Interviewed in relation to one of her earlier films, Olin describes the importance of observing "life as it is" but also that it must be presented in an appropriate form:

> I thought that life must appear as it is with all the contradictions that exist in life. And if there is one thing that film is capable of, it is to convey what a human life is and what affects a human life. And if we relate only to the lies or the sunny side of it, it is not interesting to me. These are not the movies I want to see or make.[20]

Olin's thoughts also permeate Z's *Let Me Fall*. The film sees Stella and Magnea through their first experiences with drugs, years of addiction, and times of relief, to the end when Stella decides to take her own life. I will foreground this last scene, rather than a proper precarity scene, suggesting a resemblance with Lea and her decision in *Angel*.

Most viewers will be both surprised and very distressed when Stella takes her life. She appears to have settled down, she has a job, a good home together with her partner, and many years have passed since she last used drugs or alcohol. It also seems fair, somehow, that she should have a good life. If all hope for Magnea is lost—she will never recover from her addiction—then at least one of them should make it? This film does not, however, aim to satisfy audiences' sense of fairness or wishes for a soothing closure. The end of Stella's life, and of the film, is a consequence of too many dark moments—introducing Magnea to drugs, lying to her, trading her for drugs, and so many other unforgivable and unforgettable acts. When Stella realizes this, and when viewers realize it too, suicide is graspable. It is a surprise, distressing, one of "all the contradictions that exist in life"— but nonetheless ominously true to social and psychological realism.

Conclusions

The focus so far has been on texts, precarity scenes, and their functions within the film. The analysis has concerned how precarity is screened, both revealed and concealed, and how textual strategies within general film practices are employed. This concluding discussion will include brief contextual remarks, audience figures, and notes for further research.

---

[20] Quoted from *Närbild: Margreth Olin*. Prod. Agneta Zandin/SVT2. Sweden, 2004.

The first two films are among the most successful films on their markets over the past few decades, *Journal 64* with close to 800,000 viewers in Denmark and *The 100-Year-Old Man* with over one and a half million viewers in Sweden.[21] Apart from belonging to popular genres, both films benefit from adapting top selling novels, using stars and experienced filmmakers—important parts of any package aiming for large audiences.[22] Their precarity scenes are inserted into goal-oriented plots ending with a satisfactory closure, and audiences are unlikely to leave cinemas with unsettling thoughts about the serious situations they have seen.

Both films share a focus on male protagonists, whereas all other films in this selective study have female protagonists. This suggests, unsurprisingly, an alignment between male protagonists and bigger, more popular, and more generic productions, and between female protagonists and stories told within realist or art film practices. Many of these women are young (even children), represent a marginalized race, ethnicity, or sexuality, and although not all belong to the weakest groups in society, most come from families with limited economic resources and precarious working conditions—suggesting that an intersectional perspective would be rewarding in an extended study of precarity scenes.

Following these two classically narrated genre films, *Beyond* and *Sami Blood* are realist films emphasizing serious structural conflicts in a welfare state context. The films give, practically for the first time in Sweden, a large national audience (close to 400,000 and 200,000 viewers respectively) access to Swedish minority identities (Finnish migrants and Sami) and conflicts they faced in the evolving welfare state. The focus on the past is both interesting and rewarding, showing that although Leena and Elle-Marja have now overcome structural challenges, their trauma remains. Focusing on the past may, however, suggest that all is well today—revealing past precarities but concealing contemporary structural problems.

---

21 All audience figures are from the LUMIERE Database on admissions of films released in Europe, http://lumiere.obs.coe.int.
22 Jussi Adler-Olsen and Jonas Josefsson are top bestselling authors, Christoffer Boe and, even more, Felix Herngren, are both well-known filmmakers, whereas Nikolaj Lie Kaas, Fares Fares, and Robert Gustafsson are among the many stars present in these films. It is particularly interesting to note the similarities between *Journal 64* and the immensely successful *The Girl with the Dragon Tattoo* that came a few years earlier (both Stieg Larsson's novel *Män som hatar kvinnor* (2005) and its adaptation by Niels Arden Oplev (2009)). Here too, we see racist and misogynic thoughts and actions in a contemporary crime thriller, where part of the story and crimes take place in the past. Similarly and reassuringly, here too, there appears to be far fewer perpetrators than would be expected.

Border and *Thelma* cast their precarity themes in a form blending art film, existential questions, genres, and supernatural elements with features from realism—an entertaining mix also visible in the films' trailers. A further study on marketing and reception of similar films could well include an *auteur* perspective. *Border*, marketed with its Cannes award and references to a successful previous adaptation of the same author, sold over 100,000 tickets in Sweden, a good number for an existentialist troll crime drama. Regarding *Thelma*, this is Trier's fourth feature, and since 60,000 viewers compares with his earlier art films, it seems that *Thelma's* genre elements contributed more to the film's art narration than to reaching new audience groups. In contrast to Trier, Boe—whose first films also were art films—fully embraces genre conventions, making *Journal 64* an effective crime thriller. The differences between *Thelma* and *Journal 64* are reflected in the films and in the audiences. Internationally, Trier's genre art film has a wider distribution, more festival screenings, and even a somewhat larger audience.

The Other Side of Hope and *Master Cheng* were both seen by some 50,000 viewers in Finland, a rather modest number, but still a position on the market that can be expected for films that deal with topical and weighty subjects in a mode that allows for moments of reflection, rather than one that is fully melodramatic or generic. On a European level, however, *The Other Side of Hope* reached over 800,000 viewers, facilitated by the premiere at the Berlinale and, more importantly, by the long-established position of Aki Kaurismäki as an auteur, well-known to European arthouse distributors, cinemas, and audiences. When, for example, *The Hollywood Reporter* describes him as a "filmmaker unerringly sure of his distinctive voice," known for adapting "pressing social issues to his unmistakable worldview with tonally rich results," and predicts that the film is "[s]ure to entice the Kaurismaki faithful to international movie theaters," it highlights just how important auteur following is to allow topics like this to reach an audience.[23] As a contrast, *Master Cheng*, made by a more prolific but still lessknown filmmaker, was successful (with 100,000 admissions) only on the German market, where it won an important local award, but did not reach international cinema audiences elsewhere.

The remaining three films are set in contemporary society, with a rather straightforward realist style, without any supernatural or art film elements. They are not based on literature, but on direct experiences, and they more

---

[23] David Rooney, "'The Other Side of Hope' ('Toivon tuolla puolen'): Film Review | Berlin 2017," *The Hollywood Reporter*, February 14, 2017, https://www.hollywoodreporter.com/movies/movie-reviews/other-side-of-hope-berlin-2017-975923.

generally reflect the filmmakers' ambitions to represent parts of our reality that we rarely see screened.

A film with a rough and realistic depiction of persons in vulnerable situations tends to have a small budget, a limited release, and consequently few viewers. *Angel, What Will People Say?*, and *Let Me Fall* show that this is not always true. Both *Angel* and *What Will People Say?* sold more than 100,000 tickets in Norway, and *Let Me Fall* reached over 53,000 viewers on the tiny Icelandic market—placing it among the most successful local films of any genre during the past decades. The reasons are unclear, as always. They would include the filmmakers' reputation, but also the emphatic approach to an urgent and seriously treated matter. Z has said that he

> wanted the audience to experience the same feelings [as the persons depicted]. I wanted to make a long film and I wanted the audience to suffer in the film. They are in an emotional roller coaster, holding them as long as possible, and leaving them sad after the film.[24]

In *Let Me Fall* both individual and structural conflicts remain unresolved and there is no comforting closure—there is no reason for viewers to believe that what they have just seen on the screen will not be present also in the society they return to when they leave the cinema.

To conclude, let us contrast this with *Journal 64*'s goal-oriented plot centered on investigating crimes and its poetic justice closure. Boe is right that crime thrillers can show "really bad things about ourselves as humans [but that then] the lights are turned on and you go out [. . .]. It is a lovely free pass to the cruelty of life, that still doesn't cost you more than a cinema ticket."[25]

What Boe says is true for all films and all precarity scenes discussed here; audiences are offered the cruelty of life for the price of a cinema ticket. But costs, and rewards, are not only measured in money. Depending on who the filmmaker is and on the film practices used, there can also be an emotional price to pay. And worrying insights to gain.

---

24 Sólrún Freyja Sen, "Baldvin Z – 'Alltaf ætlunin að láta áhorfendum líða illa'," *DV*, November 11, 2018, https://www.dv.is/fokus/2018/11/11/baldvin-z-alltaf-aetlunin-ad-lata-ahorfendum-lida-illa.

25 Boe, Christoffer, interviewed by Daniel Bentien. "Krimien er en dejlig fribillet til livets grumhed." Kino.dk, *Youtube*, October 18, 2018.

Bibliography

Abbasi, Ali. "Sommar: Ali Abbasi." *Sveriges radio*, August 5, 2019. https://sverigesradio.se/avsnitt/1319480.

Berggren, Henrik, and Lars Trägårdh. "Pippi Longstocking: The autonomous child and the moral logic of the Swedish welfare state." In *Swedish Modernism: Architecture, Consumption and the Welfare State,* ed. Helena Mattsson and Sven-Olov Wallenstein. London: Black Dog, 2010, 50–65.

Becker, Katrine. *Sprogø: Lidt om kvindeanstalten på Sprogø.* Slagelse: Dansk Forsorgshistorisk Museum, no year.

Boe, Christoffer, interviewed by Daniel Bentien. "Krimien er en dejlig fribillet til livets grumhed." Kino.dk, *Youtube*, October 18, 2018. https://www.youtube.com/watch?v=QO5TlR8p2BQ.

Broberg, Gunnar, and Nils Roll-Hansen, eds. *Eugenics and the Welfare State: Sterilization Policy in Denmark, Sweden, Norway, and Finland.* East Lansing, MI: Michigan State University Press, 1996.

Broberg, Gunnar, and Mattias Tydén. "Eugenics in Sweden: Efficient Care." In *Eugenics and the Welfare State: Sterilization Policy in Denmark, Sweden, Norway, and Finland*, ed. Gunnar Broberg and Nils Roll-Hansen. East Lansing: Michigan State University Press, 1996, 77–150.

Haq, Iram, interviewed by Arnau Salvadó. "Rebellious, wise and free." *Metal* (no date). https://metalmagazine.eu/en/post/interview/iram-haq-rebellious-wise-and-free.

Hilson, Mary. "The Nordic Welfare Model." In *Introduction to Nordic Cultures*, ed. Annika Lindskog and Jakob Stougaard-Nielsen. London: UCL Press, 2020, 70–83.

Langkjær, Birger. "Realism as a third film practice." *MedieKultur: Journal of Media and Communication Research*, vol. 27, no. 51 (2011): 40–54.

Online Etymology Dictionary. "Precarious." *Etymonline*. Accessed January 31, 2022. https://www.etymonline.com/search?q=precarious.

Rooney, David. "'The Other Side of Hope' ('Toivon tuolla puolen'): Film Review | Berlin 2017." *The Hollywood Reporter*, February 14, 2017. https://www.hollywoodreporter.com/movies/movie-reviews/other-side-of-hope-berlin-2017-975923.

Sen, Sólrún Freyja. "Baldvin Z – 'Alltaf ætlunin að láta áhorfendum líða illa'." *DV*, November 11, 2018. https://www.dv.is/fokus/2018/11/11/baldvin-z-alltaf-aetlunin-ad-lata-ahorfendum-lida-illa.

Thorén Björling, Sanna. "Pernilla August." *Dagens Nyheter*, March 2, 2011. https://www.dn.se/arkiv/kultur/pernilla-august/.

Trier, Joachim, interviewed by Scout Tafoya. "Video Interview: Joachim Trier on 'Thelma'." *RogerEbert.com*, November 11, 2017. https://www.rogerebert.com/interviews/video-interview-joachim-trier-on-thelma.

Trägårdh, Lars, Per Selle, Lars Skov Henriksen, and Hanna Hallin. "Inledning: Civilsamhället klämt mellan stat och kapital: välfärd, mångfald, framtid." *Civilsamhället klämt mellan stat och kapital: välfärd, mångfald, framtid*, ed. Lars Trägårdh, Per Selle, Lars Skov Henriksen, and Hanna Hallin. Stockholm: SNS förlag, 2013, 9–29.

Zophoníasson, Baldvin, interviewed by Vassilis Economou. "Baldvin Z • Director." *Cineuropa*, September 21, 2018. https://cineuropa.org/en/interview/360691.

Williams, Linda. *Screening Sex*. Durham, NC/London: Duke University Press, 2008.

Filmography

Engelen (*Angel*). Dir. Margreth Ohlin. Norway/Sweden/Finland, 2009.
Gräns (*Border*). Dir. Ali Abbasi. Sweden/Denmark, 2018.
Hundraåringen som klev ut genom fönstret och försvann (*The Hundred-Year-Old Man Who Climbed Out the Window and Disappeared*). Dir. Felix Herngren. Sweden, 2013.
Hva vil folk si? (*What Will People Say?*). Dir. Iram Haq. Norway, 2017.
Journal 64. Dir. Christoffer Boe. Denmark/Germany, 2018.
Lof mér að falla (*Let Me Fall*). Dir. Baldvin Zophoníasson. Iceland/Finland/Germany, 2018.
Män som hatar kvinnor (*The Girl with the Dragon Tattoo*). Dir. Niels Arden Oplev. Sweden/Norway/Denmark/Germany, 2009.
Mestari Cheng (*Master Cheng*). Dir. Mika Kaurismäki. Finland/China, 2019.
Närbild: Margreth Olin. Prod. Agneta Zandin/SVT2. Sweden, 2004.
Sameblod (*Sami Blood*). Dir. Amanda Kernell. Sweden/Norway/Denmark, 2016.
Svinalängorna (*Beyond*). Dir. Pernilla August. Sweden/Finland/Denmark, 2010.
Thelma. Dir. Joachim Trier. Norway/France/Sweden/Denmark, 2017.
Toivon tuolla puolen (*The Other Side of Hope*). Dir. Aki Kaurismäki. Finland/Germany, 2017.

John Hill
Working-Class Precarity and the Social-Realist Tradition in British Cinema

Although it has become common in British film studies to emphasize the variety of artistic traditions that compose the history of British filmmaking, the association of British cinema with realism has remained a recurring feature. The emergence of the realist tradition in Britain is typically associated with the rise of the documentary film movement in the 1930s and the subsequent fusion of documentary and fiction techniques in feature filmmaking during the Second World War. As Raymond Williams famously argued, the "realist intention" has been rooted in a drive towards "social extension" and the making visible of social groups hitherto underrepresented within the prevailing representational regimes.[1] As such, realism in British cinema has characteristically gravitated towards the representation of the working class and, in many cases, those sections of the working class that are seen to be the most economically and socially disadvantaged. As a result it has generally been films located within the realist, or documentary-realist, tradition that have most commonly engaged with the economic insecurity and vulnerability—or precarity—to which the working class has historically been subjected.

However, while it can be argued that a concern with the condition of the working class has been something of a constant within the British realist tradition, the modes of aesthetic practice and social outlook that have constituted this tradition have also been subject to change. As Stuart Hall has argued, referring to the documentary movement of the 1930s, the emphasis upon the observation of reality has not simply rested on the adoption of a particular "style" but also an underpinning "social rhetoric" rooted in the social and economic conditions of the time.[2] Viewed in this light, the history of realist filmmaking practice reveals a double movement that involves the revision and reworking of aesthetic practices—as conceptions of realism change and prevailing representational regimes mutate—alongside shifts in the socio-economic "rhetorics," or discursive formations, that both inform and are mobilized by such practices. The history of representing precarity in British cinema may therefore also be viewed through this prism, revealing elements of continuity but also of changing socio-historical perspective.

---

1 Raymond Williams, "A Lecture on Realism," *Screen* 18, no. 1 (1977), 63.
2 Stuart Hall, "The Social Eye of the *Picture Post*," *Working Papers in Cultural Studies*, no. 2 (1972), 100.

While debates about precarity and precariousness have gained particular momentum due to the socio-economic changes occurring since the 1980s, historians of these concepts have demonstrated their lengthy lineage. Eloisa Betti, for example, identifies references to precariousness in the work of Marx and Engels (who regarded the precarious condition of labor as a key feature of proletarianization) as well as in the writings of Victorian reformers such as Henty Mayhew and Charles Booth.[3] This awareness of the enduring character of precariousness has, in turn, generated a discussion of how far precarity may be understood to be a novel condition rather than a constant feature of capitalism. Jan Bremen and Marcel van der Linden, for example, argue that while the strengthening of labor rights and growth of social security in the third quarter of the twentieth century—especially in the Global North—considerably improved the condition of the working class, "insecurity, informality or precariousness" has remained the "real norm or standard in global capitalism."[4] Without entering into the specifics of this debate, the discussion that follows, by beginning with the 1930s, accepts the value of taking a longer view of precarity but also recognizes the significance of subsequent economic and political shifts for both the restructuring of British society and the films produced. In line with its emphasis upon the social-realist tradition rooted in changing representations of the working class, the discussion also confines itself to a consideration of the economic dimensions of precarity, and the insecurity and vulnerability it entails, rather than the more general conception of precariousness as an existential condition (that is commonly associated with the work of Judith Butler).[5]

The Documentary Movement

In his famous essay "The Course of Realism" (1938), John Grierson, the "father" of documentary, associates realism with documentary.[6] Although the more common

---

[3] Eloisa Betti, "Historicizing Precarious Work: Forty Years of Research in the Social Sciences and Humanities," *IRSH*, no. 63 (2018), 277–278.
[4] Jan Bremen and Marcel van der Linden, "Informalizing the Economy: The Return of the Social Question at a Global Level," *Development and Change* 45, no. 5 (2014), 921. In associating precariousness with a "labor regime" rather than a "social-class formation," Bremen also questions Guy Standing's conception of the "precariat" as a class-in-the-making distinct from the working class. See Jan Bremen, "A Bogus Concept," *New Left Review*, no. 84 (2013).
[5] Judith Butler, *Precarious Life: The Powers of Mourning and Violence* (London: Verso, 2004).
[6] John Grierson, "The Course of Realism," *Footnotes to the Film*, ed. Charles Davy (London: Lovat Dickson, 1938).

critical practice is to identify the conventions of realism with fiction, it was undoubtedly the documentary movement of the 1930s that established the reputation of British cinema for realist filmmaking and paved the way for the fusion of documentary and narrative techniques in British films during World War Two. In line with the impulse towards social extension, the reputation of the documentary movement in large part derived from its commitment to the presentation of the lives of ordinary, working-class people (and, in Grierson's terms, the presentation of the "workman" as an "honorable figure").[7] This could result in the de-politicization of work and economic relations. Robert Flaherty's *Industrial Britain* (1931), for example, emphasizes the contribution of "ordinary workmen" to contemporary industrial production but the film's voice-over, combined with the deployment of aestheticized imagery and "poetic" montage, is mainly concerned with establishing a continuity with rural traditions of craftsmanship and celebrating the "beautiful things" for which the "personal skill" of "English workers" is responsible. However, given the circumstances in which the documentary movement operated—an era of economic depression, mass unemployment, and working-class protest—it was also difficult to ignore the precarious conditions faced by such "ordinary workmen."

Workers and Jobs (Arthur Elton, 1935), produced for the Ministry of Labor, may have stressed the "fifteen thousand different kinds of work" available in Britain but also had to acknowledge the realities of unemployment and pressures upon those in search of work. *Housing Problems* (Arthur Elton and Edgar Anstey, 1935) vividly documented the destructive effects of slum housing in the form of poor health and the deaths of children. *Enough to Eat?* (Edgar Anstey, 1936) identifies the "millions" of working-class people who are "underfed" as a result of poverty and the ill-health and malnutrition it causes. As is often noted, the documentary movement was nevertheless constrained in its political outlook. Funded by a mix of public agencies and commercial companies, its socio-political rhetoric was reformist in character, identifying social ills that were already in the process of being addressed or alleviated. *Workers and Jobs*, for example, was also an advert for the efficiency of employment exchanges in finding work for members of the unemployed. *Housing Problems* identified the commitment of local authorities to slum clearance and the positive role of the gas industry—the film's sponsor—in providing new homes. *Enough to Eat?* looked at how the Milk Marketing Board and local councils were implementing policies designed to improve nutrition. In this respect, the films' acknowledgement of economic hardships and precarity was rooted in a fundamentally

---

7 Ibid., 152.

optimistic discourse that such problems could be alleviated through political and economic intervention. With the onset of war, this rhetoric also became embedded in the war effort and the cultivation of public morale. The mobilization of such sentiments, for example, is evident in the Ministry of Information short *The Dawn Guard* (Roy Boulting, 1941) in which two members of the Home Guard discuss what's at stake in winning the war. As one of the two men declares:

> There mustn't be no more chaps hanging around for work that don't come. No more slums neither. No more dirty filthy back streets. No more half-starved kids with no room to play in . . . We can't go back to the old way of living.

As such, ideas of the "People's War," and the experience of shared sacrifice necessitating a new form of economic dispensation, paved the way for the election of a Labour government at the end of the war committed to the nationalization of key industries, full employment, and the establishment of the welfare state. This, in turn, laid the basis of a new post-war political consensus, subscribed to by both the Conservatives and Labour parties, that rested upon a commitment to Keynesian economics, state intervention, and the proper provision of social security.

The British "New Wave" and "Affluence"

It was this new "consensus" that provided the backdrop to the next major cycle of working-class films—the British "new wave"—to emerge in the late 1950s and early 1960s. Largely welcomed for its attention to the working class in the urban-industrial midlands and north of England, films such as *Room at the Top* (Jack Clayton, 1959), *Saturday Night and Sunday Morning* (Karel Reisz, 1960), *The Loneliness of the Long Distance Runner* (Tony Richardson, 1962), and *A Kind of Loving* (John Schlesinger, 1962) portray the working class at what is taken to be a key moment of economic and social change. Although the physical reality of the cities—such as Bradford, Nottingham, and Stockport—revealed in these films provides evidence of continuing deprivation and economic inequality, the films themselves do not focus on the precarity of work or the precariousness of working-class lives, as the documentaries of the 1930s did. Workers such as Arthur Seaton in *Saturday Night and Sunday Morning* may find few satisfactions in factory work but their employment appears to be secure and relatively well-paid. The Conservative Prime Minister of the time, Harold Macmillan, had famously declared in 1957 that British people had "never had it so good" and that the country, including the "industrial towns," existed in a hitherto unknown "state of prosperity."[8] The same perception of "affluence" also informs the films of the "new wave" that generally accept the economic gains achieved by the working class but nonetheless fret about its cultural cost. To this extent, the emphasis of the films is less on the ongoing inequalities that continue to structure British society than the threat to traditional forms of working-class culture and community associated with "affluence," consumerism, mass culture, and suburbanization.

These socio-economic developments are linked with what is perceived to be a "feminization" of working-class life-styles and culture, which also means that the films extend a degree of sympathy to the virile, working-class male who pushes against the demands of embourgeoisement and social conformity. Unlike the 1930s documentaries whose forms and technologies limited their capacity to explore the inner lives of those portrayed, the "new wave" films place a new emphasis upon the relationship between economic circumstances and individual subjectivities. However, in comparison to the films that follow, it is significant that the anxieties experienced by the mainly male protagonists concern domestication and "settling down" (evident, for example, in Arthur's stone-throwing at the new housing estate at the end of *Saturday Night and Sunday Morning*) rather than the obstacles to the pursuit of "the good life" that Lauren Berlant associates with the experience of economic disadvantage and precarity in a later period.[9] For the characters of the "new wave," the economic preconditions for such a life are apparently in place but they either fail to offer a sufficient sense of personal fulfilment or are tainted by an association with the abandonment, or "betrayal," of earlier patriarchal working-class traditions (the decline of which is destined to become a recurring theme of many of the films to follow).

Post-industrial Decline

Despite their articulation of a sense of cultural loss, the films of the 1950s and 1960s still rely upon an implicit economic optimism rooted in an ideology of economic growth and increasing personal wealth. British films of the 1980s, however, begin to register a significant shift. This was, of course, the era of

---

[8] Quoted in T. F. Lindsay and Michael Harrington, *The Conservative Party: 1918–1970* (London: Allen & Unwin, 1974), 202.
[9] Lauren Berlant, *Cruel Optimism* (Durham, NC: Duke University Press, 2011).

Thatcherism and its break with the precepts of the post-war consensus. Dedicated to "rolling back" the frontiers of state and strengthening market forces, the Conservatives, under the leadership of Margaret Thatcher, embarked upon a range of measures intended to cultivate a more competitive, "flexible," internationally-oriented economy. These included the privatization of publicly owned corporations and selling-off of public assets (such as housing), the de-regulation of banking and financial services, reductions in public expenditure, tax cuts for the better-off, the weakening of trade unions and labor rights, and the abandonment of a policy of full employment. At a time when cinema audiences were shrinking, the Thatcher government, as a part of its general program, also cut state support for a weakened British film industry, making film production increasingly dependent upon television funding. The newly-launched Channel 4, in particular, was responsible for a series of "small" British films that combined the formal interests of "art cinema" with the realism and social concerns characteristic of public-service television. These films commonly sought to take the pulse of the "nation" and works such as *Letter to Brezhnev* (Chris Bernard, 1985), *Business as Usual* (Lezli-An Barrett, 1987) and *Rita, Sue and Bob Too* (Alan Clarke, 1987) followed the British "new wave" in turning to the experiences of working-class people in the north of England for a measure of what was occurring in Thatcher's Britain. Unlike the earlier films, however, the emphasis is no longer on "affluence" and consumerism but rather the urban and industrial decline, rise in unemployment and accompanying poverty resulting from the implementation of the Thatcher government's neo-liberal policies.

In this regard, the films of the 1980s and 1990s were the first films to address the more contemporary understanding of precarity as a newly emergent economic and social condition arising (in the West) from the politically-willed erosion of full employment, job security, and welfare rights (and, therefore, unlike the 1930s, occurring after a period perceived to have been economically more secure for the working class). In doing so, what the films also register is the changing gender composition of the workforce. For Guy Standing, the increasing entry of women into the workforce, often on a casual or part-time basis, has been a notable feature of the growth of precarity (and those whom he describes as members of the "precariat").[10] For the "new wave" films of the 1960s, "feminization" of the working class was associated with the rise of mass culture and consumerism. In the 1980s films, however, feminization is much more directly linked to the decline of traditional working-class jobs associated with manufacturing and heavy industry and a weakening of the ideologies of

---

10 Guy Standing, "The Precariat: From Denizens to Citizens," *Polity* 44, no. 4 (2012): 596.

masculinity that traditionally underpinned industrial labor and collective industrial action. It is therefore significant that many of the 1980s films focus primarily on the stories of working-class women in a way that contrasts sharply with the male-driven narratives of an earlier period. In *Business as Usual,* for example, the former union official, Kieran (John Thaw), has been made redundant due to the closure of the sugar refinery where he worked and is now largely house-bound, with a responsibility for domestic chores. His wife Babs (Glenda Jackson) and their son's partner Paula (Buki Armstrong), on the other hand, continue to work in the service sector—a clothes shop—but embark upon industrial action (with little encouragement from Kieran) when Babs is summarily dismissed for confronting the shop's owners over complaints of sexual harassment (Fig. 1).

Fig. 1: Business as Usual (Lezli-An Barrett, 1987).

This shifting configuration of gender roles is also evident in a later film such as *The Full Monty* (Peter Cattaneo, 1997) in which the erosion of traditional male roles and identities in the wake of de-industrialization and unemployment becomes the film's main concern. The film begins with footage of a promotional film from the early 1970s celebrating the city as the "the beating heart of Britain's industrial north" before cutting to shots of former steelworkers, Gaz (Robert Carlyle) and Dave (Mark Addy), and Gaz's son Nathan (William Snape), scavenging for scrap metal some twenty-five years later. In this respect, the film sets out to explore the economic and psychological insecurities that result from the loss of unemployment along with the role played by governmental apparatuses—the job club, the labor exchange—in instilling individual responsibility for their plight and re-equipping them for a newly flexible labor force. However, the film is only marginally interested in the injuries of economic precarity per se. In the course of the film, Gaz turns down the offer of a job made by his ex-wife while Dave runs out on his new job as a supermarket security guard. What the men need most, it appears, is not work or money so much as the recovery of a sense of pride and self-worth. Given the film's fusion of social realism and comedy, the "solution" that the film provides takes the somewhat unlikely form of a male strip show whereby the men involved regain the sense of homosocial community that industrial labor, and a shared occupational community, once provided. The ambivalence of this, of course, is that in choosing to become strippers, the men are also confronted with broadly feminist concerns relating to appearance, the body, and visual display. Thus, while the film involves the men regaining a sense of the "masculine" identity no longer to be found in work, the process of doing so also entails a degree of the re-education and feminization required by the transition from an industrial to a service economy (and to which, by implication, the men must ultimately submit despite their initial resistance to doing so).

A similar displacement of class politics onto gender politics may also be found in *Billy Elliot* (Stephen Daldry, 2000), another work combining social realism and comedy (along with elements of the film musical). The film is set against the backdrop of the key industrial dispute of the 1980s: the miners' strike of 1984–85. The miners' fight to prevent the closure of mines, protect jobs, and avoid the erosion of local working-class communities constituted the most concerted challenge to the Thatcher government's economic policies during this period and raised fundamental questions about the value of the type of society to which neo-liberal policies were leading. Although the film does show some of the economic hardships faced by the striking miners, it does little to explain the nature of the dispute or the contrasting visions of economy and society that underpinned it. Focusing on the aspirations of a young working-class lad, Billy (Jamie Bell), to become a ballet dancer, the film is guided in part by a progressive concern to challenge conventional understandings of gender roles and the association of ballet with homosexuality and effeminacy. However, in developing its critique of traditional notions of masculinity, the film not only locates the family as a site of dysfunction and incipient violence but the wider world of industrial action and political struggle as well. Thus, in the case of one arresting montage, the tranquility of Billy's dancing class is intercut with strongly contrasting shots of the strikers trying to prevent strike-breakers ("scabs") from entering the colliery and engaging in a noisy confrontation with a barrage of policemen (who, in a largely unexplained politicization of policing, have, in effect, "occupied" the mining village). In setting up the obstacles to the accomplishment of Billy's goals in this way, the film turns the resistance to neo-liberalism (and the imposition of precarity) represented by the miners' strike into an emblem of reactionary masculinism that not only stands in opposition to Billy's desire to break free of traditional social and cultural constraints but also, by extension, the liberalism, multiculturalism, and modernity associated with London where, in the film's final sequence, Billy is shown to have achieved his goal of becoming a successful ballet dancer.

Something of a riposte to this may be found in the later film, *Pride* (Matthew Warchus, 2014). Set during the same period as *Billy Elliot*, the film provides a fictionalized account of the support for the miners—and the South Wales mining village of Onilwyn—by the London-based group, Lesbians and Gays Support the Miners (LGSM). Although the film acknowledges the homophobia of the time, it also suggests the possibilities of "intersectional" forms of mutual support based upon an expanded notion of community and the shared values of fairness and justice. In doing so, the film also acknowledges the role played by women in supporting the strike and reinstates the virtues of collectivism over individualism (albeit that the trope of individual escape resurfaces in the coming-out narrative of the character nicknamed "Bromley" who succeeds in finding acceptance in a working-class village but not in his lower middle-class suburban hometown). It is also significant that the film is set partly in Wales given the symbolic importance of coalmining for Welsh national identity. Thus, while the film celebrates the building of forms of solidarity that straddle class, nationality, gender, and sexual orientation, it also provides a reminder of how the experience of neo-liberalism and de-industrialisation, promoted initially by a predominantly English Conservative government, played out differently across the nations that compose Great Britain, and contributed to a rise of civic nationalism and political devolution within both Scotland and Wales.

If British films of this period primarily identified the growth of precarity in terms of the loss of heavy industry and the consequent demise of occupational communities, it was also linked to a corresponding decline in working-class housing. The post-war settlement had involved a commitment to ending homelessness and the building of modern homes as a replacement for pre-war slums. Although there were some concerns about the breaking up of traditional working–class communities, the policy of building new estates was regarded, along with economic growth and full employment, as an important means of improving both working-class living conditions and standards. By the 1980s, however, the combination of growing unemployment, council house sales, and the lack of new building programs had led to the housing estate becoming linked in public discourse with poverty, social dysfunction, and the emergence of an "underclass" of the long-tern unemployed. In films, this led to the housing estate becoming something of an emblem of the economic and social damage wrought by neo-liberalism as well as a concrete visualization of the conditions faced by residents. By virtue of the shifts occurring in men's traditional economic and familial roles, this too possessed a gendered dimension insofar as it is often (young) women who figure more prominently within the films' storylines than hitherto and demonstrate a more active relationship to the public space around them.

This is evident, for example, in *Rita, Sue and Bob Too* (1987), director Alan Clarke's version of a play by Andrea Dunbar (whose life on the Buttershaw estate in Bradford also inspired Clio Barnard's experimental film *The Arbor* from 2010). Shot in fast-moving long takes, the young women of the film's title take over the public spaces of the estate, searching for excitement and giving expression to a physical and kinetic energy that seems to resist the oppressiveness of their run-down surroundings. In Penny Woolcock's *Tina Goes Shopping* (1998), the eponymous narrator also tours her estate, cheerfully taking orders from friends and family for her regular shoplifting expeditions. In Tina's world, no-one appears to have a proper job and most are mired in debt. It is therefore a community characterized by "grafting," or doing "what you have to do" to make ends meet, primarily in the form of thieving and drug-dealing. The film, in this respect, knowingly flirts with stereotypes of the residents of "sink estates," shown to be living off benefits and engaging in criminal acts, but avoids a moralistic tone while investing the female characters in particular with a spirit of resourcefulness and fortitude borne out of economic disadvantage.

Andrea Arnold's *Fish Tank* (2009) bears some similarities to both *Rita, Sue and Bob Too* and *Tina Goes Shopping* in its foregrounding of a female protagonist, Mia (Katie Jarvis), whose very physical being appears to be trapped within the confines of an estate (located on the edges of what was once a car factory). As such, the film relies upon many of the conventional signifiers associated with the housing estate to reinforce the sense of imprisonment felt by the main character and to indicate her desire to break free. However, the film's combination of the observational features of social realism with the stylistic foregrounding of the "art film" also invests the estate, and its surroundings, with a certain strangeness by virtue of the film's emphasis upon Mia's own subjectivity and the psychological strains imposed upon her (Fig. 2). Thematically, the film may be compared to *Billy Elliot* insofar as Mia aspires to become a dancer, albeit in this case within the world of hip-hop. However, in contrast to Billy's ultimate triumph, even this relatively modest ambition seems to be closed off following her dispiriting experience of an audition that is not what it is initially assumed to be. At the film's end, Mia decides to leave the estate, joining her traveler friend, Billy (Harry Treadaway), in a move to Cardiff; however, given her age and circumstances, there is little sense that her new life will prove any more fulfilling than the one she is hoping to escape.

Fig. 2: Fish Tank (Andrea Arnold, 2009).

The housing estate also provides the setting for Mike Leigh's *All or Nothing* (2002), a more multi-stranded work involving a range of characters. In comparison to the other films, characters may struggle financially but do have jobs, albeit lowly-paid ones in the service sector. Phil (Timothy Spall) is a taxi driver, his partner Penny (Lesley Manville) works at a supermarket checkout, their daughter Rachel (Alison Garland) is a care worker. While the film does draw attention to the economic difficulties faced by the family, as in a scene when Phil struggles to find the money to pay his minicab boss, the emphasis is on the emotional costs, for the characters, of unfulfilling work, limited prospects, and the loss of dignity. This comes to a head when Rory (James Corden) is hospitalized as a result of a heart attack and his parents, Phil and Penny, are prompted to take stock of their failing relationship. Thus, while the film does indicate the forms of support—rather than the dangers—to be found on the estate, particularly evident in the actions of neighbor and fellow supermarket worker Maureen (Ruth Sheen), it is the revitalization of the family which the film suggests provides the main psychological protection against the demoralization and inner loneliness that the characters face.

The Films of Ken Loach

However, if a range of British films may be seen to have addressed—both directly and obliquely—the consequences of the economic insecurity wrought by the neo-liberal turn in British economic policy, there can be little doubt that it is the work of Ken Loach from the early 1990s onwards that constitutes the most sustained exploration of working-class precarity in British cinema. As a film and television director who began his career in the 1960s, however, it would also be fair to say that a concern for the insecurity and vulnerability of those at the bottom of the social ladder has been a constant feature of his work. Indeed, the production that first cemented his reputation, the BBC television play, *Cathy Come Home* (1966), directly questioned the notions of "affluence" prevailing in the 1960s through its moving tale of a young couple, Cathy (Carol White) and Reg (Ray Brooks), forced into poverty and homelessness when Reg becomes unemployed due to a work injury. The play's critique of an economically divided society and a flawed system of welfare support continues to characterize Loach's later work but acquires an added bleakness in the face of the de-industrialization, mass unemployment, and anti-trade union legislation experienced during the 1980s. Given Loach's explicitly political concerns, it is the decline in trade-union strength and the capacity for collective action that emerges as an especially notable feature. In one of his most radical works of the 1960s, the television film *The Big Flame* (1969), Liverpool dockers take over and successfully run the docks before their occupation is brought to an end by the military. Although the men are defeated, they have nonetheless demonstrated the possibility of managing society differently, setting alight "the big flame" for others to follow. By the 1990s, however, the possibility of a collective challenge to the demands of de-regulated capitalism has been significantly weakened, leaving individual workers even more exposed than before to insecurity and hardship in the face of growing economic precarity.

Riff-Raff (1991) is the first of Loach's films to mark this transition, vividly demonstrating how the threat of unemployment and a loss of trade-union rights have placed an assorted group of building workers at the mercy of unscrupulous, cost-cutting employers. One of the main characters in the film, Larry, is played by Ricky Tomlinson, a former plasterer who was involved in a national strike against "the lump" in 1972 (and subsequently faced imprisonment for secondary picketing in support of the national action). Loach's film identifies how the practices associated with the "lump" have been revived, forcing casualized workers from across the UK into bogus "self-employment" and exposing them to both job insecurity and unsafe working conditions. In line with Loach's preference for casting actors with similarities to their characters, Tomlinson plays a Liverpudlian political activist who urges the men on the site to organize but is summarily dismissed when he complains to the foreman about safety conditions. In the wake of the hospitalization of Desmonde (Derek Young) as a result of a fall due to the faulty scaffolding about which Larry had complained, two of his fellow workers return at night and set fire to the site. This, however, is little more than an act of desperation that only leaves the men worse off and exposes their powerlessness to exercise effective control over the work and conditions to which they have been subjected (and will continue to be in other workplaces).

The erosion of working conditions, and lack of power to oppose this, is also apparent in *The Navigators* (2001) which focuses on the experiences of a group of South Yorkshire railway maintenance workers faced with railway privatization (a controversial set of measures involving the break-up of British Rail and the separation of track and train operations). The film charts the gradual disintegration of the team as market pressures undermine conditions at work, union agreements are scrapped, and the men take up agency employment that at first seems to be better paid but lacks any guarantee of regular work, holidays, or sick pay and requires the men to provide their own clothing and transport. In this way, the film reveals how the men continue to do more or less the same work as before but now on poorer terms and under less safe conditions. As in *Riff-Raff*, matters come to a head following an accident caused by cuts to the labor force and the men are forced into deceit in order to preserve their employment. In this way, the film not only highlights how privatization and de-regulation propel the workers towards job insecurity but also identifies the psychological toll upon those who have to struggle with the consequences of increasing precarity not only at work but also at home.

This is also the case with *Sorry We Missed You* (2019) in which the merciless demands of new forms of employment practice not only generate economic insecurity but threaten the stability of home and family life as well. The film's main character, Ricky (Kris Hitchen), is a hard-working "grafter" who initially lost his job in the building trade—and the opportunity to purchase a house—due to the financial crisis of 2008. Subsequently moving from "one shit job to another shit job," he wants to become his own boss and signs up with a delivery company as an "Owner Driver Franchisee." However, far from acquiring the control over his own destiny that he craves, he discovers how illusory his supposed "self-employment" really is as he is forced to pay for his own van, work long hours tracked by a handheld digital device (for which he is financially liable), and organize his own cover for any days missed (or else be liable to fines). By the film's end, he has been plunged into debt arising from family emergencies and a robbery that has left him badly beaten and injured. In the film's final scene, his family begs him not to go to work but he feels that he has no alternative but to do so. For those familiar with the often grim narrative logic of Loach's films, there is an expectation that Ricky, only partly able to see, will crash and make matters even worse. However, instead, the camera is held on a lengthy close-up of Ricky's battered face as he continues to drive, completely distraught but resolved to carry on (Fig. 3). Ending in this way, the film not only provides a moving critique of the pretensions of the "gig economy" (and its false promises of economic freedom and self-determination) but also leaves the spectator with a powerful image of the apparently perpetual state of economic servitude in which the precarious worker is liable to become trapped.

Fig. 3: Sorry We Missed You (Ken Loach, 2019).

What the film also delineates is the way in which such economic precarity impacts upon home and family life. Ricky's wife Abby (Debbie Honeywood) is a care worker, devoted to those she assists, but is employed on a zero-hours contract that only pays for her time with clients and not her travel time (for which she must bear the cost). As a result, her working day, like Ricky's, stretches from early morning to evening and the couple struggles to enjoy much time on their own or provide the support that their children need. Their son Seb (Rhys Stone) is a restless and troubled teenager who yearns for a better life than that of his parents and discovers an outlet for his artistic talent (and rebellious spirit) in street graffiti. His escapades, however, lead to an expulsion from school and an arrest for shoplifting that provokes tensions within the family and threaten to break it up. For the film, as with Loach's work more generally, family life is not to be understood solely in terms of the psychological or moral make-up of its members but rather the socio-economic pressures that weigh upon them and the difficult, uncomfortable choices to which they lead. This is even more evident when the main characters are unemployed. Films such as

Raining Stones (1993), *My Name is Joe* (1998), and *Sweet Sixteen* (2002) explore the consequences for those left without any jobs at all, detailing how characters struggle to get by, plunging into debt or veering into criminality, while jeopardizing their personal and familial relationships in the process. The added sting of *Sorry We Missed You*, of course, is that both adults are actually in work. However, their work is so demanding and so poorly-rewarded that it still proves insufficient to satisfy the modest expectations of basic financial—and by implication emotional—security for self and family.

If precarity in Loach's films is primarily associated with insecure employment, low pay and the worsening conditions of work, it is also linked to the failure of the social security system to ensure the wellbeing of those in need. This too has been something of a constant in Loach's work. Films such as *Cathy Come Home* (1966), *Ladybird, Ladybird* (1994), and *My Name is Joe* (1998) have often shown the ways in which the main characters—in the face of economic and social difficulty—are let down or obstructed by local council or state employees such as housing officials or social workers. In doing so, such works have identified the inadequacy of the state to tackle the problems that characters face insofar as these are generally a symptom of deep-rooted social and economic inequalities. However, in the wake of welfare cuts, the privatization of activities previously performed by the state, and the dilution of notions of collective responsibility, these forms of support are no longer regarded as simply failing those in need of them but also to be directly implicated in regulating and sustaining a neo-liberal economic order reliant upon precarity. This becomes particularly evident in *I, Daniel Blake* (2016) in which the lead character (played by Dave Johns) is unable to work due to a heart attack but nevertheless becomes enmeshed in a bureaucratic system that requires him to apply for work that he is not physically capable of undertaking. When Daniel spray-paints a protest on the walls of the Job Centre, he is supported by a passing Glaswegian who refers to the Conservative minister for Work and Pensions, Ian Duncan Smith, who was responsible for the overhaul of the benefits system and introduction of a "universal credit" specifically designed to increase "work incentives." The implementation of these changes was widely seen to have been responsible for delays in the payment of benefits and increases in economic hardship (most apparent in the rise in use of food banks run by charitable organizations and community groups). Daniel's protest, therefore, is shown to be provoked by the seemingly calculated slowness of the benefits system, the delays to his appeal against the refusal of employment support, and the economic difficulties with which he is then confronted.

However, what also emerges from the film is a more general critique of the way in which changes to the benefits system constitute a new form of "neoliberal" governance that prioritizes employability over need (and helps to sustain the precarity of both employed and unemployed). Writing in the context of the US shift from welfare to workfare, Loïc Wacquant indicates how welfare "reform" has sought to reshape "dispositions" through the "degradation of the recipient self and glorification of the working self" not only as a means of reducing public expenditure but of enhancing the supply of "pliable workers" to low-paid jobs in a deregulated labor market.[11] *I, Daniel Blake* may be seen to demonstrate such a process of governance in action. Despite his ill-health, Daniel is deemed "fit for work" as the result of a phone assessment by a private company rather than a qualified doctor. As a result, he is forced to attend a "CV Workshop" under the threat of sanction and obliged to spend (and prove he is spending) thirty-five hours a week looking for work in order to qualify for continued financial support. Unable to endure the "humiliation," and lack of respect, to which he has been subjected, he ends up deprived of state benefits and dies in poverty before his appeal has been heard. In the final scene, at Daniel's funeral, Katie (Hayley Squires), the young mother of two whom he has helped and who has herself suffered at the hands of a punitive welfare regime, reads out Daniel's now-famous declaration that he is not "a shirker, a scrounger, a beggar nor a thief" but a "citizen" who "paid his dues" and is now entitled to his "rights."

Daniel may be seen, in this regard, to belong to an older working-class tradition who took for granted the rights and benefits established in the post-war period and who still believe in the virtues of collectivism and mutual support. In *Sorry We Missed You*, Abby cares for a disabled woman who reminisces about the miners' strike and the free café that they organized but expresses her concerns about Abby's terms of work that involve a zero-hours contract and the lack of an "eight-hour day." In Loach's *It's a Free World* (2007), Geoff (played by former stevedore and union activist Colin Caughlin) is shocked to see men gathering in a public space for the chance to obtain casual work, believing such practices to be "all over." In this case, the workers are not British but migrant workers, mainly recruited from Eastern Europe by his daughter Angie (Kierston Wareing). Although these are legal migrants, her agency is primarily engaged in providing casual, low-paid work, without job security or employment rights, in factories and on building sites (while simultaneously renting low-quality accommodation to the same workers). Working through intermediaries, she comes unstuck when one of her contractors fails to pay her, leaving her unable to pay the workers for whom she is responsible. This does not, however,

---

[11] Loïc Wacquant, *Punishing the Poor: The Neoliberal Government of Social Insecurity* (Durham, NC: Duke University Press, 2009), 101.

deter her and, at the film's end, she arrives in the Ukraine, now planning to recruit illegal migrants who will, as the boss of a UK clothing factory has told her, make more compliant workers than EU nationals.

Migration and Precarity

Migrants, according to Guy Standing, are "the light infantry of global capitalism" who constitute a growing part of the global "precariat."[12] *It's a Free World* draws on the experience of economic migration that occurred following the enlargement of the European Union in 2004 (that included Lithuania and Poland) and 2007 (involving the accession of Bulgaria and Romania). While this permitted freedom of movement across the UK, the film indicates how the expectation of well-paid work and good accommodation in the UK could prove illusory, subjecting incoming workers to poor working conditions and precarity. This is even more obviously the case in those films that chart the experiences of undocumented migrants who enter the country illegally and become especially vulnerable to exploitation. This may be seen, for example, in Michael Winterbottom's *In This World* (2002) which follows a young boy Jamal (Jamal Udin Torabi) as he journeys from Pakistan to England through Iran, Turkey, Italy, and France only to end up washing dishes in a London café. Stephen Frears's *Dirty Pretty Things* (2002) fuses elements of film noir with social realism in its investigation of a twilight world in which illegal immigrants move from job to job and are exploited by employers and fellow migrants alike. The central character Okwe (Chiwetel Ejiofor) drives a cab by day and works in a hotel by night. He rents a couch from a young Turkish woman Senay (Audrey Tautou) who initially works as a cleaner in the same hotel but is forced to find other work—in a sweatshop where the owner demands sexual favors—in order to avoid the immigration authorities. The film highlights both the relative invisibility and extreme vulnerability of those working illegally in the UK while stressing the key role such workers play in sustaining the economy and providing services for the well-to-do. For the film, this predatory relationship is summed up—and allegorized—by the organ-trafficking that is revealed to take place inside the hotel. As such, the migrants are not only exploited and forced to live their lives on society's margins but are themselves turned into commodities whose body parts may be sold to wealthy clients in exchange for forged passports and other official documents.

---

12 Standing, "The Precariat," 597.

The commodification of the migrant also forms part of Nick Broomfield's *Ghosts* (2006), in which migrant workers from rural China pay to be smuggled illegally into Britain. They travel in the expectation of earning money that will allow them to support their families back home but enter a world in which their illegality condemns them to low-paid work, poor accommodation, and social isolation. The film is based on the research of the journalist Hsiao-Hung Pai, who worked undercover with undocumented Chinese workers and subsequently identified them as a "half-price army of labour" whose lack of legal rights facilitated their exploitation by landlords, employment agencies, and employers.[13] In the film, the migrants, supervised by a Chinese gang-master, are therefore shown to undertake poorly-paid agency work—packing meat or picking vegetables (for cost-cutting supermarkets)—while squashed into overcrowded but nonetheless income-draining accommodation (rented to them by an unscrupulous landlord). Eager to earn more money, some of the workers travel north to pick cockles. Based on real-life events at Morecambe Bay in February 2004, many of the group subsequently drown in the sea. In *Dirty Pretty Things*, Okwe's Chinese friend Guo Yi (Benedict Wong) comments that "only the ghosts" appear at night in the hospital mortuary where he works. In both films, the reference to ghosts not only refers to the spirits of the dead but also the spectral character of the migrants themselves whose economic contribution—as well as exploitation—within the shadow economy remains largely unacknowledged and unappreciated.

In both cases, it is significant that the films set out to foreground the experiences of the migrant workers and structures the spectator's responses in relation to their perspective. This is particularly so given the rise of anti-immigrant sentiment in host countries that blames the migrant for generating the very precarity of which they are the largely powerless victims. As Standing indicates, while it is capital that welcomes migration because "it brings low-cost malleable labour," it may also be opposed by those "squeezed by globalization" and in danger of "falling into the precariat" such as "the old (white) working class."[14] So, while *Ghosts* does provide some evidence of friendship and solidarity, as when a white woman worker sits and discusses photographs with Ai Qin (Ai Quin Lin) in the canteen in the meat-processing plant, the presence of the migrant workers is largely met with hostility. White English neighbors report their presence to the police and then throw rubbish around the house in which they live. It is also the actions of local cockle pickers in Morecambe Bay that lead the

---

13 Hsiao-Hung Pai, *Chinese Whispers – The True Story Behind Britain's Hidden Army of Labour* (London: Penguin, 2008).
14 Guy Standing, *The Precariat* (London: Bloomsbury, 2011), 120.

Chinese workers to pick cockles at night when they cannot be seen (or, indeed, saved when the tide turns). The irony, of course, is that the English workers are little better off than the migrants and it is chiefly the threat to their own precarious livelihoods that motivates them to drive the Chinese away.

This link between precariousness and racism is most starkly evident in *A Way of Life* (2004), directed by the Black woman director Amma Asante. Set in contemporary South Wales, the film, like those of Ken Loach, deals with characters confronted with the consequences of de-industrialization and unemployment. The main character, Leigh-Anne (Stephanie James), like Loach's Cathy, struggles to feed and clothe her child and lives in constant fear of the child's removal by social services (which does, in the end, prove to be the case). One of her friends, Robbie (Gary Sheppeard), who is sweet on Leigh-Anne and seeks to help her, goes for a job interview as a caretaker but is turned down due to his address and dependence upon public transport. However, unlike Cathy, Leigh-Anne is not simply the sentimentalized victim of economic circumstances but rather, as Steve Blandford puts it, a character brutalized by her environment into "a callous disregard for others and . . . a vicious racist mentality."[15] So while there is no particular evidence to back up their prejudices, Leigh-Anne and her circle largely blame foreigners—generically referred to as "Pakis"—for the poor rewards and insecurity that characterize their lives. This reaches a shocking climax when, egged on by Leigh-Anne, her brother and friends give vent to the racism underpinning their frustrations by kicking a Turkish neighbor to death in the mistaken belief that he has reported Leigh-Ann to social services. As in a Loach film such as *Riff-Raff*, this misplaced action (directed against a neighbor who is barely better off than themselves) can only make their situation worse. But, even by comparison with the political pessimism to be found in the work of Loach, this is a remarkably bleak demonstration of the ideological poison and social division which the precariousness generated by neo-liberalism can fuel.

Conclusion

As this survey suggests, there is a lengthy tradition of British films focusing on the conditions and experiences of the working class. The documentary movement of the 1930s partly discovered its mission through its attention to the precarious conditions under which so many lived and helped to pave the way for

---

15 Steve Blandford, *Film, Drama and the Break-Up of Britain* (Bristol: Intellect Books, 2007), 107.

the social and economic advances of the post-war period. The "new wave" films identified some of the ways in which lives were improved but also registered some of the anxieties that characterized a period of supposed "affluence." The neo-liberal turn in the 1980s, and the de-industrialization and unemployment that accompanied it, set the framework for the bulk of the films that followed. Although different in emphasis, such films mapped the changing contours of class (in terms of gender and ethnicity), the deteriorating conditions at work, the threat of joblessness, the growing sense of economic vulnerability, the erosion of older forms of social security, the decline of social housing, and the loss of traditional solidarities. While some of the films were able to offer a cautious welcome to the re-learning of gender roles in the face of economic downturn, they are mostly pessimistic about the prospects for political opposition and change. In a sense, this reflects how the contemporary conception of precarity has been predicated on a sense of loss—of job security, decent wages, good housing, proper welfare provision, trade-union activism—and the nostalgia or sense of mourning that the recognition of this loss entails. It has also in part been the product of the narrative and stylistic conventions of social realism that provide a concreteness to the lived realities of social and economic relationships but often in terms of a narration of victimization and environmental determinism. While there are no easy answers to how opposition to precarization may be mobilized, and how it is to be articulated with more traditional conceptions of class politics, these are nonetheless some of the tasks that a socially-critical British cinema of the future might productively address.

Bibliography

Berlant, Lauren. *Cruel Optimism*. Durham, NC: Duke University Press, 2011.
Betti, Eloisa. "Historicizing Precarious Work: Forty Years of Research in the Social Sciences and Humanities." *IRSH*, no. 63 (2018): 273–319.
Blandford, Steve. *Film, Drama and the Break-Up of Britain*. Bristol: Intellect Books, 2007.
Bremen, Jan. "A Bogus Concept?" *New Left Review*, 84 (2013): 130–138.
——, and Marcel van der Linden. "Informalizing the Economy: The Return of the Social Question at a Global Level." *Development and Change* 45, no. 5 (2014): 920–940.
Butler, Judith. *Precarious Life: The Powers of Mourning and Violence*. London: Verso, 2004.
Grierson, John. "The Course of Realism." In *Footnotes to the Film*, ed. Charles Davy. London: Lovat Dickson, 1938, 137–161.
Hall, Stuart. "The Social Eye of the *Picture Post*." *Working Papers in Cultural Studies*, no. 2 (1972): 71–120.
Lindsay, T. F. and Michael Harrington. *The Conservative Party: 1918–1970*. London: Allen & Unwin, 1974.

Pai, Hsiao-Hung, A Ghost No More. *New Statesman* 136, no. 4826 (2007): 36.
Standing, Guy. *The Precariat*. London: Bloomsbury, 2011.
——. "The Precariat: From Denizens to Citizens." *Polity* 44, no. 4 (2012): 588–608.
Wacquant, Loïc. *Punishing the Poor: The Neoliberal Government of Social Insecurity*. Durham, NC: Duke University Press, 2009.
Williams, Raymond. "A Lecture on Realism." *Screen* 18, no. 1 (1977): 61–74.

Filmography

A Kind of Loving. Dir. John Schlesinger. UK, 1962.
A Way of Life. Dir. Amma Asante. UK, 2004.
All or Nothing. Dir. Mike Leigh. UK/France, 2002.
Billy Elliot. Dir. Stephen Daldry. UK/France, 2000.
Business as Usual. Dir. Lezli-An Barrett. UK/USA, 1987.
Cathy Come Home. Dir. Ken Loach. UK, 1966.
Dirty Pretty Things. Dir. Stephen Frears. UK, 2002.
Enough to Eat? Dir. Edgar Anstey. UK, 1936.
Fish Tank. Dir. Andrea Arnold. Netherlands/UK, 2009.
Ghosts. Dir. Nick Broomfield. UK, 2006.
Housing Problems. Dir. Arthur Elton and Edgar Anstey. UK, 1935.
I, Daniel Blake. Dir. Ken Loach. UK/France/Belgium, 2016.
In This World. Dir. Michael Winterbottom. UK, 2002.
Industrial Britain. Dir. Robert J. Flaherty. UK, 1931.
It's a Free World. Dir. Ken Loach. UK/Italy/Germany/Spain/Poland, 2007.
Ladybird, Ladybird. Dir. Ken Loach. UK, 1994.
Letter to Brezhnev. Dir. Chris Bernard. UK, 1985.
My Name is Joe. Dir. Ken Loach. UK/Germany/France/Spain, 1998.
Pride. Dir. Matthew Warchus. UK/France/USA, 2014.
Raining Stones. Dir. Ken Loach. UK, 1993.
Riff-Raff. Dir. Ken Loach. UK, 1991.
Rita, Sue and Bob Too. Dir. Alan Clarke. UK 1987.
Room at the Top. Dir. Jack Clayton. UK, 1959.
Saturday Night and Sunday Morning. Dir. Karel Reisz. UK, 1960.
Sorry We Missed You. Dir. Ken Loach. UK/France/Belgium, 2019.
Sweet Sixteen. Dir. Ken Loach. UK/Germany/Spain, 2002.
The Arbor. Dir. Clio Barnard. UK, 2010.
The Big Flame. Dir. Ken Loach. UK, 1969.
The Dawn Guard. Dir. Roy Boulting. UK, 1941.
The Full Monty. Dir. Peter Cattaneo. UK/USA, 1997.
The Navigators. Dir. Ken Loach. UK/Germany/Spain, 2001.
The Loneliness of the Long Distance Runner. Dir. Tony Richardson. UK, 1962.
Tina Goes Shopping. Dir. Penny Woolcock. UK, 1999.
Workers and Jobs. Dir. Arthur Elton. UK, 1935.

Gert Jan Harkema
Relational Aesthetics of Precarity in Contemporary Dutch Documentary and Beyond

"The TV-series *Schuldig* proves: a moving documentary can achieve more than a hundred policy documents."[1] This is how the national newspaper *Trouw* headlined a long article on the popularity and impact of the documentary series right before it won the 2017 Nipkowschijf, the most prestigious award in Dutch broadcasting. The six-part documentary series *Schuldig* (*Guilt/Debt*, HOS, 2016) by Sarah Sylbing and Esther Gould was heralded as "cinematic" in terms of quality and narrative complexity. Other reviews compared the series to its US fictional equivalent *The Wire* (HBO, 2002–2008).[2] Since its release in the fall of 2016, *Schuldig*, which in Dutch can mean both "guilty" and "indebted," had a significant impact on public discourses on poverty, inequality, and the debt problem. Moreover, its successor *Klassen* (*Class/Classroom*, HOS, 2020), also created by Sylbing and Gould, which this time plays with the double meaning of "class" and "classroom," has generated as much discussion in the popular press and in politics.

In this chapter, I will argue that it is crucial to understand the relational, interpersonal concept of precarity portrayed in these documentaries, particularly in regard to the aesthetic and affective registers that it encompasses. What Sylbing's and Gould's work makes visible and palpable is the interrelation between precarity and precariousness.[3] By depicting the interconnected lives of individuals, social workers, teachers, politicians, and debt collectors in the specific location of an Amsterdam-Noord neighborhood and several micro-locations, they present a cultural geography of precarity as "a political condition that is the consequence of uneven power relations and refers to the exacerbation of the precariousness of

---

[1] Maaike Bos, "TV-serie 'Schuldig' bewijst: "Een ontroerende documentaire kan meer bereiken dan honderd beleidsstukken," *Trouw*, June 14, 2017.
[2] Hans Beerekamp, "'Schuldig' is een magistrale serie over armoede," *NRC Handelsblad*, December 6, 2016.
[3] For the differentiation between and the interrelation of the concepts of "precarity" and "precariousness", cf. Judith Butler, *Frames of War: When is Life Grievable?* London/New York: Verso, 2010, 3–5; Isabell Lorey, *State of Insecurity: Government of the Precarious* [2011], London/New York: Verso, 2015, 5–22; Guido Kirsten, "Studying the Cinema of Precarity: An Introduction" (in this volume).

Open Access. © 2022 Gert Jan Harkema, published by De Gruyter. This work is licensed under the Creative Commons Attribution-NonCommercial-NoDerivatives 4.0 International License.
https://doi.org/10.1515/9783110707816-019

some subjects compared to others."[4] Meanwhile, in terms of form and style, these documentary series show people on the move, commuting to work or searching for help and connection. Or, at other times, just wandering restlessly through the streets. Thereby they trigger emotional responses and make use of affective dimensions of precariousness, "the inherent state of vulnerability and dependence resulting from the relational structure of society," as an "artistic-political strategy."[5] While *Schuldig* is illustrative of a shift in the representation and aesthetics of precarity in Dutch screen culture, it needs to be situated within a broader, ongoing discussion of precarity in Dutch society. The series is also part of a wider set of fictional and documentary representations that demonstrate an increasing sensibility for precarity. These films and series seek to register and address issues of poverty and social insecurity by finding new forms. Hence the critical success of *Schuldig* is symptomatic of the emergence of a set of forms and framings that address different affective registers and focus on precariousness and the politics of vulnerability in contemporary Dutch society. Like so many other Western European countries, the Netherlands has seen an increasing precarization, particularly of labor but also in terms of a broader set of social insecurities related to migration and identity, accessible and affordable health care, the pension system, and more.[6] Research on this has mainly focused on the rise of temporary, short-term, and so-called flexible contracts, and the unstable career patterns among young adults entering the job market after the 2000s.[7] From a broader perspective and following the work of Robert Castel and others, researchers from many different fields recognize the increasing dangers of poverty and social inequality, albeit from a centralist and bourgeois perspective. The middle-class, meanwhile, is still

---

[4] Ella Harris and Mel Nowicki, "Cultural Geographies of Precarity," *Cultural Geographies* 25, no. 3 (March 2018): 387.

[5] Ibid.; Mieke Bal, "Affectively Effective: Affect as an Artistic-Political Strategy," in *How to Do Things with Affects: Affective Triggers in Aesthetic Forms and Cultural Practices*, ed. Ernst van Alphen and Tomáš Jirsa (Leiden/Boston: Brill-Rodopi, 2019).

[6] Peter van Lieshout, ed., *Sociale (on)zekerheid: De voorziene toekomst* (Amsterdam: Amsterdam University Press, 2016); Dirk Geldof, *Onzekerheid: Over leven in de risicomaatschappij* (Leuven/The Hague: Acco, 2021).

[7] See Marlous de Lange, Maarten Wolbers, and Wout Ultee, "United in Precarious Employment? Employment Precarity of Young Couples in the Netherlands, 1992–2007," *European Sociological Review* 29, no. 3 (June 2013); Dirk Witteveen, "Precarious Early Careers: Instability and Timing within Labor Market Entry," in *Precarious Work*, ed. Arne L. Kalleberg and Steven P. Vallas (Bingley: Emerald Publishing, 2018); Ruud Luijkx and Maarten Wolbers, "The Impact of Employment Precarity on Early Labour Market Careers and Family Formation in the Netherlands," in *Flexible Employment and the Welfare State in Europe*, ed. Paolo Barbieri (Cheltenham: Edward Elgar, 2018).

in a relatively stable situation, although, in the words of the Scientific Council for Government Policy, "they have to work harder for that, while they have to accept a higher degree of insecurity."[8] Hence we recognize on a national scale what Isabell Lorey describes from an international perspective as the normalization of precarity reaching the middle of society.[9] The true effects of the ongoing precarization can be recognized at the lower-class regions of society where we see an increase in poverty, or in fact an inability to get out of situations of deprivation, and a sharp increase in problematic, structural debts while the living conditions of the people in low-income areas worsen.[10]

This process of precarization did not just emerge with the European debt crisis of 2010, nor did it start with the financial crisis of 2008. The current precarization of labor and the rise of social insecurity is the result of more than twenty years of neoliberal governing resulting in constant welfare reform since the mid-1990s.[11] Historically, postwar Netherlands was marked by a progressive political agenda which achieved a system of social security and a solid welfare state that was, for a long time at least, considered in line with that of northern European countries like Denmark and Sweden. With this policy, center-left governments successfully managed to decrease inequality up until the 1990s, resulting in a stable and robust middle-class society.[12] On this basis, the government started implementing more neoliberal policies. At the heart of these policies lays, as financial geography scholar Ewald Engelen observes, a far-reaching cost-benefit paradigm in which political decision-making is left in the hands of "econocrats," an aggregation of economists and technocrats.[13]

Since 2008, the national government has branded this restructuring of the post-welfare state as the "participation society" or the "do-democracy." The role of the citizen is that of a "social entrepreneur," an *individual* who determines their own chances and invests in a better future. Illustrative for this is an annual

---

[8] Godfried Engbersen, Erik Snel, and Monique Kremer, *De Val Van De Middenklasse?: Het Stabiele En Kwetsbare Midden. Verkenningen* (The Hague: WRR, 2017).
[9] Lorey, *State of Insecurity*, 63.
[10] Cor Vrooman, "Armoede, naar Nederlandse maatstaven," *Sociale Vraagstukken*, December 19, 2011; Matthijs Uyterlinde, "Dalende leefbaarheid is geen nieuws, wel prioriteit," *Sociale Vraagstukken*, November 17, 2018.
[11] For an overview, see Lei Delsen, *Exit Polder Model?: Socioeconomic Changes in the Netherlands* (Westport/London: Praeger, 2002); and Wim Vermeersch, "Het is klasse, suffie, niet identiteit – interview met Ewald Engelen," *Samenleving en Politiek* 25, no. 8 (October 2018).
[12] Bas van Bavel and Ewout Frankema, "Wealth and Inequality in the Netherlands, c. 1950–2015," *Tijdschrift voor sociale en economische geschiedenis* 14, no. 2 (2017).
[13] Ewald Engelen, *Ontwaak! Kom uit uw neoliberale sluimer* (Amsterdam: Atheneum, 2021). The term "econocrats" originated from the work of Peter Self.

report by the Raad van Maatschappelijke Ontwikkeling (Council of Societal Development), a central governmental advisory board, which in 2006 had the title *Een verschil maken: Eigen verantwoordelijkheid na de verzorgingsstaat* (*Making a Difference: Own Responsibility after the Welfare State*). During the past two decades, the Dutch welfare system has slowly evolved from security to flexibility, or to *flexicurity*, while the monthly allowance for social assistance benefits has been structurally reduced on a yearly basis (and is planned to decrease further until 2030).[14] Meanwhile, as studies show, there has been a decline in solidarity, particularly between different classes and different generations.[15] *Schuldig*, and films and documentaries such as *De Tegenprestatie* (*Quid Pro Quo*, Monique Lesterhuis and Suzanne Raes, 2015), *New Kids Turbo* (Flip van der Kuil and Steffen Maas, 2010), *The Domino Effect* (Paula van de Oest, 2012), and others that will be discussed below, can be interpreted as responses to this new political and social reality.

Particularly in the last five years, the country has seen a renewed political awareness of precarity although we are yet awaiting materialization of this in terms of a new government (which is, and has been, formed by a center-right coalition). The search for new forms and frames in cinema and television production marks a counter discourse that uses concepts of precariousness and vulnerability to defy the state's governing of precarity. Whereas the political discourse has been constructing the concept of a so-called participation society in which the role of the state is significantly diminished, a widespread counter discourse recognizable in film and television addresses the increasing feelings of insecurity in society. I am following Raymond Williams' notion of "structures of feeling" here, which entails art's and popular culture's unique capacity "to capture social dynamics before they are rationalized, classified, and institutionalized."[16] Predating current political discussions on precarity and poverty by several years, the work of Sylbing and Gould should be understood in relation to a broad spectrum of comedies, documentaries, and arthouse productions in contemporary film and television addressing the fundamental social, interpersonal, and affective dynamics of insecurity and precarious lives.

---

14 Albert Jan Kruiter, Femmianne Bredeworld, and Marcel Ham, eds., *Hoe de verzorgingsstaat verbouwd wordt: Kroniek van een verandering* (Amsterdam: Van Gennep and Sociale Vraagstukken, 2016).
15 Femke Roosma, "Wie verdient nog onze solidariteit?: Veranderingen in solidariteitsgevoelens met ouderen, zieken en gehandicapten, werklozen en immigranten in de 21ste eeuw," *Mens en Maatschappij* 94, no. 4 (November 2019).
16 Adriana Margareta Dancus, Mats Hyvönen, and Maria Karlsson, "Mobilizing Vulnerability in Scandinavian Art and Culture," in *Vulnerability in Scandinavian Art and Culture*, ed. Adriana Margareta Dancus, Mats Hyvönen, and Maria Karlsson (London: Palgrave Macmillan, 2019), 3.

Documentary, Television, and Generating Impact

The documentary miniseries *Schuldig* consists of six one-hour episodes in which we follow in a mosaic narrative a group of individuals who either encounter financial problems or deal with debt collection, home evictions, or general politics. Problems of stress, anxiety, alcoholism, underperformances at school, inequality, class, etc. are related to the financial troubles. The depiction of precarity in *Schuldig* is thus not limited to job insecurity, but also includes the typical aspects that Brett Neilson and Ned Rossiter broadly define as "questions of housing, debt, welfare provision and the availability of time for building affective personal relations."[17] Some of the represented subjects experience multiple precarity while others are part of the system in positions such as debt collector or welfare workers. The series was broadcasted in November and December 2016 on the Dutch public television station NPO2 by the broadcast organization HUMAN. In the Dutch broadcast system, different broadcasters serving different religions and/or ideologies have their own airtime based on the number of members of that organization. HUMAN, ideologically inspired by humanism, was added to the public broadcasting structure in 1989.[18] Today, nearly all documentaries are in some way or other coproduced with funding from individual public broadcasters, nationally or regionally, and practically all productions are shown on the public channel and online within half a year after their release. Historically, this production method has

---

17 Brett Neilson and Net Rossiter, "Precarity as a Political Concept, or, Fordism as Exception," *Theory, Culture & Society* 25, no. 7/8 (2008): 52.
18 Explicitly drawing on the philosophy of Spinoza, Erasmus, and Coornhert, HUMAN explains its motto as: "Inspiring the mind, touching the heart," as explained on their website (https://www.human.nl/over-human/humanisme.html, accessed January 31, 2022). As a result of a public broadcasting system formed by different organizations serving the different "pillars" of society, content, perspective, and relevance were very important from the outset, when most broadcasters started on radio. Huub Wijfjes, *Omroep in Nederland: vijfenzeventig jaar medium en maatschappij, 1919–1994* (Zwolle: Waanders, 1994). This approach of providing multiple perspectives on society and providing bandwidth for different voices based on religions and philosophies of life was transferred to television broadcasting in the 1950s. In the 1960s, the broadcasting structure was opened to new organizations that, according to the numbers of registered members, could convince the board that they complemented the system. To this day, new broadcasters are added to the arrangement every few years. This focus on content and multiple perspectives in television has influenced Dutch documentary filmmaking significantly since the 1970s. Broadcasters such as the VPRO (and later HUMAN) encouraged filmmakers to make documentaries that were less aesthetically pleasing and more politically progressive while the makers often showed a personal engagement. Bert Hogenkamp, *De Nederlandse documentairefilm, 1965–1990: De ontwikkeling van een filmgenre in het televisietijdperk* (Amsterdam: Boom, 2015).

led to several documentaries that we can label "neighborhood films" and that are, in many respects, predecessors to contemporary documentary series like *Schuldig* and *Klassen*.[19] These neighborhood films zoom in on the impact of policymaking, often from a progressive standpoint, in which a local situation serves as an analogy to discuss a broad range of societal problems. The four-part television documentary series *Lijn 6* (*Line 6*, 1983) by Vincent Monnikendam, for example, addresses issues such as the dilapidation of housing and the general decline of everyday life in neighborhoods along a tram line in The Hague. The three-part documentary series *De Straat* (*The Street*, Netty van Hoorn and Ireen van Ditshuyzen, 1986) is geographically closer to *Schuldig*. It portrays the gradual decline in social cohesion of the Pieter Vlamingstraat in Amsterdam from an everyday perspective. A slightly different, yet equally important predecessor to *Schuldig* is the 2015 documentary *De Tegenprestatie*, which similarly exemplifies the crossover of film and television in documentary filmmaking. Also produced by the television broadcaster HUMAN, the film won the Gouden Kalf award for best Dutch documentary. The film is a discomforting experience to watch as it presents a series of conversations between welfare agents from the Rotterdam municipality and unemployed people who, due to a stricter regime, are now told to do all kinds of trainings, internships, and communal service to "deserve" their welfare check. Without any narrative structure, without any voice-over, and from a static camera perspective, we see individuals who are told that they are responsible for being in their situation and that "*you* have to change the tide." Only at the end of the film does the camera setup change: then we see unemployed people in reflective gear picking up street garbage at a public square right in front of the city hall. Whereas the television format has its limitations in terms of length and form, its biggest advantage is television's present tense and wide availability (which has increased with web broadcasting).

Documentary series on television thus have the capacity to engage audiences for several weeks in a row and in that way to stir public and political debate. As John Caughie summarizes, "the extension of interrupted time gives us forms of engagement, involvement, and subjectivity specific to television."[20] *Schuldig*, like similar progressive documentary programs, was produced with an "impact coordinator" in the team while it was established as a cross-media product.

---

[19] The term "neighborhood documentaries" is my own, but for an in-depth discussion on these films and their impact on the history of documentary filmmaking, see Hogenkamp, *De Nederlandse documentairefilm*, 345–357.
[20] John Caughie, *Television Drama: Realism, Modernism, and British Culture* (Oxford: Oxford University Press, 2000), 205.

On-site screenings and debate evenings featuring professionals, academics, and politicians were organized throughout the country with a special final demonstration in the streets of The Hague, the governmental capital.[21] The series was also accompanied by an eight-episode podcast, a special magazine, and a call to action as viewers could register to volunteer in a welfare organization. A similar cross-media structure was organized for the 2020 series *Klassen*, although all live events were cancelled due to Covid-19.

An Aesthetics of Time and Place and the Spatio-Temporalities of Precarity

The impact of *Schuldig*, *Klassen*, *De Tegenprestatie* and other documentaries portraying issues of precarity is, of course, not only due to their cross-media compatibilities. Rather, we can identify some recurring forms and motifs that contribute to the emotional impact of these documentaries on the viewer. By focusing on the spatio-temporalities of precarity, for example by zooming in on daily life in one particular neighborhood, the documentaries visualize the affective atmosphere of precarity. *Schuldig* follows seven key individuals who are all living or working in a small urban neighborhood, De Vogelbuurt in Amsterdam-Noord (nicknamed "Debt Village" in the first episode).[22] Separated from the rest of Amsterdam by the body of water IJ, Amsterdam-Noord is historically known as a working-class neighborhood. Only in the last decade has Noord been subject to gentrification. Attracting more upper-class and creative elites, the neighborhood is now oftentimes considered a prime example for the process of gentrification. However, since it has been closed-off for such a long time, it has remained a largely poor neighborhood with an increasing amount of higher-educated wealthy newcomers forming a parallel society. The spatial dimension of the small neighborhood is important for the intertwining narratives in the documentary. Aerial, high-angle shots are used to signify the spatial organization of the neighborhood. In it there are a few key locations inhabited by recurring characters,

---

[21] The "*Schuldig* on Tour" series of events was financially supported by an insurance company, a public-academic think-tank, and Ministry of Social Affairs and Employment.
[22] The documentary series actually followed from an ethnographic study that Sylbing and Gould did for the municipality of Amsterdam, published as Esther Gould and Sarah Sylbing, *Dubbeltjes & kwartjes: een onderzoek naar schulden en dreigende huisuitzetting in Amsterdam* (Amsterdam: Gemeente Amsterdam and Delta Lloyd Foundation, 2015).

such as Dennis' pet store and the office of the social worker Paul, which function as recurring points of recognition where characters of individual storylines meet. Hence from the outset it is communicated that this is an area where people live together. More importantly, the problems that these individuals encounter are particular but related. The series presents an economy of debt where everyone has their own private problems while, at the same time, there is a structure of shared suffering and support. The images arouse feelings of control and recognition as the viewer slowly enters the documentary storyworld. Moreover, they address a nostalgia for a time when people coincidentally met on the street and had a shared sense of community. In a somewhat melancholic tone, Esther Gould's voice-over follows this process from nostalgia to harsh reality: "It is a village within a city, a neighborhood like so many other. A place where people still greet each other. With a pet store, a Foodbank, and with inhabitants with debts. Many, many debts." Sylbing and Gould have been working together since 2006, always in the same neighborhood of De Vogelenbuurt. For an art festival organized at the crossroads of the rich and the poor part of Amsterdam-Noord, they teamed up to make the short documentary *50 Cent* (2007), an intimate portrait of the eight-year-old Giovanni shot in a predominantly observational mode with an occasional voice-over by Giovanni himself introducing his family. We follow him wandering around the neighborhood, always on the move. Sometimes at the place of his mother (a desperate, slightly alcoholic mother of three young kids), then at his father's friend's guest address (a friendly and homeless person using alcohol and drugs). Giovanni is always in search for a little money that he spends on buying soda, toys, and a DVD version of *Get Rich or Die Tryin'* (Jim Sheridan, 2005) featuring the rapper 50 Cent. Yet Giovanni is represented as a kid who, devoid of parental supervision, manages his own life in the streets, at school, and at the local shopping mall. He is hopeful and sees no obstacles even though the living situation will evidently hinder, or even prevent him from reaching the wealthy life that he dreams of.

Giovanni appears in presence through absence (he refuses to appear onscreen as he is facing youth detention) in a subsequent, longer documentary that Sylbing and Gould released five years later. *De rekening van Catelijne (Catelijne's Bill,* 2012) focuses on the family's mother who, now reconciled with Giovanni's father, faces ongoing stress while taking care of her kids. Over the course of several days, we follow Catelijne in her everyday life and witness daily moments when the washing machine is breaking down, when she's talking on the phone at home, or at the office of a welfare worker, or when she is writing e-mails to a welfare organization or checking her account at the ATM.

"Precarity is often understood as a temporal or rhythmic phenomenon defined by erratic and uncertain rhythms as well as by a necessitated short-termism,"[23] Ella Harris and Mel Nowicki conclude in their article about cultural geographies of precarity. The aesthetics of *50 Cent* and *De rekening van Catelijne* make the spatio-temporalities of precarity tangible. These affective-aesthetic forms are also relevant to the success of *Schuldig* and *Klassen*. Hence the spatio-temporalities of precarity should be an important object of investigation. Precarity, in this respect, can be imagined and visualized as having an impact on everyday rhythms and mundane situations, on movements and mobilities. While precarious living conditions are a constant, the articulation of these circumstances, the stress and impact that this situation has on daily life, is felt in specific moments and places. Both films display an aesthetics of spatial movement as characters like Giovanni and his mother Catelijne are frequently *on the move*. The film about Catelijne opens and closes with the main character jogging. The shots of key characters Ramona and Ron on their Vespa have probably become the most iconic images of *Schuldig*. In *Klassen* the motif of people on the move is most evident in scenes where Anyssa travels with her grandfather (with whom she lives as her mother lost custody) in a quadricycle (Fig. 1). These images of people restlessly changing places illustrate the fantasy that, according to Lauren Berlant, "[u]nder capitalism, being in circulation denotes being in life."[24] And yet, this movement leads nowhere, it is both a symptom and a cause of restlessness and anxiety that typifies the affective atmosphere of a local, shared precarity of bodies and individuals. There is no surplus, no solution and no relief of sorrow.

The intertwinement of daily life with stressful situations is related to this motif of movement. Moments of stress, precarity, and anxiety are situated *within* the rhythms of everyday life at home, at work, in moments of caretaking and social contact. In episode two, for example, we tune into a conversation of a group of women on a street corner. Instead of everyday small-talk, these women talk about debt restructuring and a financial counselor they *love to hate*. Or we see how Ron's and Ramona's daughter is given a figure of the princess Anna from the animated musical fantasy *Frozen* (Chris Buck and Jennifer Lee, 2013) for her birthday; the same puppet reappears, a few scenes later, in a shot of a home eviction. Or, Dennis, the man with the local pet shop who is enjoying his pigeons in one moment, while in the next shot he is negotiating with a debt collector on the

---

[23] Harris and Nowicki, "Cultural Geographies of Precarity," 389. See also Louise Waite, "A Place and Space for a Critical Geography of Precarity?" *Geography Compass* 3, no. 1 (2009).
[24] Lauren Berlant, *Cruel Optimism* (Durham, NC: Duke University Press, 2011), 42.

Fig. 1: Anyssa and her grandfather riding through the neighborhood in their quadricycle in *Klassen* (Class/Classroom, HOS, 2020).

phone. This recurring intertwinement of recognizable cheerful, heartwarming, and familial scenes with moments of stress and concern gives *Schuldig* and *Klassen* their affective force. Precarity as a socio-economic problem is embodied by "people of flesh and blood, whom we all start to love," as a reviewer wrote.[25] The characters are never simply sad or miserable but always complex, multifaceted personalities with a range of emotions, behaving rationally as well as irrationally.

What is shown is a deeply human condition marked by inhumane anxiety. The effect of these images reaches further or deeper than mere identification with the characters. Viewers do not necessarily feel for the misery of individual characters, but rather get involved or respond affectively to the mood of precariousness that the series presents. Moods, as Charles Altieri explains, are "modes of feeling where the sense of subjectivity becomes diffuse and sensation merges into something close to atmosphere, something that seems to pervade an entire scene or situation."[26] According to Mieke Bal, mood is therefore located within the relational intensity between the images and the viewer.[27] What these documentaries establish, then, is an affective space of intensity, through which the works "become more serious, effective, and stronger utterances than any news item or political debate—these days reduced to tweets anyway—can effectuate."[28] It is this mode of intensity that is affectively effective in the work of Sylbing and Gould.

---

[25] Kim van der Meulen, "Klassen, nieuwe serie in Noord: 'Er wordt absurd vroeg geselecteerd'," *Het Parool*, November 28, 2020.
[26] Charles Altieri, *The Particulars of Rapture: An Aesthetics of the Affects* (Ithaca, NY: Cornell UP, 2003), 48.
[27] Bal, "Affectively Effective," 196.
[28] Ibid., 187.

Intertwined Lives and Precarious Living

Schuldig and *Klassen* represent life as a networked collection of interactions. Precarity, as economically vulnerable existence, is systemic. No one is individually held responsible for the current situation. In *Schuldig*, one of the central characters is Ed, a debt collector who, together with a housing organization, evicts Ron and Ramona. But even this *antagonist* is human, since he cares for people and is part of a larger system. What the works of Sylbing and Gould repeatedly challenge, in the end, is the notion that the welfare state is functional and that it protects all citizens equally. These documentaries visualize how the Dutch neoliberally shaped post-welfare state keeps precarious living situations existing. "The stability of welfare-state protection never exists equally for all," as Lorey observes, and in the case of *Schuldig* it becomes clear that the commercial interests of creditors as owners of capital are better protected than the lives of debtors or non-owners.[29] The damages caused by this exploitative relation are felt across generations. As the series shows, an unresolved debt of €6,000 ruins the lives of a complete family. The parents and children are evicted and have to move in with the grandparents. As a result of the ongoing levels of stress and trauma, the children underperform at school while the grandparents experience physical and mental effects of the uncertain living conditions. It shows that in this system of governing, to phrase Carolina Odd, "The reverse side of the 'right to life' here is always the exclusion or destruction of life."[30]

An aesthetic representation of the increasingly large share of the population that runs the risk of dropping out of protective state regulation can also be found in *The Paradise Suite* (Joost van Ginkel, 2015). In several respects, van Ginkel's film, which won the 2015 Gouden Kalf for Best Feature Film, can be seen as an important precedent to *Schuldig*, albeit from a fictionalized perspective. *Paradise Suite* tells the story, in a mosaic narrative, of six immigrants coming to Amsterdam. Its thematic originality lies in linking the experience of the *successful new citizen*, of whom the metropolitan city is so proud, to stories of the marginalized, unprotected, and often invisible migrant. Each of these six characters faces setbacks or personal disasters up to the extent that the two illegal migrants almost lose their status as humans. Hence, *The Paradise Suite* shows not only the global circulation of labor, money, and individuals in late

---

29 Lorey, *State of Insecurity*, 57; Maurizio Lazzarato, *The Making of the Indebted Man* (Los Angeles: Semiotext(e), 2012), 23.
30 As cited in Lorey, *State of Insecurity*, 37.

capitalism, it also critiques that system by presenting a global circulation of broken dreams and shattered lives.

From a different perspective, *The Domino Effect* (Paula van de Oest, 2012) also thematizes the international circulation of money and the interdependence of people in a globally networked society. Inspired by the 2008 financial crisis, van der Oest's film focuses on the reliance of middle-class families, spread across different continents, on the international flows of money. The film presents a kind of *glocal* precariat as it shows local lives of people whose dreams, ambitions, and personal self-worth have become dependent on a fragile yet exploitative system of international capital. In the Netherlands, for example, we follow Nick, an ex-convict who gets the chance to work in a restaurant owned by welldoers Kai and Antoinette, only to find out that the restaurant faces bankruptcy due to a loss of financial trust somewhere in the global capital market. In another plotline we see the impact of the financial crisis on the wedding-cake business of an Indian immigrant family in the US. These knock-on effects are the core of the film as the narrative portrays the interwoven lives of a South African student, a British investor, his father who is drawn to British nationalist politics, a Chinese laborer supporting his family living in the rural countryside, and more. The film visualizes the effects of financial capitalism on everyday lives in this kaleidoscope of personal tragedies. *The Domino Effect* thereby shows a global village filled with struggling individuals whose lives and dreams are marked by an increasing amount of interdependence.

The Domino Effect and *The Paradise Suite*, like *Schuldig*, represent the destructive nature of the governing of precarity in late capitalism. However, as these films indicate, our only hope to overcome that exploitative system is equally found in our fundamentally social and relational being-in-the-world. At the same time, these fiction films allow for a somewhat melodramatic resolution in working toward narrative closure. Absent in *The Paradise Suite* is any form of authority or state agency. Rather, the film focuses on individual responsibility. Living socially, recognizing the other's needs and vulnerability against a background of exploitation and a Hobbesian Leviathanism in which only the strongest survive. At the end of the film, Jenya, an illegal sex-worker from Bulgaria, returns traumatized to her home where she finds her loving mother. Or, in an extreme case, the African immigrant Yaya sacrifices his own life to safe Jenya from an international network of sex traffickers. These strangers, foreigners in an unknown land of their broken immigrant dreams, are dependent on each other. These melodramatic narrative devices of sacrifice and survival, told by way of an aestheticized cinematography, arouse an engaging viewer experience but refract from a more explicit political message. Instead, both *The Paradise Suite* and *The Domino Effect* are ultimately about an existential conception of precariousness which, in the words of Judith Butler, "implies living socially, that is, the fact that one's life is always in the hands of the other. It implies exposure, both to those we know and those we do not know; a dependency of people we know, or barely know, or not know at all."[31]

This practice of considering precarity in relation to unknown, and often foreign others remains a recurring topic in other Dutch arthouse fiction films like *La Holandesa* (*Messi and Maud*, Marleen Jonkman, 2017) and *In Blue* (Jaap van Heusden, 2017). These two films present two strikingly similar narratives about independent, middle-class, Western women who, travelling abroad, confront their own precarious lives in encountering a child who they think needs help. *La Holandesa* confronts the themes of white saviorism and Western privilege with society's normative ideas about motherhood. In the film we see Maud (Rifka Lodeizen), a woman in her early forties, backpacking through Chile. In the wake of a personal existential crisis concerning her unfulfilled desire for motherhood, she starts to take care of a young boy named Messi who, she presumes, is neglected by his parents. Yet, as it turns out, the boy actually has a loving and caring family that is searching for him while he has been abducted by this unidentified Western woman. *In Blue*, subsequently, tells a similar story of an air hostess in her mid-forties who develops a complex relationship with a 15-year-old homeless boy in Bucharest. This relationship between Lin and Nico hovers between surrogate parenting and a romantic affair until Nicu, the street boy, ends it on his own terms by taking her money. Both films focus on the intercultural recognition of precarity between individuals who care for each other. At the same time, these films criticize this idealization of recognition and care by showing the uneven relations of dependency. After all, the Western protagonists overcome their existential crisis or heal their trauma by taking care of the foreign other on whom they project their needs and desires. What remains, in the end, is a lack of understanding and a final solution as both films end with a safe return flight to the Netherlands.

The various fiction films that I have mentioned are illustrative of the landscape of representation of precarity in which *Schuldig* partakes; for instance, they all present complex mosaic narratives. It is striking that both *Schuldig* and *Klassen* have been mainly compared to fiction film and television in the press, and directors Sylbing and Gould agreed that they had analyzed *The Wire*, *Narcos* (Netflix, 2015–2018), and *Top Boy* (Channel 4/Netflix, 2011–present) for their storytelling techniques.[32] There are no good guys, and no bad ones either,

---

31 Butler, *Frames of War*, 14.
32 "Schuldig (HUMAN): Winnaar Zilveren Nipkowschijf 2017," *Nipkowschijf.nl*. http://nipkow schijf.nl/schuldig-human/.; Belinda van de Graaf, "Kan school het verschil maken? Bij Gianny en Anyssa uit de docuserie 'Klassen' is het de vraag," *Trouw*, November 30, 2020.

just as in those fiction films and TV series. However, there *is* a responsibility to act as humans. That is, to acknowledge the Other as human by admitting their precarious living. And to act accordingly politically, which is why there are always politicians as part of the narrative.[33]

Most importantly, what this handful of contemporary documentary features and fiction films portray is the broad range of dependencies that we have as humans. From different perspectives, these films illustrate how the changes made in the welfare state systematically destabilize these relations of dependency. Films like *Schuldig* and *The Paradise Suite* are, in Berlant words, "aesthetic reenactments of the impact of neoliberalism on the everyday lives of formerly protected classes."[34] It is in this process of enacting the human body and its systems of relations as vulnerable that resistance and political action begin, or as Judith Butler observes:

> By theorizing the human body as a certain kind of *dependency* on infrastructure, understood complexly as environment, social relations, and networks of support and sustenance by which the human itself proves not to be divided from the animal or from the technical world, we foreground the ways in which we are vulnerable to decimated or disappearing infrastructures, economic supports, and predictable and well-compensated labor.[35]

Conclusion

The landscape of framings and visualizations of precarity and poverty in contemporary Dutch film and television is more diverse than the films under discussion. Whereas *Schuldig, Klassen, De Tegenprestatie,* and fiction films like *The Paradise Suite* and *The Domino Effect* relate to an affective register of recognition and care, there are other, more cynical, essentialist, or conservative framings operative in Dutch visual culture. From a larger perspective, I think, the framings of precarity and vulnerability discussed above should be seen as a response to a kind of neoliberal or conservative framing that has been dominant

---

[33] *Klassen* has an aftershow, called *Nablijven*. Airing immediately after each episode (though on a different public channel), politicians and experts discuss the show.
[34] Berlant, *Cruel Optimism*, 191.
[35] Judith Butler, "Rethinking Vulnerability and Resistance," in *Vulnerability and Resistance*, ed. Judith Butler, Zeynep Gambetti, and Leticia Sabsay (Durham, NC/London: Duke University Press, 2016), 21.

for several decades. Filmmakers Sylbing and Gould, for example, have explicitly addressed this lack of real people instead of caricatures.

The most striking examples of the mainstream caricaturizing of poverty from a middle-class perspective can be found in *low-class comedy* films like *Flodder* (Dick Maas, 1986) and *New Kids Turbo*. These comedy features are still among the top hits in recent Dutch film history.[36] While ridiculing, in the end, also the hypocrisy of the upper-class, *Flodder* presents a happy-go-lucky image of poverty in which social change and equality remain impossible. The Flodder family that is at the center of the story is poor, but that does not seem to bother them (so it should not bother us either). Even when, in a kind of experiment, they get relocated to an upper-class neighborhood, they neither change nor do they do grow bitter. *New Kids Turbo* is in many ways similar, although it presents a more complex and contradictory framing of poverty. A satire, this comedy is about a group of seemingly antisocial low-lifes on which the welfare system has turned its back, who start to refuse to pay for anything and initiate a revolt. In the end, the film remains a celebration of violence with ingredients of *white male victimage,* in which masculinity is presented as being under threat by a bureaucratic system.[37] The resolution of the film basically revolves around one of the characters trying to get to have sex with his girlfriend while all potentially political causes of the protest remain unaddressed.

It is against these caricatures of precarized people that *Schuldig* should be understood. For a long time, as these films indicate, the welfare state has been treated as a laughing matter in Dutch cinema. Yet, as I argued in this chapter, we can recognize an increased sensitivity for issues of precarity and precariousness in film and television. The critical acclaim and widespread popularity of *Schuldig* and *Klassen* signifies this trend. The impact of these series is felt both in politics as well as in the popular framing of issues of social security, equality, and the governing of precarity. An important strategy to make representations of precarity "affectively effective" is the focus on the cultural geography of precarity and the visualization of the spatio-temporalities of precarity within the everyday.[38] In the end, the purpose of these newly developed frames on poverty is to *move* the spectator, not just metaphorically but also politically and physically. As Mieke

---

36 Peter Verstraten, "Low-class Comedies," in *Humour and Irony in Dutch Postwar Fiction Film* (Amsterdam: Amsterdam University Press, 2016).
37 Paul Elliot Johnson, "Walter White(ness) lashes out: *Breaking Bad* and male victimage," *Critical Studies in Media Communication* 34, no. 1 (October 2016): 14–18.
38 Bal, "Affectively Effective."

Bal reminds us, if viewers are to be affected politically, they must first "float away."[39] We need to leave our fixed positions to perceive the face of the other.

Bibliography

Altieri, Charles. *The Particulars of Rapture: An Aesthetics of the Affects*. Ithaca, NY: Cornell University Press, 2003.
Bal, Mieke. "Affectively Effective: Affect as an Artistic-Political Strategy." In *How to Do Things with Affects: Affective Triggers in Aesthetic Forms and Cultural Practices*, ed. Ernst van Alphen and Tomáš Jirsa. Leiden/Boston: Brill-Rodopi, 2019, 179–199.
Beerekamp, Hans. "'Schuldig' is een magistrale serie over armoede." *NRC Handelsblad*. December 6, 2016.
Berlant, Lauren. *Cruel Optimism*. Durham, NC: Duke University Press, 2011.
Bos, Maaike. "TV-serie 'Schuldig' bewijst: Een ontroerende documentaire kan meer bereiken dan honderd beleidsstukken." *Trouw*, June 14, 2017.
Butler, Judith. *Frames of War: When is Life Grievable?* London/New York: Verso, 2010.
——. "Rethinking Vulnerability and Resistance." In *Vulnerability in Resistance*, ed. Judith Butler, Zeynep Gambetti, and Leticia Sabsay. Durham, NC/London: Duke University Press, 2016, 12–27.
Caughie, John. *Television Drama: Realism, Modernism, and British Culture*. Oxford: Oxford University Press, 2000.
Dancus, Adriana Margareta, Mats Hyvönen, and Maria Karlsson, eds. *Vulnerability in Scandinavian Art and Culture*. London: Palgrave Macmillan, 2019.
De Lange, Marlous, Maarten Wolbers, and Wout Ultee. "United in Precarious Employment? Employment Precarity of Young Couples in the Netherlands, 1992–2007." *European Sociological Review* 29, no. 3 (June 2013): 503–516.
Delsen, Lei. *Exit Polder Model?: Socioeconomic Changes in the Netherlands*. Westport/London: Praeger, 2002.
Engbersen, Godfried, Erik Snel, and Monique Kremer. *De Val Van De Middenklasse?: Het Stabiele En Kwetsbare Midden. Verkenningen*. The Hague: WRR, 2017.
Engelen, Ewald. *Ontwaak! Kom uit uw neoliberale sluimer*. Amsterdam: Atheneum, 2021.
Geldof, Dirk. *Onzekerheid: Over leven in de risicomaatschappij*. Leuven/The Hague: Acco, 2021.
Gould, Esther, and Sarah Sylbing. *Dubbeltjes & kwartjes: een onderzoek naar schulden en dreigende huisuitzetting in Amsterdam*. Amsterdam: Gemeente Amsterdam and Delta Lloyd Foundation, 2015.
Harris, Ella, and Mel Nowicki. "Cultural Geographies of Precarity." *Cultural Geographies* 25, no. 3 (March 2018): 387–391.
Hogenkamp, Bert. *De Nederlandse documentairefilm, 1965–1990: De ontwikkeling van een filmgenre in het televisietijdperk*. Amsterdam: Boom, 2015.

---

39 Bal, "Affectively Effective," 190.

Johnson, Paul Elliot. "Walter White(ness) lashes out: *Breaking Bad* and male victimage." *Critical Studies in Media Communication* 34, no. 1 (October 2016): 14–18.
Kruiter, Albert Jan, Femmianne Bredeworld, and Marcel Ham, eds. *Hoe de verzorgingsstaat verbouwd wordt: Kroniek van een verandering*. Amsterdam: Van Gennep and Sociale Vraagstukken, 2016.
Lazzarato, Maurizio. *The Making of the Indebted Man: An Essay on the Neoliberal Condition*, trans. Joshua David Baron. Los Angeles, CA: Semiotext(e), 2012.
Lieshout, Peter van, ed. *Sociale (on)zekerheid: De voorziene toekomst*. Amsterdam: Amsterdam University Press, 2016.
Lorey, Isabell. *State of Insecurity: Government of the Precarious*. London/New York: Verso, 2015.
Luijkx, Ruud, and Maarten Wolbers. "The Impact of Employment Precarity on Early Labour Market Careers and Family Formation in the Netherlands." In *Flexible Employment and the Welfare State in Europe*, ed. Paolo Barbieri. Cheltenham: Edward Elgar, 2018, 1–33.
Neilson, Brett and Net Rossiter. "Precarity as a Political Concept, or, Fordism as Exception." *Theory, Culture & Society* 25, no. 7/8 (2008): 51–72.
Roosma, Femke. "Wie verdient nog onze solidariteit?: Veranderingen in solidariteitsgevoelens met ouderen, zieken en gehandicapten, werklozen en immigranten in de 21ste eeuw." *Mens en Maatschappij* 94, no. 4 (November 2019): 483–505.
Uyterlinde, Matthijs. "Dalende leefbaarheid is geen nieuws, wel prioriteit." *Sociale Vraagstukken*. November 17, 2018. https://www.socialevraagstukken.nl/dalende-leefbaarheid-geen-nieuws-wel-prioriteit/.
Van Bavel, Bas, and Ewout Frankema. "Wealth and Inequality in the Netherlands, c. 1950–2015." *Tijdschrift voor sociale en economische geschiedenis* 14, no. 2 (2017): 29–62.
Van de Graaf, Belinda. "Kan school het verschil maken? Bij Gianny en Anyssa uit de docuserie 'Klassen' is het de vraag." *Trouw*, November 30, 2020. https://www.trouw.nl/cultuur-media/kan-school-het-verschil-maken-bij-gianny-en-anyssa-uit-de-docuserie-klassen-is-het-de-vraag~b7e01716/?referrer=https%3A%2F%2Fwww.google.com%2F.
Van der Meulen, Kim. "Klassen, nieuwe serie in Noord: 'Er wordt absurd vroeg geselecteerd'." *Het Parool*. November 28, 2020.
Van Lieshout, Peter, ed. *Sociale (on)zekerheid*. Amsterdam: Amsterdam University Press, 2016.
Vermeersch, Wim. "Het is klasse, suffie, niet identiteit – interview met Ewald Engelen." *Samenleving en Politiek* 25, no. 8 (October 2018): 36–43.
Verstraten, Peter. *Humour and Irony in Dutch Postwar Fiction Film*. Amsterdam: Amsterdam University Press, 2016, 45–82.
Vrooman, Cor. "Armoede, naar Nederlandse maatstaven." *Sociale Vraagstukken*. December 19, 2011. https://www.socialevraagstukken.nl/armoede-naar-nederlandse-maatstaven/.
Waite, Louise. "A Place and Space for a Critical Geography of Precarity?" *Geography Compass* 3, no. 1 (2009): 412–433.
Wijfjes, Huub. *Omroep in Nederland: vijfenzeventig jaar medium en maatschappij: 1919–1994*. Zwolle: Waanders, 1994.
Witteveen Dirk. "Precarious Early Careers: Instability and Timing within Labor Market Entry." In *Precarious Work*, ed. Arne L. Kalleberg and Steven P. Vallas. Bingley: Emerald Publishing, 2018, 365–398.

Filmography

50 Cent. Dir. Sarah Sylbing and Esther Gould. VPRO. Netherlands, 2007.
De rekening van Catelijne (*Catelijne's Bill*). VPRO. Netherlands, 2012.
De Straat (*The Street*). Dir. Netty van Hoorn and Ireen van Ditshuyzen. NOS. Netherlands, 1986.
De Tegenprestatie (*Quid Pro Quo*). Dir. Monique Lesterhuis and Suzanne Raes. HUMAN. Netherlands, 2015.
Flodder. Dir. Dick Maas. Netherlands, 1986.
Get Rich or Die Tryin'. Dir. Jim Sheridan. US, 2005.
In Blue. Dir. Jaap van Heusden. Netherlands, 2017.
Klassen (*Class/Classroom*). HOS. Netherlands, 2020.
La Holandesa (*Messi and Maud*). Dir. Marleen Jonkman. Netherlands, 2017.
Lijn 6 (*Line 6*). Dir. Vincent Monnikendam. NOS. Netherlands, 1983.
Narcos. Dir. Carlo Bernard, Chris Brancato, Doug Miro. Netflix, USA, 2015–2018.
New Kids Turbo. Dir. Flip van der Kuil and Steffen Maas. Netherlands, 2010.
Schuldig (*Guilt/Debt*). HOS, Netherlands, 2016.
The Domino Effect. Dir. Paula van der Oest. Netherlands, 2012.
The Paradise Suite. Dir. Joost van Ginkel. Netherlands, 2015.
The Wire. HBO, USA, 2002–2008.
Top Boy. Channel 4/Netflix, UK, 2011–.

Contributors

Zane Balčus is a PhD candidate and Junior Research Assistant at the Latvian Academy of Culture. She co-authored the books *Inscenējumu realitāte. Latvijas aktierkino vēsture* (*Reality of Fiction. History of Latvian Fiction Film*, 2011), *Rolanda Kalniņa telpa* (*Cinematic Space of Rolands Kalniņš*, 2018), and *Latvijas kino: jaunie laiki. 1990–2020* (*Latvian Cinema: Recent History, 1990–2020*, 2021), and she works as a curator and as a freelance film critic for various publications.

Özgür Çiçek is a film scholar based in Berlin. Currently she is a Philipp Schwartz Fellow at Freie Universität Berlin, Cinepoetics: Center for Advanced Film Studies. She received her PhD from Binghamton University, New York in 2016. Her research interests include national/transnational cinemas, minor cinemas, migrant cinemas, memory studies, and documentary filmmaking. In her current project she is examining the motivations and dynamics behind Kurdish filmmaking in Germany.

Elisa Cuter is a PhD candidate and Research Associate at the Emmy Noether research group "Cinematic Discourses of Deprivation" of the Film University Babelsberg (Potsdam). She has worked as a film critic for several magazines and collaborated with various festivals in Italy and Germany, is chief editor of the online magazine *Il Tascabile*, and author of *Ripartire dal desiderio* (2020), and has had articles published in peer-reviewed journals and edited collections.

Christian Ferencz-Flatz is a researcher at the Alexandru Dragomir Institute for Philosophy. He teaches at the National University of Theatre and Film in Bucharest. His research concerns phenomenology, critical theory, philosophy of history, and film and media theory. With Julian Hanich, he edited the journal issue Studia Phaenomenologica: *Film and Phenomenology* (2016). His latest monographs: *Sehen Als-ob. Ästhetik und Pragmatik in Husserls Bildlehre* (2016) and *Filmul ca situație socială* (2018).

Manuel Garin is Senior Lecturer in Film and Media Studies at Universitat Pompeu Fabra, Barcelona. He has been a visiting scholar at various institutions including the Tokyo University of the Arts, the University of Southern California, and Columbia University. Author of the monograph *El gag visual* (Cátedra, 2014), his research focuses on the historical, political and aesthetic dimensions of cinema and audiovisual media.

Marcy Goldberg is a Lecturer in film, media, gender, and cultural studies at the Lucerne University of Applied Arts and a freelance writer, curator, and translator. She holds an M.F.A. from York University (Toronto), with a thesis on documentary film and the philosophy of the everyday, and is a doctoral candidate at the University of Zurich film studies department, with a dissertation in Swiss film history. Together with Simon Spiegel and Andrea Reiter, she co-edited *Utopia and Reality: Documentary, Activism and Imagined Worlds* (2020).

Gert Jan Harkema teaches film at the University of Amsterdam. His main research interest is in the concept of *presence* and aesthetic experiences in (early) cinema. His most current research, however, focuses on the critical dimensions of social and ecological precarity in Dutch film and television.

John Hill is Professor of Media at Royal Holloway, University of London. He is the author or editor of a number of books including *Sex, Class and Realism: British Cinema 1956–1963* (1986), *The Oxford Guide to Film Studies* (co-ed. 1998), *British Cinema in the 1980s* (1999), *Cinema and Northern Ireland: Film, Culture and Politics* (2006), *Ken Loach: The Politics of Film and Television* (2011), *Film Policy in a Globalised Cultural Economy* (co-ed. 2018), and *A Companion to British and Irish Cinema* (ed. 2019).

Ursula-Helen Kassaveti is an adjunct tutor at the department of Primary Education of the National and Kapodistrian University of Athens. Her research has focused on aspects of visual culture, cultural theory, visual ethnography, and popular culture. She holds an MA in Cultural Studies and an MA in History and Folklore (UOA). Her PhD thesis revolved around the 1980s VHS culture in Greece. She has undertaken extensive research for the Greek Institute of Small Businesses (GSEVEE) on representations of employment of small merchants in Greek cinema (1950s–2018).

Guido Kirsten is Principal Investigator of the Emmy Noether Research Group "Cinematic Discourses of Deprivation" at the Film University Babelsberg KONRAD WOLF (Potsdam). He is the author of books on cinematic realism (2013) and on the notion of *découpage* (2022). Together with Margrit Tröhler he edited *Christian Metz and the Codes of Cinema* (2018).

Nino Klingler earns his living at a philanthropic NGO and works as a freelance film critic and filmmaker in his spare time. He studied film and philosophy at Freie Universität Berlin and Bilgi University Istanbul and was a fellow at the Graduiertenschule of the University of Art Berlin. Most of his German-language texts can be found online on critic.de. His most recent film *Ununterbrochen Reden* (with Frédéric Jaeger) premiered at the Hof International Film Festival in 2021.

Melanie Letschnig studied theater, film, and media studies with a focus on European ethnology at the University of Vienna, where she has a permanent position as Lecturer for Film Theory and Analysis. She is an assistant (prae-doc) at Kunstuniversität Linz and a trainer for German as second language at bfi Wien. Her recent publications include several articles in *Eine eigene Geschichte. Frauen Film Österreich seit 1999* (ed. Isabella Reicher, 2020).

Anders Marklund is Senior Lecturer in Film Studies at Lund University. His research, as well as his teaching and work as primary editor of *Journal of Scandinavian Cinema*, revolves around Swedish and Nordic cinema from perspectives that include industry, representation, and narration. Another lasting research interest concerns contemporary European popular cinema, currently primarily with a focus on how it draws on, and contributes to, cultural and historical memory.

Ewa Mazierska is Professor of Film Studies at the University of Central Lancashire. She has published over thirty monographs and edited collections about film and popular music, focusing on Eastern European and British cinema and music. Among them are several books about the representation of work, such as *From Self-Fulfilment to Survival of the Fittest: Work in European Cinema from the 1960s to the Present* (2015/2020). Mazierska is also editor of the journal *Studies in Eastern European Cinema*.

Aleksandra Miljković studied Art History at the Philosophical Faculty in Belgrade, Serbia, where she completed her master's degree with a focus on contemporary art and film. Her texts have been published in the magazine of the *Yugoslav Film Archive*. She is currently pursuing an MA degree in Film Culture Heritage and working as a research assistant on the project "Cinematic Discourses of Deprivation" at the Film University Babelsberg KONRAD WOLF in Potsdam, Germany.

Katarína Mišíková is Associate Professor at the Film and Television Faculty of the Academy of Music and Dramatic Arts in Bratislava, Slovakia. She lectures on film history, cognitive film theory and film analysis. Her current field of research is storytelling in contemporary Slovak cinema, hybrid films, and issues of realism. She has published numerous studies and articles as well as a monograph on cognitive narrative theory (*Mysl a příběh ve filmové fikci*, 2009). Her professional activities also include the popularization of cinema among students and pupils.

Eva Näripea is Director of the Film Archive of the National Archives of Estonia and deputy editor of *Studies in Eastern European Cinema* (Routledge). Her research interests range from spatial representations in Soviet Estonian cinema and histories of Eastern European genre film to reflections of neoliberalism in recent Estonian cinema. She has contributed over 40 articles to internationally published volumes, and (co)edited several publications on Eastern European film cultures.

Hanna Prenzel is a scientific/artistic PhD candidate and Research Associate of the Emmy Noether research group "Cinematic Discourses of Deprivation" at the Film University Babelsberg KONRAD WOLF (Potsdam). Her areas of interest include collective filmmaking, documentary-based film forms, postcolonial theory, and feminist film theory. She is co-founder of the *TINT Filmkollektiv* and works as a freelance documentary filmmaker.

Martin O'Shaughnessy is Professor of Film Studies at Nottingham Trent University. He is the author of *Jean Renoir* (2000), *The New Face of Political Cinema* (2007), *La Grande Illusion* (2009), and *Laurent Cantet* (2015). He co-edited, with Graeme Hayes, *Cinéma et engagement* (2012) and he is just completing *Looking Beyond Neoliberalism: French and Belgian Cinema in the Crisis*, which will be published by Edinburgh University Press in 2022.

László Strausz is Assistant Professor in Film Studies at Eötvös Loránd University in Budapest. His work focuses on contemporary East/Central European screen media, cultural memory, and the politics of style. Since the publication of his monograph *Hesitant Histories on the Romanian Screen* (2017), he has been working with state-produced educational films made during the state socialist decades. He is the associate editor of the journal *Studies in Eastern European Cinema*.

Renata Šukaitytė is Associate Professor of Film and Media Studies, Head of The Centre for Journalism and Media Research at Vilnius University, Faculty of Communication. She is co-author of a book about the post-Communist transformation in Lithuanian documentary cinema, TV and video which was published in 2020 by Vilnius University Press and author of 50 publications, including book chapters and peer-reviewed articles for culture, art, and film journals.

Index

Abbasi, Ali 307
Adaman, Fikret 126
Agamben, Giorgio 59
Alakoski, Susanna 305
Albert, Barbara 219
Alemany, Lucía 50
Almodóvar, Pedro 50
Altieri, Charles 356
Álvarez Lopez, Cristina 72
Álvarez, Mercedes 49f., 61
András, Ferenc 187
Andreotti, Giulio 88
Anstey, Edgar 327
Antal, Nimród 193
Arendt, Hannah 55
Arnold, Andrea 5, 9, 334f.
Arslan, Savas 127
Asante, Amma 343
Aspioti, Myrto XV
Audiard, Jacques 40
August, Pernilla 303, 305
Aulenbacher, Brigitte 18, 217 fn 1, 221

Bacsó, Péter 191
Bahrani, Ramin 14
Baillif, Frédéric 246
Bajić, Darko 165
Baker, Sean 21
Bal, Mieke 356, 362
Baldauf, Anette 218
Ballús, Neus 50
Bardan, Alice 12, 15, 96, 251 fn 3
Bardem, Juan Antonio 54
Barrett, Lezli-An 330f
Begić, Aida 172
Benjamin, Walter 40f
Benna, Zyed 41
Benyamina, Houda 37
Berggren, Henrik 303
Berlanga, Luis García 53
Berlant, Lauren 2, 12–16, 20, 34, 49, 54, 59, 73 fn 26, 98, 248, 251 fn 3, 329, 355, 360
Bernard, Chris 330

Bertolucci, Bernardo 96
Bianchi, Pietro 89
Biedermann, Karl 6
Bilge, Deniz 130
Billingham, Richard 5
Blaževičius, Andrius 292
Boe, Christoffer 307, 309, 319–321
Bogdán, Árpád 192
Boldi, Massimo 93
Bollaín, Icíar 50
Bollók, Csaba 192
Bong Joon-ho 22, 234
Booth, Charles 326
Boroš, Rasťo 206
Bortzmeyer, Gabriel 16, 19, 44
Borzęcka, Ewa 276–281
Böszörményi, Géza 189
Boulting, Roy 328
Bourdieu, Pierre 16, 23f, 58 fn 21, 61, 105, 182, 218
Brasla, Varis 295
Brecht, Bertolt 60, 74–77, 154
Bremen, Jan 326
Brizé, Stéphane 34, 36
Brizzi, Fausto 94f
Broomfield, Nick 342
Brown, Wendy 38
Bruegel, Pieter 279
Bruno, Massimiliano 34, 96
Büchner, Christiane 252
Bučka, Jana 213
Bukodi, Erzsébet 181f.
Buñuel, Luis 49, 52
Buraja, Oksana 299
Burkovska Jacobsen, Ilze 293
Butler, Judith 20, 31, 43–45, 171, 230, 326, 358, 360

Cabot, Xesc 50
Caligari, Claudio 98f
Cantet, Laurent 4, 13f., 32, 35f., 73 fn 26
Căpățână-Juller, Laura 149
Caranfil, Nae 144
Carrasco, Luis López 50

Castel, Robert 16, 18f, 218, 230, 348
Cattaneo, Peter 206, 331
Caughlin, Colin 340
Celma, Una 295
Cerdán, Josetxo 53
Černovaitė, Olga 299
Cervini, Alessia 86f., 90
Chaplin, Charlie 127, 129
Chiarla, Lucia 22
Chiotaki-Poulou, Irini 109
Chiriac, Andra 149f
Citti, Sergio 98
Çınar, Gizem 137
Clarke, Alan 330, 334
Clayton, Jack 328
Coers, Matthias 263
Comas, Ramón 53
Comencini, Luigi 95
Conde, José Antonio Nieves 49, 53
Cordeiro, Margarida 66
Cortellesi, Paola 95f.
Costa, José Filipe 65f., 72
Costa, Pedro 66, 78–80
Crewdson, Gregory 79
Culková, Andrea 204
Cvejić, Marko 166, 168

Daković, Nevena 172
Daldry, Stephen 332
Dalianidis, Giannis 111
Dardenne brothers 5, 7f., 12–14, 32, 34–37, 39, 73 fn 26, 200
Day, Dorothy 272
De Gaetano, Roberto 100
de Lauretis, Teresa 218
de Oliveira, Manoel 66
de Paz, Castro 53
De Sica, Christian 93f.
De Sica, Vittorio 87, 89 fn 12
Deák, Krisztina 193
Debruge, Peter 89
del Castillo, Juan Miguel 50
Delépine, Benoît 42, 45
Deleuze, Gilles 57, 87
Demian, Iosif 143
Derflinger, Sabine 220
Dević, Goran 166

Di Giacomo, Federica 99
Dimitrijević, Branislav 146, 165
Dos Santos, José Pedro 70
Dresen, Andreas 252
Drunga, Saulius 292
Dumont, Bruno 34
Dunbar, Andrea 334

Echeverría, Arantxa 50
Eder, Jens 7
Eisenstein, Sergei 212
Elton, Arthur 327
Emmer, Luciano 96
Enciso, Eloy 50
Engels, Frederick 1f., 5–7, 10
Erdőss, Pál 187
Exarchou, Sofia 106, 113f.

Fansa, Samira 263
Farocki, Harun 22
Fassbinder, Rainer Werner 264
Faur, Anna 192
Faus, Pau 56
Fellini, Federico 96
Ferreri, Marco 53
Ferry, Isidoro Martínez 53
Filipović, Stevan 172
Flaherty, Robert 327
Fornay, Mira 199 fn 3, 207, 211
Frears, Stephen 341
Frisch, Max 238
Frye, Northrop 55

Gahigiri, Kantarama 246
Gárdos, Péter 188
Garrido, Pep 50
Garrone, Matteo 89
Gébová, Dana 204
George, Sylvain 37f., 40–42, 45
Golik, Krešo 164
Golubović, Srdan 169
Gomes, Miguel 66, 74, 78
Goretta, Claude 234
Gould, Esther 347, 350, 353 fn 22, 354, 356f., 359, 361
Graeber, David 49, 62
Grierson, John 326f.

Grifi, Alberto 97
Grigoriou, Grigoris 110
Grófová, Iveta 207
Grozeva, Kristina 157
Grunert, Andrea 25
Grunwalsky, Ferenc 189, 190 fn 28
Guédiguian, Robert 34, 36, 38f.
Guerín, José Luis 49, 58
Guyer, Jane 272
Guzmán, Mireia Sanjaume 263

Haggis, Paul 21
Halbheer, Michelle 241
Hall, Stuart 325
Hanák, Dušan 202
Haneke, Michael 158
Haq, Iram 312f.
Harlan, Thomas 69–71, 77 fn 40
Haroun, Mahamat-Saleh 37
Harris, Ella 355
Hauptmann, Gerhart 6
Hermann, Michael 236f.
Herngren, Felix 307, 311, 319
Hjort, Mette 236
Holenstein, André 235
Holland, Agnieszka 275
Hongisto, Ilona 57
Honneth, Axel XII, 146, 155f.
hooks, bell 218
Hübner, Carl Wilhelm 1–3, 5f.
Hufnagl, Klemens 226

Ikić, Ivan 172
Imbach, Thomas 239–241
Imhoof, Markus 233, 243
Irigoien, Maier 50

Janeček, Vít 203
Jelača, Dijana 171–174
Jiránský, Zdeněk 203
Jonkman, Marleen 359
Jonynas, Ignas 292
Jordà, Joaquim 50
Jude, Radu 152
Jūra, Sandris 295
Jušić, Hana 172, 174

Kaboš, Ladislav 213
Kalleberg, Arne 145
Kamalzadeh, Dominik 74
Kamieńska, Irena 276f.
Kamondi, Zoltán 191
Karabasz, Kazimierz 275
Karanović, Srđan 165
Karapetian, Aik 299
Kassovitz, Mathieu 33, 35
Kaurismäki, Aki 315f., 320
Kaurismäki, Mika 316
Kechiche, Abdellatif 32, 35, 37
Keedus, Sulev 298
Keil, Judith 252
Kern, András 191, 193
Kernell, Amanda 307, 311
Kervern, Gustave 42, 45
Keyder, Çağlar 126, 132
Kézdi-Kovács, Zsolt 188
Kirchhoff, Robert 199 fn 2, 205
Klein Svoboda, Lucia 206
Klein Svoboda, Petr 206
Klotz, Nicolas 36
Kluge, Alexander 56, 60
Klusák, Vít 203
Knappik, Christian 224
Kohan, Jenji 21
Koller, Xavier 233
Kolosi, Tamás 181
Koundouros, Nikos 110
Kovalik, József 193
Krauze, Krzysztof 281f.
Krawicz, Mieczysław 274
Krekovič, Miloš 200
Krisiūnas, Justinas 296
Kristóf, György 192, 200 fn 3, 208
Kroske, Gerd 252
Kruska, Antje 253
Kuld, Ergo 298
Kursietis, Juris 296
Kuster, Brigitta 260

Lacuesta, Isaki 50
Laki, László 181
Langkjær, Birger 305–307, 309
Lapinskė, Laura 289

Lazzarato, Maurizio 31, 43, 281
Lehotský, Juraj 199 fn 2, 209, 210
Leigh, Mike 335
León, Fernando de Aranoa 15, 50
Leščák, Marek 201
Lesterhuis, Monique 350
Levi, Angelika 253, 263–267
Levinas, Emanuel 39
Ležaić, Nikola 172
Liiv, Urmas Eero 298
Lioret, Philippe 33
Liová, Zuzana 208
Loach, Ken 9f., 14f., 336, 338–340, 343
Lokshina, Yulia 252
Longinović, Tomislav 161 fn 1, 165
Łopacka, Bożena 283
Lorey, Isabell 24, 31, 43, 260, 266f., 349, 357
Lužytė, Lina 295
Ly, Ladj 37
Lyssy, Rolf 233

Maár, Gyula 187
Maas, Dick 361
Maas, Steffen 350
Macher, Karin 220f., 223
Mader, Ruth 223f., 230
Majmurek, Jakub 283
Marković, Goran 165
Martin, Adrian 72, 73
Martinsons, Māris 295
Marx, Karl 17, 87, 326
Matanić, Dalibor 170
Mateus, Marta 66
Matter, Mani 247
Mayhew, Henty 326
Meier, Ursula 243f
Melgar, Fernand 245–247
Menart, Ursa 172
Mendelson, Jordana 52
Milani, Riccardo 95
Miloš, Maja 172
Minervini, Roberto 88–90
Mladenović, Ivana 154
Möderndorfer, Vinko 169
Moeschler, Olivier 235

Molina, Catalina 220
Monnard, Pierre 241
Monnikendam, Vincent 352
Morató, Jordi 50
Moreno, Victor 49, 58, 159
Mortezai, Sudabeh 220, 225–228
Motakef, Mona 165f.
Moutout, Jean-Marc 32
Muhu, Meelis 298
Mulvey, Laura 4, 218
Munch, Edvard 212
Munck, Ronaldo 31, 43
Mungiu, Cristian 14, 147
Musić, Goran 166f.

Nakache, Olivier 37f
Nanau, Alexander 152f.
Negoescu, Paul 148
Negri, Anna 97
Neilson, Brett 351
Netzer, Călin Peter 144
Ngai, Sianne 55
Nicolaescu, Sergiu 151
Nikolić, Živko 165
Niola, Gabriele 91
Noulelis, Grigoris 112
Novák, Erik 193
Novković, Oleg 166, 169
Nowicki, Mel 355

Odd, Carolina 357
Oiz, Iker 50
Ökten, Zeki 126
Olin, Margreth 317f.
Östlund, Ruben 158
Ostrochovský, Ivan 212
Õunpuu, Veiko 291, 292 fn 10
Öztürk, Ahu 125, 137f.

Paakspuu, Liina 292
Pai, Hsiao-Hung 342
Panayotopoulos, Nikos 111
Papadopoulos, Dimitris 54
Papić, Krsto 164
Pascal, Gabriel 4
Paskaljević, Goran 161

Pasolini, Pier Paolo 98
Paulick, Richard 262
Pavičić, Jurica 162
Pejó, Róber 192
Pekarčík, Pavol 214
Persico, Daniela 90
Péter, Gábor 191
Pethke, Kathrin 22
Petrie, Duncan 236
Petrova, Ralitsa 146
Pichler, Barbara 223
Pichler, Gabriela 158
Pietrangeli, Antonio 96
Pimpare, Stephen 4f.
Pinho, Pedro 76–78
Pintilie, Lucian 147
Pogačić, Vladimir 163
Porumboiu, Corneliu 147
Poškus, Juris 292
Precarias a la deriva 4, 23, 261, 266
Pribačić, Vedrana 166, 167 fn 21
Prikler, Mátyás 209
Prušinovský, Jan 203
Puiu, Cristi 147

Radlmaier, Julian 5
Radunović, Aleksa Stefan 172
Raes, Suzanne 350
Rancière, Jacques 80
Ray, Lolita 305
Reichardt, Kelly 14
Reis, Antonio 66
Reisz, Karel 328
Remo, Miro 212
Remunda, Filip 203
Richardson, Tony 328
Richet, Jean-François 37
Rico, Celia 50
Róbert, Péter 181
Rodrigues, Roberto 66
Rohrwacher, Alice 91
Rosales, Jaime 50
Rossiter, Ned 351
Rothe, Katrin 22, 259, 263
Rudolf, Péter 194
Rumanová, Mária 206

Rusnoková, Daniela 209
Russbach, Antoine 36
Ryan, Kate 156
Rychlíková, Apolena 204

Sabuncu, Başar 125, 130
Sadowska, Maria 283f.
Sáez, Isabel 50
Sakellariou, Alexandros 109
Salamon, András 191
Salmane, Ieva 295
Salomonowitz, Anja 219f.
Samulionytė, Jūratė 295
Sander, Helke 257
Schabus, Robert 220
Schaub, Martin 237–239, 247
Schäublin, Cyril 247f.
Scheiring, Gábor 195
Schiop, Adi 154
Schlesinger, John 328
Schmid, Hans-Christian 9, 252
Schröder, Stefanie 260
Schulte Westenberg, Gertrud 263
Sciamma, Céline 37
Scola, Ettore 98
Seidl, Ulrich 219
Seiler, Alexander 237
Seničić, Maša 127
Sequeria Brás, Patricia 77
Servetas, Giorgos 106, 117, 119
Sezer, Kıvanç 135, 136
Silhol, Nicolas 36
Simon, David 21
Siri, Florent-Emilio 37
Sitaru, Adrian 144
Skalar, Siegmund 220, 229
Škanata, Krsto 164
Škop, Marko 209
Sláma, Bohdan 203
Šlauka, Juraj 206
Ślesicki, Władysław 275
Soldini, Silvio 19
Sólyom, András 191
Sönmez, Sevcan 130
Sontag, Susan 51, 60
Sööt, Andres 298

Söth, Sándor 187
Standing, Guy 8, 16 fn 44, 19–22, 24f., 43, 75 fn 32, 101, 105f., 109, 112f., 117, 120, 145, 162 fn 7, 165, 172, 252, 259, 272, 326 fn 4, 330, 341f.
Steiner, Michael 233
Sticchi, Francesco 8, 16, 20, 44, 251 fn 3
Stiegler, Bernard 173
Strugar Mitevska, Teona 170
Stuber, Thomas 252
Šulík, Marek 205, 213
Šulík, Martin 214
Survila, Mindaugas 299
Surzhikova, Alyona 298
Sviličić, Ognjen 172
Sylbing, Sarah 347, 350, 353 fn 22, 354–357, 359, 361
Szabó, István 179, 188
Szalai, Erzsébet 194
Szombati, Kristóf 195
Szomjas, György 189–191
Szurdi, Miklós 187

Tanner, Alain 234, 243
Tanović, Danis 5
Tasios, Pavlos 111
Tatasopoulos, Stelios 110
Taylor, Charles 9
Thalheim, Robert 252
Thatcher, Margaret 330, 332
Toledano, Eric 37f.
Tóth, Tamás 191
Trägårdh, Lars 303
Traoré, Bouna 41
Traykova, Eldora 157
Třeštíková, Helena 203
Trier, Joachim 312, 314, 320
Tsianos, Vassilis 54
Tubarões, Os 79
Turanskyj, Tatjana 22, 251, 253, 255 fn 15, 257–259, 266f.
Tzavella, Sophia 157
Tzitzis, Stratos 106, 116f.

Václav, Petr 203
Valchanov, Petar 157
Valuch, Tibor 181f.

van de Oest, Paula 350, 358
van der Kuil, Flip 350
van der Linden, Marcel 326
van Ditshuyzen, Ireen 352
van Ginkel, Joost 357
van Heusden, Jaap 159, 359
van Hoorn, Netty 352
Vanzina brothers 93
Vatansever, Ali 126, 133f.
Veldstra, Carolyn 252, 257
Vij, Ritu 12, 15
Villaverde, Teresa 66, 71–74
Vimba, Renārs 295
Virzì, Paolo 5, 97
Visconti, Luchino 87
Vojtek, Jaro 208, 210
Völker, Susanne 217f.
Volpe, Petra 242f.
von Hodenberg, Christina 3, 6
von Osten, Marion 256
Voulgaris, Pantelis 111
Vranik, Roland 192
Vuletić, Bojan 170f.

Wacquant, Loïc 340
Warchus, Matthew 333
Weingartner, Katharina 219
Werenfels, Stina 234
Werkgruppe 2 252
Williams, Linda 320
Williams, Raymond 325, 350
Winterbottom, Michael 341
Wittgenstein, Ludwig 9 fn 26, 68f.

Xantus, János 187

Zambrano, Benito 50
Zaniello, Tom 15, 291
Zhangke, Jia 14
Žilnik, Želimir 164–168
Živković, Ivan 169
Zonka, Erick 36
Zonta, Dario 88
Zophoníasson, Baldvin 317
Zsigmond, Dezső 191
Zviedris, Ivars 293, 295
Zvirbulis, Armands 295

www.ingramcontent.com/pod-product-compliance
Lightning Source LLC
Chambersburg PA
CBHW061928220426
43662CB00012B/1840